Debtor Diplomacy

To Julie

Debtor Diplomacy

*Finance and American Foreign Relations
in the Civil War Era 1837–1873*

JAY SEXTON

Oxford University Press is a department of the University of Oxford.
It furthers the University's objective of excellence in research, scholarship,
and education by publishing worldwide.

Oxford   New York
Auckland   Cape Town   Dar es Salaam   Hong Kong   Karachi
Kuala Lumpur   Madrid   Melbourne   Mexico City   Nairobi
New Delhi   Shanghai   Taipei   Toronto

With offices in
Argentina   Austria   Brazil   Chile   Czech Republic   France   Greece
Guatemala   Hungary   Italy   Japan   Poland   Portugal   Singapore
South Korea   Switzerland   Thailand   Turkey   Ukraine   Vietnam

Oxford is a registered trade mark of Oxford University Press
in the UK and certain other countries.

Published in the United States of America by
Oxford University Press
198 Madison Avenue, New York, NY 10016

© Jay Sexton 2005

First issued as an Oxford University Press paperback, 2014.

All rights reserved. No part of this publication may be reproduced, stored in a
retrieval system, or transmitted, in any form or by any means, without the prior
permission in writing of Oxford University Press, or as expressly permitted by law,
by license, or under terms agreed with the appropriate reproduction rights organization.
Inquiries concerning reproduction outside the scope of the above should be sent to the Rights
Department, Oxford University Press, at the address above.

You must not circulate this work in any other form
and you must impose this same condition on any acquirer.

Library of Congress Cataloging-in-Publication Data
Sexton, Jay, 1978–
Debtor diplomacy : finance and American foreign relations in the Civil War era, 1837–1873 / Jay Sexton.
pages cm . (Oxford historical monographs)
Includes bibliographical references and index.
ISBN 978-0-19-928103-9 (hardcover); 978-0-19-021258-2 (paperback)
1. United States—History—Civil War, 1861–1865—Finance. 2. Debts, External—United States—History—19th
century. 3. United States—Foreign economic relations—Great Britain. 4. Great Britain—Foreign economic
relations—United States. 5. United States—Economic conditions—19th century.
6. United States—Foreign relations—19th century. I. Title.
HC105.6.S49   2005
327'.7304109034—dc22   2005482008

CONTENTS

List of Figures — vii

Acknowledgments — viii

Introduction: Finance and Foreign Relations in the Mid-nineteenth Century — 1

1. The Baring Years, 1837–1861 — 20
2. Union Finance and Diplomacy — 82
3. Confederate Finance and Diplomacy — 134
4. "Were it not for our Debt," 1865–1873 — 190

Conclusion — 242

Bibliography — 255

Index — 277

LIST OF FIGURES

1. The National Debt, 1853 and 1869 — 10
2. Foreign Investment in the United States, 1853 and 1869 — 11
3. U.S. Bonds in London, 1848–1861 — 59
4. U.S. Bonds in London during the Civil War — 97
5. Confederate Erlanger Bonds in London, 1863–1865 — 170
6. Virginia 6% Bonds in London, 1861–1865 — 178
7. U.S. 5-20 Bonds in London, 1865–1872 — 207
8. Massachusetts and Virginia 5% Bonds in London, 1869–1873 — 232
9. U.S. Bonds in London, 1848–1873 — 244

ACKNOWLEDGMENTS

Having written a book about Americans indebted to Britons, I am particularly aware of the need to acknowledge my debts to those who have made this book possible.

First, I would like to thank Lawrence Goldman. If he had not been generous with his time all those years ago (breaking, if I remember, a pledge to his wife to cut down on his teaching hours!), this project would have ended before it began. Throughout my postgraduate years, Lawrence had an uncanny knack for timely assistance and could be counted on for that nugget of information. He lent a hand, as well, in the production process. I am deeply grateful.

Others at Oxford, Cambridge, and elsewhere provided indispensable advice, assistance, and encouragement. Richard Carwardine and John Thompson read the whole manuscript and pushed me to explore the implications of my argument and detail. I owe a special thanks to Mel Leffler, who took me under his wing and helped me situate the project in the historiography of American foreign relations. Several others read part of the manuscript or had a hand in the course of this project: Eric Rauchway, Mary Klayder, John Killick, Ted Wilson, Denny Wood, Martin Crawford, Richard Blackett, Gareth Davies, Donald Rakestraw, Dan Howe, and Tony Badger.

I would also like to thank the staffs of several libraries and archives on both sides of the Atlantic. John Orbell and Moira Lovegrove at the ING Barings Archive and Melanie Aspey at the Rothschilve Archive have helped from the beginning. I gratefully acknowledge both archives for granting me permission to visit and to reproduce my findings in this book. I am also indebted to the staffs of the following libraries for their special assistance: the Bodleian, the Rhodes House, the Vere Harmsworth Library, the Massachusetts Historical Society, the Manuscript Reading Room in the Library of Congress, and the British Library.

Parts of this book have been reproduced from the following journal articles: "Transatlantic Financiers and the Civil War," *American Nineteenth Century History*, 2:3 (Autumn 2001), 29–46; and "The Funded Loan and the *Alabama* Claims", *Diplomatic History*, 27:4 (Autumn 2003), 449–78. I am grateful to both *ANCH* and *Diplomatic History* for granting permission for republication. Funding provided by the Marshall Commission and the Mellon Fund made this book possible.

Support from friends and family has been priceless. My parents maintained an interest in my work from the beginning—with my mother even lending a hand with research in the Peabody papers. My sister and brother-in-law took me in during several weeks of research in New York. Months of research in Washington over the years would have been impossible without the hospitality of old Kansas friends Stephen, Katie, Steve, and Lynne. Alex, Becky, Brad, Laura, and Malani helped in more ways than they will ever know.

Above all, I would like to thank my wife Julie, to whom this book is dedicated. Not only did she provide encouragement and support, but she also read the manuscript and helped me restructure it at a critical point. Most importantly, she forced me to take a vacation to the isle of perspective at several points when work was getting the better of me.

JS
Oxford, January 2005

Introduction:
Finance and Foreign Relations in the Mid-nineteenth Century

"The natural resource of new countries," *The Economist* of London proclaimed in the mid-nineteenth century, "is to borrow the capital of old countries."[1] The "new" country that *The Economist* primarily had in mind was the United States. Lacking the resources to develop the nation and to fund the wars necessary to expand and then preserve it, the United States looked to Europe for investment capital. This desire to obtain European capital greatly influenced American foreign policy, principally relations with Britain. The intersection of finance and diplomacy was particularly evident during the Civil War when both the North and the South integrated attempts to procure loans from European banks into their larger international strategies. Furthermore, the financial needs of the United States (and the Confederacy) imparted significant political power to an elite group of London-based financiers who became intimately involved in American foreign relations during this period. It is the purpose of this study to explore and assess how the United States' need for capital influenced its foreign relations in the tumultuous years wedged between the two great financial crises of the nineteenth century, 1837 to 1873.

American foreign relations in the mid-nineteenth century have attracted little scholarly attention in recent decades. The topic, Kinley Brauer has asserted, is the "Great American Desert" of U.S. historiography and its neglect "has been scandalous."[2] The works that have been produced often "stand alone as discrete monographs that appear to have little relation to each other or any broad understanding of the period."[3]

---

[1] *The Economist*, 18 May 1872, p. 605.
[2] Kinley Brauer, "The Great American Desert Revisited: Recent Literature and Prospects for the Study of American Foreign Relations, 1815–1860," in Michael J. Hogan (ed.), *Paths to Power: The Historiography of American Foreign Relations to 1941* (Cambridge, 2000), pp. 49, 77.
[3] See Lawrence Kaplan, "Introduction," *Journal of the Early Republic*, 14 (Winter 1994), pp. 453–7.

Further frustrating is the failure of those historians who do delve into the period to formulate a thesis to explain what happened.[4] Paul Varg, one of only a handful of historians to publish a monograph on early and mid-nineteenth-century foreign relations, admitted that he could find "no over arching theory to explain what took place."[5]

Despite the inadequacy of scholarship, historians have reached something of a consensus interpretation of mid-nineteenth-century foreign relations. Inspired by Norman Graebner's 1955 work, *Empire on the Pacific*, scholars promote "the close relationship between territorial and commercial expansionism."[6] The chief aim of this interpretive school is to relate the consolidation of the "continental empire" to overseas commercial expansion. Westward expansion, according to this view, was largely driven by the need to acquire deep-water ports on the Pacific coast. These ports, it was hoped, would serve as the entrepots from which American commerce could expand into the profitable, though not yet adequately open, East Asian market. Accordingly, commercial agreements were negotiated with China (1844) and Japan (1854) and strategic stopping points, such as the Aleutian and Midway Islands, were annexed to serve as way stations for trade with Asia. Commercial expansion into Latin America, the Mediterranean, and even the Near East also occurred at this time (and even earlier in the century). The Walker Tariff of 1846 and the Marcy–Elgin Treaty of 1854 also demonstrated that American statesmen were aware of their largest and closest markets—Britain and Canada. Particularly after the Civil War when the American economy began producing a surplus of agricultural and, to a lesser extent, manufactured goods, American statesmen viewed the expansion of the nation's export markets as the central objective of their diplomatic strategies.[7]

---

[4] Kinley Brauer, "The Need for a Synthesis of American Foreign Relations, 1815–1861," *Journal of the Early Republic*, 14 (Winter 1994), pp. 467–76.

[5] Paul Varg, *United States Foreign Relations, 1820–1860* (Michigan, 1979), p. xv.

[6] Quoted from Brauer, "The Need for a Synthesis of American Foreign Relations, 1815–1861," pp. 467–76. Norman Graebner, *Empire on the Pacific* (New York, 1955). See also Ernest Paolino, *The Foundations of the American Empire* (Ithaca, 1973); William Earl Weeks, *Building the Continental Empire* (Chicago, 1996); Walter LaFeber, *The American Age* (New York, 1994); Charles Vevier, "American Continentalism: An Idea of Expansion, 1845–1910," *American Historical Review*, 65 (January 1960), pp. 323–35; Edward P. Crapol, "John Tyler and the Pursuit of National Destiny," *Journal of the Early Republic*, 17 (Fall 1997), pp. 467–91; John Belohlavek, "Economic Interest Groups and the Formation of Foreign Policy in the Early Republic," *Journal of the Early Republic*, 14 (Winter 1994), pp. 476–85.

[7] Kinley Brauer, "The United States and British Imperial Expansion, 1815–1860," *Diplomatic History*, 12 (Winter 1988), pp. 19–37.

"Widening old markets and opening new ones, expanding production, and promoting industry," Kinley Brauer argues, "became the central concerns of American diplomats and statesmen."[8] Part of the appeal of this interpretation is its retrospective clairvoyance. Scholars typically have been eager to demonstrate that the aggressive turn in American foreign policy in 1898 was not a sudden aberration but, rather, the climax of decades, if not a century, of territorial and commercial expansion. "The overseas empire that Americans controlled in 1900," Walter LaFeber argues, "was not a break in their history, but a natural culmination."[9] Expansionism—both as an ideology and as a practice—clearly had its roots in the mid-nineteenth century.

Historians have also emphasized commerce and trade in their work on American relations with European states, specifically Britain, during this period. Indeed, the heyday of Anglo-American trade is dated not during the formal mercantilism of the eighteenth century but in the years wedged between the Treaty of Ghent and the shots at Fort Sumter. During these years each nation was the other's most important trading partner. On average, the United States shipped half of its exports to Britain while receiving forty percent of its imports from its former colonial master. In terms of computed real value, British imports of American goods were double their nearest rival, the British East Indies. On the other side of this trade, the United States was the leading market for British goods. Again in terms of real value, exports to the United States were nearly one and one-half times as large as the value of those shipped to the East Indies. Augmented by new shipping lines that reduced the costs of the transatlantic passage, Anglo-American trade was the hallmark of what one historian has labeled "a single, integrated Atlantic economy."[10]

---

[8] Kinley Brauer, "Diplomacy of American Expansionism, 1821–1860," in William Becker and Samuel Wells (eds.), *Economics and World Power* (New York, 1984), p. 59. Brauer maintains, however, that "America's assault on the British Empire and attempt to establish an informal empire of its own generally failed before the Civil War." See Brauer, "The United States and British Imperial Expansion, 1815–1860," p. 34.

[9] Walter LaFeber, *The New Empire* (Ithaca, 1963), p. vii.

[10] J. Potter, "Atlantic Economy, 1815–60: The U.S.A. and the Industrial Revolution in Britain," in L.S. Pressnell (ed.), *Studies in the Industrial Revolution* (London, 1970), p. 239. For more on Anglo-American trade, see Frank Thistlethwaite, *The Anglo-American Connection in the Early Nineteenth Century* (Philadelphia, 1959), pp. 9–13; Thistlethwaite, "Atlantic Partnership," *Economic History Review*, 7 (1954), pp. 1–17; H. C. Allen, *The Anglo-American Relationship since 1783* (London, 1959), pp. 53–94; and Norman Buck, *Anglo-American Trade, 1800–1850* (New Haven, 1925).

At the heart of the Atlantic economy, of course, was the cotton picked by slaves in the American South. From the years 1825 to 1860, American cotton perennially amounted to between three-quarters and four-fifths of British imports of the staple. Britain's textile industry, in turn, was one of the pillars of the Victorian economy that, according to an 1853 estimate of *The Economist*, directly and indirectly sustained one-fifth of the population of Britain.[11] The commercial links of the Atlantic economy were comprised of more than cotton fibers. Following the repeal of the Corn Laws in 1846, American grains poured into Britain in unprecedented amounts. Although the United States did not enjoy a monopoly in corn as it did in cotton, American farmers, particularly during periods of agricultural difficulty or political unrest in Europe (the prime example being the Crimean War, 1854–6), were able to export their crops across the Atlantic.[12] The foreign exchange generated by these agricultural exports, in turn, enabled Americans to purchase British manufactured goods.

This commercial connection has often served as the window through which historians view U.S. relations with Britain in the mid-nineteenth century. Writing at the beginning of the Cold War during the height of the "special relationship," scholars reassessed Anglo-American relations in the nineteenth century and concluded that these economic links established a vital connection between the two nations that prevented squabbles such as border disputes, shipping controversies, and the assertion of national honor from erupting into war. The work of H. C. Allen, Frank Thistlethwaite, and others all pointed to the existence of a nascent "special relationship" in the nineteenth century, one that primarily extended from economic interdependence.[13] As Kenneth Bourne argues, Atlantic trade functioned as a powerful "peace factor" that preserved Anglo-American amity during the diplomatic disputes of the era and paved the way for the rapprochement of the coming century.[14]

---

[11] *The Economist*, 21 May 1853, p. 561. This estimate assumed that every worker would have three dependents. See Frank Owsley, *King Cotton Diplomacy* (Chicago, 2nd ed., 1959), pp. 8–9. Another historian estimates that 16.6 percent of Britain's population was sustained by the cotton trade and textile industry. See Douglas Ball, *Financial Failure and Confederate Defeat* (Urbana, Ill., 1991), p. 66.

[12] Potter, "Atlantic Economy," pp. 249–51.

[13] See, for example, H. C. Allen, *Great Britain and the United States: A History of Anglo-American Relations, 1783–1952* (London, 1954); Thistlethwaite, *The Anglo-American Connection in the Early Nineteenth Century*; H. G. Nicholas, *Britain and the United States* (London, 1963); Charles Campbell, *From Revolution to Rapprochement: The United States and Great Britain, 1783–1900* (New York, 1974).

[14] Kenneth Bourne, *Britain and the Balance of Power in North America, 1815–1908* (London, 1967), pp. 410–11.

Historians' emphasis on commerce and trade has illuminated our understanding of American expansionism and foreign policy. The scholarship, however, is not without its shortcomings. Although historians have done well to document the instances when American statesmen were concerned with promoting export expansion, a convincing case has yet to be made that this objective was decisive, that the "glut theory" of overproduction consistently fueled overseas expansion. In several recent works, David Pletcher has cogently demonstrated that American efforts to expand overseas economic interests were disjointed, inconsistent, arranged on an ad hoc basis, and marked by little cooperation between business and government. "Evidence does not support the claim of a single overarching policy, a 'way of life,'" Pletcher concludes, challenging the interpretation of William Appleman Williams. Although economics remain at the heart of Pletcher's studies, the picture that emerges is much less clean, much more nuanced than the view that economic forces consistently propelled the United States outward.[15]

The prevailing emphasis on commercial expansion has also oversimplified the complex and at times contradictory relationship between economics and foreign policy by ignoring how financial considerations often tempered American diplomacy. As the recent scholarship of Niall Ferguson, P. J. Cain, and A. G. Hopkins on nineteenth-century European relations and British imperialism suggests, the role of economics in foreign policy formations needs to be viewed not only from the traditional commercial perspective, but also from a financial one.[16] In response to William Appleman William's *The Tragedy of American Diplomacy* and other "New Left" revisionist works, scholars of twentieth-century American foreign relations have also recognized that the economic engine behind foreign policy was fueled by more than just the desire for commercial expansion.[17]

[15] David M. Pletcher, "Rhetoric and Results: A Pragmatic View of American Economic Expansionism, 1865–1898," *Diplomatic History* 5 (Spring 1981), pp. 93–104; idem, *The Diplomacy of Trade and Investment: American Economic Expansion in the Hemisphere, 1865–1900* (Columbia: University of Missouri Press, 1998); idem, *The Diplomacy of Involvement: American Economic Expansion across the Pacific, 1784–1900* (Columbia: University of Missouri Press, 2001); idem, *The Awkward Years: American Foreign Relations under Garfield and Arthur* (Columbia: University of Missouri Press, 1962). Quote from *The Diplomacy of Trade and Investment*, p. 4. "Way of life" refers to William Appleman Williams, *Empire as a Way of Life* (Oxford: Oxford University Press, 1980).

[16] Niall Ferguson, *The House of Rothschild*, 2 vols. (London, 1998–9); and *The Cash Nexus* (London, 2001); P. J. Cain and A. G. Hopkins, *British Imperialism: Innovation and Expansion, 1688–1914* (London, 1993).

[17] For this point, see Bradford Perkins, "*The Tragedy of American Diplomacy*: Twenty-Five Years After," *Reviews in American History*, 12 (March 1984).

It is clear that scholars of mid-nineteenth-century American foreign relations have devoted far too little attention to the other international economic concern of the mid-nineteenth century: efforts to attract European investment to the United States, particularly to finance the government debt. In need of capital to fund internal improvements, the Mexican War, and, above all else, the Civil War, the U.S. government (and the governments of various states) was forced to look abroad for its financial needs. Abroad increasingly meant Britain, as London developed into the world's financial center by the middle of the century. "Our country is sometimes called the workshop of the world," the London *Bankers' Magazine* reported in 1869, "It might, with even great truth, be called its cash-box."[18]

How exactly the United States' need for capital related to its foreign relations in the mid-nineteenth century, particularly with Britain, is the question that frames this study. In many instances, this is not a complex issue. Throughout the period of this study, the State and Treasury Departments in Washington dispatched agents to Europe and corresponded with banks across the Atlantic to negotiate foreign loans. In this sense, policies of international finance were a component of American foreign relations, with the Treasury Department often taking a leading role. The manner in which American leaders conducted this financial diplomacy, particularly during the Civil War, is a central theme of this study.

The relationship between finance and diplomacy, however, was not always so clear. In times of diplomatic crisis, plans to procure a foreign loan were often shelved. Moreover, international finance rarely appears in the official diplomatic correspondence of the era—accounting, perhaps, for the lack of scholarship on the topic. This problem can largely be solved by the sources used. Although diplomatic correspondence provides the historian with a detailed account of the process of conducting foreign policies, it alone does little to expose the forces behind the decisions of nineteenth-century statesmen. In contrast, the private correspondence of political leaders and, more importantly, the records of banks such as Baring Brothers and the Rothschilds highlight the connection between the financial needs of the United States and the formation of American foreign policy. Bank records, it should be noted, include not only ledger and accounting books, but also correspondence in which the views of political leaders on both sides of the Atlantic are either stated in a

---

[18] *Bankers' Magazine*, vol. 29, April 1869, p. 421.

private note or, as is often the case, recorded by a banker after an unofficial meeting behind closed doors. As has been recently recognized, the archives of the leading international banks, typically located in London, are an underused historical source that provide a new lens through which to view the international history of the nineteenth century.[19]

This approach reveals the considerable extent to which financial considerations shaped American foreign policy. The United States' need to attract foreign investment often guided the actions of American statesmen and provides the backdrop from which the diplomacy of the era must be viewed. American leaders were acutely aware of their nation's financial needs and were well informed of the sensitivity of the bond market in London to unfavorable political and diplomatic developments. "It is no doubt unpleasant," *The Nation* reported in 1869, "to be thus obliged to count in advance the cost of every shift in our foreign policy."[20] Consequently, the financial needs of the United States provided a powerful incentive for American statesmen to pursue a conciliatory foreign policy, particularly in relations with Britain, the nation's chief creditor. Just as trade served as a "peace factor" in Anglo-American relations, the creditor–debtor relationship of Britain and the United States bonded the two nations together and gave them the common interest of avoiding war. Although historians have been correct to highlight the role of conciliatory British leaders (such as Lord Aberdeen in the 1840s and William Gladstone in the 1870s) in maintaining Anglo-American peace during this period,[21] this study shall concentrate on how financial considerations shaped the decisions of American statesmen, especially those of the Whig and Republican Parties, and led them to pursue peaceful relations with Britain and other European powers in order to promote foreign investment.

The foreign indebtedness of the United States, however, did not always pave the way to harmonious foreign relations. European capital, as we shall see, helped finance American expansion, particularly during the Mexican War. Furthermore, Anglo-American relations were strained by the state defaults of the 1840s, the joint effort of the State and

---

[19] For a discussion of the advantages of using the records of financial institutions as a source for international history, see Ferguson, *The House of Rothschild*, I, pp. 1–10.
[20] *The Nation*, vol. 9, 12 August 1869, p. 124.
[21] See, for instance, Charles S. Campbell, *From Revolution to Rapprochement: The United States and Great Britain* (New York, 1974); David Dykstra, *The Shifting Balance of Power: American-British Diplomacy in North America, 1842–1848* (Maryland, 1999); Wilbur D. Jones, *The American Problem in British Diplomacy, 1841–1861* (London, 1974).

Treasury Departments to recover Confederate property in Europe after the Civil War, and various frauds perpetrated by American railroad and canal companies. Hence, though largely a "peace factor," British investments in the United States also had the potential to incite controversy. Such controversies did not necessarily involve both or either of the two nations' governments. This brings up an important point: the foreign indebtedness of the United States was more than just a foreign policy issue. The various relationships between European creditors and American debtors (which included not only the national government, but also states, merchant firms, and railroad and canal companies) serve as reminders that foreign relations are composed of more than just the diplomacy of national governments. International finance had a bearing in one way or another on matters as diverse as state politics in Mississippi, evangelicals' discussions of morality in Pennsylvania, the fate of the Confederacy, and the severity of stock market panics on Wall Street. In this sense, foreign investment in the United States needs to be considered not only in relation to foreign policy decisions, but also as a component of the nation's larger relationship with the wider world, and with Britain in particular.

On the surface, it may be surprising that the United States' foreign indebtedness and its desire to attract more overseas investment would influence American foreign policy in the mid-1800s. After all, the United States became the world's greatest debtor at the end of the nineteenth century, not in the middle of it. Foreign investment in the United States multiplied from $2.5 billion in 1895 to more than $7 billion on the eve of the Great War in 1914.[22] In contrast, foreign investment in the period of this study grew from a modest $110 million in 1838 to $1.5 billion in 1873.[23] (All figures of foreign investment, it should be noted, include only long-term investment, not short-term loans and letters of credit issued by European banks to American merchants, and, therefore, understate the United States' reliance on foreign capital.) Furthermore, economic historians have dispelled the notion that foreign investment fueled American economic growth in the nineteenth century. The recent work of Lance Davis and Robert Cull reveals that only five percent of the

---

[22] Mira Wilkins, *The History of Foreign Investment in the United States to 1914* (Cambridge, Mass., 1989), p. 147.
[23] Ibid., pp. 50–1, 91.

almost $60 billion increase in the nation's capital stock between 1799 and 1900 came from abroad.[24]

Though not the fuel of the nineteenth-century economy, in certain periods foreign investment was an essential lubricant without which the economic engine of the United States might have stalled. In the same works, Davis and Cull contend that although foreign investment in the aggregate did not dictate American economic development, inflows of foreign capital were at times significant factors in economic growth. Chief among these periods were the 1830s and 1840s and the decade immediately following the Civil War when foreign investment accounted for between fifteen and twenty-two percent of the nation's net capital formation.[25] Mira Wilkins has placed the figure at twenty-seven percent for the boom year of 1869.[26] Moreover, had Union and Confederate statesmen succeeded in their financial diplomacy of the Civil War, economic historians might have labeled the mid-nineteenth century as "the era of foreign investment"—which was only temporarily broken by the depression of the mid-1840s when several state governments defaulted and/or repudiated their debts.

In addition to the economic significance of foreign capital in the mid-nineteenth century, the type of foreign investment in the United States also played a role in the merging of finance and diplomacy. In contrast to the turn of the century when foreign investment was placed almost exclusively in the stock of railroads, mining companies, and other private enterprises, a high percentage of foreign investment in the United States at mid-century was placed in government securities. Despite Andrew Jackson's remarkable feat of paying off the national debt in 1835, the federal government's fiscal needs, particularly during the Mexican and Civil Wars, led the Treasury to issue its bonds abroad. Treasury reports in 1853 and 1869 revealed that nearly half of the national debt was held overseas, principally in Britain.

The Treasury in Washington was not the only American government body indebted to foreign capitalists. Of importance in the early years of

---

[24] Lance E. Davis and Robert J. Cull, "International Capital Movements, Domestic Capital Markets, and American Economic Growth, 1820–1914," in Stanley Engerman and Robert Gallman (eds.), *The Cambridge Economic History of the United States: The Long Nineteenth Century* (Cambridge, 1996–2000), pp. 733–812; Davis and Cull, *International Capital Markets and American Economic Growth, 1820–1914* (Cambridge, 1994), p. 111.

[25] Davis and Cull, "International Capital Movements, Domestic Capital Markets, and American Economic Growth, 1820–1914," p. 734; Davis and Cull, *International Capital Markets*, p. 111.

[26] Wilkins, *Foreign Investment*, p. 153.

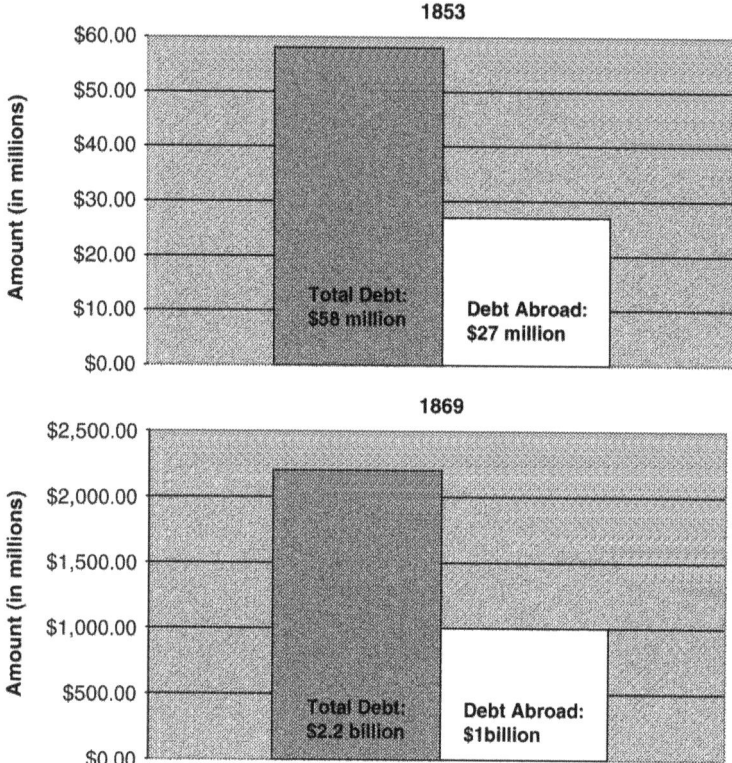

Figure 1   The National Debt, 1853 and 1869
(Source: Mira Wilkins, *The History of Foreign Investment in the United States to 1914*. Cambridge, Mass., 1989, pp. 76–7, 137.)

this study are the state debts of the antebellum era. Denied federal assistance by Jacksonian Democrats for projects such as the building of roads and canals, individual state and municipal governments took it upon themselves to fund internal improvements, which, given Americans' aversion to taxation, often meant public borrowing. By 1853 foreign investment in state and municipal securities totaled $132.5 million. When the federal debt overseas is added to this figure, seventy-two percent of all foreign investment in 1853 was placed in public debt (federal, state, or municipal). The proportion of foreign investment in public securities was even higher in 1869. Of a total foreign indebtedness of $1.39 billion, $1.11 billion, or approximately eighty percent, was owed to foreign capitalists

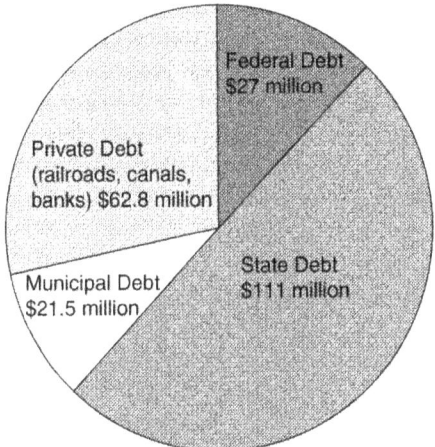

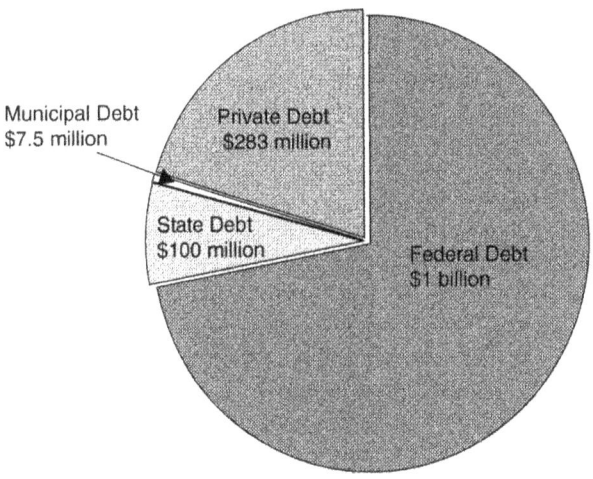

Figure 2 Foreign Investment in the United States, 1853 and 1869
(Source: Mira Wilkins, *The History of Foreign Investment in the United States to 1914*. Cambridge, Mass., 1989, pp. 76–7, 110.)

by a government body. With foreign investment largely placed in government debt in this period, it should come as little surprise that financial, political, and diplomatic issues were closely intertwined.

The unprecedented power of an elite group of investment banks and international financiers also contributed to the convergence of finance and diplomacy. The mid-nineteenth century witnessed the great British-based banking houses reach the pinnacle of their power and influence in American affairs. Led by Baring Brothers, the Rothschilds, and George Peabody and Co. (the predecessor to the house of J. P. Morgan), banks in the City of London were the architects of nearly every facet of the Atlantic economy. In addition to negotiating loans and marketing American securities abroad, banks such as the Barings and Rothschilds underwrote transatlantic trade, provided insurance, exchanged currencies, and compiled influential market reports.[27] Directing the westward flow of capital across the Atlantic, however, remained the central function of the leading transatlantic banks. Lured by high interest rates and the perceived fidelity of fellow Anglo-Saxon debtors, these London-based banks connected Britain and the United States through their (and their clienteles') investments in American securities. Ninety percent of the United States' foreign indebtedness in 1861 was of British origin.[28]

The financial and commercial power of leading transatlantic financiers extended to them significant political and diplomatic influence on both sides of the Atlantic. In addition to possessing the power to bail out foreign governments in financial straits, leading British bankers, such as Thomas Baring, Lionel de Rothschild, and William Brown (head of the Liverpool firm Brown Brothers), also served as members of Parliament. "There are six great powers in Europe," a French statesmen declared in 1818, "England, France, Prussia, Austria, Russia and Baring Brothers."[29] The Barings and Rothschilds, Lord Byron asserted in *Don Juan*, "are the true lords of Europe."[30] Recent British scholarship has emphasized the political power of financiers in the City and their close links to politicians and statesmen in Westminster. The work of Niall Ferguson, P. J. Cain, and A. G. Hopkins all point to the existence of a politically active group of financial leaders who helped shape British foreign policy, imperial expansion, and, in the larger picture, the diplomacy of Europe's great powers.[31]

---

[27] Ralph Hidy, "The Organization and Functions of Anglo-American Merchant Bankers, 1815–60," *Journal of Economic History*, 1 (1941), pp. 53–66.

[28] Davis and Cull, *International Capital Markets*, p. 17. This percentage only declined to 83 percent in 1875.

[29] Philip Zeigler, *The Sixth Great Power: Barings, 1765–1929* (London, 1988).

[30] Byron quoted in Ferguson, *The Cash Nexus*, p. 289.

[31] Cain and Hopkins, *British Imperialism*, p. 13; Ferguson, *The Cash Nexus*; and Ferguson, *The House of Rothschild*.

In the United States, as well, leading figures possessed connections to both the financial and political spheres. American agents of the top British firms, such as August Belmont, the Rothschilds' representative based in New York, and Barings' consultants in Massachusetts, Thomas Wren Ward and Daniel Webster, were also highly influential politicians and lobbyists. Belmont, after a brief stint as U.S. minister to Belgium, served as the chairman of the Democratic National Committee (from 1860 to 1872), while Webster, in addition to being a leading Whig politician of the era, twice served as secretary of state (1841–3, 1850–2). Similarly, American expatriate bankers in London, such as Joshua Bates of Baring Brothers and George Peabody and his partner J. S. Morgan (father of J. P.), served as conduits between financial and political leaders on both sides of the Atlantic. Maintaining intimate relations with leaders in both nations, men such as Bates are the forgotten, though vitally important, actors in nineteenth-century American foreign relations. Indeed, New York bankers and merchants of the period so considered themselves experts in foreign affairs because of their experience in international trade and finance that they referred to themselves as "statesmen."[32]

These transnational banks established a network of high finance and high politics that connected Britain and the United States and merged international finance with international relations. The involvement of these financiers, many of whom were British, in American politics was nothing new. Baring Brothers, for example, had long served as the official financial agency of the U.S. Government in Europe and extended credit to Washington for purposes ranging from the Louisiana Purchase in 1803 to propping up the Bank of the United States in the 1820s and 1830s. The direct participation of financial leaders in the diplomatic settlements of the mid-nineteenth century, however, superseded this previous overlapping of finance and diplomacy. At several times in the years of this study—namely the Webster–Ashburton Treaty of 1842, the Joint Claims Commission of 1853–5, and the preliminary talks of the Treaty of Washington in 1870—financiers doubled as diplomats and were directly involved in negotiating international agreements.

In these instances, financiers sought to promote Anglo-American peace by assisting and, at times, prompting policy-makers to calmly and

---

[32] For a recent study that highlights the overlap and connection between leaders in finance and politics during this period, see Sven Beckert, *The Monied Metropolis: New York City and the Consolidation of the American Bourgeoisie, 1850–1896* (New York, 2001). Quote from p. 64.

rationally disentangle cantankerous and oftentimes complex diplomatic disputes in isolation from the extreme demands made by public opinion. "I consider your interest and mine, and that of the country," Ward informed Bates during the Maine boundary dispute, "identical with soundness and stability and good order."[33] At other times financial interests functioned as behind-the-scenes lobbyists and planted favorable articles in the British and American press. All of this, of course, was in addition to their normal duty of deciding whether and on what conditions to grant loans requested by the federal and state governments of the United States. However, as we shall see, though the intervention of the financial lobby and the objective of restoring confidence in the financial markets helped preserve peace and often laid the groundwork for treaties, this did not always translate into thorough and far-sighted diplomatic agreements.

There can be little question that the political and financial power of European financiers made them key figures in mid-nineteenth-century international relations. Accordingly, their views regarding American politics, diplomacy, and, of course, investment opportunities are central to this study. Even in issues concerning domestic American politics, the views of financiers across the Atlantic yielded direct consequences. For example, outside investment in the American South after the Civil War was essential to Republican plans for the economic and political reconstruction of the former Confederate states. Indeed, the Republican state governments in the South might have been able to cling to power longer had European financiers been willing to provide investment capital for Southern states and railroads, thereby assisting Republican efforts to modernize the Southern economy and mitigating the effects of the Panic of 1873. How foreign capitalists viewed the South and why they chose not to invest in the region after the war, therefore, is a question of great significance—a question, it should be added, that historians have not only failed to answer, but one that they have generally failed to even ask.[34] In this sense, European financiers were players on the international stage who, though not always given a leading role in treaty negotiations and policy decisions, were vital supporting actors who shaped the course of mid-nineteenth-century foreign relations.

---

[33] Ward to Bates, 6 January 1839, Thomas Wren Ward Papers, Massachusetts Historical Society.
[34] For a work that does briefly consider this issue, see Mark Summers, *Railroads, Reconstruction, and the Gospel of Prosperity: Aid under the Radical Republicans, 1865–1877* (Princeton, 1984).

At no time was the power of leading financiers in London more apparent, nor Americans' need for foreign capital greater, than during the Civil War. Lacking the infrastructure and the means to fund a protracted war, both the Union and the Confederacy sought foreign financial assistance. Each side quickly integrated plans to attract foreign capital into their larger diplomatic strategies. Within weeks of the bombardment of Fort Sumter and even before Congress had authorized a foreign loan, U.S. Secretary of the Treasury Salmon P. Chase dispatched Rothschild American agent August Belmont across the Atlantic to negotiate a loan with a British banking house. The newly formed Confederacy was not far behind as Southern emissaries in Britain sought takers for Confederate bonds in the war's first year. Even after these early efforts failed to attract foreign investment, Union and Confederate statesmen attempted throughout the war to procure the financial backing of a European bank. Other financial operations—such as denigrating the other side's finances and obstructing the enemy's purchasing operations—also became significant components of the international strategies of the Union and the Confederacy.

Given the importance of finance and diplomacy in determining the war's outcome, it is surprising that more attention has not been devoted to this subject. It is also surprising given the recent wave of publications on the international dimensions of the Civil War. British public opinion, Confederate diplomacy, and the threat of European intervention have all been the subject of recent monographs.[35] Despite this scholarly interest in the international history of the war, however, the financial aspects of the conflict remain largely neglected. Indeed, it has been more than twenty years since Richard Burns admitted that "one of the oddest aspects of Civil War historiography is the lack of good studies of the war's economic impact overseas."[36] Some "economic" aspects of the war, of course, have attracted the attention of historians. The so-called "cotton

---

[35] For recent work on the international dimensions of the Civil War, see Howard Jones, *Union in Peril* (Chapel Hill, 1992); R. J. M. Blackett, *Divided Hearts: Britain and the American Civil War* (Baton Rouge, 2001); Alfred Grant, *The American Civil War and the British Press* (Jefferson, N.C., 2000); Charles Hubbard, *The Burden of Confederate Diplomacy*, (Knoxville, 1998); Howard Jones, *Abraham Lincoln and a New Birth of Freedom* (Lincoln, Neb., 1999); Dean Mahin, *One War at a Time* (Washington, 1999); Robert Young, *Senator James Murray Mason: Defender of the Old South* (Knoxville, 1998); Martin Crawford, *The Anglo-American Crisis of the Mid-Nineteenth Century: The Times and America, 1850–1862* (London, 1987). The standard works on the topic remain D. P. Crook, *The North, the South, and the Powers, 1861–1865* (New York, 1974); and Brian Jenkins, *Britain and the War for the Union*, 2 vols. (London, 1974–80).

[36] Richard Burns, *Guide to American Foreign Relations since 1700* (Oxford, 1983), p. 293.

famine" in Lancashire and the "King Corn" versus "King Cotton" dispute have been historiographical battlegrounds that have witnessed extensive scholarly debate.[37] Again, however, scholarly interest in economics has focused on commerce and trade, ignoring banking and finance. Despite the heated debate concerning British public opinion during the war, historians have ignored the views of the vitally important financial class. Although it is methodologically impossible to come up with a precise figure for the financial support each side obtained in Europe, this study shall evaluate the financial diplomacy of the Union and Confederacy and the instances when the two sides succeeded in finding takers for their war bonds on European stock exchanges.

Westward flows of capital across the Atlantic during the war were significant for more than just financial reasons. The nineteenth-century bond market, as Niall Ferguson maintains, can serve the historian as "a kind of daily opinion poll, an expression of confidence in a given regime."[38] This certainly held true on British stock exchanges during the Civil War as the price of Union and Confederate bonds fluctuated in accordance with military and political developments in the warring states. Indeed, Union diplomats (and more recently, economic historians) used quotations of the Confederate cotton bonds as a gauge to measure British support for the South.[39] However, this form of an "opinion poll," as Ferguson is quick to point out, is highly unrepresentative. Only the views of those wealthy and, as a consequence, powerful enough to have money to invest in foreign securities are reflected in the fluctuations of the bond market.

The wealthy and powerful of Britain, of course, were the very people that the Union and Confederacy hoped to enlist as supporters. Both sides

---

[37] The "cotton famine" is considered by Norman Longmate, *The Hungry Mills* (London, 1978); Eugene Bradey, "A Reconsideration of the Lancashire 'Cotton Famine,'" *Agricultural History*, 37 (July 1963), pp. 156–62; and Nigel Hall, "The Liverpool Cotton Market and the American Civil War," *Northern History*, 34 (1998), pp. 149–69. For the debate regarding "King Corn" versus "King Cotton," see Louis Schmidt, "The Influence of Wheat and Cotton on Anglo-American Relations during the Civil War," *Iowa Journal of History and Politics*, 16 (July 1918), pp. 400–39; Amos Khasigian, "Economic Factors and British Neutrality, 1861–1865," *Historian*, 25 (August 1963), pp. 451–65; Eli Ginzberg, "The Economics of British Neutrality during the American Civil War," *Agricultural History*, 10 (October 1936), pp. 147–56; and Robert Jones, "Long Live the King?" *Agricultural History*, 37 (July 1963), pp. 166–9.

[38] Ferguson, *The House of Rothschild*, I, p. 6.

[39] See, for instance, William Brown and Richard Burdekan, "Turning Points in the U.S. Civil War: A British Perspective," *Journal of Economic History*, 60 (March 2000), pp. 216–31.

recognized that a loan from a British bank, backed by the public issuance of bonds on the London Stock Exchange, would engender support for their cause by creating a class of bondholders in Britain who had a vested interest in the permanence of their government. Once such a class of partisan bondholders was established, it was presumed, diplomatic favors, such as the recognition of the Confederacy or, alternatively, the maintenance of neutrality, would be forthcoming. Hence, attempts to arrange a foreign loan were motivated just as much by diplomatic and political considerations as they were by the obvious financial ones. As William Aspinwall, a Union financial agent in Britain, put it in 1863, "I think every bond sold on this side of the water becomes a bond of sympathy. Men are governed by steel or gold."[40] In this sense the financial component of each sides' foreign policy was an integral part of Civil War diplomacy. That both sides largely failed to procure a sizable foreign loan (the exception being the relatively modest Confederate Erlanger loan of 1863) should not deter scholarship on this neglected aspect of Civil War diplomacy. As we shall see, although British banks remained remarkably financially neutral during the war, they were anything but politically impartial.

When viewed in this light, it is clear that the United States' need for foreign capital was inextricably linked to foreign policy issues and extended considerable leverage to London-based financiers who became important actors in Anglo-American relations. This thesis, however, should not be taken too far. As scholars have long argued, geopolitics, commercial expansion, Atlantic trade, domestic politics, ideology, and prevailing views of race all influenced the formation of U.S. foreign policy. This work attempts not to impose a template upon all U.S. foreign policy in the mid-nineteenth century, but seeks to explore a neglected theme in American foreign relations. By using finance to connect periods of U.S. diplomatic history rarely viewed together and to consider the foreign relations of both the Union and the Confederacy, it is hoped that this work will shed new light on Anglo-American relations and draw attention to an important, though ignored, dimension of mid-nineteenth-century American foreign relations.

It should also be added that the policy objective of obtaining foreign capital and the political influence of European capitalists was by no means

---

[40] Aspinwall to Chase, 8 May 1863, Chase Papers, University Publications of America, Library of Congress.

popular amongst most Americans. Foreign financiers, many Americans believed, were corrupt parasites who fed off the work of honest men and, by meddling in American politics and foreign relations, threatened to undermine the nation's republican institutions and to thwart America's "manifest destiny." Not surprisingly, the Democratic Party, inspired by Anglophobic and anti-financier ideologues such as Andrew Jackson and Lewis Cass, most often articulated these concerns. This study does not aim to deny the rhetorical power of Anglophobia in mid-nineteenth-century politics, nor the influence of such ideas to the construction of American foreign policy.[41] Rather, it seeks to deepen our understanding of the period by demonstrating that these ideas did not on their own determine diplomacy, that interests—particularly financial ones—also factored into the formation of foreign policy. Even the Democrats in the 1840s, as we shall see, recognized the benefits of foreign investment and, when push came to shove and the Treasury required funds, proved willing to swallow the bitter pill of cooperating with the foreign financial interests that they publicly deplored. Nonetheless, the Democrats' cooperation with European capitalists during periods of financial exigency, should not be confused with the more Anglophilic, business-friendly policies of Whigs and Republicans such as Daniel Webster and Hamilton Fish. The reader will be well served, therefore, to keep in mind that though attracting foreign investment was often a policy objective—even of the belligerent Polk administration—it was a goal that produced political controversy at home and was never popular amongst hard-line Democrats.

Finally, it should be explicitly stated that in no way does this work advance the argument that the United States, through its debts to British capitalists, was in some way incorporated into an "informal" British empire. The extent to which such an "informal" empire existed is itself a highly controversial topic in British historiography.[42] However, even

---

[41] For Anglophobia during this period, see Sam W. Haynes, "Anglophobia and the Annexation of Texas: The Quest for National Security," in Haynes and Christopher Morris (eds.), *Manifest Destiny and Empire: American Antebellum Expansionism* (Arlington, Tex., 1997), pp. 115–45. For a work that explores the relationship between British economic dominance and Anglophobia in the United States in the second half of the nineteenth century, see, Edward P. Crapol, *America for Americans: Economic Nationalism and Anglophobia in the Late Nineteenth Century* (Westport, Conn., 1973).

[42] For the classic articulation of the "informal" empire thesis, see Jack Gallagher and Ronald Robinson, "The Imperialism of Free Trade," *Economic History Review*, 6 (1953). For a work that takes issue with the "informal" empire thesis, see D. C. M. Platt, *Finance, Trade, and Politics in British Foreign Policy, 1815–1914* (Oxford, 1968).

proponents of the notion agree that Britain "had less influence" in the United States than elsewhere in the world in the nineteenth century.[43] At only one time in the period of this study—during the state debt crisis of the mid-1840s—did British capitalists interfere in domestic American affairs to an extent characteristic of informal imperialism. However, this was an isolated instance that would not be repeated again. The British government, as articulated by every foreign secretary in the 1840s, declined to assist capitalists in their efforts to recover their defaulted and repudiated American investments. Moreover, as we have seen, the United States was never as dependent on British capital as were some states under imperial influence. After 1795 the U.S. national debt was always denominated in dollars, unlike less autonomous governments that often had their debt in pounds sterling.[44] As the largely domestic financing of the Civil War demonstrated, the United States was financially independent of Britain. It would not be long before New York would supplant London as the world's capital of capital.

It was not British "informal imperialism," but the combination of American "debtor diplomacy" and a financial class in Europe, primarily London, that was often eager to invest in U.S. securities that accounts for the intersection of finance and foreign relations in this period. Requiring capital to finance the government debt and internal improvements, American statesmen were forced to look to Europe for the nation's financial needs. The pages that follow explore how this influenced American foreign relations.

[43] Cain and Hopkins, *British Imperialism*, pp. 314–15.
[44] See Wilkins, *Foreign Investment*, p. 617.

I

The Baring Years, 1837–1861

"Ask about anything" concerning American securities, one American traveler in Britain remarked in the 1850s, "and the reply is, 'What does Mr. Thomas Baring say or think?'"[1] Indeed, contemporaries and historians alike have not disputed the prominent position Baring Brothers bank enjoyed in American finance in the decades before the Civil War.[2] The London firm dominated its European rivals in the business of American securities and, in the early years of this period, was one of the leading merchant houses in the cotton trade. Barings were kept informed of political and economic developments across the Atlantic through their correspondence with scores of American banks and agents. The bank's position in American finance was further underscored by its position as the official financial agency of the U.S. Government in Europe. Barings enjoyed a comparable status with several states, canal companies, and railroads. The firm's supremacy in Anglo-American business was so complete that in 1846 Joshua Bates, an American partner in the London house, declared that "as we now stand the permanent means of the House would enable us to buy out all our competitors and have a half million to spare."[3]

What is rarely mentioned, however, is that the financial and commercial prominence of Baring Brothers imparted tremendous political and diplomatic influence to the firm. It was no accident that the bank became intimately involved in American politics and foreign relations during this period. Correspondence between Joshua Bates in London and the bank's agent in the United States, Thomas Wren Ward, was as concerned with politics and diplomacy as it was with finance and business. Moreover, the firm maintained close relationships with leading statesmen on both sides of the Atlantic, particularly with the Whig leader from Massachusetts

---

[1] Ward to Bates, 1 June 1852, Thomas Wren Ward Papers, Massachusetts Historical Society (henceforth MHS).
[2] For the best works on the Barings, see Ralph Hidy, *The House of Baring in American Trade and Finance* (Cambridge, Mass., 1949); Philip Zeigler, *The Sixth Great Power: Barings, 1762–1929* (London, 1988).
[3] Bates to Ward, 5 April 1846, Ward Papers, MHS.

Daniel Webster. Given the power and influence of the firm, it is impossible to understand American foreign relations, particularly with Britain, without considering the prominent role played by Baring Brothers. Other British-based banks also developed relationships with the United States in this period. Firms such as George Peabody and Co. and, in later years, the Rothschilds entered the American market and became active in both financial and political matters.

The formation of American foreign policy in the decades preceding the Civil War, of course, was not determined by decisions taken in the headquarters of London banking houses. The ideology of "Manifest Destiny,"[4] the desire to obtain Pacific ports and expand the nation's export markets,[5] and the aspirations and anxieties of leading statesmen and propagandists[6] dominated the era and merged, particularly under the Polk administration, to fuel the remarkable extension and consolidation of the United States' continental empire. American foreign policy in this period, as one historian has aptly put it, was "the diplomacy of annexation."[7] The very process of this expansion, combined with the need to develop the nation's infrastructure, however, necessitated large sums of foreign capital. The twenty-five years preceding the Civil War thus witnessed an unprecedented increase in the nation's foreign indebtedness. As we shall see, the United States' reliance on foreign capital created problems for American diplomats during the border disputes of the 1840s and the attempts to construct an isthmian canal in the 1850s. Moreover, the depression that followed the Panic of 1837 led several states to default and/or repudiate their debts—actions that not only provoked foreign creditors to intervene in state politics, but that also led European capitalists to differentiate the states north of the Mason–Dixon line from those south of it in the run-up to the Civil War.

---

[4] Albert Katz Weinberg, *Manifest Destiny: A Study of Nationalist Expansionism in American History* (Baltimore, 1935); Reginald Horsman, *Race and Manifest Destiny: The Origins of American Racial Anglo-Saxonism* (Cambridge, Mass., 1981); Anders Stephanson, *Manifest Destiny: American Expansionism and the Empire of Right* (New York, 1995).

[5] Norman Graebner, *Empire on the Pacific: A Study in American Continental Expansion* (New York, 1955); Kinley Brauer, "Diplomacy of American Expansionism, 1821–1860," in William Becker and Samuel Wells (eds.), *Economics and World Power* (New York, 1984).

[6] Frederick Merk, *Manifest Destiny and Mission in American History: A Reinterpretation* (New York, 1963); Thomas Hietala, *Manifest Design: American Exceptionalism and Empire* (Ithaca, 2003).

[7] David Pletcher, *The Diplomacy of Annexation: Texas, Oregon and the Mexican War* (Columbia, Mo., 1973).

FINANCIAL AND DIPLOMATIC CRISIS

Andrew Jackson was no friend to financiers on either side of the Atlantic. Determined to dismantle the power of a cabal of moneyed interests who, the president argued, were exploiting the average American, Jackson lashed out against the financial institutions and prevailing notions of political economy of his day. The former general and hero of the War of 1812 campaigned against the national debt, arguing that it enriched bondholders—one-third of whom were foreign, principally British, when he took office in 1828—at the expense of taxpayers.[8] Accordingly, Jackson cut spending and began paying down the debt, a feat that he remarkably accomplished in his second term. The liquidation of the national debt in 1835, Richard Sylla recently remarked, was "an exceptional occurrence in world history."[9]

Jackson's hostility to centralized finance and foreign capitalists did not end with the elimination of the national debt. Early in his first term, Jackson vetoed a bill that extended federal funding to the construction of the Maysville Road, a proposed turnpike in Kentucky. The action was a historic triumph over Henry Clay and his Whig allies who argued that the federal government should sponsor internal improvements such as the building of roads and canals. Most famous, of course, was Jackson's veto of the renewal of the charter of the second Bank of the United States. By ending the federal government's association with the bank, Jackson struck at the very symbol of, as he called it, the "monied aristocracy" of the Northeast and Europe (thirty percent of the stock of the bank was held abroad, primarily in Britain).[10] Indeed, Jackson's fear that European investors' stake in the bank would subject the United States to the unchecked power of foreign financiers was one of the major reasons he vetoed the bank bill. Foreign ownership of the bank, Jackson declared, "would be far more formidable and dangerous than the naval and military power of the enemy."[11]

---

[8] Of the $58.4 million national debt in 1828, $19.1 million was held abroad ($14.15 million in Britain). See Mira Wilkins, *The History of Foreign Investment in the United States to 1914* (Cambridge, Mass., 1989), p. 53.

[9] Richard Sylla, "The United States: Financial Innovation and Adaptation," in Michael Bordo and Robert Cortes-Conde, *Transferring Wealth and Power from the Old to the New World* (Cambridge, 2001).

[10] Quoted in John Steele Gordon, *Hamilton's Blessing* (New York, 1997), p. 59. For foreign ownership of the second Bank of the United States, see Wilkins, *Foreign Investment*, p. 61.

[11] Quoted in Wilkins, *Foreign Investment*, p. 84. For a critique of Jackson's economic policies, see Bray Hammond, *Banks and Politics in America from the Revolution to the Civil War* (Princeton, 1957), pp. 326–450.

The irony of these actions was that in some instances they imparted power and influence to the very interests Jackson hoped to weaken. Denied federal assistance for vitally important internal improvements, state legislatures—aware of the political consequences of raising taxes—had no choice but to turn to private banks for assistance. As there was a dearth of financial institutions in the United States capable of underwriting expensive internal improvement projects, this often meant that states and canal companies were forced to look overseas for their financial needs. Thus, the 1830s were years of unprecedented foreign investment in American public securities despite the elimination of the national debt. Often fronting for infant banks, canals, and railroads, state governments marketed large bond issues both at home and abroad. In the years 1836-8 alone, states accrued more debt than they had in the previous fifty years.[12] By 1838, foreign investment in the United States reached an unprecedented $110 million, the majority of which was placed in state bonds.[13] "The barometer of the American money market," one congressman remarked, "hangs up at the stock exchange in London."[14]

From the perspective of British capitalists, American securities were a very attractive investment. Evinced in the repayment of the national debt, the developing and prospering United States appeared a relatively safe destination for British capital compared to the unstable governments of Latin America (many of which had defaulted on their foreign loans in the 1820s). Such financial probity confirmed stereotypes that, as fellow Anglo-Saxons, Americans could be trusted in pecuniary matters. Perhaps more importantly, American securities typically bore twice the interest rate of British consols (government bonds) that yielded only three percent. All of these factors led leading transatlantic banks, such as Baring Brothers and George Peabody and Co., to buy American securities on their own account and to serve as brokers in placing new issues in the capital markets of Europe. The prominence of these financial intermediaries extended further credibility to American stocks and bonds, while eliminating the logistical difficulties of investing in foreign securities. "Nearly all investments in Europe," one American observed, "are made by or in the advice of Bankers who, to a great extent, control the market."[15]

[12] B. U. Ratchford, *American State Debts* (Durham, N.C., 1941), pp. 80-3.
[13] Wilkins, *Foreign Investment*, p. 59. By 1838, thirty-eight percent of all American state bonds were held abroad, principally in England.
[14] Quoted in Ron Chernow, *The House of Morgan* (London, 1990), p. 4.
[15] Walker to Chase, 26 February 1864, Chase Papers, Collection No. 121, Historical Society of Pennsylvania. For a contemporary's view of American securities, see An Anglo-American, *American Securities* (London, 1860).

Barely had the boom in American securities began before the Panic of 1837 altered the way in which European investors viewed the United States. Traditionally, historians—following the lead of Jackson's contemporary critics such as John C. Calhoun—blamed the president for bringing on the financial crisis. The veto of the charter of the second Bank of the United States and the subsequent reallocation of federal funds from the bank into smaller "pet banks" crippled the nation's already weak banking system. Unchecked by any central authority, state-chartered pet banks multiplied their note issues and, in the words of a conservative Boston financier, engaged in "the most extended and wild speculations in property."[16] Jackson's Specie Circular of July 1836, a measure intended to curb this land speculation by requiring all public land to be purchased in coin, further set the stage for a financial crisis by removing gold from circulation. Subsequent runs on banks, the argument goes, led to the suspension of specie payments and contributed to an atmosphere of panic.

Although Jackson's policies no doubt contributed to the financial crisis of 1837, it is clear that the president should not bear all of the blame for a panic whose origins lay largely outside of his control. The decision in London in 1836 to raise interest rates, revisionists argue, led more to the financial crisis than did the Specie Circular.[17] Appalled by the depletion of gold reserves in London, which was partly the result of the boom in British investment in the United States, the Bank of England twice raised its discount rate in the summer 1836. Higher rates at home and the Bank's subsequent decision to withdraw credit from several banks involved in American finance led British firms to call in their outstanding loans in the United States.[18] This, of course, pinched American banks, particularly those that had irresponsibly speculated in land. The international origins of the crisis were also evinced in the collapse in the price of cotton. In March 1837, the month of the panic, cotton fell from fourteen to five cents per pound.[19] Denied the foreign exchange generated by cotton exports and unable to meet the demands of British creditors, an American banking panic was all but inevitable.

[16] Henry Lee to Baring Brothers, 1837, HC5.1.23. ING. Baring Archive (henceforth BA), London.

[17] For this interpretation, see Peter Temin, *The Jacksonian Economy* (New York, 1969); Hidy, *The House of Baring*, pp. 207–35; Hammond, *Banks and Politics in America*, pp. 500–48. For a discussion of the historiography of the Panic of 1837, see Jeremy Atack and Peter Passel, *A New Economic View of American History* (New York, 1994), pp. 96–102.

[18] *North American Review*, 58 (January 1844), p. 119.

[19] Hidy, *The House of Baring*, pp. 219–20.

The Panic of 1837 had both immediate and long-term economic implications. In the short term, American banks were forced to suspend specie payments in May 1837, not to resume until the following spring. Fledging banks in the American South, many of which had been established by the influx of foreign capital into state securities in the 1830s, were particularly hard hit. Across the Atlantic, three major Anglo-American firms, the so-called "three W's" of George Wildes and Co., Thomas Wilson and Co., and Timothy Wiggin and Co., also went under.[20] Brown, Shipley and Co., a leading transatlantic merchant bank based in Liverpool, only survived the crisis after being bailed out by a £2 million loan from the Bank of England.[21] Indeed, Baring Brothers was the only major Anglo-American firm that escaped the crisis unscathed (the Rothschilds were only just entering the American market at this point as August Belmont appointed himself as the firm's agent during the panic). Barings' strength in a time of financial turmoil, their American agent Thomas Wren Ward wrote from Boston, made the house "the sheet anchor of the commercial world."[22] It would not be long before the bank's unmatched financial power translated into increased diplomatic and political influence.

In the larger picture, the crisis of 1837 initiated a depression that lasted well into the next decade. This did not seem the case a year after the panic as most banks had resumed specie payments (although some in the South and West remained in suspension) and cotton prices and land sales returned to pre-panic levels. The crisis seemed to be contained and states, canal companies, and banks, in need of fresh capital, sent agents to Britain to market new bond issues. In fact, from 1837–9, state debts increased by more than forty percent and an estimated $100 million of American stocks and bonds were hawked on the London money markets.[23] This reckless expansion endangered the fragile recovery, particularly when wary British capitalists stopped buying American securities in 1839. The second financial crisis in as many years ensued in October 1839 when the Bank of the United States, now operating under a Pennsylvania charter and unsuccessfully marketing several bond issues in Europe, failed.

[20] Ralph Hidy, "The Origin and Functions of Anglo-American Merchant Bankers, 1815–1860," *Journal of Economic History*, 1 (1941), p. 64.
[21] Frank Thistlethwaite, *The Anglo-American Connection in the Early Nineteenth Century* (Philadelphia, 1959), p. 18.
[22] Quoted in Hidy, *The House of Baring*, p. 234.
[23] Reginald McGrane, *Foreign Bondholders and American State Debts* (New York, 1933), p. 18; Hidy, *The House of Baring*, pp. 236–7; Wilkins, *Foreign Investment*, p. 68.

Thus, the 1840s began with the United States in the midst of a financial crisis. The nation's banking system was in disarray, merchants were short on credit, and victims of the panic fled west to start a new life on the other side of the Mississippi. Deeply indebted states, however, could not escape from their problems. With revenue down and budget deficits increasing, many on both sides of the Atlantic began to worry that indebted states might not be able to meet their obligations. Rumors circulated in London that states legislatures lacked legal authority to contract foreign debts and would not be bound to redeem bonds held by European creditors. Such reports led Baring Brothers to ask their legal consultant in the United States, the Whig senator from Massachusetts Daniel Webster, "has the legislature of one of the American states legal and constitutional power to contract loans at home and abroad?" Webster, an advocate of internal improvements and a friend of British capitalists, wasted no time in responding with a resounding yes before privately encouraging his employers to purchase more American securities.[24] Baring Brothers was not convinced. Still wary of the ability and desire of states to meet their obligations and barred from filing suits against states in federal courts by the Eleventh Amendment, the bank issued a circular in 1840 that urged Congress to issue a "national pledge" to guarantee state debts.[25]

The idea that the federal government should assume state debts—as it had done after the Revolution—was not unique to British capitalists. Determined to preserve the financial integrity of the nation and to continue to attract foreign investment, the Whig leader from Maryland William Cost Johnson called for the issuance of a $200 million national loan, backed by increased federal land sales, to allow the federal government to cover state debts during the depression.[26] Predictably, Democrats outspokenly denounced the plan. Calhoun labeled it a "wild and ruinous" scheme that would condemn the federal government to an insurmountable debt (not to mention undermine states'

---

[24] Baring Brothers to Webster, 12 October 1839, in Charles Wiltse (ed.), *The Papers of Daniel Webster: Personal Correspondence* (henceforth *DWPC*), vol. 4 (London, 1974–86), pp. 401–2; Webster to Baring Brothers, 16 October 1839, *DWPC*, 4, pp. 404–7. Webster later warned the Barings to invest cautiously in some states. See Webster to Bates, 26 March 1840, *DWPC*, 5, pp. 23–4.
[25] Hidy, *The House of Baring*, p. 283. For the Eleventh Amendment and the legal standing of state debts, see William English, "Understanding the Costs of Sovereign Default: American State Debts in the 1840s," *American Economic Review*, 86 (March 1996), pp. 259–75.
[26] House Report No. 296, 27th Congress, 3rd session, vol. 4, pp. 1–15.

rights).[27] However, more than just economic and legal issues were at stake. To assume state debts, Missouri Senator Thomas Hart Benton argued in 1840, would be "to the enormous and undue advantage of foreign capitalists." Catering policy to European financiers would only induce "foreigners to interfere in our affairs, and to bring all the influences of a moneyed power to operate upon public opinion, upon our elections, and upon State and Federal legislations, to produce a consummation so tempting to their cupidity, and so profitable to their interest."[28] Democrats repeated Benton's nationalistic arguments across the country, particularly during the election of 1840 when they warned voters that a Whig victory would be tantamount to the takeover of the U.S. Government by foreign financiers.[29] Although they won the presidency in 1840, few Whigs sought to spend their political capital on an unpopular scheme for federal assumption of state debts and Johnson's plan foundered in Congress in 1842-3.

Denied federal assistance and jolted by the bankruptcy of the Bank of the United States in February 1841, states began to default on the interest payments of their outstanding debts. By 1842, eight states and one territory had defaulted: Arkansas, Illinois, Indiana, Louisiana, Maryland, Michigan, Mississippi, Pennsylvania, and Florida (which would become a state in 1845). For most of these states, defaulting was seen as a temporary action resorted to only because of the financial exigencies of the depression. British creditors, however, rightly pointed out that few such states had made any attempt to increase revenue or cut spending to make funds available for servicing their debt. Other states, particularly those in the South, made no effort to appease foreign capitalists before they defaulted. Echoing the xenophobia of Thomas Hart Benton, Governor Alexander McNutt of Mississippi attacked the states' foreign creditors, namely the Jewish Rothschilds. "The blood of Judas and Shylock flows" in their veins, McNutt declared before warning of a Rothschild conspiracy to "mortgage our cotton fields and make serfs of our children."[30] Another Mississippi politician encouraged the fleecing of British investors, vowing that he would rather "slap John Bull in the face than to quail before his power."[31]

---

[27] Calhoun to Thomas Clemson, 14 February 1843, in Robert Meriwether (ed.), *The Papers of John C. Calhoun* (South Carolina, 1959), vol. 16, p. 667.
[28] Senate Doc. 18, 26th Congress, 1st Session, vol. 2, pp. 1-2.
[29] For more on this issue during the election of 1840, see Wilkins, *Foreign Investment*, pp. 84-5.
[30] McNutt quoted in A Member of the Boston Bar, *An Account of the Origin of the Mississippi Doctrine of Repudiation* (Boston, 1842).
[31] Quoted in McGrane, *Foreign Bondholders*, p. 34.

Such remarks did little to comfort British capitalists. Fearing that the prevailing hostility to public debts and foreign financiers in America would lead states to repudiate their debts outright, European capitalists took action. In early 1841 leading European banks, headed by Baring Brothers, the Rothschilds, and the Dutch house of Hope and Co., privately urged President John Tyler and now Secretary of State Daniel Webster to pressure delinquent states to resume interest payments on their debts. The Tyler administration did not respond to the petition, although Webster privately assisted Barings' agent Thomas Wren Ward in pressuring state politicians to increase taxation.[32] With action through official channels yielding no results, European capitalists began to take matters into their own hands. As early as October 1841, Baring Brothers urged Ward to use "all gentle means" to get defaulting states to pay.[33] Hope and Co. suggested that all European banks unite in not granting credit to any American body until the state debt issue was resolved.[34] Although this plan was never formally executed, the early and mid-1840s saw an almost complete cessation of European investment in the United States. As one Rothschild declared, "let us get rid of that blasted country ... it is the most blasted & the most stinking country in the world."[35] Not only did Barings refuse new loan offers, but the firm also dumped one-third of its American holdings between 1843 and 1848.[36]

It was not only the leading banks, however, that were burned by the defaulting states. "Many persons of small incomes," a U.S. Treasury report conceded, "have invested their whole estates in American securities, because they paid a greater dividend; and failure to pay any part of the interest has left many families in utter destitution."[37] This was particularly the case with holders of defaulted Pennsylvania bonds. Twenty-four million out of the state's $34 million outstanding debt was held abroad.[38] Many of these bondholders were small investors and pensioners who had invested in the securities on the advice of their bankers. One such investor was Reverend Sydney Smith, the former

[32] Belmont to N.M.R. and Sons, 22 April 1841, T54/137, Rothschild Archive (henceforth RA), London; McGrane, *Foreign Bondholders*, p. 31; Hidy, *The House of Baring*, p. 294.
[33] Quoted in McGrane, *Foreign Bondholders*, p. 48.
[34] Baring Brothers to Hope and Co., 27 May 1842, Baring Papers (henceforth BP), Library of Congress [microfilm].
[35] Quoted in Ferguson, *The House of Rothschild*, I, p. 375.
[36] Hidy, *The House of Baring*, p. 368.
[37] House Doc. No. 197, 27th Congress, 3rd Session, pp. 1–6.
[38] These figures are the estimates of Nicholas Biddle. See Biddle to Webster, 20 April 1843, *DWPC*, 4, pp. 295–6.

editor of the *Edinburgh Review* and the Canon of St. Paul's in London, who petitioned Congress to right the wrongs committed by delinquent states.[39] The delinquency of Pennsylvania inspired Smith to compose a petition to the U.S. Congress. "I never met a Pennsylvanian at a London dinner without feeling a disposition to seize and divide him," Smith declared, "How such a man can set himself down at an English table without feeling that he owes two or three pounds to every man in company I am at a loss to conceive; he has no more right to eat with honest men than a leper has to eat with clean men."[40] Smith's anger was echoed by Poet Laureate William Wordsworth, whose family also had the misfortune of investing in Pennsylvania bonds. In two little-known poems composed in the 1840s, Wordsworth criticized the state for its financial and moral infidelity:

> All who revere the memory of Penn
> Grieve for the land on whose wild woods his name
> Was fondly grafted with a virtuous aim,
> Renounced, abandoned by degenerate Men
> For state-dishonour black as ever came
> To upper air from Mammon's loathsome den.[41]

If 1837 can be regarded as the date that Anglo-American financial relations began to deteriorate, it can also be viewed as the year that initiated a series of diplomatic disputes between Britain and the United States that would not be resolved for nearly a decade. After an unsuccessful rebellion against British rule in Canada, a small band of Canadian rebels, led by William Lyon Mackenzie, fled to Buffalo, New York, to regroup. Once there, Mackenzie recruited sympathetic Americans who used the *Caroline* to ship supplies to the rebels who were now gathering on Navy Island (on the St. Lawrence River), presumably to launch another attack into Canada. In December 1837, a Royal Navy officer ordered a pre-emptive attack on the *Caroline*, which was moored in American waters. The British-Canadian force boarded the *Caroline* (killing an American in the process) and then set the ship ablaze and drifted it down Niagara Falls. Americans were furious, though President

---

[39] Smith invested £1,000 in Pennsylvania securities. See Everett to Webster, 18 April 1845, *DWPC*, 6, pp. 83–4.
[40] Sydney Smith, *Letters on American Debts* (London, 1844), p. 15.
[41] William Wordsworth, "To the Pennsylvanians" (1845). See also Wordsworth, "Men of the Western World" (1842). Wordsworth worried that his family would "be in their graves before [repayment] comes." For more, see Francis Gribble, *What America Owes Europe* (London, 1932).

Van Buren calmly dispatched General Winfield Scott to upstate New York to prevent vigilante retaliation. American anger found a target in 1840 when Canadian Alexander McLeod boasted in a Buffalo tavern of killing an American during the attack. Local authorities arrested McLeod and, despite British warnings, threatened execution. "McLeod's Execution would produce War," Foreign Secretary Lord Palmerston vowed, "war immediate and frightful in its Character."[42]

The *Caroline* and McLeod controversies were accompanied by a Northeastern border dispute that had festered since the Treaty of Paris in 1783 failed to clearly mark the division between Canada and Maine. The United States did little to help resolve the issue when the Senate rejected the arbitration ruling of the King of the Netherlands in 1832. At issue were some 12,000 square miles of land important for its timber, access to fisheries, and, most importantly, as a strategic route to the interior of Canada when the St. Lawrence was frozen. In 1839 the so-called "Aroostook War" erupted over this disputed land in the Aroostook Valley. Opposing groups of Maine and New Brunswick lumberjacks took turns crossing the border and arresting each other (in one instance, an American was arrested for whistling "Yankee Doodle" on the Canadian side) before engaging in a drunken bar-brawl. Although the episode, as its historians have put it, was "nearly comical," it illustrated the potential for the unresolved border to inflame local passions, which, in turn, might further heighten tensions between the two nations.[43] "We are in a good deal of anxiety," Baring Brothers wrote to their New York correspondents, "for in spite of the pacific disposition of the two Governments, the border population may go to war and eventually involve the two countries."[44]

Finally, Southern states were brought into the fray during the *Creole* incident of 1841. Difficulties arose when slaves aboard the *Creole*, a ship involved in the legal internal slave trade between Virginia and New Orleans, commandeered and redirected the ship to the British West Indies where slavery had been outlawed since 1833. Once there, British officials freed the slaves without consulting their American owners.

---

[42] Quoted in Howard Jones and Donald Rakestraw, *Prologue to Manifest Destiny: Anglo-American Relations in the 1840s* (Wilmington, Del., 1997), p. 47. This monograph is an amalgamation of the authors' previous work. See Howard Jones, *To the Webster-Ashburton Treaty: A Study in Anglo-American Relations, 1783–1843* (Chapel Hill, 1977); Donald Rakestraw, *For Honor or Destiny: The Anglo-American Crisis over the Oregon Territory* (New York, 1995). See also Kenneth Stevens, *Border Diplomacy: The* Caroline *and McLeod Affairs in Anglo-American-Canadian Relations, 1837–1842* (London, 1989).

[43] Jones and Rakestraw, *Prologue to Manifest Destiny*, pp. 8–19.

[44] Baring Brothers to Grinnell, Minturn and Co., 19 October 1841, BP.

Predictably, Southerners demanded compensation from the British Government for their confiscated property.

Although the causes of these disputes were varied, their effect on the financial markets was singular. As Joshua Bates put it, "The Maine Boundary Question has again become a matter of deep anxiety to all engaged in commercial transactions." The fear that local passions in Maine and New Brunswick would ignite a wider controversy became evident on British stock exchanges where investors would not touch American securities. "The injury to our country in a pecuniary point of view in every month," Bates reported to Secretary of State Webster, "is the value of all of the wild land in Maine."[45] British capitalists as well had an economic interest in avoiding a war over wild land in Maine. As the Rothschilds' American agent August Belmont wrote to his superiors in London, "England, in a war with this country, her largest debtor, the consumer of her manufacturers, has all to lose and nothing to gain."[46]

The onus of resolving these disputes and restoring confidence in American securities in Britain fell upon the shoulders of Daniel Webster. More than any other statesmen of the era, Webster sought to cultivate peaceful relations with Britain. As his most recent biographer put it, Webster was "an ardent, indeed rabid Anglophile."[47] In a speech in Oxford during his trip to Britain in 1839, Webster pointed to his arm before proclaiming, "I am proud to know what blood flows in these veins."[48] Such words were intended as more than a mere celebration of his Anglo-Saxon heritage (though Webster was certainly proud of this). The archetypal Whig, Webster was the nation's leading advocate for the development of the nation through internal improvements such as the building of canals, turnpikes, and railroads. Denied federal funds by his Democratic rivals and unable to rely on nascent American investment banks, Webster believed that the nation must turn to foreign, primarily British, capitalists for assistance.[49]

---

[45] Bates to Webster, 26 April 1840, *DWPC*, 5, pp. 30–1. See also Baring Brothers to Ward, 18 November 1841, BP.
[46] Belmont to N.M.R. and Sons, 5 April 1840, T54/112, RA.
[47] Robert Remini, *Daniel Webster* (New York, 1997), p. 484. See also Charles Wiltse, "Daniel Webster and the British Experience," *Proceedings of the Massachusetts Historical Society*, 85 (1973), pp. 58–77.
[48] Quoted in Remini, *Daniel Webster*, p. 494.
[49] Webster, historian Robert Carey contends, "paid a high tribute to the part foreign capital had played in the development of American banking, internal improvements, and industry." Robert Carey, *Daniel Webster as an Economist* (New York, 1966), p. 113.

In seeking financial help from abroad, Webster argued, the nation was not placing itself at the mercy of a decadent European elite, but was simply following the trail blazed by economic nationalists such as Alexander Hamilton and Albert Gallatin. "From the commencement of the government, it has been thought desirable to invite... the introduction of foreign capital," Webster maintained in an 1832 Senate speech, "whatever State has created a debt has been willing that foreigners should become purchasers, and desirous of it." Webster countered Andrew Jackson's claim that foreign ownership of the second Bank of the United States threatened national security by accurately pointing out that federal law precluded foreign stockholders from serving as directors.[50] Moreover, Webster argued that foreign investment kept down interest rates by enlarging the market for American securities and was therefore economically advantageous for the whole of the nation at the expense of American capitalists—a theme he hoped would counter Democratic accusations that Whig policies were designed to benefit the wealthy. "If the introduction of foreign capital," Webster declared in his 1832 speech at the National Republican Convention in Worcester, Massachusetts,

be discountenanced and discouraged, the American moneylender may fix his own rate anywhere from five to twelve per cent. per annum. On the other hand, if the introduction of foreign capital be countenanced and encouraged, its effect is to keep down the rate of interest, and to bring the value of money in the United States so much the nearer to its value in older and richer countries. Every dollar brought from abroad, and put into the mass of active capital at home, by so much diminished the rate of interest; and by so much, therefore, benefits all the active and trading classes of society, at the expense of the American capitalists.[51]

Webster's racial, diplomatic, and economic views thus all converged and led to one conclusion: maintaining Anglo-American peace was essential to the nation's development and prosperity. In this sense, Webster was both a theorist and, during his tenure as secretary of state in the early 1840s, a key protagonist of debtor diplomacy. However, promoting foreign investment was more than just a political goal for Webster. In 1831 Baring Brothers hired Webster as a legal and financial consultant,

---

[50] Daniel Webster, "Veto of the Bank Bill," in Charles Wiltse (ed.), *The Papers of Daniel Webster: Speeches and Formal Writings*, vol. 1 (London, 1986), pp. 511–3. See also Wilkins, *Foreign Investment*, p. 83.

[51] Daniel Webster, "Speech at the National Republican Convention at Worcester," in Wiltse (ed.), *The Papers of Daniel Webster: Speeches and Formal Writings*, vol. 1, pp. 541–2. See also Daniel Walker Howe, *The Political Culture of the American Whigs* (Chicago, 1979), p. 141.

a position he would hold for the remainder of his life. The Massachusetts Whig advised the London bank on political and legal issues and alerted the firm to profitable investment opportunities in the United States. In the course of this work, Webster developed close relationships with Baring executives Thomas Wren Ward in Boston, the American expatriate in London Joshua Bates, and the firm's head, Thomas Baring. While secretary of state, Webster regularly corresponded with these financiers, relying on Bates in particular for inside information concerning political and financial developments in Britain. Barings paid Webster a retainer fee for his services (typically £1,000), in addition to giving him kickbacks such as $500 to help fund his trip to England in 1839.[52] It should not be overlooked that the Panic of 1837 ruined Webster financially and he spent the remainder of his political career attempting to cover his debts. Even while he was secretary of state and negotiating a treaty with Britain, Webster attempted to profit from volatile capital markets (and perhaps his inside information regarding the status of Anglo-American relations) by selling his holdings of American securities in London "at a higher than market rate" through Baring Brothers.[53]

Webster's commitment to preserving Anglo-American peace led him to remain at his post of secretary of state after the death of President William Henry Harrison in April 1841 (the rest of the cabinet resigned soon after John Tyler assumed the presidency).[54] It also led him to privately press New York Governor William H. Seward to release Alexander McLeod, the Canadian subject accused of killing an American during the *Caroline* incident. Although Seward refused to budge for political reasons, the war that Palmerston had threatened was avoided when a New York jury acquitted McLeod in 1841. The Northeastern border question proved more problematic as local tensions remained high and continued to threaten to erupt into war. Fortunately, Webster would not have to resolve this thorny dispute by himself. In December 1841 Sir Robert Peel, the British prime minister, named Lord Ashburton a special emissary to resolve all outstanding disputes with the United States.

---

[52] "Subscription for Webster," *DWPC*, 4, pp. 559–60; Hidy, *The House of Baring*, p. 100.
[53] During his negotiations with Lord Asburton, Webster asked Thomas Wren Ward to sell his Illinois securities in London. See Ward to Bates, 2 July 1842, Ward Papers, MHS. Webster was also a consultant to the Bank of the United States (to which he was also deeply indebted) and had no problem reminding Nicholas Biddle that his retainer needed to be "renewed or refreshed as usual." See Remini, *Daniel Webster*, pp. 261–2, 511.
[54] Bradford Perkins, *The Creation of a Republican Empire, 1776–1865* (Cambridge, 1993), p. 212.

A self-proclaimed "messenger of peace," Ashburton had a history of personal, financial, and political involvement with the United States.[55] Known prior to his ascension to the peerage as Alexander Baring, Ashburton served as head of Baring Brothers bank until his retirement in 1831. Under Ashburton's leadership, the bank expanded its holdings and operations in the United States, particularly its relationship with the second Bank of the United States. The expansion of Baring Brothers' American business was in part a result of Ashburton's personal interests. He was married to the daughter of Pennsylvania Senator William Bingham and, on his first trip to the United States, purchased over one million acres of real estate in Maine (none of which, it should be noted, was the territory in contention). Politically, Ashburton served as a Tory MP from 1806 to 1835 and was known for his pro-American views, particularly his opposition to war with the United States in 1812. "A more acceptable selection of a person for the important mission could not have been made," the head of the U.S. legation in London Edward Everett wrote to Webster, "even the credit of American Securities has somewhat improved."[56] As Lady Ashburton put it to Webster, "if you don't like him we can send you nothing better."[57]

Although scholars have acknowledged the amazing fact that the 1842 Webster–Ashburton Treaty was negotiated by two men who were both intimately connected with Baring Brothers bank, financial considerations play no role in the narratives of the diplomacy between Webster and Ashburton.[58] As we shall see, negotiations concerning the Northeastern boundary were anything but smooth or predetermined by some secret backroom deal brokered in Barings' London headquarters. Moreover, as Joshua Bates pointed out at the time, Ashburton had already secured his personal fortune (estimated at £2.5 million), had sold most of his American holdings, and, therefore, held little personal financial interests in the negotiations.[59] Similarly, accusations that Webster received £10,000 from Baring Brothers to secure the Senate's passage of the treaty have been proven false.[60]

[55] Ashburton to Webster, 2 January 1842, in Kenneth Shewmaker (ed.), *The Papers of Daniel Webster: Diplomatic Papers*, 2 vols. (London: University Press of New England, 1983–7) (hereafter *DPDW*), 1, pp. 486–8.
[56] Everett to Webster, 31 December 1841, *DPDW*, 1, pp. 173–7.
[57] Lady Ashburton to Webster, 12 January 1842, *DPDW*, 1, pp. 490–1.
[58] See, for instance, Jones and Rakestraw, *Prologue to Manifest Destiny*; Jones, *To the Webster-Ashburton Treaty*; Stevens, *Border Diplomacy*.
[59] See Bates to Ward, 3 and 10 January 1842, Ward Papers, MHS. See also Jones and Rakestraw, *Prologue to Manifest Destiny*, p. 183.
[60] Remini, *Daniel Webster*, pp. 616–17.

By narrowly focusing on the personal interests of Webster and Ashburton, however, historians have missed the larger point. The Barings' connection with the Anglo-American diplomacy of 1842 exemplified the nexus between finance and foreign relations that led statesmen on both sides of the Atlantic to avoid war at all costs. Ashburton's view that "the material interests of the two countries call loudly for peace and friendship" was representative of the thinking of Peel and other Tories in Britain who believed that it was more in the national interest to preserve and expand the economic relationship with the United States than it was to defend national honor by demanding territory in far-off Maine (the policy preferred by Palmerston).[61] Such a view was the perfect complement to Webster's commitment to Anglo-American peace and his attempts to attract British investment to the United States. Considering this shared objective, it should come as little surprise that executives of Baring Brothers had a hand in policy decisions and helped to lay the groundwork for a diplomatic agreement in the buildup to the negotiations. Joshua Bates, for example, confidentially passed information from Webster's letters to British statesmen in order to influence their decision regarding whom to appoint as special emissary.[62] This contributed—perhaps even led—to Peel's selection of Ashburton. Baring agents also regularly corresponded on the diplomatic issue, serving as an informal conduit through which Webster and Ashburton could sound out proposals prior to their talks.[63]

New evidence also reveals that in the run-up to the Webster–Ashburton negotiations the Barings offered their services in brokering a loan to the United States. Significantly, this offer was conditional on the success of the two diplomats' treaty talks.[64] Just as Ashburton prepared to sail across the Atlantic to discuss the Northeastern boundary and other outstanding disputes, Joshua Bates informed Webster that the bank would be willing to issue a five percent $12 million loan on behalf of the United States once "the result of Lord Ashburton's mission is known to be favourable." Given the federal government's need for capital at this time (the Treasury, as we shall see, attempted to procure a foreign loan a few months

---

[61] Ashburton to Webster, 2 January 1842, *DPDW*, 1, pp. 486–8. For this point, see Kenneth Bourne, *The Foreign Policy of Victorian England, 1830–1902* (Oxford, 1970), p. 50.
[62] See Bates to Ward, 3 January 1842, Ward Papers, MHS; Everett to Webster, 3 January 1842, *DPDW*, 1, pp. 488–90.
[63] See, for example, Webster's recommendations contained in Ward to Bates, 16 May 1842, Ward Papers, MHS. See also Bates to Ward, 17 September 1841, Ward Papers, MHS.
[64] Bates to Webster, 15 April 1842, Ward Papers, MHS; Baring Brothers to Hope and Co., 27 May 1842, BP.

later to cover government deficits) and Webster's political views, this was a very attractive offer. Indeed, Webster had already informally inquired whether the Barings would be interested in brokering a new U.S. loan.[65] However, "should [Ashburton] fail," Bates added, "it will be *impossible* for anyone in the United States to negotiate a loan abroad." As he put it more succinctly in a letter to Ward, "No one will venture to saddle themselves with the loan while the relations between the two countries give rise to war speeches in Congress and there is any chance that the mission of Lord Ashburton will fail."[66] Furthermore, Bates hinted to Webster that without a new loan to guarantee the credit of the United States, Barings might resign its position as the financial agency of the U.S. Navy. Thus, on the eve of the Webster–Ashburton negotiations, Bates used both a carrot and a stick to press upon the U.S. secretary of state the financial imperative of resolving Anglo-American diplomatic disputes.

Despite their mutual interest in maintaining peace and this extra incentive for a deal, Webster and Ashburton struggled to resolve the border dispute when negotiations began in the summer 1842. The issue was complicated both by Webster's decision to include delegates from Maine and Massachusetts in the negotiations and by a revision of Ashburton's instructions that demanded more land for a proposed military road linking Halifax and Quebec.[67] Moreover, the two statesmen's respect for each other did not prevent them from resorting to the old tricks of diplomacy. In what Howard Jones and Donald Rakestraw label the "Machiavellian prelude to negotiations," Webster concealed maps that upheld British territorial claims from Ashburton and used secret service funds to finance propaganda and the lobbying of state officials in Maine.[68] For his part, Ashburton secretly consulted with New Brunswick representatives who demanded all of the disputed area of Madawaska. By July talks stalled and Ashburton begged Webster to allow him out of the summer heat of Washington, D.C. "I must throw myself on your compassion to contrive some how or other to get me released," Ashburton wrote to Webster, "I continue to crawl about in these heats by day and pass my nights in a sleepless fever."[69]

---

[65] Ward to Bates, 30 October 1841 and 16 May 1842, Ward Papers, MHS.
[66] Bates to Ward, 20 May 1842, Ward Papers, MHS.
[67] See Webster to Everett, 16 May 1842, *DPDW*, 1, pp. 560–1; Ashburton to Aberdeen, 26 April 1842, *DPDW*, 1, pp. 544–7.
[68] Jones and Rakestraw, *Prologue to Manifest Destiny*, pp. 97–119.
[69] Ashburton to Webster, 1 July 1842, *DPDW*, 1, p. 604.

That the two diplomats succeeded in negotiating what became known as the Webster–Ashburton Treaty in these circumstances illustrates their desire to preserve peace and to promote economic intercourse between the two nations. Although financial matters were not within the purview of the treaty, the political and economic views of the two negotiators led them to persist in their talks even when the differences between them— namely the ownership of Madawaska—appeared insurmountable. Both diplomats recognized that a failure to resolve the diplomatic controversy would have costs far greater than anything to be gained from the territory and issues in dispute. A breakdown in the talks would result in a complete suspension of British investment in the United States, a reduction in transatlantic trade, and a possible run on banks because of the fear of war. As Bates reminded Webster during the negotiations, only the settlement of Anglo-American differences could "produce a favourable change" in American securities on the London Stock Exchange.[70] Thus did the goal of the negotiators shift from resolving all outstanding disputes between the two nations to the more attainable objective of successfully negotiating a treaty—even if it left some issues unresolved. As Ashburton put it during the negotiations, "For my own part what seems most important is that there should be a settlement of some sort, and I do not attach all the importance which some do to the precise terms." Webster certainly agreed, having already stated that "No difference shall be permitted seriously to endanger the maintenance of peace with England."[71]

Ratified by the Senate on 20 August 1842, the Webster–Ashburton Treaty was the product of mutual compromise and diplomatic sidestepping. Although the United States received a slight majority of the disputed land (7,015 of the 12,000 square miles) along with the strategic position of Rouse's Point, Ashburton secured enough territory for a British military road. This establishment of the Maine–Canadian border, along with the marking of the border in the Lake of the Woods region (in modern day Minnesota), constituted the central achievement of the treaty. The other provisions of the agreement are more notable for how they glossed over persisting disagreements than for how they definitively resolved differences. For example, Webster dropped demands for reparations to the American owners of the escaped slaves aboard the *Creole* in exchange for a British assurance not to interfere with future American vessels brought by "accident or by violence" to British ports. Indemnity

---

[70] Bates to Webster, 13 June 1842, *DWPC*, 5, pp. 218–20.
[71] Both quoted in H. C. Allen, *Great Britain and the United States: A History of Anglo-American Relations, 1783–1952* (London, 1954), p. 397.

payments were also avoided in settling the *Caroline* and McLeod disputes when the two diplomats merely exchanged notes that served as expressions of regret for their respective government's role in the affairs. Both of these issues, as we shall see, would resurface during the Joint Claims Convention of the 1850s. The exchange of position papers delineating each government's stance on impressment served as the treaty's "resolution" to this historically inflammable issue. Article 8 of the treaty, which pledged both nations to maintain a naval force off the coast of Africa to prevent the illegal slave trade, also soon proved hollow when the U.S. Congress cut funding for this commitment and successive secretaries of the Navy (many of whom were Southerners) showed little enterprise in giving the necessary orders.[72] Perhaps most significantly, Webster and Ashburton postponed controversy when they avoided establishing a border in the contested Oregon territory.

Thus, through its emphasis of style over substance, the Webster–Ashburton Treaty succeeded more in covering up the symptoms—rather than eliminating the sources—of Anglo-American differences. It may be useful to remember that compromise, as Jones and Rakestraw argue, "is the essence of diplomacy."[73] This was no doubt the case in 1842 as mutual compromises enabled both sides to maintain their national honor and preserve their national interests (despite the predictable opposition of nationalists in both countries). The burden of establishing the Oregon border, Webster and Ashburton decided, could fall on the shoulders of future compromisers. However, it should also be pointed out that in international relations appearances are often as important as realities. In this sense, Webster and Ashburton's success lay not so much in the specific provisions of the treaty (many of which would prove inadequate), but in how the agreement restored confidence—particularly to the British capitalists who were wary of investing in American securities—that peace would be maintained. In this way, Webster and Ashburton's mutual interest in using diplomacy to advance economic objectives helps account for the curious end product of the negotiations.

It stands as a great irony, therefore, that the treaty did not yield the financial benefits that the two diplomats had anticipated. This was the result of an issue outside of the control of Webster and Ashburton: the depressed state of the American economy. The Barings shelved their plans to issue a U.S. loan when American states defaulted on their

---

[72] See Jones and Rakestraw, *Prologue to Manifest Destiny*, p. 142.
[73] Jones and Rakestraw, *Prologue to Manifest Destiny*, p. 138.

interest payments in 1842. Despite the easing of diplomatic tension, Barings informed one of their New York correspondents, "no new loan shall be introduced here while there is any one of the states as a defaulter."[74] The Barings were not the only financiers in Britain who maintained that the failure of several states to honor their commitments impaired the credit of the United States as a whole. American securities became known as "American insecurities" on the London Stock Exchange.[75] "As long as there is one state in the Union in default," George Peabody maintained, "no U.S. Government bonds can be negotiated [in Britain]."[76] An American expatriate banker in Britain, Peabody experienced British anger regarding defaulting states firsthand when he was blackballed from the London Reform Club. Even astute observers at home could foresee that the unsettled condition of the state debts made it unpropitious to introduce a loan on the European markets. "It is certain that no negotiation could be effected there but at usurious interest," John C. Calhoun declared on the Senate floor, "and on a considerable extension of the time for redemption."[77]

Ignoring these warnings, Secretary of the Treasury Walter Forward dispatched William Robinson to Europe shortly after the ratification of the Webster–Ashburton Treaty to negotiate a multimillion dollar loan to cover the deficits the government had run since 1837.[78] There was little chance that the Robinson mission would succeed in the prevailing climate of anti-Americanism in the City. "No house, however strong or influential in the money market of Europe," Robinson soon reported back to Washington, "dare venture to present an American loan to the British public, with the slightest hope that any portion of it would be taken off their hands." Overend, Gurney and Co. of London informed Robinson that they would consider the offer only if the proceeds of the loan were used to redeem defaulted state bonds. In Paris, James de Rothschild was even more skeptical of the proposal. "You may tell your government that you have seen the man who is the head of finances of Europe," the banker

---

[74] Baring Brothers to Grinnell, Minturn and Co., 18 May 1842, BP. See also Baring Brothers to Grinnell, Minturn and Co., 19 September 1842, BP.
[75] Bates to Webster, 15 April 1842, Ward Papers, MHS.
[76] Peabody to Unknown, estimated 1840–5, Peabody Papers, B197 F1, Essex Institute, Salem, Mass.
[77] Calhoun speech to Senate, 22 January 1842, in Meriwether (ed.), *The Papers of John C. Calhoun*, vol. 16, p. 74. See also Calhoun speech to Senate, 12 April 1842, pp. 220–33.
[78] Forward to Tyler, 18 April 1842, Record Group 56, Entry 4, National Archives II (henceforth NAII), College Park, Md. Young to Haggerty, 2 September 1842, RG56, E29, NAII.

bluntly informed another American agent, "and that he has told you that they cannot borrow a dollar, not a dollar."⁷⁹ "The condition of American credit in Europe," Robinson concluded, "is a source of deep humiliation to every American who visits that section of the world."⁸⁰

RESTORING AMERICAN CREDIT

Despite the humiliation of Americans abroad, it was European creditors, not American debtors, who labored to correct the actions of the nine defaulting American states. As we have seen, leading European banks unsuccessfully pressed the Tyler administration to exert its influence on the delinquent states in 1841. The following year British holders of defaulted American securities composed an "Appeal by Holders of American State Stocks" in the London *Times* and petitioned Edward Everett, head of the U.S. legation in London, and Foreign Secretary Lord Aberdeen to censure the offending states. Again, nothing came of the appeal except Aberdeen's statement that the British Government had "no concern with the securities in question and no power to compel payment of the sums required."⁸¹ Even the nationalistic Foreign Secretary Lord Palmerston stated that "British subjects who buy foreign securities do so at their own risk and must abide the consequences."⁸² In his famous circular of 1848, Palmerston informed British capitalists that the government would not help them recover their defaulted investments in foreign securities that could have been employed "in profitable undertakings at home."⁸³

With no hope of assistance from the British government, leading investment banks in London took matters into their own hands. Baring Brothers first urged Daniel Webster to push "some strong Resolutions against repudiations" through Congress.⁸⁴ Preoccupied with his negoti-

---

⁷⁹ Duff Green to Calhoun, 24 January 1842, in Meriwether (ed.), *The Papers of John C. Calhoun*, vol. 16, pp. 83–6. See also Bates to Ward, 1 August 1842, Ward Papers, MHS; Leland H. Jenks, *The Migration of British Capital 1875* (London, 1927), p. 105.

⁸⁰ For Robinson's mission, see House Doc. No. 197, 27th Congress, 3rd Session, pp. 1–6.

⁸¹ McGrane, *Foreign Bondholders*, pp. 51–2.

⁸² Quoted in Reginald McGrane, "Some Aspects of American State Debts of the Forties," *American Historical Review*, 38 (July 1933), pp. 673–86.

⁸³ For Palmerston's circular, see *The Economist*, 21 April 1849, p. 436; D. C. M. Platt, *Finance, Trade and Politics in British Foreign Policy, 1815–1914* (Oxford, 1968), pp. 34–41, 398–9.

⁸⁴ Bates to Webster, 13 June 1842, DWPC, 5, pp. 218–20; Bates to Webster, 15 April 1842, Ward Papers, MHS.

ations with Lord Ashburton, however, Webster chose not to expend the political capital that would be needed to secure passage of the forthcoming treaty on a very unpopular resolution that was nakedly in the interests of foreign capitalists, particularly his employers. Denied access to the corridors of power in Washington, Barings opted to go public with their grievances against defaulting states. In the age of rigid Victorian morality and piety, Barings American agent Thomas Wren Ward hoped "acting on the public sentiment through the press and keeping up a constant annoyance and moral pressure" might be the best tactic to get states to resume the interest payments on their debts.[85]

The state of Pennsylvania offered a perfect testing ground for such an approach. If there was a state that could be compelled to honor its financial obligations through moral and religious appeals, it was Pennsylvania, home of the Quakers and a hotbed of religious revivalism. The state was also one of the wealthiest in the Union and, in Philadelphia, housed many of the nation's leading banks and merchant firms. Furthermore, Barings "had a large stake with the Pennsylvania Banks" and, as we have seen, more than two-thirds of the state's $34 million debt was held abroad.[86] Accordingly, Baring Brothers earmarked £2,000 for a public campaign to restore the financial integrity of Pennsylvania in June 1843. Within weeks, five other European investment banks, including Hope and Co., Overend, Gurney and Co., and Jones, Lloyd and Co., joined Barings and pledged funds to the propaganda campaign to compel defaulting states to resume payment.[87] Organized under the rubric of the "Committee on State Debts," these banks engineered a "restoration campaign" comprised of public meetings of bondholders, insertions into the press, the lobbying of state officials, and the enlisting of "the clergy to point out from the pulpit the moral wrong and danger to the people of not acting honestly."[88]

Barings' agent Thomas Wren Ward executed this campaign from his office in Boston. Politically connected, yet aware of the need to be "kept out of sight" to avert the charge of foreign meddling in American affairs, Ward was ideally suited for such a task.[89] Within weeks, the Boston

---

[85] Ward to Baring Brothers, 30 January 1844, BP.
[86] Bates to Ward, 18 April 1842, Ward Papers, MHS.
[87] Baring Brothers to Ward, 3 July 1843, BP. The two other banks were Denison and Co. and Reid, Irving and Co.
[88] Bates to Ward, 3 October 1843, Ward Papers, MHS; Baring Brothers to Ward, 18 July 1842, BP.
[89] Ward to Baring Brothers, 25 July and 1 August 1843, BP.

banker established a network of prominent figures from politics, the pulpit, and the press to carry out his instructions from London. Ward convinced many Presbyterian and Baptist leaders in Pennsylvania of the need for "the religious world to speak out" against the sin of financial infidelity. Led by Francis Wayland of Brown University, religious leaders distributed antirepudiation literature to their congregations and inserted similar articles into their church publications.[90] Politically, Ward hired William B. Reed, a former state senator, and Elihu Chauncey, a prominent Whig banker, as special aides in his behind-the-scenes lobbying and petitioning of the state government. For the public dimension of the campaign, Ward appointed Nathaniel Hale, the editor of the Boston *Daily Advertiser*. Under Hale's leadership the *Advertiser* became the organ of foreign and domestic financial interests and espoused the moral, legal, and economic benefits of the repayment of state debts. Hale's articles soon began to reappear in journals in New York, Baltimore, and even New Orleans after Ward would send newspaper editors clippings along with a check. Payments were typically $10 for the insertion of an article that advocated the resumption of payments on state debts and $20 for an editorial.[91]

As Ward's efforts in the press demonstrate, the campaign in Pennsylvania soon became an effort on a national scale to condemn financial delinquency and to encourage all defaulting states to honor their commitments. Once the Pennsylvania campaign was underway, Ward turned his attention to Maryland. In addition to financing the Chesapeake and Ohio Canal Company and the Baltimore and Ohio Railroad Company, Baring Brothers was the foreign agent of the state. "It is the only state," Joshua Bates wrote, "which our fame would suffer by in case of default."[92] Unfortunately for Bates, the state did default even after a bailout loan from Barings in January 1842.[93] After corresponding with the state's treasurer, Ward went straight to the governor with his message that the only "important point is to get the state to commence paying its interest."[94] Ward received assistance in the Maryland campaign from John H. B. Latrobe, a Baltimore attorney, and Louis McLane, the president of the

---

[90] Hidy, *The House of Baring*, pp. 318–19. For Whig evangelicals and the state debt issue, see Richard Carwardine, *Evangelicals and Politics in Antebellum America* (Knoxville, 1997), pp. 78–9.
[91] Ward to Unknown, 13 January 1844, BP.
[92] Bates to Ward, 3 November 1841, Ward Papers, MHS.
[93] Maryland Treasury to Ward, 27 March 1843, BP; Baring Brothers to McLane, 18 January 1841, BP.
[94] Ward to Baring Brothers, 6 December 1842, BP.

Baltimore and Ohio Railroad and former secretary of state and secretary of the treasury under Andrew Jackson (McLane had supported the Bank of the United States to the annoyance of his superior). Coordinating his efforts with the larger campaign, Latrobe inserted reprints of Nathaniel Hale's articles into the Baltimore press, distributed pro-resumption literature to state politicians, and drafted memos and bills that influential friends introduced in the state legislature. Baring Brothers was not the only British bank that had a vested interest in Maryland's financial integrity. George Peabody, who began his business career in Baltimore, was also one of the state's largest creditors. In 1845, Peabody joined Barings in contributing £1,000 to the Whig party and to the gubernatorial campaign of Thomas E. Pratt, who advocated full repayment of the state's debt.[95]

Two prominent articles published in the *Democratic Review* and the *North American Review*, and republished as pamphlets on both sides of the Atlantic, were the most visible products of the restoration campaign. Authored by Alexander Everett and future Supreme Court justice Benjamin Curtis, respectively, these publications were secretly commissioned by British banks and were based on outlines provided by Thomas Wren Ward.[96] "The providence of God," Curtis's piece in the *North American Review* averred, "persuades us not to repay [His] kindness by breaking His law of justice." There were more than just religious and moral reasons, however, for states to resume debt repayment. "The conduct of a few States," Curtis accurately pointed out,

has not only destroyed their own credit, and left their sister States very little to boast of, but has so materially affected the credit of the whole Union, that it was found impossible to negotiate in Europe any part of the loan authorized by Congress in 1842.... It is the truth, and it should enter into the heart of every American, that this loan was refused because Europe doubted the honor of this country.[97]

This argument was particularly close to the heart of Daniel Webster. After his successful negotiations with Ashburton failed to materialize into the loan Baring Brothers promised, Webster offered his services to Ward in the restoration campaign in order to further his cause of attracting

---

[95] Dorothy Adler, *British Investment in American Railways, 1834–1898* (Charlottesville, 1970), p. 15; McGrane, *Foreign Bondholders*, p. 97; Baring Brothers to Ward, 18 July 1845, BP.

[96] Curtis took no money for his article. See Ward to Baring Brothers, 29 November and 8 December 1843, BP.

[97] *North American Review*, 58 (January 1844), p. 150.

British investment to the United States. Webster, however, was also motivated by another consideration. "He is desirous of sustaining his reputation as a great statesman and in all he does will have a view to that," Ward reported to Barings' headquarters in London, "but, he wants and must have *money*—and will in what he does or omits look very much to its result to himself."[98] Webster was, Ward would later put it, "a sort of public property."[99] In need of money to resume his political career after resigning as secretary of state, Webster saw the Barings' campaign as an opportunity to advance both his political agenda and his private interests.

Accordingly, Webster condemned defaulting states in a public speech and offered his opinion to Barings regarding the legality of the Maryland debt. He then sent a bill to Ward along with a recommendation for Barings to issue a loan on behalf of a canal company of which he also served as legal counselor.[100] "It is a humiliating fact," Ward wrote, "that the first talents in the country even must be bought and paid for in the highest causes." Because of his high asking price and the bank's fears that "the fact of his being paid would lessen his influence," Webster's services were never fully used during the campaign.[101] After all, Webster's position regarding state debts was set: as a Whig who advocated investment for internal improvements, he would condemn the defaulting states regardless of whether he was paid for it. Barings recognized this and, in order to avoid charges of bribery and meddling in American politics, kept Webster at an arm's length during the restoration campaign. In this matter, the Barings were both politically and financially shrewd.

Even without the assistance of their most powerful American ally, Baring Brothers' campaign to restore the financial integrity of the United States began to pay off by the middle of the decade.[102] In Pennsylvania, a plan advocating increased taxation drawn up by Ward provided the basis for a bill passed by the state legislature. The state began to partially

---

[98] Ward to Baring Brothers, 15 September 1843, BP.

[99] Ward to Bates, 15 January 1846, Ward Papers, MHS.

[100] Ward to Baring Brothers, 21 September 1843, BP; Ward to Bates, 14 November 1843, Ward Papers, MHS; Webster's legal opinion, 019184, BP. Webster served as legal counselor for the Chesapeake and Ohio Canal Co. He urged Barings to issue a loan on behalf of the company "in efforts to restore the credit of Maryland, and to enable her to complete her great work." See Webster to Bates, 30 July 45, *DWPC*, 6, pp. 91–4; Webster to Ward, 31 July 1845, *DWPC*, 6, pp. 95–6; Webster to Baring Brothers, 14 October 1845, *DWPC*, 6, pp. 98–9.

[101] Quoted in McGrane, "Some Aspects of American State Debts of the Forties," pp. 673–86; Ward to Baring Brothers, 30 March 1844, BP. See also Bates to Ward, 4 November 1844, Ward Papers, MHS.

[102] Important, as well, was the end of the economic depression.

meet the interest payments due on its debt in 1845 (much to the chagrin of European capitalists, half of each coupon was paid in paper money) before fully resuming its obligations in 1847. In Maryland, a resumption bill passed in 1847, but only after Latrobe kept one legislator sober enough to vote and blackmailed a few more.[103] Illinois, Indiana, and Louisiana resumed payments in the mid-forties, though the Barings were less active in promoting resumption in these states. In Michigan, the matter was complicated by the failure of the state's financial agencies (the Bank of the United States and the Morris Co.), which went under owing the state roughly $2 million dollars of a bond issue it marketed. The state resumed interest payments on the bonds it had received payment from in 1846 but refused to do the same for the unpaid bonds. In 1855, the state partially converted these bonds to new issues but, in the process, repudiated a portion of its debt.[104] We shall return later to the debts of Mississippi, Arkansas, and Florida.

The resumption campaign of the 1840s illustrates at once both the United States' need for foreign capital and the power and influence yielded by British banks, particularly Baring Brothers. Despite prevailing hostile attitudes to foreign capitalists, few Americans resisted the intervention of European financiers into the internal affairs of several states. Part of this was a result, no doubt, of the care Barings and others took to stay out of public view. However, this was also a consequence of the simple fact that American leaders, even those at the state level, recognized that they would need foreign capital in the future. "It appears that states repaid," the economic historian William English maintains, "in order to maintain their access to international capital markets."[105] Repudiation was simply not a viable option for a developing nation that was in need of investment during a transportation revolution. To make this point to American leaders, Baring Brothers was willing to spend tens of thousands of dollars on a behind-the-scenes lobbying and propaganda campaign. The bank's ability to do all of this—collaborate with its European competitors, use its network of American correspondents, enlist the support of prominent journalists, politicians, and even evangelicals—illustrates that it had political, as well as financial, capital in the United States.

[103] Hidy, *The House of Baring*, p. 328.
[104] Ratchford, *American State Debts*, pp. 112–14; McGrane, *Foreign Bondholders*, pp. 143–67. Michigan repudiated an estimated $2 million of its debt.
[105] English, "Understanding the Costs of Sovereign Default," pp. 259–75. See, for example, Morris to Corcoran, 19 September 1843, Corcoran Papers, Library of Congress.

What Baring Brothers could not seem to do, however, was to prevent cantankerous border disputes from jeopardizing its business in American securities. Similar to the jittery reaction of British capitalists to the Northeastern border controversy earlier in the decade, controversy surrounding the annexation of Texas and the Northwestern border in the Oregon territory left its mark on the financial markets. Because of the threat of conflict developing from these issues, British dealers of American securities were unable to reap the rewards of their restoration campaign that had produced action against repudiation in the high-profile state of Pennsylvania in 1845. "It would be a pity," Joshua Bates admitted, "to disturb this state of things by any doubts about the relations between the two countries."[106] The depression in American securities in London, however, was not without its advantages. Baring Brothers was on the lookout for bargain deals so the bank "can make money, for American stocks are very cheap."[107] Aside from such speculations, the diplomatic disputes were neither in the interests of British capitalists nor their American debtors.

In contrast to the Webster–Ashburton negotiations of a few years earlier, financial interests found themselves largely on the diplomatic sidelines, particularly in the United States, during the Texas and Oregon questions. The triumph of the darkhorse Democratic candidate James Polk in the election of 1844 and clamor in the Democratic press about the nation's "Manifest Destiny" put expansionism at the top of the agenda. To be sure, American capitalists were attracted to the possibility of acquiring new land, markets, and ports on the Pacific and were thus not entirely opposed to territorial expansion.[108] However, particularly amongst the nation's financial leaders who were intimately connected with European creditors, the overriding objective of maintaining international peace mitigated the appeal of Manifest Destiny. Thus, American financiers collaborated with their European partners in an effort to guide the currents of expansionism in a direction that would avoid the great calamity of Anglo-American war. This was no easy task, least of all because traditional transatlantic financial interests such as the Barings had few ties with the Democratic Polk administration.

Nonetheless, the Barings did what they could to promote policies that would maintain Anglo-American peace. In regard to the potential Ameri-

---

[106] Bates to Ward, 3 May 1845, Ward Papers, MHS.
[107] Bates to Ward, 1 December 1845, Ward Papers, MHS.
[108] For the fullest presentation of this argument, see Graebner, *Empire on the Pacific*; and Hietala, *Manifest Design*.

can annexation of Texas, Thomas Wren Ward articulated the familiar position that the national interest of avoiding war—with Mexico, Britain, or any other potential rival—far outweighed any territorial advantages that were to be had.[109] Ward was fortunate that this was also the position of the Whig party and, in particular, presidential candidate Henry Clay. In his public "Raleigh Letter" of April 1844, Clay argued that annexation would upset domestic and sectional harmony, divert resources from development, and, most of all, run the risk of provoking a war with Mexico. Considerations of public finance also factored into the opposition to annexation. In the same letter, Clay contended that the financial condition of the United States made it unpropitious to assume the debts of Texas, a likely consequence of annexation.[110] Although Clay's opposition to annexation struck a chord amongst conservative financiers such as Ward and may have helped him energize the Whig base in certain Northern states in the election of 1844, it failed to counter in electoral and political terms the Democratic position that annexation would extend individual liberty without upsetting domestic harmony.[111]

With expansionism gaining ground in the United States, the position of British capitalists on the Texas question became all the more important. Although the prospect of a free-trading Texan republic appealed to capitalists in Britain (as did a potential antislavery bulwark to American expansion), their support of British involvement in Texas was limited. As Lelia Roeckell has shown, British financiers were more interested in protecting their investments in Mexico than they were in schemes to incorporate Texas into their economic orbit (indeed, Alexander Baring had represented British holders of Mexican bonds in the 1830s).[112] To be sure, an independent Texas promised future profits and, by ending the conflict with Mexico, could be the best means of restoring stability in the region and protecting British investments. Thus, British bondholders

[109] See, for example, Ward to Baring Brothers, 11 December 1843, 22 and 29 April 1845, BP.

[110] Henry Clay, "To the Editors of the Washington *Daily National Intelligencer*," 17 April 1844, in Melba P. Hay (ed.), *The Papers of Henry Clay*, vol. 10 (Lexington: University Press of Kentucky, 1991), pp. 41–6.

[111] For the Texas issue in domestic politics, see Michael A. Morrison, "Westward the Curse of Empire: Texas Annexation and the American Whig Party," *Journal of the Early Republic*, 10 (1990), pp. 221–49. For the view that Clay's opposition to annexation might have helped him in the North in the election of 1844, see Lex Renda, "Retrospective Voting and the Presidential Election of 1844: The Texas Issue Revisited," *Presidential Studies Quarterly*, 24 (1994), pp. 837–54.

[112] Lelia Roeckell, "Bonds over Bondage: British Opposition to the Annexation of Texas," *Journal of the Early Republic*, 19 (Summer 1999), pp.257–78.

supported diplomatic efforts to secure and guarantee the republic's independence and were involved in an effort for Texas to assume a portion of Mexico's debt in exchange for British mediation in 1840.[113] Nonetheless, the limited nature of British financial involvement in Texas should be stressed. There is no evidence in the records of the major transatlantic banks, for instance, that suggests they were involved in schemes to extend a loan to Texas in exchange for emancipation, a staple of Democratic pro-annexation propaganda. Nor did their limited involvement in Texan finance constitute a threat to American national security (though the perception amongst Democrats that they did comprise a threat no doubt contributed to the appeal of annexation). Indeed, as the annexation drama unfolded and the futility of British policy became clear in the mid-1840s, British capitalists backed away from supporting Texan independence. When Tyler signed the joint resolution that annexed Texas in early 1845, the Barings in London contended that the British government should acquiesce to the action in order to promote Anglo-American harmony.[114]

Overall, the Barings and other transatlantic financial interests played little role in the Texas question. This was primarily the result of the limited scope of British economic interests there and a reflection of how the annexation controversy only tangentially concerned Anglo-American relations and the foreign indebtedness of the United States.[115] The Barings were much more active in the Oregon dispute, which directly threatened their business as dealers of American securities in Britain.

"I think I could settle the Oregon question very soon," Bates declared, "but professed diplomatists will never settle it."[116] The dispute, however, was more complex than Bates was willing to admit. Attempts to establish the border during the Anglo-American Convention of 1818 foundered

---

[113] For this episode, see Roeckell, "Bonds over Bondage," pp. 264-5.

[114] For Barings and Texas, see Baring Brothers to Ward, 4 April 1845; Ward to Baring Brothers, 1 June 1845, BP. For Anglo-American relations and the Texas issue, see Sam Haynes, "Anglophobia and the Annexation of Texas: The Quest for National Security," in Haynes and Morris, *Manifest Destiny and Empire: American Antebellum Expansionism* (Arlington, Tex., 1997), pp. 115-45; Lelia Roeckell, "British Interests in Texas, 1825-1846," D.Phil. dissertation, University of Oxford, 1993; Ephraim D. Adams, *British Interests and Activities in Texas, 1838-1846* (Baltimore, 1910). For an interpretation that stresses the activism of British policy, see Pletcher, *The Diplomacy of Annexation*.

[115] Roeckell contends that "British influence was minimal" in Texas and that "few direct trading links were established between Britain and Texas." See Roeckell, "Bonds over Bondage," p. 275.

[116] Bates to Ward, 3 May 1845, Ward Papers, MHS.

when American statesmen demanded all territory south of the 49th parallel, while their British counterparts were willing only to have the 49th as the border as far as the Columbia River. Controversy over the disputed area north of the Columbia and south of the 49th increased in the following decades when the British Hudson's Bay Company set up shop in the area and American merchants and businessmen demanded access to the deep water port of Juan de Fuca Strait, particularly after a naval mission concluded that the mouth of the Columbia River was too shallow to serve as a port.[117] Matters were further complicated in the years after the Panic of 1837 when thousands of unemployed Americans sought a better life in the West and blazed the Oregon Trail. The White–Hastings wagon train of 1842 alone doubled the American population in the Oregon territory.[118] The explosion of the American population in Oregon served as the basis of John C. Calhoun's policy of "masterly inactivity" during his brief stint as secretary of state in 1844–5. Ownership of the disputed territories, Calhoun calculated, would be solved not by diplomats but by the natural westward migration of American citizens.

Newly elected President James Polk was more proactive in his efforts to secure American demands in Oregon. In his inaugural address, Polk declared that American claims in Oregon were "clear and unquestionable."[119] Despite this provocative rhetoric, in the summer 1845 Secretary of State James Buchanan offered Richard Pakenham, the British minister to the United States, all territory north of the 49th parallel, in addition to the whole of Vancouver Island. Although Britain had consistently rejected similar offers in the past, American statesmen hoped that the boom in American settlers in the region might lead the British to reconsider. Pakenham, however, rejected the offer and insulted the Polk administration in the process by not consulting his superiors in London before doing so. Polk responded by withdrawing the offer, an action that escalated tensions and appeared to express his solidarity with Midwestern Democrats who, in their slogan of "Fifty-four forty or fight," were demanding the entire Oregon territory (which extended to the northern latitude of 54° 40"). Polk's growing belligerence was confirmed in his annual address to Congress in December 1845 in which he revived the Monroe Doctrine (which had laid dormant since 1823) and asserted

---

[117] For more on Pacific ports and the Oregon controversy, see Norman Graebner, *Empire on the Pacific* (New York, 1955).
[118] Jones and Rakestraw, *Prologue to Manifest Destiny*, p. 175.
[119] Quoted in Jones and Rakestraw, *Prologue to Manifest Destiny*, p. 202.

American claims to the entire territory. "The only way to treat John Bull," Polk declared, "was to look him straight in the eye."[120]

Staring down the British Government, however, was not the best way to treat British investors. Polk's message sent American securities tumbling on the London Stock Exchange, countering the improvement that followed the peaceful annexation of Texas in early 1845. "Business," Joshua Bates reported, "becomes less safe."[121] Accordingly, financial interests pressed statesmen on both sides of the Atlantic to find a compromise to avert war. Once again, agents of Baring Brothers were at the center of this behind-the-scenes lobbying effort. In the United States, Thomas Wren Ward personally pleaded with Polk to peacefully resolve the dispute in 1845.[122] Daniel Webster, having regained his seat in the Senate, publicly called for the now compromise border of the 49th parallel while he privately advised British leaders to "avoid sharp points" regarding Oregon with the United States.[123] Across the Atlantic, Joshua Bates pushed for a compromise plan of the 49th parallel as the boundary line, sugarcoated with free navigation of the Columbia River for the duration of the charter of the Hudson's Bay Company (which would expire in 1859).[124] Upon Bates' prompting, the British economist Nassau Senior endorsed this plan in a prominent article in the *Edinburgh Review*, which drew the support of Foreign Secretary Lord Aberdeen.[125] The new U.S. minister to Britain Louis McLane, who, prior to being appointed to his post, had assisted the Barings in the restoration campaign in Maryland, also favored the compromise offer of the 49th parallel.

In addition to the standard economic arguments for avoiding war, transatlantic financiers pointed to the likelihood that a decrease in tariffs would occur on both sides of the Atlantic if diplomats could settle the border dispute. Both Peel's Tory and Polk's Democratic governments desired to lower trade barriers between the two nations. Indeed, both the repeal of the Corn Laws in Britain and the low-duty Walker Tariff in

---

[120] Quoted in Walter LaFeber, *The American Age* (New York, 1994), p. 113.

[121] Bates to Ward, 3 May 1845, Ward Papers, MHS.

[122] Hidy, *The House of Baring*, p. 127.

[123] Webster to Denison (forwarded to Lord Aberdeen), 26 February 1846, *DWPC*, 6, pp. 126–7; Webster to Haven, 2 February 45, *DWPC*, 6, pp. 73–4; Pletcher, *The Diplomacy of Annexation*, p. 304.

[124] Bates to Ward, 1 December 1845 and 16 January 1846, Ward Papers, MHS; David Dykstra, *The Shifting Balance of Power: American-British Diplomacy in North America, 1842–1848* (Lanham, Md., 1999), pp. 85, 104, 120.

[125] Frederick Merk, *The Oregon Question* (Cambridge, Mass., 1967), p. 287; Pletcher, *The Diplomacy of Annexation*, p. 250; Paul Varg, *New England and Foreign Relations 1789–1850* (London, 1983), p. 182.

the United States were enacted in the summer 1846 just after the settlement of the Oregon controversy. The economic benefits of freer trade between the two nations—which would facilitate the British importation of American grains to help feed the starving Irish who were in the midst of the Great Potato Famine—seemed to far outweigh the advantages to be gained in acquiring extra territory in the remote wilderness of Oregon. "I should hope those belligerent Gentlemen in Congress would feel quite ashamed of their war speeches," Joshua Bates declared, "when they find they are to have such a market opened to them."[126] There was also the question of how the United States would fund a war against Britain, its largest creditor. "It should be remembered that monied men, for the most part, think very unfavorably of belligerent measures for the acquisition of Oregon," one American pamphleteer wrote, "and would not deem it prudent to invest money in any government stock issued for the purpose of asserting a claim to a worse than useless territory on the coast of the Pacific."[127] "The merchants, traders, shipowners, and capitalists of America are opposed to war," *The Economist* opined, "the politicians alone are in favour of it!"[128]

Thus, as in the Anglo-American treaty deliberations concerning the Northeastern boundary a few years earlier, there were powerful economic incentives to peacefully resolve the Oregon dispute. Though the drive for more territory and access to ports on the Pacific coast, as Norman Graebner famously argued, pushed Americans westward, economic considerations also cut the other way and provided a motive for compromise—particularly if statesmen could arrange a deal in which territory and ports were equitably distributed to both sides. Such was the plan advocated by Joshua Bates and other financial leaders. This is not to contend, it should be stated, that financial concerns were decisive to the settlement or that some secret free-trade bargain led to the Oregon settlement (a contention disproved by historians).[129] Unlike four years earlier

---

[126] Bates to Ward, 3 February 1846, Ward Papers, MHS. Even before the repeal of the Corn Laws, the Peel government used Baring Brothers to arrange for £100,000 of American corn to be shipped to Ireland during the famine. Baring Brothers to Ward, 3 December 1845, BP; Merk, *The Oregon Question*, p. 312.

[127] A Disciple of the Washington School, *Oregon: The Cost, and the Consequences* (Philadelphia, 1846).

[128] *The Economist*, 3 January 1846, pp. 4–5.

[129] Graebner, *Empire on the Pacific*, pp. 137–41; Merk, *The Oregon Question*, pp. 309–36. For the view that trade issues led directly to the Oregon settlement, see Thomas P. Martin, "Free Trade and the Oregon Question, 1842–1846," in Arthur H. Cole, A. L. Dunham, and N. S. B. Gras (eds.), *Facts and Factors in Economic History: Articles by Former Students of Edwin Francis Gay* (Cambridge, Mass., 1932), pp. 470–91.

when a pro-British, pro-business secretary of state, and a pro-American British financier negotiated the Webster–Ashburton Treaty, the Oregon dispute was dominated by the bellicosity of Midwestern Democrats and threats of a third Anglo-American war. "I only regret sometimes," Thomas Ward lamented during the Oregon dispute, "that my influence is not in some degree commensurate with my conviction of the importance of the views I entertain as to the policy of both countries."[130] Although Ward and other financiers may have felt powerless to individually shape policy, there can be little question that the larger financial and commercial interdependence of Britain and the United States that they embodied connected the two nations to such an extent that leaders on both sides of the Atlantic desired to avoid war at all costs. Even Democratic leaders such as John C. Calhoun and Thomas Hart Benton recognized by late 1845 that Oregon was not worth a war with Britain and pushed for a compromise settlement at the 49th parallel.[131] In sum, as Joshua Bates put it, "for America and England to go to war would be perfect madness."[132]

It would also be madness for the United States to get involved in two wars, fought on two fronts, at the same time. A conflict with Mexico loomed in the immediate future in the spring 1846 and, combined with Britain's deployment of thirty warships to North American waters, prompted American leaders to reconsider their position on the Oregon territory. Seeking a way to resolve the crisis without losing face, Polk deferred the decision to the Senate. On 18 June 1846, the Senate passed the Oregon Treaty by the comfortable margin of 41 to 14. The final settlement looked much like the plan advocated by Joshua Bates in the preceding years: the 49th parallel marked the division between the United States and Canada, Britain received Vancouver Island, and the Juan de Fuca Strait and the Columbia River remained open to both nations (but the latter only until 1859). Thus, for the second time in less than five years, cool heads prevailed during a diplomatic crisis. National honor and interest were maintained for both sides, while the disastrous economic consequences of an Anglo-American war were avoided.

[130] Ward to Baring Brothers, 22 April 1845, BP.
[131] For the conciliatory views of some Southern Democrats, see Joseph A. Fry, *Dixie Looks Abroad: The South and U.S. Foreign Relations, 1789–1973* (Baton Rouge, 2002), pp. 60–1.
[132] Bates to Ward, 1 January 1846, Ward Papers, MHS.

With the Oregon question settled and the state debt crisis largely resolved, British banks anticipated a new boom in investment in American securities. As Baring Brothers had reported a year earlier, when "the Texas and Oregon questions are settled and Pennsylvania pays her August dividends, we should look for some demand for American stock for there is great want of employment for capital."[133] Indeed, as soon as the Senate passed the Oregon Treaty, Barings began to inquire about negotiating a new loan for the U.S. Government.[134]

THE MEXICAN WAR LOAN OF 1848

Renewed European interest in U.S. securities came none too soon as the federal government was in need of cash following the outbreak of the Mexican War in May 1846. Within months, the government's inlays were insufficient to cover the increased expenses of arming and supplying armies engaged in offensive operations in central Mexico. In 1847, the U.S. Government ran a deficit of more than $30 million, its largest to date. The Treasury, under the leadership of Robert J. Walker, responded by issuing an $18 million, six percent loan. The Polk administration gave first priority on the new loan to the Washington, D.C. firm of Corcoran and Riggs, headed by the Democratic supporter William Corcoran. The bank soon purchased $14.7 million of the issue and attempted to resell the six percent bonds to American investors at a premium. Although there was much initial demand for the new loan on American markets, by January 1848 Corcoran and Riggs encountered difficulty in finding takers for the bonds. British banks, in trouble of their own during the London financial crisis of 1847, were in no position to bale Corcoran out.[135] Only Walker's cooperation in postponing the Treasury's collection date, combined with the firming of the market in the United States, saved the firm from bankruptcy.[136]

[133] Baring Brothers to Ward, 18 June 1845, BP.
[134] Baring Brothers to Ward, 13 July 1846, BP; Baring Brothers to Grinnell, Minturn and Co., 3 June 1847, BP.
[135] See, for example, Peabody to Corcoran, 18 October 1847, Corcoran Papers, Library of Congress (henceforth LC).
[136] This paragraph draws from Henry Cohen, *Business and Politics in America from the Age of Jackson to the Civil War: The Career Biography of W. W. Corcoran* (Westport, Conn., 1971), pp. 31–61; Timothy Roberts, "The American Response to the European Revolutions of 1848," D.Phil. dissertation, University of Oxford, 1998; Timothy Roberts and Daniel Walker Howe, "The United States and the Revolutions of 1848," in R. J. W. Evans and

Corcoran would not forget this experience a year later when Walker sought takers for another national loan. In need of capital to fund the costs of the war (and the possible annexation of all of Mexico, which Walker advocated), Congress authorized a further $16 million, six percent loan on 31 March 1848. Once again Corcoran bid for a majority of the loan, this time taking $14 million of the issue.[137] However, when Walker requested an advance needed for the indemnity payment to Mexico (a product of the Treaty of Guadalupe Hidalgo) and an increase in the army's pay recently authorized by Congress, Corcoran was willing to cooperate only on the condition that he be allowed to seek the assistance of British capitalists. "If a portion of this Loan could be placed in London," Corcoran argued, "the effect on the market would be felt at once. Confidence would be restored.... You may rely upon it, there is no other mode to accomplish your wishes."[138] Anxious to ensure the loan's success and wary of the prospects at home, Walker had little choice but to authorize Corcoran to market U.S. bonds in Europe.[139] Accompanied by the former governor of Massachusetts John Davis (who was selected because of his previous advocacy of resumption and his relationship with Barings), Corcoran sailed to Britain in the summer 1848 to find takers for the new U.S. loan.[140]

The response of European capitalists to Corcoran's mission can be understood only when viewed in light of the social and political unrest that engulfed Europe in 1848. The continental revolutions of that year constituted, as Niall Ferguson has illustrated, "the biggest crisis on the European bond market in the nineteenth century."[141] Political instability, fears of radical social revolution, and rumors of massive defaults (particularly by the French government) led European government bonds to spectacularly crash in the spring. French *rentes* fell by sixty percent from their high two years earlier; Austrian five percents were down by almost half; and even the cornerstone of the nineteenth-century financial world, British consols, fell by nearly a quarter (though this decline largely

---

Hartmut Pogge Von Strandmann (eds.), *The Revolutions in Europe, 1848–1849* (Oxford, 2000), pp. 157–79; James Shenton, *Robert John Walker: A Politician from Jackson to Lincoln* (New York, 1961), pp. 92–7.

[137] Cohen, *Business and Politics in America from the Age of Jackson to the Civil War*, p. 53.

[138] Corcoran to Walker, 4 August 1848, Corcoran Papers, LC.

[139] See Walker to Corcoran, 5 August 1848; Walker to Bancroft, 9 August 1848, Corcoran Papers, LC.

[140] For Corcoran's appointment and the selection of Davis, see Walker to Corcoran, 5 August 1848; Ward to Corcoran, 27 July 1848, Corcoran Papers, LC.

[141] Niall Ferguson, *The Cash Nexus* (London, 2001), pp. 189, 292.

occurred before the revolutions during the financial crisis of 1847).[142] With European money markets in chaos whilst the political situation remained in flux, there was little chance that a new U.S. loan would meet with success. "The continent politically [is] in great confusion," Thomas Wren Ward informed Corcoran, "and no one can tell what is to come of it... the English buy little or nothing."[143]

However, despite the tumult on European exchanges, there were advantages to be had for the U.S. Treasury. As many contemporaries recognized, the revolutions of 1848 provided the stimulus needed to revive European interest in American securities after the state debt imbroglio of the preceding decade. With the very fate of European governments hanging in the balance (and consequently their ability to honor their pecuniary engagements), the bonds of the U.S. Government—despite the sordidness of several of its state governments—began to look more attractive. After all, the federal government, in contrast to many European states, had never defaulted. Because of "the shocks recently given to the public funds of the several nations of Europe," *The Economist* reported, "many persons are now looking to the American stocks as a means of profitable investment."[144] Even "a great many Englishmen" suffering from the London panic of 1847, Bates noted, "wish themselves in the United States."[145] Further encouraging was the relatively quick victory of U.S. armies in Mexico achieved by early 1848 and, not to be forgotten, the discovery of gold in California that reminded Europeans of America's unrivalled natural resources.

Corcoran and his collaborators lost no opportunity to impress these points upon the minds of British capitalists. In a letter distributed to British banking houses, Abbott Lawrence, a leading Massachusetts businessman and Whig, promoted Corcoran's mission. The United States, Lawrence reminded his readers, was "now at peace with all of the world" and its resources were plentiful enough "to supply even the luxurious and avaricious wants of man." In contrast to the instability in Europe, there was "nothing to disturb the U.S.—the Union cannot be severed." Lawrence also reminded British capitalists that Americans "are too Anglo-Saxons—and the example of our ancestors taught us long ago that

---

[142] For an informative chart of European bonds before and after the revolutions of 1848, see Ferguson, *The House of Rothschild*, I, p. 461.
[143] Quoted in Timothy Roberts, "The American Response to the European Revolutions of 1848," pp. 159–65. See also Bates to Ward, 12 May 1848, Ward Papers, MHS.
[144] *The Economist*, 5 May 1849, p. 490.
[145] Bates to Ward, 15 December 1848, Ward Papers, MHS.

national credit is national honor and individual interest."[146] The notion that the social and political turmoil in Europe made the United States a safe destination for capital was made more explicitly by August Belmont, the Rothschilds' American agent. In March 1848, Belmont informed his superiors in London that U.S. securities

> now *may be considered the safest of any government.* . . . I should think that it would be a very desirable thing for yourselves to invest a portion of your fortune in the securities of a country, which experience has shown not to be subject to the revolutions, the growing radicalism of Europe, threatening to involve more or less every country of southern and western Europe. . . . [the United States'] resources are so vast and inexhaustible that no event can happen during our generation at least which could in any way endanger securities. . . . the resources have increased in a ratio unprecedented in the history of nations and must increase at a still greater proportion in the future.[147]

Thus, the 1848 revolutions had contradictory implications for Corcoran's hopes of placing U.S. bonds in Europe. On the one hand, European capitalists were in no mood for a risky venture, particularly with a nation composed of defaulting states that had burned investors just a few years earlier. On the other hand, the relative political stability and natural resources of the United States made its securities an attractive investment when contrasted to the bonds of endangered European governments. The response of European banking houses to the new U.S. loan clearly evinced both of these notions. Much to Corcoran's dismay, no bank was willing to take all or a majority of the $10 million in bonds he intended to sell. Despite this caution, however, several firms recognized that investors' views of American securities had changed and thus were willing to buy small portions of the loan to offer to the public.

Leading the way, not surprisingly, were the houses traditionally associated with the United States. Barings agreed to take $1.25 million of the issue at the bargain price of 93 ¾. By January 1849 the bank was selling the bonds at 105.[148] Similarly, George Peabody and Overend, Gurney and Co. made large profits marketing their portions of the loan.[149] The largest single subscriber to the loan, however, was a house not known for

---

[146] Lawrence to Bates, 14 August 1848, Corcoran Papers, LC.

[147] Belmont to N.M.R. and Sons, 20 March 1848, T54/275, RA. See also Belmont to N.M.R. and Sons, 29 May 1849, T54/291, RA.

[148] *The Economist*, 20 January 1849, p. 74; Baring Brothers to Ward, 28 April 1848, BP; Hidy, *The House of Baring*, pp. 386–9.

[149] Baring Brothers to Ward, 25 August 1848, BP; Muriel Hidy, *George Peabody* (New York, 1978), pp. 290–1.

its risk-taking in American securities: the Rothschilds. Estimates place the Rothschilds' stake in the loan at between three and four million dollars.[150] Part of this was, no doubt, due to Belmont's persistence in promoting the issue to his superiors. The Rothschilds' interest in the U.S. loan was also a product of European, not just British, demand for American securities. Uniquely situated to market the issue across Europe, the Rothschilds were merely reflecting changing market attitudes by purchasing U.S. securities. Indeed, as Baring Brothers would later report, many of the investors buying U.S. bonds in 1848–50 were French and German, not just English.[151] The London Rothschilds again entered territory usually reserved for the traditional Anglo-American banks when the firm joined Barings and Peabody a few months later in brokering the $15 million U.S. indemnity payment to Mexico for lands ceded under the terms of the Treaty of Guadalupe Hidalgo. This Rothschild activity initiated the bank's large-scale involvement in American finance and elevated the social and political status of Belmont, who would soon become a leading figure in the Democratic Party.

The success of the Mexican War loan restored the financial standing of the United States in Europe. "The lean years" of the 1840s, the economic historian Mira Wilkins argues, "were over."[152] European investment in U.S. Treasury bonds returned to levels not seen since before the presidency of Andrew Jackson. Paradoxically, the distension of the national debt held abroad was begun by a Democratic administration under a president whose political views and nickname, "Young Hickory," invoked the persona of "Old Hickory" himself. As is often the case, the financial exigencies of war led to political compromises. The Democrats and Polk, however, were not entirely responsible for European investment in U.S. Treasury bonds that also occurred under the Whig administrations of Zachary Taylor and Millard Fillmore. Moreover, there is little evidence to suggest that the U.S. Government or even the Treasury Department was fully responsible for overseas holdings of the national debt. It appears that, with the exception of the bonds brought to Britain by Corcoran in 1848, the Treasury bonds held in Europe were not placed there by the U.S. Government, but were independently brought across the Atlantic by British firms such as the Barings, Rothschilds, and

---

[150] Hidy, *The House of Baring*, p. 384; Wilkins, *Foreign Investment*, pp. 664 n. 216.
[151] Baring Brothers to Ward, 12 July 1850, BP. See also Belmont to N.M.R. and Sons, 28 January 1851, T54/335, RA.
[152] Wilkins, *Foreign Investment*, pp. 75–6.

Peabody.[153] There was an obvious incentive for these firms to do this considering the high demand for U.S. Government bonds in Europe. By the summer 1851, U.S. six percent bonds were quoted on the London Stock Exchange at 113, the peak price for federal government securities in the forty years of this study.[154] Large European holdings of U.S. bonds were confirmed by an 1853 Treasury report that found that $27 million out of the $59 million national debt—or forty-six percent—was held abroad.[155] Thus, less than two decades after Jackson's elimination of the national debt, half of the government's obligations were once again in the hands of foreign capitalists.

The boom in U.S. bonds overseas that began in 1848 had another irony: British capitalists, who generally opposed American expansion because of the strain it placed on Anglo-American relations, helped finance a war (and the subsequent indemnity payment to Mexico) that constituted the climax of U.S. continental expansion. It should be noted that this paradox was not without precedent. Baring Brothers, for instance, had advanced the necessary funds to the Jefferson administration to underwrite the Louisiana Purchase of 1803. American acquisition of the Louisiana territory established a precedent for expansion that would contribute to the Anglo-American rivalry of the mid-nineteenth century. In this regard, the Mexican War loan of 1848 was just another example of how complementing financial interests could bond together an unlikely partnership between nationalistic Democrats and European capitalists and, in the larger picture, the expansionist United States and established Great Britain.

The 1853 Treasury report—the most reliable estimate of foreign investment in the United States in the antebellum period—reported that this mutually profitable bond was deepening. Similar to the 1830s, the decade before the Civil War witnessed a boom in overseas investment in state and railroad securities. Despite the defaulting states of the previous decade, European holdings of American state securities ballooned to $111 million. Many of these securities, it must be said, were the old (and, in some instances, repudiated) issues of the 1830s. Nonetheless, the return of European capitalists to state securities indicated just how much the financial situation had changed in less than ten years. Mira Wilkins estimates that fifty-eight percent of all state debts were held

---

[153] See Peabody to Corcoran, 29 December 1848, Corcoran Papers, LC.
[154] *The Economist*, 6 August 1851.
[155] U.S. Senate, *Report of the Secretary of the Treasury*, 33rd Cong., 1st sess., 1854, Exec. Doc. 42. This document is reproduced in full in Mira Wilkins (ed.), *Foreign Investments in the United States* (New York, 1977). See also *The Economist*, 26 December 1857, p. 1427.

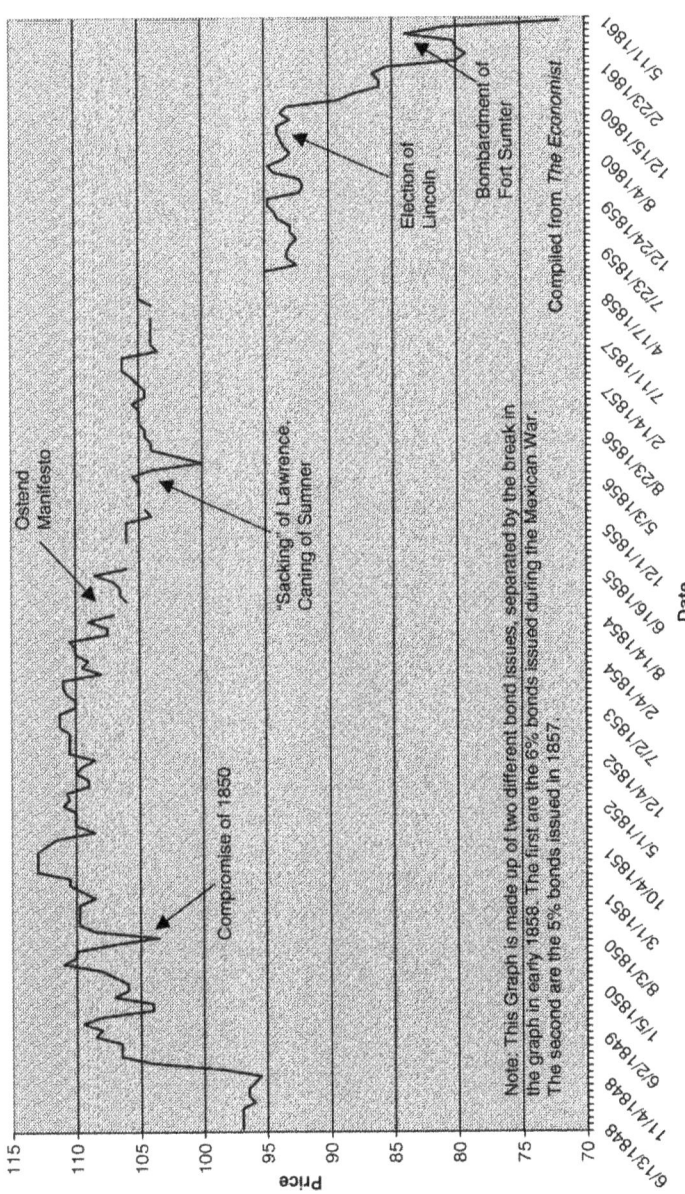

Figure 3 U.S. Bonds in London, 1848–1861

abroad in 1853.[156] By December 1852 Pennsylvania five percents were listed at 96 and Maryland fives at 98 1/2 on the London Stock Exchange (securities of both states were quoted in the 20s and 30s a decade earlier).[157]

Likewise, the early 1850s witnessed an explosive increase in the popularity of American railroad securities in Europe. Although American capital funded the majority of railroads constructed in this period, foreign investment was crucial to the construction of several significant lines, such as the Illinois Central and the New York and Erie. Funds obtained in Britain were often required to purchase superior British steel that was in high demand in the United States in the 1850s. For a brief period following their initial public issuance abroad in 1852, American railroad bonds were "the prime glamour issue" in London.[158] The 1853 Treasury report estimated European holdings of American railroad securities at $44 million. This estimate might be too low. Dorothy Adler contends that between 1848 and 1852 British investment in American railroads doubled from £12 to £24 million ($60 to $120 million).[159] In all, the Treasury estimated that total foreign investment in the United States in 1853 amounted to $222 million—seventy percent of which was placed in public (federal, state, municipal) securities. "All seems to me at present a high prosperity mark," Thomas Baring reported back to London during his 1852 trip to the United States, because of "an easy money market in Europe and sale of the Railway bonds."[160]

There is little question that this renewed European interest in American securities was encouraged by political and diplomatic developments. The Compromise of 1850 confirmed the prevailing belief amongst European capitalists that, despite being an experimental democracy, the United States could peacefully resolve its political problems, in contrast to continental Europe, which seemed to experience destructive revolutions every few decades. "As regards the slavery question," August Belmont somewhat naively informed the London Rothschilds, "not the slightest apprehension need be entertained from it."[161] On the diplomatic

---

[156] Wilkins, *Foreign Investment*, p. 617.

[157] *The Economist*, 4 December 1852.

[158] Quoted in D. C. M. Platt, *Foreign Finance in Continental Europe and the United States* (London, 1984), p. 159.

[159] Adler, *British Investment in American Railways*, p. 24. See also A. W. Currie, "British Attitudes toward Investment in North American Railroads," *Business History Review*, 34 (1960), pp. 194–215.

[160] Baring to Baring Brothers, 20 September 1852, HC1.20.4. ING. BA.

[161] Belmont to N.M.R. and Sons, 5 March 1850, T554/314, RA.

front, relations with Britain steadily improved following the Oregon settlement of 1846. The Clayton–Bulwer Treaty of 1850, though an inadequate agreement as we shall see, initially appeared to signify an end to the border confrontations of the previous decade. An 1854 trade reciprocity agreement between the United States and Canada further served as evidence to British capitalists of an Anglo-American rapprochement. With the causes of conflict with Britain largely eliminated, European capitalists hoped that the United States could now get to work, with their assistance, on developing its infrastructure and exploiting its unmatched natural resources.

THE CLAYTON–BULWER TREATY AND THE JOINT
CLAIMS CONVENTION

The United States emerged from the Mexican War with vast new territories and improved credit. To the Whig administration of Zachary Taylor, the latter could help the development of the former. A chief goal of Whigs and American business interests at mid-century, particularly after the discovery of gold in California in 1848, was to create a transportation network to connect the Atlantic seaboard to the Pacific west. In order to avoid the long and expensive sea voyage around Cape Horn, many lobbied for the construction of a transoceanic canal across the isthmus of Central America. Far from just facilitating transportation, an isthmian canal became the Whigs' symbol of choice for the potential for commercial expansion to promote economic development, international cooperation and Christian civilization across the world. In words that foreshadowed the "open-door" policy of the turn of the century, one Whig diplomat declared,

It is our mission to extend commerce, the pioneer of civilization and child of peace to all parts of the world—to cultivate friendly relations with all to bring the distance near—and to illustrate by our example the elevating effects of Christianity. There is a fitness in our union for the purposes of opening a great channel of communication, saving a distance of more than ten thousand miles; given up to the use of the world, dedicated to peace, and working out incalculable benefits to mankind. Let us construct the work on the only practicable basis, and invite all nations to join in the guarantee of its neutrality, that neither now nor hereafter jealousies may arise on the part of those who may be the recipients of its benefits.[162]

[162] Lawrence to Palmerston, 14 December 1849, RG59, M30, National Archives (henceforth NA).

In this nascent "open-door" spirit, Secretary of State John Clayton invited Britain to enter into an agreement for the joint establishment of a canal in 1849.[163]

Behind this lofty American rhetoric, of course, lay contingencies and material interests that demanded Anglo-American co-operation in Central America. Embroiled in the domestic dispute over the extension of slavery that would culminate in the Compromise of 1850, American leaders were in no position to provoke Britain by unilaterally digging and fortifying a canal in Central America. Anglo-American relations were already strained by the two nations' jockeying for mastery in Nicaragua, which offered the most promising canal route because of the pre-existing waterways of Lake Nicaragua and the San Juan River. In 1848 the British, who had century-old interests in Central America, extended their protectorate over the Miskito Indians on the Atlantic coast of Nicaragua to include the strategically important port city of San Juan (renamed Greytown), and, a year later, occupied Tigre Island on the Pacific side as a guarantee for a British loan to Honduras. American statesmen interpreted these actions as the opening moves in a British effort to control an isthmian canal. In fact, the British were in part responding to the 1846 Panamanian–American Bidlack Treaty, which conferred transit rights to the United States.

Nonetheless, American officials on the ground in Central America further escalated tensions in a race to secure control over the territory of a future canal. The American diplomat Elijah Hise responded to British actions in June 1849 by negotiating an unauthorized treaty with Nicaraguan officials that extended exclusive control over a future isthmian canal to the United States in exchange for an American guarantee of Nicaragua's territory, which undermined the British protectorate on the Mosquito Coast. The following year, a second American emissary, Ephraim Squier, negotiated a similar treaty with Nicaragua that also ceded Tigre Island to the United States and granted special privileges to Cornelius Vanderbilt's Atlantic and Pacific Ship Canal Company.

---

[163] Given historians' interest in delineating the antecedents of the "open-door" policy, it is surprising that little attention has been given to the Clayton–Bulwer Treaty. The Clayton–Bulwer episode also would be an illuminating window into the rise of Anglo-Saxonism, which has been documented by historians such as Thomas Hietala and Reginald Horsman. "England was the home of my forefathers," Clayton informed Bulwer during the treaty negotiations, "and the blood of the Anglo-Saxon forms the basis of the population of this country." Clayton to Bulwer, 15 February 1850, John M. Clayton Papers, Library of Congress. The best work on the Clayton–Bulwer Treaty remains Mary Wilhelmine Williams, *Anglo-American Isthmian Diplomacy, 1815–1915* (London, 1916).

Thus, the two nations were on a collision course in Central America by the time the Taylor administration took office. Fearing that Anglophobic Democrats would jeopardize prospects for domestic compromise on the slavery issue while "dishonoring England" by demanding an aggressive policy in Central America, the Whigs sought to pre-empt political and diplomatic controversy by arranging a quick settlement with Britain.[164]

An equally important motive behind the American offer of joint action in Central America was the United States' need to attract British investment for the construction of a canal, a massive project that was certain to carry an unprecedented price tag.[165] An Anglo-American treaty would lay the groundwork for the political stability in Central America that investors on both sides of the Atlantic viewed as a precondition to financing any isthmian enterprises. Private American entrepreneurs who sought investment for isthmian canal and railroad companies, such as Cornelius Vanderbilt in Nicaragua and William Aspinwall in Panama, lost no opportunity to convey the financial advantages of co-operating with the British to American statesmen.[166] Whig leaders, not surprisingly, required little lobbying on this point. The new U.S. minister in London Abbott Lawrence, who had promoted the Mexican War loan of 1848 to British capitalists the previous year and had corresponded with the Barings for years, closely monitored the price of stock in Aspinwall's Panama railroad company on the London Stock Exchange.[167] Lawrence explicitly stated that Britain and the United States needed to reach an agreement on the canal issue because "capital, always timid, would shrink from it without such guaranty."[168] Indeed, in order to secure British investment for the canal, Lawrence, Clayton and other Whigs were prepared to scrap the yet unratified Hise and Squire treaties with Nicaragua and, more significantly, to forbid American expansion in Central America if the

---

[164] Lawrence to Clayton, 25 January 1850; Clayton to Bulwer, 15 February 1850, Clayton Papers, LC. For a work that places the Clayton-Bulwer Treaty in the context of the domestic crisis of 1850, see Samuel Flagg Bemis, *A Diplomatic History of the United States* (New York, 1955), pp. 250–2. For a recent and concise interpretation, see David Pletcher, *The Diplomacy of Trade and Investment: American Economic Expansion in the Hemisphere, 1865–1900* (Columbia, Mo., 1998), pp. 116–25.

[165] "The United States," the historian Lawrence A. Clayton argues, "simply did not have the capital to go it alone on such a grandiose project." See Lawrence A. Clayton, "The Nicaragua Canal in the Nineteenth Century: Prelude to American Empire in the Caribbean," *Journal of Latin American Studies*, 19 (November 1987), pp. 323–52.

[166] Kinley Brauer, "Diplomacy of American Expansionism, 1821–1860," in William Becker and Samuel Wells (eds.), *Economics and World Power* (New York, 1984), pp. 106–8.

[167] Lawrence to Clayton, 23 November 1849, Clayton Papers, LC.

[168] Lawrence to Palmerston, 14 December 1849, RG59, M30, NA.

British would reciprocate. Intended to curb British influence and as a reassurance to investors on both sides of the Atlantic that the two nations would avoid crossing swords in Central America, this position contradicted American diplomatic tradition by limiting the United States' potential to expand. It was, the historian William Earl Weeks maintains, "one of the few examples in American history of the United States agreeing not to seek control over a region in the Western Hemisphere."[169]

Despite the generosity of the Whigs, the Central American question resembled other Anglo-American disputes of the era in proving difficult to settle. Secret negotiations in Washington between Clayton and British emissary Sir Henry L. Bulwer (which occurred without full consultation with either nation's cabinet) invoked the contentious issues of mastery in the Caribbean, the viability of the Monroe Doctrine, the legitimacy of British "gunboat diplomacy," and, never to be underestimated, the national honor of both parties. At the heart of the dispute lay the question of whether the British protectorate over the Miskito Indians was legitimate and whether Britain could be persuaded to withdraw from the area that would most likely become the Atlantic terminus of the proposed canal. If Britain would not join the United States in compromising its territorial interests and ambitions in Central America, Clayton asserted in March 1850 when talks with Bulwer stalled, the Taylor administration might respond by placing the Squire treaty before the Senate for ratification. No agreement, Clayton made clear, could be made if Britain retained territory through which the canal might run.[170] Accompanying this hardline position emanating from Washington were pleas from Lawrence in London that Britain must reciprocate the enlightened self-interest of the United States in order to facilitate capital investment in a canal. "In order to give full confidence to the capitalists of Europe and America," the U.S. minister informed Palmerston,

> neither the United States nor Great Britain should exercise any political power over the Indians, or any of the States of Central America. The occupation of Grey Town, and the attempt to establish a protected independence of Mosquito, throw at once obstacles in the way, excite jealousies and destroy confidence without which capital can never flow in this channel.[171]

The compromise reached by Clayton and Bulwer in the spring 1850 revealed that the short-term objective of promoting investment in an

---

[169] William Earl Weeks, *Building the Continental Empire* (Chicago, 1996), p. 156.
[170] Clayton to Lawrence, 15 February 1850, Clayton Papers, LC.
[171] Lawrence to Palmerston, 14 December 1849, RG59, M30, NA.

isthmian canal project constituted the central aim of the discussions regarding Central America. The infamous Article I of the treaty forbade either nation from seeking to "obtain or maintain for itself any exclusive control" over a canal and banned attempts to "occupy, fortify, or colonize, or assume or exercise any dominion" in Central America. Whether this meant that Britain had to relinquish its pre-existing claim on the Mosquito Coast was left deliberately unclear. As Bulwer wrote to Clayton in response to an earlier draft of the treaty that specifically bound Britain to withdraw from the Mosquito Coast, "words... which cannot but be more or less offensive to us, which will be alarming to Capitalists, and of which you can express the real value in other terms, cannot but be words that, on all accounts, had better be changed." At this critical point in the negotiations, Bulwer adroitly alluded to the fact that a treaty tough on Britain "will not draw closer the relations between the two states, nor engage persons to advance their money."[172] This was language Clayton understood. The Secretary of State (and Lawrence), despite the opposition of many within the cabinet, came to the conclusion that an interpretively flexible treaty would promote investment in a canal project while sidestepping the combustible Miskito issue.[173] The hope that the agreement would facilitate the quick construction of a canal was made more explicit elsewhere in the Clayton–Bulwer Treaty. In contrast to the ambiguous first article, Article V made both nations' commitment to investors crystal clear by guaranteeing that the "canal may forever be open and free, and the capital invested therein secure," while Article VII extended special privileges to a pre-existing canal company—presumably that of Cornelius Vanderbilt.[174] As Zachary Taylor put it in his endorsement of the treaty to congress, "It yields protection to the capitalists who may undertake to construct any canal or railroad across the Isthmus."[175]

---

[172] Bulwer to Clayton, 21 April 1850, Clayton Papers, LC.

[173] For opposition within the cabinet, see Samuel Flagg Bemis (ed.), *The American Secretaries of State and Their Diplomacy*, vol.6 (New York, 1928), pp. 55, 59–60. For the desirability of an elastic treaty, see Lawrence to Clayton, 5 April 1850, RG59 M30, NA; Wilbur Jones, *The American Problem in British Diplomacy* (London, 1974), p. 88. The treaty, Jones writes, is "one of the most splendid examples of ambiguity every penned by a British or American diplomat, a marvel of verbiage which was to confound interpreters in both countries during the next decade."

[174] For the text of the Clayton–Bulwer Treaty, see William Malloy, *Treaties, Conventions, International Acts, Protocols and Agreements between the United States of America and Other Powers* (Washington, 1910), vol. 1, pp. 659–63.

[175] James Richardson (ed.), *A Compilation of the Messages and Papers of the Presidents, 1789–1897*, vol. 6 (Washington, D.C.: 1917–25), pp. 2580–1.

Thus was the genesis of one of the most inadequate and unpopular treaties in American history. Within weeks of the signing of the agreement, Lawrence acknowledged the need for a supplemental treaty to "define exactly the respective rights of the several parties claiming upon the isthmus."[176] No supplemental agreement was negotiated and Britain's protectorate on the Mosquito Coast and other possessions in Central America, combined with American aggression and filibustering in the area, would bedevil Anglo-American relations for a decade. Democrats, led by Stephen Douglas and Lewis Cass, openly condemned the treaty as a "truckling to Great Britain" that violated the Monroe Doctrine and vowed to ignore the limits it placed on U.S. expansion.[177] These attacks were perhaps unfair. Not only did the treaty put an end to future British expansion in Central America but, by the end of the 1850s, Britain had largely retreated from the region by ceding the Bay Islands to Honduras and withdrawing from the Mosquito Coast after Nicaraguan officials agreed to respect the rights of the Miskito Indians and preserve Greytown as a free port.[178] However, relative to the expansionism of the previous decade, this was little consolation for "Young Americans" and other nationalists.

Perhaps a more cogent criticism of the treaty is that it failed to achieve its central aim—ensuring the construction of an isthmian canal. In their defense, Clayton and Bulwer cannot be blamed for the difficulties encountered in the rugged topography of Central America and the further diplomatic complications that followed the Costa Rican demand for a share of all transit profits. Clayton, however, did reject a proposal by Palmerston for a joint survey of possible canal routes that might have clarified such issues, expressing his laissez-faire view that results "can best be attained by means of the sagacity and enterprise of individuals or companies."[179] The subsequent efforts of Cornelius Vanderbilt to "git the English banks to help us" might have made Clayton think otherwise.[180] Although Vanderbilt's newly rechristened Accessory Transit Company did profit from transporting passengers across the isthmus

---

[176] Lawrence to Clayton, 7 June 1850, RG59, M30, NA.

[177] Douglas quoted in Edward P. Crapol, *America for Americans: Economic Nationalism and Anglophobia in the Late Nineteenth Century* (Westport, Conn., 1973), p. 11. See also Paul Varg, *United States Foreign Relations, 1820–1860* (Michigan, 1979), pp. 214–35.

[178] For the Central American issue in the 1850s, see Jones, *The American Problem in British Diplomacy*, p. 77–185.

[179] Clayton to Lawrence, 14 December 1850, RG59, M30, NA.

[180] Quoted in Aurthur D. Howden Smith, *Commodore Vanderbilt* (London, unavailable date), p. 164.

sans a canal in the 1850s, the American businessman failed to achieve the Anglo-American financial co-operation that the architects of the Clayton–Bulwer Treaty viewed as a prerequisite for the construction of an isthmian passage. Vanderbilt alienated British capitalists during his 1850 fundraising trip to Europe with his tobacco chewing. Perhaps more decisively, the Barings, Rothschilds, and other prominent banks became skeptical of the enterprise when Vanderbilt opted to go cheap on the canal construction by making it only seventeen feet deep—much too shallow for the large packet-liners that British investors presumed would make the project turn a profit.[181] Thus, business ineptitude and political instability in Central America ensured that an isthmian canal would remain an unfulfilled dream of commercial expansionists on both sides of the Atlantic until the next century.[182]

In a final paradox of the Clayton–Bulwer Treaty, when the technology and investment capital was finally available for constructing a canal, the treaty stood as an obstacle to American statesmen who felt no obligation to collaborate with the British in the United States' backyard. Ironically, the burden of annulling the treaty fell upon Secretary of State John Hay, himself the author of the open-door notes, so that the United States could unilaterally build, occupy, and fortify an isthmian canal in Panama.

If the Clayton–Bulwer Treaty stands as a failure of American debtor diplomacy, the joint claims convention of 1853–5 illustrates the ability of private financiers to help resolve complex and long-standing Anglo-American disputes. In the 1850s, the time of diplomats in both countries was increasingly spent on supporting the claims of individuals from one country against that of the other.[183] Accordingly, U.S. minister to Britain Joseph Reed Ingersoll and British Foreign Secretary Lord John Russell agreed in 1853 to establish a binational court, presided over by one representative from each nation plus an umpire with the tie-breaking vote, to settle all claims of individuals, corporations, and companies against the other government since 24 December 1814. All compensation

---

[181] For Vanderbilt and other business schemes in Nicaragua in this period, see Clayton, "The Nicaragua Canal in the Nineteenth Century," pp. 325–7; Pletcher, *The Diplomacy of Trade and Investment*, pp. 118–22.

[182] For a more positive view of the Clayton–Bulwer Treaty, see K. Jack Bauer, *Zachary Taylor: Soldier, Planter, Statesman of the Old Southwest* (Baton Rouge, 1985), pp. 283–6. The treaty, Bauer rightly points out, did succeed in blocking future British expansion in Central America.

[183] See, for instance, the complaints in Everett to Ingersoll, 27 December 1852, RG59, M30, NA.

would be paid by one government to the other. "A speedy and equitable settlement of all such claims," the agreement stated, "will contribute much to the maintenance of the friendly feelings which subsist between the two countries." The U.S. Senate concurred and ratified the treaty on 20 August 1853.[184]

The success of the claims convention hinged upon the decisions of the umpire who would arbitrate what was certain to be a large percentage of split votes between the American and British representatives. Accordingly, U.S. commissioner Nathaniel Upham and British commissioner Edward Hornby spent much of their first two months together selecting the umpire. After ex-president Martin Van Buren declined the offer, the two commissioners agreed on the selection of senior Barings partner Joshua Bates. As an American partner of a British bank, Bates was thought to have an equal stake in both nations (something that George Peabody, whom the commissioners also considered, did not). Bates' "long residence in England and his great success has established him here permanently as his adopted home," Upham argued in his endorsement of the expatriate banker, "and has given a standing and character that should impart full confidence to the claimants of both countries."[185]

The majority of the claims the commissioners considered were far from politically charged. Rulings relating to property disputes, maritime issues, and customs fraud composed the majority of the roughly $330,000 awarded to U.S. citizens and $280,000 compensated to British subjects. Behind some of these pedestrian disputes, however, lay explosive controversies that had brought the two nations to the brink of war. One claimant was Alexander McLeod, the Canadian acquitted of murdering an American citizen during the *Caroline* incident of 1837, who sought compensation from the state of New York for his prolonged imprisonment. After a predictable split decision by Upham and Hornby, Bates disallowed McLeod's case because his claim was against a state, rather than the federal government.[186] Bates came to an identical decision in a claim that involved an issue in which he had a personal interest: the case of British holders of repudiated state bonds (in this case, Florida).

---

[184] For the agreement, see RG 76, Entry 195, National Archives, Washington, D.C.; Malloy, *Treaties, Conventions*.... vol. 1, pp. 664–8. See also Jones, *The American Problem in British Diplomacy, 1841–1861*, p. 124.

[185] Upham to Hornby, 31 October 1853, RG 76, Entry 195, NA.

[186] McLeod was later awarded an annual pension of £200 from the British Government. See Jones and Rakestraw, *Prologue to Manifest Destiny*, p. 69; Stevens, *Border Diplomacy*, p. 170.

Although he had no choice but to disallow the claim because it was again directed against a state government, Bates did not waste the opportunity to condemn financial delinquency while adding "that sooner or later the people of Florida will discover that honesty is the best policy and that no State can be called respectable that does not honourably fulfill its engagements."[187]

The most controversial decision of the convention involved the claims of American owners of the escaped slaves aboard the *Creole* in 1841. Legal precedent left Bates with no choice other than to award the slave-owners $110,330 for their lost property. The decision gave great satisfaction to Southerners such as James Henry Hammond who had condemned the "unprincipled and cowardly Sec. of State Webster" who was "in the pay of the great English Bankers, the Barings," for failing to protect their interests back in 1841–2.[188] It was fitting to Southerners that it was a partner of Baring Brothers—in many ways the symbol of the Yankee–British financial power that took a cut out of their profits from the cotton trade—who awarded compensation to slave-owners. Despite his ruling in favor of slaveholders, Bates used his position as umpire as a platform to articulate his belief that the peculiar institution was "odious and contrary to the principles of Justice and Humanity." In this statement, Bates spoke not only for himself and for Baring Brothers, but also for the majority of European capitalists.

THE COMING CRISIS

The Slavery Abolition Act marked the end of involuntary servitude within British dominions in 1833. The act was the culmination of decades of lobbying, petitioning, and agitation orchestrated by various abolitionist and religious organizations. Thus, early in the nineteenth century, Britain could proudly assume the leading role in the struggles to end slavery, serfdom, and other forms of forced labor. Despite this prevailing anti-slavery sentiment, British capitalists had little ethical problem with investing in the securities of Southern states during the boom of the 1830s. Baring Brothers' $7 million loan to Louisiana in 1831 was the largest it brokered on behalf of a state in the thirty years preceding the Civil War.[189]

[187] All quotes from Bates come from RG 76, Entry 195, NA.
[188] Diary of James H. Hammond, 21 March 1842, Carol Bleser (ed.), *Secret and Sacred: The Diaries of James Henry Hammond, a Southern Slaveholder* (London, 1988), pp. 88–9.
[189] Hidy, *The House of Baring*, p. 110; HC5.1.2, Louisiana State Loan, ING. BA.

"If the credit of the State was good and friends recommended its bonds," the Barings' historian Ralph Hidy asserts, "the Barings found slavery no bar to the marketing of securities."[190]

For financial reasons first, and ethical ones second, this began to change in the 1840s. Financially, European capitalists preferred Northern states' practice of using the proceeds of bond issues to finance internal improvements (which promised to generate revenue once completed). In contrast, Southern states often issued bonds overseas to finance state-backed banking institutions.[191] Although these new Southern banks planned to make profits through land deals and the clearing of fields to produce cotton, British investors were notoriously suspicious of the practices of these new banks, which often, as one Boston lawyer put it, "pursued business with the spirit of a lunatic gambler."[192] The Panic of 1837, as we have seen, burst this speculative bubble and ruined many of the new banks in the South.

Many European capitalists blamed slavery for the financial imprudence of these banks and, in the larger picture, of the Southern states themselves. Slavery, it was argued, was not only immoral, but it also corrupted the culture and the economy of the South. Slaveholders who kept a race of people in bondage were expected to be equally unscrupulous in their financial dealings. European capitalists feared that there was little to prevent a man who did not respect basic human rights from disregarding his commitment to his creditors. As early as 1797, Alexander Baring declared that "to the south of Baltimore, I understand there is nobody worth trusting."[193] In terms of the bottom line, as well, slavery raised as many questions as it answered. On a macroscale, the peculiar institution inhibited the intensive growth and diversification of the Southern economy. The production and exportation of cotton, of course, was profitable and had made many Southern planters and British merchants and textile mill-owners wealthy. However, an economy dependent upon one commodity was not attractive to British investors. Concerns about drought, soil exhaustion, slave rebellions, and, as some pessimists were beginning to prognosticate by the mid-1850s, a civil war with the North all made the

[190] Hidy, *The House of Baring*, p. 151.
[191] Thistlethwaite, *The Anglo-American Connection*, p. 21. In Louisiana, for example, fifty-two percent of the capital invested in the states' sixteen new banks was foreign, again, primarily British. See Wilkins, *Foreign Investment*, p. 62.
[192] A Member of the Boston Bar, *An Account of the Origin of the Mississippi Doctrine of Repudiation* (Boston, 1842).
[193] Quoted in Philip Ziegler, *The Sixth Great Power: Barings, 1765–1929* (London, 1988), p. 65.

bonds of Southern states a risky investment. Slavery, in short, made the South an unsafe destination for European capital. "The existence of even a minute fraction of the population in bondage," the *Westminster Review* proclaimed in 1850, "places the government of that state at a serious disadvantage in the money market. This mistrust arises from a shrewd calculation of the dangers, in both a moral and physical sense, which hang over a state of society whose foundations are laid in injustice and violence."[194]

An 1839 investors' manual written by British capitalist Alexander Trotter exemplified how slavery tarnished the standing of Southern state bonds in Europe.[195] To Trotter, the manner in which Northern states expended foreign capital (canals, turnpikes, railroads, etc.) would produce a much healthier economy than the South's practice of creating speculative state banks to underwrite the clearing of new cotton fields.[196] The United States, Trotter informed his readers, was a nation of two separate—though not incompatible, it should be added—economies. This bifurcation engendered larger, cultural divergences between the North and South that had financial implications. "The business-like habits of the people of the northern states," Trotter asserted in words that foreshadowed the self-help doctrines of Samuel Smiles,

are calculated to inspire confidence in their engagements; and living in a country where almost everyone is employed in some profitable pursuit, and where idleness or an expensive appearance must be injurious to credit, it is likely that their general character for industry and thriftiness will be maintained until greater advances at least have been made in the realisation of wealth, when luxury and its demoralising consequences may interfere to deteriorate it.[197]

In contrast, slavery tainted Southerners and made them less trustworthy in their pecuniary engagements:

The moral degradation which the system of slavery stamps both on master and slave, the effects of an enervating climate, and the carelessness which often

---

[194] *Westminster Review*, Volume 52, 1850, p. 213. The increasing concentration of Southern wealth in slaves also presented a legal problem to British investors who sought to invest in the South. It was a felony under English law to lend money to a person or institution to be used either directly or indirectly in aiding the cause of slavery. See Platt, *Foreign Finance in Continental Europe and the United States*, p. 146; Wilkins, *Foreign Investment*, p. 71.

[195] Alexander Trotter, *Observations on the Financial Position and Credit of Such of the States of the North American Union as Have Contracted Public Debts* (London, 1839).

[196] Ibid., pp. 71, 84.

[197] Ibid., p. 361.

accompanies the uncertainty of life in the unhealthy marshes of the south, which all conspire to promote reckless habits, to loosen moral restraints, and this greatly to modify the more favourable character which the inhabitants of the north have earned for themselves.[198]

"Such distinctions," Trotter concluded, "should not be lost sight of in forming an estimate of the credit to which the different states are separately entitled."[199]

Trotter's words proved prophetic in the 1840s as three of the nine states that had defaulted on their interest payments repudiated their debts altogether. Significantly, all three were south of the Mason–Dixon line: Mississippi, Arkansas, and Florida (Michigan's repudiation, as we have seen, was only partial). Repudiation was mostly a consequence of the failure of state-supported banks that, owing to unsound practices and overspeculation, became insolvent. The offending states, of course, defended repudiation on legal grounds. Mississippi politicians argued that $5 million of Mississippi Union Bank bonds and $2 million of Planters' Bank bonds had been unconstitutionally sold and, therefore, the state was not legally required to assume the debts of the state-backed institutions. Similarly, Florida, which became a state in 1845, disavowed its commitment to $3.9 million in bonds (which were marketed in Europe by the aptly named John Gamble) on the premise that its territorial legislature lacked authority to issue them. Arkansas leaders justified repudiation by claiming that the state's bonds had been unlawfully hypothecated abroad for a fraction of their value. The repudiated debts of these three states (most of which were held in Britain) amounted to $11.5 million, a sum greater than the amount of U.S. bonds William Corcoran marketed in Europe in 1848.[200]

The justifications of the repudiating states did little to allay the anger of British bondholders. In their eyes repudiation was a very simple issue: capital had been lent to states that were now refusing to honor their commitment to repay the loans. Mississippi was particularly targeted after it was reported in Britain that, though the state courts ruled against repudiation, politicians refused to resume payment on the state's debt. "The abject political hacks of Mississippi seem determined to lose no opportunity of degrading the American name," *The Times* opined.[201]

---

[198] Ibid., pp. 361–2.
[199] Ibid., p. 362.
[200] Ratchford, *American State Debts*, pp. 105–12.
[201] *Times*, 26 March 1852.

"The bold and barefaced want of principle which Mississippi has thus shown," August Belmont declared to the Rothschilds, who themselves held $1.5 in repudiated Mississippi bonds, "must necessarily create the deserved indignations, not only of the European holders of American securities, but also of the larger majority in this country."[202] As we shall see, European financiers would not forget their experience with these three Southern states when the Confederate States of America came calling for a loan during the Civil War.

The divide between European capitalists and the South was widened by the diplomatic events of the 1850s. The proposed creation of a Caribbean empire open to slavery that Southern leaders planned in the 1850s threatened to undermine U.S. relations with Europe. The threat to annex Cuba issued by American diplomats in Ostend, Belgium, in 1854 confirmed European suspicions that proslavery ideologues were plotting to spread their institution into areas where slavery was in the retreat.[203] Similarly, *The Economist* attributed William Walker's filibustering expedition in Nicaragua to the "political demoralization of the great community of Southern states." "The politics of slavery first led to the politics of annexation," the publication contended, "and now the politics of annexation have led to the politics of undisguised rapacity."[204] Fears that James Buchanan, who had been an architect of the Ostend Manifesto, would favor Southern expansion led *The Economist* and other British capitalists to support the first Republican presidential candidate, John C. Frémont, in 1856—a remarkable endorsement when one considers the protectionism of the Republican Party.[205]

The issue of American expansion into the Caribbean, however, revealed that transatlantic financiers were not a monolithic body, always in harmony over international issues. August Belmont, the Rothschilds' American agent who served as U.S. minister to The Hague under the Pierce administration, advocated expansion into the Caribbean and even played a

---

[202] Belmont to N.M.R. and Sons, 22 November 1841, T54/144, RA. For the Rothschilds' holdings of Mississippi bonds, see Wilkins, *Foreign Investment*, p. 665 n. 221.

[203] The signatories of the Ostend Manifesto were Pierre Soulé of Louisiana, James Mason of Virginia, and James Buchanan of Pennsylvania. See Gavin Henderson (ed.), "Southern Designs on Cuba, 1854–1857, and Some European Observations," *Journal of Southern History*, 5 (August 1939), pp. 371–85. The best work on Southern expansion in the decade before the Civil War remains Robert E. May, *The Southern Dream of a Caribbean Empire, 1854–1861* (Baton Rouge, 1973). See also May, *Manifest Destiny's Underworld: Filibustering in Antebellum America* (Chapel Hill, 2002).

[204] *The Economist*, 6 February 1858, p. 139.

[205] *The Economist*, 6 September 1856, p. 980; Morgan to Peabody, 17 September 1860, J. S. Morgan Papers, Morgan Library, New York.

behind-the-scenes role in attempts to purchase Cuba from Spain.[206] As Belmont put it in a letter to the Rothschilds, "the sooner our manifest destiny brings Mexico, Cuba and Central America under the wings of the American Eagle, the better it will be for the civilization, progress and commerce of the world."[207] Despite this provocative rhetoric, Belmont was not prepared to risk war—and the debilitating implications it would have for his business in promoting American securities to European capitalists—to achieve such territorial objectives. His involvement in ventures pertaining to the acquisition of Cuba focused on exploiting his connections with the Rothschilds to purchase the island on behalf of the United States, rather than the "wrestling" of the territory from Spain called for in the Ostend Manifesto. Indeed, Belmont envisioned U.S. acquisition of Cuba not as an act of belligerence, but rather a step in the path of economic modernization that would promote international commerce and provide new investment opportunities for European and American capitalists. This position was clearly not shared by Belmont's superiors in London, nor other European financiers, who expressed little interest in his plans to purchase the island. Nonetheless, the advocacy of expansion by one of the nation's leading capitalists demonstrated the economic appeal of overseas expansion and foreshadowed the position many American businessmen and statesmen would take later in the century.[208]

Belmont's involvement in schemes to purchase slaveholding Cuba also suggests that transatlantic capitalists' distaste for slavery and investing in Southern states, even after repudiation in the 1840s, should not be exaggerated. Throughout the antebellum years, Southern states continued to market their bonds abroad and some, as in the case of Virginia, did so quite successfully. Moreover, leading banks in London established a network of correspondents and agents in the commercial cities of the South such as New Orleans, Mobile, and Charleston in this period. The South's advocacy of tariff reductions, of course, appealed to transatlantic financial and commercial interests.[209] Nonetheless, there is little question

---

[206] For Belmont's involvement in Cuban annexation schemes, see Irving Katz, *August Belmont: A Political Biography* (New York, 1968), pp. 22–50; and May, *The Southern Dream of a Caribbean Empire*, p. 42.

[207] Belmont to N.M.R. and Sons, 2 November 1858, T55/101, RA.

[208] For an exploration of the economic drive behind expansion in the late nineteenth century, see Walter LaFeber, *The New Empire: An Interpretation of American Expansion, 1860–1898* (Ithaca, 1963). Indeed, Belmont also advocated commercial expansion, devoting much of his energies while minister to The Hague to negotiating a commercial agreement that would open up the Dutch East Indies to American commerce.

[209] See, for example, *The Economist*, 12 December 1846, p. 1611.

that slavery and repudiation tarnished the reputation of the Southern states in the eyes of European capitalists. Nowhere was this more evident than on the London Stock Exchange in the 1840s and 1850s. Although there are no reliable figures regarding the amount of British investment in the two sections of the United States, it is clear that the bonds of Northern states were in much higher demand than those of the South. Northern state securities frequently sold at or above par in Britain whereas those of the Southern states, tainted by slavery and the specter of repudiation, were often quoted at significant discounts.[210] "If the whole country was like New England," Joshua Bates lamented, "it would be the happiest country in the world."[211] Where British capital went, financial institutions followed. All of the principal American agents and branches of transatlantic banking houses were Northern: Joshua Bates and Thomas Wren Ward of Barings were from Boston; Belmont made his home in New York; and George Peabody and his partner J. S. Morgan were both New Englanders.

This London–Wall Street connection was also evinced in British investment in American railroads. Ten railroads before the Civil War, for example, had $1 million or more of its stock held abroad.[212] Only one of these railroads was in a Southern state, despite the South possessing 35 percent of the nation's railroad mileage in 1860.[213] Although most promising lines in a pecuniary sense were in Northern states, British preference for these railroads was also in part the product of the anti-slavery investment tactics of British capitalists. As Harriet Martineau wrote in 1857, "It would be useful to us to consider railways, both philosophically and economically, as exponents of the social systems under which they arise, and are intended to work."[214] Accordingly, lines

---

[210] On an average day in 1851, for example, Northern state bonds were quoted much higher than Southern state bonds on the London Stock Exchange. New York fives were quoted at 96, Massachusetts fives at 106, and Ohio sixes at 104. Conversely, South Carolina fives were quoted at 89, Louisiana fives at 90, and Tennessee sixes at 90. These bonds were selected because they yielded similar rates and none of the states had defaulted in the 1840s. *The Economist*, 6 December 1851. See also McGrane, *Foreign Bondholders*, p. 11.
[211] Bates to Ward, 17 October 1841, Ward Papers, MHS.
[212] Adler, *British Investment in American Railways*, pp. 66–7.
[213] These ten railroads were the Philadelphia and Reading; New York and Erie; Western of Massachusetts; Pennsylvania; Camden and Amboy; Ohio and Mississippi (Eastern Division); South Carolina; Illinois Central; Baltimore and Ohio; and Belvidere and Delaware. See Adler, *British Investment in American Railways*, p. 66. See also *The Economist*, 7 February 1857, p. 141.
[214] Elisabeth Sanders (ed.), *Harriet Martineau in the London* Daily News (London, 1994), pp. 84–90. This column appeared on 10 February 1857.

such as the Illinois Central became favorites of British liberals who recognized that improved infrastructure in the North would promote free labor and, by connecting American farms to Atlantic ports, free trade. Sixty-six percent of the stock of the Illinois Central was held in Britain, most notably by antislavery, free traders John Bright and Richard Cobden (whose trip to the United States in 1859 was undertaken not to observe American democracy, but to inspect the Illinois Central on behalf of its British shareholders).[215] An Illinois lawyer named Abraham Lincoln protected the interests of the railroad and its British shareholders.

Fortunately for the Southern states already discriminated against on European capital markets, the Panic of 1857 did not have the same debilitating effects on their financial standing as did the crisis of two decades earlier. The collapse of the New York branch of the Ohio Life Insurance and Trust Company in August 1857 precipitated a stock market crash and a panic that led hundreds of banks to close their doors. Poor administration of railroads and banks alike intensified what initially appeared to be an isolated instance of mismanagement.[216] Railroad stock and confidence in the nation's monetary institutions plummeted. Four days after the failure of Ohio Life Insurance, the stock of the Illinois Central dropped by twenty percent, leading the railroad to default later in the year.[217] The crisis reached its nadir in October and November 1857 as unemployment rose and bank failures continued.

Like the crisis in 1837, malfeasant American leaders and banks alone were not entirely responsible for a panic whose origins lay in events beyond their control. Revisionist historians contend that the end of the Crimean War and the subsequent reintroduction of Eastern European and Russian grains into Britain triggered a decrease in agricultural prices that depressed both the farming and merchant communities in the United States and left an unstable economy vulnerable to any banking crisis.[218] The ensuing trade deficit led to a drain in specie that depleted

---

[215] For the Illinois Central's stock abroad, see Wilkins, *Foreign Investment*, p. 96. See also Thomas P. Martin. "The Upper Mississippi Valley in Anglo-American Anti-Slavery and Free Trade Relations: 1837–1842," *The Mississippi Valley Historical Review*, 15 (September 1928), pp. 204–20; and *idem* "Cotton and Wheat In Anglo-American Trade and Politics, 1846–1852," *Journal of Southern History*, 1 (August 1935), pp. 293–319.

[216] Peter Temin, "The Panic of 1857," *Intermountain Economic Review*, 6 (Spring 1975), pp. 1–12.

[217] James Huston, *The Panic of 1857 and the Coming of the Civil War* (London, 1987), p. 14.

[218] For the revisionist view, see James Huston, "Western Grains and the Panic of 1857," *Agricultural History*, 57 (1983), pp. 14–32.

American holdings of gold.[219] Moreover, as in the 1830s, an increase in interest rates in Britain provided extra incentive for British capitalists to sell their plummeting American securities.[220] The further decline in American security prices abroad led to the failure of European firms from Glasgow to London to Hamburg who dealt in U.S. issues.[221] Waves of British creditors calling on their American investments nearly drowned George Peabody and Co. Like the Browns in 1837, the survival of Peabody's bank was owed to a £1 million loan advanced by the lender of last resort, the Bank of England.[222] Unlike the crisis of twenty years earlier, however, the Panic of 1857 did not prompt a protracted depression. The crisis was most severe in the West as a three-year decline in grain prices depressed American agriculture until 1859–60. The results of the panic were less prolonged in other regions of the nation. Northeastern employment levels, industries, and banks recovered by the following year and the Southern economy—which enjoyed unprecedented exports of cotton in the five years preceding the Civil War—emerged from 1857 relatively unscathed.

Despite this quick recovery, European interest in American securities steadily waned in the run-up to the Civil War. This was more a result of the intensifying sectional dispute than a prejudice against American securities after the panic. Indeed, initially after the troubles of 1857, British investors purchased depreciated American railroad bonds on the assumption that the securities would soon regain their value. Political disputes regarding the extension of slavery, however, soon led foreign investors to reconsider sinking capital into a nation on the brink of civil war. In particular, the bloody battle over whether Kansas would be admitted as a free or slave state demonstrated the potential for the sectional controversy to turn violent. August Belmont deplored "the fanatics and demagogues on the extremes of the anti and pro slavery parties" in Kansas, while Joshua Bates waited for another great

---

[219] For more on "specie drain" in 1857, see George W. Van Vleck, *The Panic of 1857* (New York, 1943), pp. 53–8.

[220] In October 1857, the Bank of England raised its discount rate from six to eight percent. See Hidy, *The House of Baring*, p. 459; Robert Sobel, *Panic on Wall Street* (London, 1970), p. 104.

[221] Niall Ferguson, *The House of Rothschild*, II, p. 82.

[222] British banks offered to float loans to Peabody and Co. in 1857 on the condition that Peabody relocate his firm to the United States. Fortunately for Peabody, the Bank of England intervened. For background on Peabody and Co. (which would later become the House of Morgan) see Franklin Parker, *George Peabody: A Biography* (Nashville, 1971); Murial Hidy, *George Peabody Merchant and Financier, 1829–1854* (New York, 1978).

compromise.²²³ The sacking of Lawrence, John Brown's Pottawatomie massacre, and the caning of Charles Sumner in the Senate by South Carolina Congressman Preston Brooks led U.S. bonds to fall to par in London for the first time in nearly eight years in the early summer 1856. Although U.S. bonds quickly recovered, the threat of civil war led them to drop below par in 1859, where they would stay until after Reconstruction (see Figure 3). Not surprisingly, none of the U.S. loan of 1857, issued to cover government deficits resulting from declining customs revenue after the panic, was formally marketed abroad and few of the issues made their way across the Atlantic.²²⁴ "I don't like the looks of things ahead," J. S. Morgan informed George Peabody, "nobody has confidence in the Political future."²²⁵ Despite the decline of British interest in American securities in the late 1850s, the boom years of the mid-fifties had increased foreign investment to $444 million by the eve of the Civil War in 1861.²²⁶

The quarter century preceding the Civil War was a period of unprecedented foreign investment in the United States. As we have seen, American foreign indebtedness increased from $110 million in 1838 to $444 million in 1861. The nation's need for capital to fund internal improvements and, later, the Mexican War, was not lost on American statesmen. Daniel Webster premised his foreign policy on attracting European investment and, during his negotiations with Lord Ashburton in 1842, recognized the financial benefits of Anglo-American peace. During the Clayton–Bulwer negotiations as well, the United States' need for British capital provided a powerful incentive to make unprecedented diplomatic compromises. Even on the state level, the need for foreign investment influenced political decisions—particularly after European capitalists made it clear that future loans hinged upon the renewal of old obligations. Baring Brothers bank was involved in nearly every issue of transatlantic significance in this period. From marketing American securities in Britain

---

[223] Belmont to N.M.R. and Sons, 5 February 1858, T55/82, RA; Bates to Young, 24 June 1854. HC1.20.8. ING. BA.

[224] Mira Wilkins has disproved the myth that the late 1850s witnessed massive European investment in federal securities. See Wilkins, *Foreign Investment*, pp. 94–5.

[225] Morgan to Peabody, 30 March 1860, Morgan Papers, Morgan Library.

[226] Wilkins, *Foreign Investment*, p. 152. A similar estimate put the United States' total foreign debt in 1861 at £100 million. See *The Economist*, 19 January 1861, p. 71; and Adler, *British Investment in American Railways*, p. 24. See also H. C. Allen, "Civil War, Reconstruction and Great Britain," in Harold Hyman (ed.), *Heard Round the World* (New York, 1969), p. 22; Jenks, *The Migration of British Capital to 1875*, p. 413.

to lobbying statesmen on both sides of the Atlantic during diplomatic crises to arbitrating disputes in the claims convention of the 1850s, Barings functioned as a powerful nineteenth-century multinational in both political and financial terms. However, as economic and political considerations led the firm to reduce its American business, the era of Barings' dominance in American finance and politics was over by 1861.

The Civil War, however, did not catch Barings or their European competitors off guard. Cautious European capitalists had reduced their American holdings in the late 1850s as it became clear that the United States was not the safe destination for capital that it had appeared to be during the revolutions of 1848. Indeed, the financial implications of the sectional dispute were made evident in a panic on American stock exchanges that followed the election of Lincoln and the secession of South Carolina in late 1860. Unlike the crises in 1837 and 1857, the Panic of 1860, *The Economist* maintained, was "in its origin wholly political."[227] The stock market crash in New York triggered a corresponding panic in Europe. American securities in London depreciated by an average of ten percent in the month following Lincoln's election, while U.S. Treasury bonds "were quoted lower than ever before" in Frankfurt.[228] As Lord Overstone, one of the largest British holders of American securities, remarked, "I doubt whether we are not as deeply interested in the matter as the parties themselves."[229]

The impending conflict resulted in the further repatriation of American securities by British capitalists. Baring Brothers instructed their agents to stop purchasing American securities in April 1861, while selling much of their American holdings "although the price is very low."[230] "The anticipation of a bloody conflict between the North and the South," George Peabody observed a month before the war began, "has already destroyed confidence in the U.S. Government and State securities and millions have within a few months been sent home for a market in consequence."[231] It is estimated that $200 million worth of American securities—almost half of those held abroad—were sent back across the

---

[227] *The Economist*, 8 December 1860, p. 1357.
[228] *The Economist*, 10 November 1860, p. 1243; Ricker to Black, 25 February 1861, RG 59, Main 161, NA.
[229] Overstone to Norman, 15 January 1861, in D. P. O'Brien (ed.) *The Correspondence of Lord Overstone*, vol. 2 (London, 1971), pp. 937–8.
[230] Baring Brothers to Ward, 20 April 1861, BP.
[231] Peabody to Sherman, 9 March 1861, Peabody Papers, B197 F2, Essex Institute, Salem, Mass.

Atlantic during 1860–3.[232] This was not a promising sign to either side as leaders in the North and South looked abroad for financial help in the war's first years.

The political response of British financial leaders during the secession crisis was to help the quarrelling Americans find a compromise to avert war. As they had done during the diplomatic crises of the preceding decades, financiers worked behind-the-scenes to prevent, as Joshua Bates put it, "a long and bloody war that will be destructive to commerce and will naturally reduce the profits of Baring Brothers."[233] Thomas Baring urged Foreign Secretary Lord John Russell to act as a mediator in the sectional dispute in December 1860.[234] Similarly, upon the recommendation of August Belmont, Lionel de Rothschild, head of the English Rothschilds and a Liberal MP, promoted British arbitration in the conflict during an 1861 meeting with Russell and Prime Minister Palmerston.[235] George Peabody penned a letter that was reprinted in his hometown *Boston Courier*, arguing that the only hope to "restore our credit" in Europe was "by concession on the part of the North and a compromise which will secure the best feelings of the border-states."[236] Even *The Economist* printed "An Earnest Appeal against Civil War" days after news of the Confederate bombardment of Fort Sumter reached Britain.[237]

However, unlike the preceding decades when statesmen on both sides of the Atlantic took the views of transatlantic financiers into account, the pleas of the financial lobby fell upon deaf ears in 1860–1. The roots of the conflict were too deep and passions on both sides were too high for economic rationales for conciliation to carry the day—a lesson that Wall Street leaders similarly learned when their support of compromise proposals failed to forestall war. When the sectional conflict turned into all-out war, many European financiers, particularly Anglo-American banking

---

[232] Lance E. Davis and Robert J. Cull, *International Capital Markets and American Economic Growth, 1820–1914* (Cambridge, 1994), p. 7; Richard Bensel, *Yankee Leviathan: The Origins of Central State Authority in America, 1859–1877* (New York, 1990), p. 249. It should be noted that Davis and Cull question this exact figure. Nonetheless, the point remains that the early years of the Civil War witnessed a repatriation of American securities abroad and, certainly, a cessation of the flow of capital across the Atlantic.

[233] Diary of Joshua Bates, 28 April 1861, DEP 74, Vols. 7–10, ING. BA.

[234] Baring to Russell, 27 December 1860, Russell Papers, PRO 30/22/39. Russell, of course, declined the offer to mediate in the Civil War.

[235] N.M.R. and Sons to Messrs. August Belmont and Co., 7 May 1861, RA. See also Belmont to N.M.R. and Sons, 16 April 1861, T55/183, RA.

[236] Peabody to Sherman, 9 March 1861, Peabody Papers.

[237] *The Economist*, 18 May 1861, pp. 533–4.

houses, were forced to choose a side. Although neutrality was a feasible policy for the Palmerston government, many British financiers were too intimately involved in the American economy to remain on the sidelines and the warring parties would bring them into the conflict by requesting war loans. Opting to support the Union or the Confederacy was not simple as the major banks were deeply divided in their sympathies. The two American partners of Baring Brothers were split on which side to support. Joshua Bates staunchly advocated the cause of the Union, while Russell Sturgis, though a New Englander, supported the South. The firm's loyalty to the Union was tested as early as the autumn 1861 when Governor Francis Pickens of South Carolina requested a loan for the procurement of arms.[238] The Rothschilds were also split on which side to support. Their American agent, August Belmont, vowed to "stand by the Government at any sacrifice in order to subdue this atrocious heresy of secession," while Salomon de Rothschild, who was visiting the United States from Paris during the secession controversy, urged his family to "recognize the Republic of the Southern Confederacy as quickly as possible."[239] George Peabody and partner J. S. Morgan, though New Englanders and sympathetic to the Union, doubted the North's ability to conquer the South and feared the economic consequences of a protracted war.[240]

Which side these financiers would support would hold both financial and diplomatic implications in the coming Civil War. The business relationships and investment patterns of the antebellum period, of course, were essential in shaping the responses of European financiers to the war. But so too were the international strategies and financial diplomacy of the Union and Confederacy.

[238] Pickens to Winans, 3 October 1861, 204327, ING. BA.
[239] Belmont to N.M.R. and Sons, 24 May 1861, T55/189, RA; Salomon de Rothschild to N.M.R. and Sons (Paris), 20 April 1861 in Sigmund Diamond, *A Casual View of America: The Letters of Salomon de Rothschild, 1859–1861* (London, 1962), pp. 123–4.
[240] See *New York Times*, 23 December 1869; and Diary of John Bigelow, 10 September 1861, John Bigelow Papers, New York Public Library.

2

Union Finance and Diplomacy, 1861–1865

The Civil War placed unprecedented financial burdens on the U.S. Government. The Treasury's outlays totaled a mere $63 million in the year before the war. By 1865, the government spent this amount every twenty days. To meet this massive increase in expenditure, Union leaders were forced to introduce new measures in addition to relying on traditional sources of revenue. Early in 1861 Congress took the first of several steps to raise funds when it passed the Morrill Tariff, which dramatically increased customs duties, and, later that summer, enacted the nation's first ever income tax, a progressive three percent tax on annual incomes greater than $800. The Internal Revenue Act of the following year revised the income tax upward[1] and, more significantly, set regressive taxes on nearly every good that Northerners consumed. Although taxes would provide the Treasury with twenty-one percent of the revenue needed to finance the war, the majority of the government's inlays—some two-thirds—would come from loans. Given the nation's lack of a central bank to coordinate its finances and its historic reliance on foreign capital, it is not surprising that Union leaders looked across the Atlantic for financial assistance during the Civil War.

If European financiers presented the Treasury with a potential ally, European statesmen represented the greatest threat to the State Department. Union statesmen worried that European states, led by Britain, might recognize or support the Confederacy because of their reliance on Southern cotton, sympathy for struggles of self-determination, and desire to divide and weaken a rival nation. Thus, Union foreign policy sought to prevent European diplomatic intervention in the conflict. Secretary of State William H. Seward pronounced this strategy of isolating the Confederacy in his famous dispatch number ten on 21 May 1861, in which he instructed U.S. minister to London Charles Francis

---

[1] All annual incomes between $600 and $10,000 were taxed at three percent and all incomes greater than $10,000 at five percent.

Adams to inform British leaders that "intercourse of any kind with the so-called commissioners [of the Confederacy] is liable to be construed as a recognition of the authority which appointed them." Recognition of the Confederacy, Seward warned, would mean that "we from that hour, shall cease to be friends and become once more, as we have twice before been forced to be, enemies of Great Britain."[2]

The Union's international objectives, therefore, were twofold: to obtain financial and material support abroad while blocking European powers from recognizing and assisting the Confederacy. The second of these two goals clearly took precedence during the conflict. Obtaining a foreign loan would mean little to the Union if Britain recognized the Confederacy. Moreover, Union leaders, particularly after their initial overtures to European capitalists failed in 1861, were disinclined to arrange a foreign loan for the financial reason of keeping interest payments on the debt at home and for the political and symbolic reason of conducting the war without the help of those who expressed little interest in the Union cause. Nonetheless, the financial exigencies of the war, combined with the desire to secure the political and diplomatic benefits that would accompany the presence of a contingent of Union bondholders in Europe, led leaders in Washington to seek foreign financial assistance at several points during the conflict. The Treasury made repeated attempts to arrange a foreign loan and conducted other operations abroad to prevent the Confederacy from doing the same. This section shall explore the Union effort to attract foreign capital to its cause and the attempts of Northern diplomats and agents to block European commercial and financial support of the Confederacy.

THE SEARCH FOR FRIENDS IN THE CITY

Salmon P. Chase inherited in early 1861 a Treasury Department that had run a deficit of more than $7 million the previous year. Increasing the government's revenues did not get off to a good start in the winter 1861 when Chase encountered difficulty in persuading American banks to purchase government bonds and to accept noninterest bearing Treasury notes for remittance. Arranging ad hoc loans from banks, however, was

---

[2] Seward to Adams, 21 May 1861, *Foreign Relations of the United States* (Washington, 1865; hereafter *FRUS*), 1861, pp. 71–4; Norman Ferris, *Desperate Diplomacy: William H. Seward's Foreign Policy, 1861* (Knoxville, 1976), pp. 21–3.

not a viable fiscal policy once the Civil War erupted in April. A Treasury report soon projected massive federal deficits to the tune of $11 million by August. Leading members of the House and Senate Finance Committees conferred with Chase and Lincoln in the days preceding the special session of the 37th Congress to find a solution to the Treasury's financial problems. Their answer, which Congress unanimously approved, was to issue a $250 million national loan bearing up to 7.3 percent interest. This loan was uniquely both a popular and a bank loan. After extended negotiations Chase persuaded banks in New York, Philadelphia, and Boston to advance the Treasury three installments of $50 million in specie. The Treasury would then reimburse the banks through the proceeds of seven-thirty bonds sales (known as such because they were three-year notes bearing 7.3 percent interest) or, if sales lagged, with the bonds themselves. The first national loan of the war—thanks in part to the marketing tactics of an unknown Philadelphia financier named Jay Cooke—soon became one of the Union's greatest successes of 1861.[3]

The same could not be said of the second component of the first loan bill. Congress authorized Chase to place "any portion of [the] loan, not exceeding $100,000,000" abroad.[4] Given the historic links between British capitalists and the U.S. Government, it was natural for Union leaders to look across the Atlantic for funds—particularly when American banks were being less than cooperative with the government. Furthermore, it was hoped that a foreign loan would yield both financial and diplomatic advantages. First, an influx of foreign gold would bolster reserves at home as well as establish the nation's credit abroad from the war's beginning. Both would be needed in a potentially long war. Second, a successful loan issued on the London Stock Exchange would demonstrate support for the North amongst the influential financial class of Britain who, in order to protect their investment returns, would likely oppose any diplomatic move that favored the Confederacy. With British statesmen skeptical of the North's ability to forcibly reunify the nation, the Union could use powerful friends in London.

Chase was so eager to arrange a foreign loan that he empowered August Belmont, the Rothschilds' American agent who was already crossing the

---

[3] For the specifics of the loan bill, see *Congressional Globe*, 37th Congress, 1st session, Appendix, pp. 60–1. This paragraph also draws from Heather Cox Richardson, *The Greatest Nation of the Earth: Republican Economic Policies during the Civil War* (Cambridge, Mass., 1997), pp. 31–45.

[4] *Congressional Globe*, 37th Congress, 1st session, Appendix, pp. 60–1.

Atlantic on business, to sound out the idea on European capitalists before Congress passed the loan bill.[5] With Chase's approval, Belmont planned to issue $50 million in six percent bonds, with principal and interest payable in London, under the auspices of a leading banking house, preferably one with agencies in Britain and on the continent. This bank would market the securities—ideally in denominations as low as $20 to attract small investors who would likely hold antislavery views—on European stock exchanges at its own discretion and would earn a commission for its services.[6] This was the standard procedure for government loans in the nineteenth century and had been recently employed by Russia, Austria, and Brazil on the London market. It was agreed that the mission be kept confidential (Belmont left under the guise that his wife sought medical treatment in Europe) in the event that it should be unsuccessful. The failure to attract European capital, Belmont admitted, "would affect very materially our home-markets" in addition to being a diplomatic setback.[7]

Like most Union agents sent to Europe during the war, Belmont was an excellent choice. His knowledge of international finance and European capitalists was unrivalled in the United States. If any American could persuade European financiers to advance credit to the Union, it was the Rothschilds' agent who had experience in finance, politics (Belmont was the chairman of the Democratic National Committee), and diplomacy (he had served as minister to Belgium under the Pierce administration). The major drawback to selecting Belmont—he was a Democrat who was hostile to Lincoln's election—could also be viewed as another one of his strengths. The support of the Northern war effort from a leading Democrat demonstrated the national, bipartisan nature of the war and countered the prevailing view abroad that the Union cause was radical, the word feared most by European capitalists. Indeed, Belmont would loyally serve the Union, even collaborating with his old New York political nemeses William Seward and Thurlow Weed during his time in Europe. Although Belmont would later oppose many Republican policies and, as we shall see, would even be willing to entertain negotiated peace proposals with reunion as the basis, his services to the Lincoln

---

[5] Chase dispatched Belmont in late June. Congress passed the loan bill on 15 July.
[6] Belmont to Chase, 24 June 1861, in August Belmont, *A Few Letters and Speeches of the Late Civil War* (New York, 1870); Belmont to Chase, 3 July 1861, Belmont Papers, Library of Congress (hereafter LC).
[7] Belmont to Chase, 3 July 1861, Belmont Papers, LC.

administration during his mission to Europe personified War Democrats' commitment to the Union cause in 1861–2.[8]

Belmont's loyalty to his nation was matched by his loyalty to his employers. Although he vowed to act "not as the Banker and correspondent of foreign Banking firms, but as an American citizen," it is clear that Belmont hoped to arrange the loan through his employer, the Rothschilds.[9] The largest and most influential bank in the world, the Rothschilds had a history of assisting governments in their hour of need. The firm had recently arranged national loans for Britain, France, and Turkey during the Crimean War.[10] Although the bank's interests in North America remained relatively insignificant throughout the nineteenth century, the Rothschilds had briefly served as the European agent of the U.S. Government in the 1840s and had granted credit to Washington during the Mexican War. Belmont's personal ambitions complemented the obvious allure of arranging the loan through the world's leading bank. The New York financier had repeatedly attempted to expand the Rothschilds' American business before the war and brokering a national loan would cement the firm's future interest in the United States.[11] Furthermore, a Rothschild loan engineered by the ever-ambitious Belmont would enhance the banker's reputation at home and help him launch a political career after the war. For all of these reasons, Belmont urged his superiors in London to sponsor the Union loan:

> stocks of our federal Government at par ought to prove, even in the present distracted state of our country, a very desirable investment to your capitalists.... Under your auspices they would be eagerly taken in London, Paris, Amsterdam and Frankfurt. In England particularly I should think that among the rich Quakers and antislavery capitalists ready takers would be found for the loan of our Government, now engaged in a struggle not for the lawless destruction of slavery and slave property, but for the purpose of preventing the extension of this baneful institution.[12]

---

[8] For the Democrats and the Civil War, see Joel Silbey, *"A Respectable Minoriotу": The Democratic party in the Civil War Era, 1860–1868* (New York, 1977). Silbey finds Belmont a leader of the "Legitimist" wing of the party who consistently opposed the "Purist" faction led by Clement Vallandigham.

[9] Belmont to Chase, 3 July 1861, Belmont Papers, LC.

[10] See Niall Ferguson, *The House of Rothschild: The World's Bankers, 1849–1999* (New York, 1998), pp. 72–7.

[11] For Belmont's attempts to expand Rothschild business in the United States before the war, see Belmont to N.M.R. and Sons, 7 December 1840, T54/123; Belmont to N.M.R. and Sons, 15 July 1847, T54/262; Belmont to N.M.R. and Sons, 9 October 1849, T54/306, Rothschild Archive (hereafter RA), London.

[12] Belmont to N.M.R. and Sons, 17 June 1861, T55/194, RA.

Unfortunately for the North, the Rothschilds did not agree with Belmont's analysis. The bank expressed no interest in their agent's offer, stating that "the present moment is far from propitious for bringing out an American loan, for if the war should continue, it can only be carried on at a monumental expense, and loan would have to follow loan in order to provide the means."[13] Other London banks gave Belmont a similar reply. British capitalists were so wary of investing in Union bonds that the *Bankers' Magazine* declared that the only way the North would be able to borrow money in Britain would be to pledge "the best public lands" as security.[14] Perhaps *The Economist* best summed up the mood when it tersely stated "Mr Chase will obtain no money in Europe."[15] All of this convinced Belmont that though "small amounts will here and there be taken by capitalists," a large loan could not "be effected with any of the leading Banking houses." Without the backing of such a bank to exert influence on the financial markets, it would be impossible to successfully promote a Union loan in Europe. "Any direct or indirect attempt on the part of our Government to do so," Belmont reported to Chase, "would be worse than useless, and you will have to look for all wants to our home markets."[16]

Having failed to gain the financial support of the City, Belmont attempted to secure its political and moral backing. Winning the war of sympathies, Belmont recognized, could pave the way to a future loan and, perhaps more importantly, would block a financial or diplomatic move that favored the Confederacy. Not surprisingly, Belmont focused much of his lobbying efforts on the financially and politically influential Rothschilds. Seeking to counter the pro-Confederate views of Salomon de Rothschild (who was visiting the South at the time) and to retract his earlier suggestion that the Rothschilds should press the British cabinet to offer to mediate in the conflict,[17] Belmont urged his employers to embrace the cause of Union. Particularly worrying to Belmont was the Queen's proclamation of neutrality, issued on 13 May 1861. The proclamation officially pronounced Britain's neutrality in the coming war and prevented British subjects from enlisting in foreign services and from constructing war vessels for the belligerents in British shipyards. Like

[13] N.M.R. and Sons to Belmont, 11 June 1861, RA.
[14] *Bankers' Magazine*, October 1861, pp. 688–91.
[15] *The Economist*, 24 August 1861, p. 927.
[16] Belmont to Chase, 31 October 1861, Belmont Papers, LC. See also Henrietta Larson, *Jay Cooke: Private Banker* (Cambridge, Mass., 1936), p. 117.
[17] Belmont to N.M.R. and Sons, 19 April 1861, RA.

many Northerners, Belmont feared that by categorizing the rebellious states as belligerents the proclamation was "an initial step towards recognizing the Southern Confederacy." In an effort to portray the rebellion as illegitimate and unlawful, Belmont rebutted the prevailing argument that the South was fighting for the right to self-determination as Greece, with the support of Britain, had done against the Ottomans earlier in the century. Unlike the Greeks who were "a Christian people oppressed by fanatical Moslemism," the Southern states "were free and voluntary parties to a compact of Union which was declared to be perpetual." The North, he argued to his superiors, had not violated a "single right guaranteed to [the South] under the Constitution."[18]

There were financial reasons as well, Belmont maintained, for the Rothschilds and, in the larger picture, for Britain not to side with the Confederacy. Deploying an argument that would later become a staple of Union financial diplomacy, Belmont denigrated the credit of the new Confederacy to dissuade the Rothschilds from advancing a loan to the South. As evidence Belmont recalled the repudiation of the debts of Southern states in the 1840s:

> Who will take a dollar of a Confederacy of states of which 4 have already repudiated their debt... unless it be that the name of Jefferson Davis, notwithstanding his advocacy of repudiation in his own State of Mississippi, should have a sweeter sound to European capitalists than I think.[19]

There was little chance, as we shall later see, that a British bank would attempt to profit from the Civil War by arranging a loan to the Confederacy. However, what British financiers and the British government wanted from the South, of course, was cotton. Belmont countered the argument that recognizing the Confederacy was in Britain's economic self-interest in two ways. First, the New Yorker reminded the Rothschilds that the Confederacy, as even its vice-president Alexander Stephens openly proclaimed, was "based upon slavery." Confederate leaders had called for the expansion of slavery before the war and would likely reopen the slave trade, that "nefarious traffic in human flesh." "The only ground upon which they justify their rebellion," he argued, "is a fear that their peculiar institution of slavery may hereafter be interfered with." Belmont hoped that linking the rebellion with slavery—which was not often done in Europe in the early stages of the war as Lincoln's

---

[18] Belmont to N.M.R. and Sons, 21 May 1861, RA.
[19] Belmont to N.M.R. and Sons, 21 May 1861, RA.

pronounced war aim was reunion, not emancipation—would garner the support of the antislavery Rothschilds.

Second, Belmont pointed out that by harping on their need for cotton, British leaders "threaten to prolong the war by giving hope and comfort to the rebels." The longer the rebels held out, the longer Lancashire would have to survive without American cotton. Moreover, Belmont hinted that "interference or one sided neutrality" might lead to a war between the North and Britain that would "entail ruin...upon the material interests of the commerce of the world."[20] A third Anglo-American war was and always had been the nightmare of financiers who profited from the transatlantic peace that followed the Treaty of Ghent in 1815. As *The Economist* avowed, "a war with either of the belligerents would be a terrible calamity, but a war between England and the *Northern* states of America would be the most affecting misfortune which could happen to civilization."[21] British shipping and investments in the Northern states, as well as Britain's largest commercial market, would all be endangered by such a war. Although the recognition of the Confederacy would end the South's cotton embargo and might bring immediate economic benefits to Britain (and to the banks that underwrote the cotton trade), a pro-Confederate move would also infuriate American leaders in Washington and lead to a war whose costs would be far greater than the cotton famine. Britain's economic interests, in other words, demanded peace with the North—and thus a policy of neutrality during the war—more than an alliance with the cotton-producing Confederacy. This pragmatic assessment of national interest, as we shall see, would provide a powerful disincentive to British intervention in the conflict when such a policy was under consideration in the autumn 1862.

Belmont did not have to campaign on behalf of the Union in the house of the Rothschilds' greatest rivals, the Barings. That job had already been done by Joshua Bates. Countering the pro-Confederate position of rival partner Russell Sturgis, Bates persuaded his colleagues to uphold the cause of their long-time client, the U.S. Government. As Bates averred, "the Union is to be preserved whatever the cost and all are traitors who talk of secession."[22] Bates was convinced, even after the humiliating

---

[20] Belmont to N.M.R. and Sons, 21 May 1861, RA.
[21] *The Economist*, 1 June 1861, p. 590.
[22] Bates to Young, 2 October 1861, HC1.20.8, 1856–62, Letters of Joshua Bates, ING. Barings Archives (hereafter BA), London. For more on Bates, see Stanley Chapman, "Ethnicity and Money Making in Nineteenth Century Britain," *Renaissance and Modern Studies*, 38 (1995), pp. 20–38.

Union defeat at Bull Run in the summer 1861, that the North's superior resources would eventually lead to the restoration of the Union.[23] The certainty of a Northern victory demanded the advancement of loans to the U.S. Government. Bates argued that there "is nothing illegal or dishonourable in sending money to the United States," citing the precedent of the bank's loans to Buenos Aires during the Argentinean Revolution. Although he conceded that it was not propitious to broker a sizeable advance so early in the war, Bates maintained that it was in the firm's best interests to grant, at the very least, a symbolic loan to the Union. "If we refuse to have anything to do with American securities," he wrote to a partner, "we may damage the future business of the House."[24] Past prosperity and future profit, Bates recognized, could determine the sympathies of ambivalent partners. The future prospects of the firm, Bates privately revealed in his diary, had already been compromised by the pro-Confederate stance of Sturgis.[25] Indeed, the "disloyalty" of Sturgis led the American legation in London and the Treasury Department in Washington to "think seriously of transferring its business to some other House."[26]

Such action was unnecessary as Baring Brothers, under the leadership of Bates, became the staunchest supporter of the North in British financial circles. In the war's opening months, the firm advanced funds to George Schuyler, a Union arms purchasing agent in Europe.[27] Later in 1861, Barings financed the propaganda mission of Thurlow Weed, a longtime ally and advisor to Seward. With the funds provided by Barings, Weed wined and dined British statesmen, published pro-Union columns and pamphlets, and assisted in Union arms-purchasing operations.[28] Thomas Baring, the firm's head, politically supported the Union from his seat in Parliament, particularly, as we shall see, during the *Alabama*

---

[23] Diary of Joshua Bates, 25 August 1861, DEP 74, Vols. 7–10, ING. BA.
[24] Bates to Young, 1 October 1861, HC1.20.8, 1856–62, Letters of Joshua Bates, ING. BA.
[25] Diary of Joshua Bates, 4 October 1863, DEP 74, Vols. 7–10, ING. BA.
[26] Chase to Forbes, 14 June 1862, in John Niven (ed.), *The Salmon P. Chase Papers*, 5 vols. (Kent, Ohio, 1993–8), 3, pp. 210–11; Diary of Benjamin Moran, Library of Congress. Moran was secretary to the American legation in London.
[27] Bates to Baring, 5 October 1861, HC1.20.8, 1856–62, Letters of Joshua Bates, ING. BA; Baring Brothers to Ward, 8 October 1861, Baring Papers (hereafter BP), Library of Congress [microfilm]; 204333, ING. BA; *The Times*, 26 June 1871.
[28] Weed to Baring Brothers, 3 December 1861, Thurlow Weed Papers, Library of Congress. See also Thurlow Weed, *Life of Thurlow Weed* (New York, 1883), p. 638. Weed soon discovered that, "to see people right," he must live "more expensively than intended." See Weed to Seward, 6 December 1861, Seward Papers, Rochester University [microfilm].

dispute later in the war. Baring Brothers' support for the North did not sit well with the Confederacy. "The United States had their Treasury Department in England," the Confederate agent James Bulloch later complained, "at the office of bankers whose leading partner was a member of Parliament, who was bound by his oath...to follow...her Majesty's Proclamation of Neutrality."[29]

Baring Brothers' support for the Union, however, was not without its limits. Apart from Bates, the firm expressed no interest in Belmont's loan proposal. With even the agency of the U.S. Government rejecting his offer, Belmont suspected that European banks had joined together under the belief that "by withholding all aid from us, they may force us into a settlement of some kind with the Southern States."[30] There is no evidence in the bank records, however, to suggest that this was the case. The failure of Belmont's mission, as the Rothschilds clearly stated, was more a result of the uncertainties of the financial and military situation in the United States than a premeditated and coordinated agreement between competing banks to force the Lincoln administration into a settlement with the Confederacy. As *The Economist* put it, "Federations at a crisis of revolutionary disunion cannot hope to have credit abroad."[31] Particularly damaging to Belmont's cause was the humiliating Union defeat at Bull Run in July 1861—the news of which reached Europe through the famous reports of *The Times'* foreign correspondent William Howard Russell just as Belmont sought takers for the loan.

The Bull Run disaster also increased the threat of British recognition of the Confederacy, a move that would impart legal, diplomatic, and moral legitimacy to the South's rebellion. "Bull Run," Prime Minister Palmerston quipped, should be called "Yankee's Run."[32] With the forces of the Confederacy able to repel an invading army, many in Britain began to consider the division of the Union a *fait accompli* that Britain should recognize. Belmont took it upon himself to meet with British leaders to dismiss such thoughts, despite being given no diplomatic authority by Seward. With the help of Lionel de Rothschild, Belmont arranged an informal meeting with Palmerston in a private gallery in the Commons. Belmont's attempts to appeal to Palmerston's antislavery sympathies got him little more from the Prime Minister than a succinct synopsis of the

---

[29] James Bulloch, *The Secret Service of the Confederate States in Europe*, 2 vols. (London, 1883), I, p. 364.
[30] Belmont to Chase, 3 July and 15 August 1861, Belmont Papers, LC.
[31] *The Economist*, 18 January 1862, p. 57.
[32] Quoted in Howard Jones, *Union in Peril* (Chapel Hill, 1992), p. 57.

British position: "We do not like slavery, but we want cotton, and we dislike very much your Morrill tariff."

"I think this phrase comprises the whole policy of this government in the present war," Belmont informed Seward, "and from what I have seen and heard since my arrival, I am more than ever convinced that we have nothing to hope from the sympathy of the English government and people in our struggle."[33] All that could be done to change these views, the free trade advocate Belmont concluded, was to repeal the Morrill Tariff. Although Belmont's political views and prominent position within the Democratic Party no doubt influenced this recommendation, there were valid diplomatic justifications for reconsidering the Morrill Tariff. The measure alienated British capitalists and liberals who were inclined to support the North and provided Confederate agents with ammunition for their propaganda that argued that the tariff, not slavery, was at the heart of the sectional dispute. Even friends of the North in Britain scoffed at the tariff, which John Bright called "a stupid and unpatriotic act."[34] The Morrill Tariff, *The Times* retorted, should be called the "immoral tariff."[35] "The protectionists are actually inviting the world to support the Confederate cause," a perplexed Harriet Martineau wrote in the London *Daily Star*.[36] A repeal in the tariff, Belmont informed Chase and Seward, would be "worth more to our cause [in Britain] than the most brilliant victory which our arms could achieve over the rebels."[37] The Republican's political and ideological commitment to the tariff, combined with Chase's desperate need for funds, trumped considerations of international opinion. Indeed, far from repealing the tariff, the Republican-led Congress increased it several times during the war.

---

[33] For Belmont's meeting with Palmerston, see Belmont to Seward, 30 July 1861, Belmont, *Letters, Speeches and Addresses*; Belmont to Chase, 15 August 1861, Belmont Papers, LC; David Black, *The King of Fifth Avenue: The Fortunes of August Belmont* (New York, 1981), pp. 210–12; Irving Katz, *August Belmont* (New York, 1968), pp. 100–3; and Louis Sears, "August Belmont: Banker in Politics," *The Historical Outlook*, 15 (April 1924), pp. 151–4. Belmont followed up his meeting with Palmerston with an appeal to Foreign Secretary Russell to "revoke the Queen's Proclamation of neutrality in the American conflict and show your detestation of slavery by openly espousing the cause of the North." See Belmont to Dunfermline (forwarded to Russell), 19 August 1861, Russell Papers, 30/22/39, Public Records Office, Kew, England.

[34] Quoted in R. J. M. Blackett, *Divided Hearts: Britain and the American Civil War* (Baton Rouge, 2001), p. 21. See also Diary of Joshua Bates, 21 March 1861, DEP 74, Vols. 7–10, ING. BA.

[35] *The Times*, 17 April 1861.

[36] *Daily Star*, 15 July 1862.

[37] Belmont to Chase, 31 October 1861, Belmont Papers, LC. See also Belmont to Seward, 26 November 1860, Seward Papers.

The Morrill Tariff was also a thorny subject for another advocate of the Union in Britain, George Francis Train. Publisher of the antislavery and free trade journal the *London American*, Train viewed protectionism as a blight on the otherwise noble cause of the Union. "We shall advocate," a lead editorial in the *American* asserted, "the repeal of this impolitic measure [the Morrill Tariff] as injurious alike to the moral and material interests of the United States and the commercial interests of nearly every nation of Europe."[38] In an effort to garner British support for the North, Train soon revised this position and argued that financial exigencies necessitated a tempory tariff, which would both fund the Union cause and illustrate the deleterious effects of protectionism to American politicians. "Paradoxical as it may seem," the *American* held, "we regard [the Morrill Tariff] as the first and, perhaps, necessary step toward the universal recognition of the soundness of the Free-trade doctrine."[39]

Such legerdemains were typical of Train, one of the loudest, yet least recognized by historians, advocates of the Union in Britain. An American promoter of the Atlantic and Great Western Railroad in London, Train established in 1860 the *London American*, a weekly journal covering transatlantic trade and investment.[40] Mirroring its editor who applauded the "spread-Eagleism" of the expansionist, jingoistic, and democratic Young America movement of the 1850s, the publication was also unabashedly radical.[41] The editorial page was commonly filled with pieces that promoted democracy and denounced slavery and the European aristocracy. It came as little surprise, therefore, that when the Civil War erupted a year later the *American* became the North's semi-official propaganda organ in Britain. "War has arrived, and it is utterly useless to say we cannot find where the responsibility rests," the *American* declared, "it is directly on the heads of the leading Southern politicians."[42] Although Train's nationalism and hatred of the European aristocracy made him a controversial figure in Britain, leaders in Washington soon recognized the utility of a pro-Union newspaper that landed on the breakfast tables of London financiers.[43] Seward contributed $100 to the publication in 1862

[38] *London American*, 20 March 1861.
[39] Ibid., 17 April 1861.
[40] The idea of establishing an American newspaper in London was not new. Joshua Bates considered backing such an operation in the 1840s. See Bates to Ward, 4 October 1841, Thomas Wren Ward Papers, Massachusetts Historical Society.
[41] See, for instance, George Francis Train, *Young America in Wall Street* (London, 1857).
[42] *London American*, 1 May 1861.
[43] For Train's nationalism, see Donaldson Jordan and Edwin Pratt, *Europe and the American Civil War* (New York, 1931), p. 179; Edward L. Widmer, *Young America: The Flowering of Democracy in New York City* (New York, 1999), pp. 202–3.

to help it become "a permanent thing in England" and corresponded with A. W. Bostwick, the *American's* editor.[44]

Until Train's return to the United States led to its abrupt discontinuation in early 1863, the *London American* helped coordinate pro-Union activity in Britain. Train's publication sponsored and advertised pro-Union rallies in London while connecting the struggles of British radicals, such as John Bright and Richard Cobden, against the "the bankrupt monarchies of Europe" to the Northern crusade against the "men who claim merit and superiority for being shameless advocates of human oppression and bondage."[45] Train's pro-Union public speeches were reproduced in special addenda to the *American* and, though controversial for their radical political views, were widely circulated in Britain. The publication never completely forgot its main audience, the financial community, and appealed to merchants and financiers on both sides of the Atlantic to help those in Britain who were suffering from the North's blockade. Americans were encouraged to donate money to the unemployed cotton operatives in Lancashire while capitalists in both nations were urged to enter into investment schemes for establishing cotton production in India, Central America, and border states in the Union.[46]

Not surprisingly, the *American* became the North's quasi-official organ for promoting Union war bonds overseas. If anyone in Britain would buy into a possible Union loan, it would be the readers of the *American* who likely subscribed to the journal for its coverage of transatlantic commerce and finance. "The question has been raised, whether, in view of the present difficulties in the United States, the Government will be enabled to borrow money on as good terms as formerly," the newspaper asked, "Can any reasons be given why it cannot?" The publication assured its readers that Lincoln would "restore the ... financial credit of the great American nation" and that Chase "may fairly lay claim to the laurels which have been so lavishly strewn over the graves of the great William Pitt, and the more crafty and less patriotic Sir Robert Peel." These endorsements, however, had little effect. The *American* was baffled at

---

[44] Train to Seward, 19 October 1862, Seward Papers. See also George Francis Train, *My Life in Many States and in Foreign Lands* (New York, 1902), p. 273. See also Jay Monaghan, *Diplomat in Carpet Slippers* (New York, 1945), p. 104. Bostwick to Seward, 7 October and 22 November 1862, Seward Papers.

[45] George Francis Train, *Train's Union Speeches* (London, 1862), p. 28; *London American*, 5 June 1861.

[46] *London American*, 5 February and 17 July 1861, 19 November 1862. Such recommendations contrasted favorably to the *Index's* (the Confederate propaganda organ) advocacy of the Confederacy's cotton embargo.

the repatriation of U.S. securities from Europe in 1861, asserting that "the past and present state of panic in the American stock markets of Europe is utterly groundless and unjustifiable." When American investors eagerly purchased the seven-thirties of the first national loan in the autumn 1861, the *American* changed its view of a foreign loan. "It must be a source of gratification to every loyal American," the publication contended, "that sufficient capital can be spared from the ordinary channels of business to meet the want of the Government. It is certainly desirable that everything relating to the rebellion should be kept at home if at all possible."[47]

THE *TRENT* AFFAIR

Keeping the rebellion at home became a difficult task after U.S. Navy Capt. Charles Wilkes boarded a British steamer, the *Trent*, and removed two of its passengers, Southern agents James Mason and John Slidell, who were en route to Europe to lobby for the recognition of the Confederacy. This act, which was not authorized by the Lincoln administration, was in violation of international law.[48] It was also an insult to British honor. Reports of Americans, who were desperate for a victory of some sort after the humiliations of 1861, celebrating Wilkes' act stoked the flames of British anger. As an irate Palmerston declared in an emergency cabinet meeting on 28 November 1861, "I don't know whether you are going to stand this, but I'll be damned if I do!"[49] Palmerston's determination to reprimand the United States showed up in Foreign Secretary Lord Russell's dispatch to Washington, which, though toned down by Prince Albert days before his death, demanded the immediate release of the two captives and a formal apology. "What we want," Russell informed the British minister to Washington Lord Lyons, "is a plain Yes or No to our very simple demands, and we want that plain Yes or No within seven days of the communication of the despatch."[50] If the answer

---

[47] *London American*, 13 November, 13 March, 17 April, 15 May, and 4 September 1861.

[48] For a discussion of international law and the *Trent* affair, see Jones, *Union in Peril*, pp. 80–99. The act violated international law because human beings had never been considered the embodiment of diplomatic dispatches (which could legally be seized) and Wilkes did not take the *Trent* to a prize court for a ruling.

[49] Quoted in Gordon Warren, *Fountain of Discontent: The* Trent *Affair and Freedom of the Seas* (Boston, 1981), p. 109.

[50] Quoted in Jones, *Union in Peril*, p. 85.

was no, Britain was making preparations for war. Military and naval strategists planned the defense of Canada and a blockade of the Northern states as the government blocked the exportation of saltpeter (which was used in gunpowder) to the United States.[51]

As could be expected, the political fallout from the *Trent* affair produced a transatlantic financial crisis. Securities plummeted on both sides of the Atlantic. When news of the crisis hit the floor of the London Stock Exchange, *The Times* reported that "after a few moments, during which it was deemed almost incredible, the result on the funds was a fall of one per cent."[52] The drop in consol prices was nothing compared to the ten percent collapse in the price of U.S. bonds in London.[53] In Frankfurt as well, the U.S. consul reported that the *Trent* crisis "is rendering American stock entirely unsaleable."[54] Even Canadian securities plummeted as British investors feared that Lincoln would divert a portion of his massive army northwards.[55] In New York news of the British demand to release Mason and Slidell ignited a stock market panic on 16 December. Investors dumped their Treasury bonds, preferring gold, dry goods, war supplies, or anything other than securities of a government that might soon be involved in a two-front war. The panic on Wall Street contributed to a run on banks in New York that exacerbated the city's already short supply of gold. A hard-money advocate, Chase had insisted that banks literally pay the $50 million advances of the first national loan to the Treasury in gold (rather than allowing the banks to keep the reserves on a government account). This left banks with dangerously low reserves and fueled rumors of an imminent suspension of specie payments. So dire was the situation that New York banks reneged on their pledge to advance the Treasury the third $50 million installment of the first national loan that was due in mid-December.

To make matters worse, the normally conciliatory financial lobby took sides during the *Trent* crisis. George Francis Train chose a poor time and place to reveal his American nationalism, brashly declaring in front of a London audience that if he were the president "he would have convicted [Mason and Slidell] of high treason; he would have hanged them— [hisses]—and then sent them to England, if England insisted on their

[51] Kenneth Bourne, "British Preparations for War with the North, 1861–1862," *English Historical Review*, 76 (October 1961), pp. 600–32.
[52] *The Times*, 28 November 1861.
[53] See *The Economist*, 30 November and 7 December 1861.
[54] Murphy to Seward, 2 December 1861, RG 59, Main 161, National Archives (hereafter NA).
[55] *The Economist*, 14 December 1861, p. 1374.

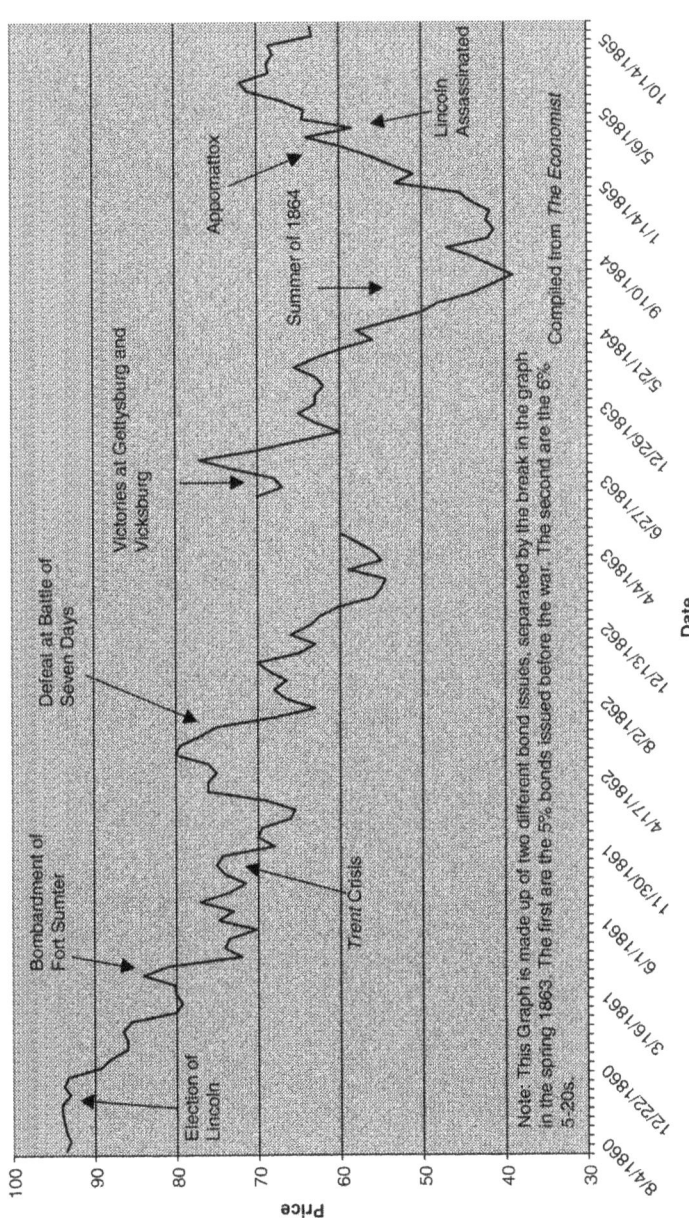

Figure 4 U.S. Bonds in London during the Civil War

being given up."⁵⁶ Union propagandist Thurlow Weed informed Seward that Baring "is against us 'flat-footed'" and "Peabody tries to see both sides—ours dimly."⁵⁷ Even the conservative Rothschilds were swept up in the nationalism. "As much as war is deprecated," the London bankers wrote to their New York correspondents August Belmont and Co., "every support will be given to our Ministers, if you force us into it."⁵⁸ War appeared so imminent that the Barings and Rothschilds suspended all business in the United States, the latter going as far as to transfer all of the English Rothschilds' American holdings to the French house out of the fear that the United States would confiscate holdings of British subjects during an Anglo-American war.⁵⁹

The financial implications of the *Trent* crisis were not good news to Salmon Chase. The British demand to release Mason and Slidell and to apologize for the *Trent* affair reached Washington just after Chase issued his annual Treasury report on 9 December 1861. Despite the failure of Belmont's mission and warnings from Wall Street that American capitalists would not back another loan, Chase's report proposed more borrowing to finance the war effort. After downward revisions in projections of tax revenue, ninety percent of the Treasury's inlays for the coming year were expected to come from loans.⁶⁰ However, as Chase soon recognized, it would be difficult to cajole investors into buying into another massive national loan when existing government securities were plummeting because of fears of an imminent Anglo-American war. Furthermore, alarming shortages of specie in New York threatened a suspension of payments and led Chase—as early as his December report—to recommend the federal chartering of banks that could issue notes backed by Treasury bonds (as opposed to gold reserves). Restructuring the currency system and banking structure, however, would have to wait. In the meantime, war with Britain needed to be averted or else a financial, as well as a diplomatic and military, disaster would ensue. Lest Chase miss this point, a Wall Street broker reminded him that business leaders "trust you will have allayed this excitement with England . . . one war at a

---

⁵⁶ Quoted in D. P. Crook, *The North, the South and the Powers, 1861–1865* (New York, 1974), p. 139. See also Train, *Train's Union Speeches*.

⁵⁷ Weed to Seward, 5 December 1861, Seward Papers, Rochester. See also Crook, *The North, the South and the Powers*, p. 138.

⁵⁸ N.M.R. and Sons to Messrs. August Belmont and Co., 3 December 1861, RA.

⁵⁹ Belmont to N.M.R. and Sons, 3 December 1861, T55/214, RA; Baring Brothers to Ward, 4 December 1861, BP. See also *The Economist*, 7 December 1861, pp. 1345–6.

⁶⁰ For the Treasury report, see *The Economist*, 28 December 1861, pp. 1429–30; John Niven, *Salmon P. Chase* (New York, 1995), p. 271.

time is enough."⁶¹ As *The Economist* put it, "Is it possible that a nation whose finances are [in disarray]—who is engaged in a civil war—can venture on a war with Great Britain?"⁶²

It was in this context that the Lincoln cabinet met on Christmas Day 1861 to formulate its response to the British demands. In addition to violating international law and contradicting the nation's traditional advocacy of neutral shipping rights, to not release Mason and Slidell would lead to a war with Britain. Such a war would almost certainly result in the independence of the Confederacy. Financial concerns also provided a powerful incentive to compromise. Significantly, both cabinet members who recorded their reflections on the Christmas Day meeting listed the precarious state of the Treasury as a reason to release the Confederate envoys. As Attorney General Edward Bates put it, a "war with England is to abandon all hope of suppressing the rebellion... our trade would be utterly ruined and our treasury bankrupt. In short,... we must not have war with England."⁶³ Not surprisingly, Chase agreed. "The surrender of the two men and a disavowal of [the] act," the Secretary of the Treasury confided in his diary, "is gall and wormwood to me... but we cannot *afford delays while the matter hangs in uncertainty, the public mind will remain disquieted*, our commerce will suffer serious harm, our action against the rebels must be greatly hindered, and *the restoration of our prosperity... must be delayed*" (emphasis added).⁶⁴ Letters from John Bright and Richard Cobden that Charles Sumner read aloud to the cabinet reinforced such sentiments. "If you are resolved to succeed against the South," Bright maintained, "have no war with England; make every concession that can be made... rather than give another nation a pretense for assisting in the breaking up of your country."⁶⁵ The Lincoln administration took this advice and released Mason and Slidell in late December 1861. The onus of drafting an apology fell on Seward, who seized the moment to applaud Britain for finally supporting neutral shipping rights before inserting an admission of wrongdoing shrouded in the convoluted language of international law. Seward's

⁶¹ Quoted in Brian Jenkins, *Britain and the War for the Union*, vol. 1 (London, 1974), p. 224.
⁶² *The Economist*, 28 December 1861, pp. 1429–30.
⁶³ Quoted in Dean Mahin, *One War at a Time* (Washington, D.C., 1999), p. 78.
⁶⁴ Chase diary, 25 December 1861, in David Donald (ed.), *Inside Lincoln's Cabinet: The Civil War Diaries of Salmon P. Chase* (New York, 1954).
⁶⁵ Bright to Sumner, 14 December 1861, in Massachusetts Historical Society *Proceedings*, 45 (1912), p. 155.

dispatch was good enough for the Palmerston cabinet and war was averted.

The diplomatic resolution, however, did not lead to an improvement in the Union's financial condition. Three days after Seward composed his famous dispatch, New York banks suspended specie payments. The Treasury had no choice but to follow suit the next day (31 December 1861). The immediate cause of suspension was the run on banks triggered by the *Trent* crisis and Chase's policy of requiring banks to transport gold to a federal depository when advancing the Treasury funds for the $150 million loan. Furthermore, the loss of foreign exchange generated by the exportation of cotton led to a negative balance of payments in 1861.[66] In the larger picture, Chase's policy of relying on short-term loans to finance the war could not, in the words of the historian John Niven, "withstand a sustained breach of public confidence"—which is exactly what occurred after the poor performance of the Union armies in 1861.[67] With investor confidence flagging and gold reserves disappearing, the Treasury was unable to meet its obligations. As Lincoln rued, "the bottom is out of the tub. What shall I do?"[68]

There was no hope that the President and Chase could count on capitalists across the Altantic to plug the hole in the bottom of the Treasury. British financiers were appalled by Chase's 9 December proposal to fund the war almost completely from borrowing. This contrasted to Britain's experience during the Crimean War a few years earlier. William Gladstone, who served as Chancellor of the Exchequer during the war, stated in 1854 that loans "practiced wholesale systematic deception upon the people" and attempted to finance the war exclusively through annual revenue.[69] Only when taxes failed to bring in enough capital did the government resort to a Rothschild loan in 1855. Most in Britain did not believe that Northerners had adequately employed taxation before resorting to issuing massive national loans. The fallacy of this policy, it was argued, was exposed when frightened depositors withdrew their savings rather than allow their banks to purchase more Union bonds that might never be repaid.[70] The resulting suspension of specie pay-

---

[66] Lawrence Officer, "The Floating Dollar in the Greenback Period: A Test of Theories of Exchange-Rate Determinism," *Journal of Economic History*, 41 (September 1981), pp. 629–50.
[67] Niven, *Salmon P. Chase*, p. 273.
[68] Quoted in James McPherson, *Battle Cry of Freedom* (New York, 1988), p. 444.
[69] Quoted in Ferguson, *The House of Rothschild*, II, p. 73.
[70] See *Bankers' Magazine*, February 1862, p. 108.

ments made Union bonds even more unattractive to British capitalists. Lord Overstone (Samuel Jones Lloyd) joked that "if the NY Banks suspend specie payments will the Old Lady do the same—and issue Lead instead of Gold?"[71] The suspension of specie payments, however, was far from a laughing matter to most Victorians. British adherence to hard money was evinced in the Bank Act of 1844, which limited the Bank of England's power to issue notes not backed by gold and discouraged all other banks from distributing their own paper notes. Furthermore, the suspension of specie payments, as *The Economist* clearly outlined, would have implications for British holders of American securities:

> Those persons whose securities are payable in dollars will receive fewer pounds sterling for their dividends, if those dividends are paid in depreciated paper. All the securities of the Federal Government are so payable, and the tendency of the measure must be to lower their value.[72]

The concern that interest on government bonds would be paid in devalued paper, which was obviously shared by Wall Street bankers, shaped the debate in Washington regarding the establishment of a paper currency. Accordingly, the bill that emerged in February 1862 stipulated that the new national currency—the so-called "greenbacks"—would be legal tender for all transactions except the interest on government bonds and, to pay for this provision, customs duties. It was hoped that this exception would make the $500 million in six percent bonds authorized in conjunction with the passage of the Legal Tender Act attractive to investors. Although the interest in gold provision enabled financier Jay Cooke to successfully market the new five-twenty bonds at home (known as such because they were callable between five and twenty years), it did not have the same effect abroad. Indeed, it appears that many European capitalists were unaware of this provision.[73] Making this known, as we shall see, was one of the main objectives of Treasury agent Robert J. Walker during his 1863 mission to Europe.

Even had British capitalists realized this, there was little chance that a Union loan would have met with success on the London Stock Exchange after the passage of the Legal Tender Act in February 1862. Paper greenbacks, British economists argued, would lead to uncontrollable

---

[71] Overstone to Norman, 31 December 1861. D. P. O'Brien (ed.), *The Correspondence of Lord Overstone*, vol. 3 (Cambridge, 1971), 3, p. 981. The reaction in Frankfurt was similar. See Murphy to Seward, 20 January 1862, RG 59, Main 161, NA.
[72] *The Economist*, 18 January 1862, p. 57.
[73] See, for example, *The Economist*, 14 March 1863, p. 285.

inflation and financial ruin. The creation of millions of dollars of wealth (nearly $450 million in all by the war's end) by the fiat of the government appeared to be an act of desperation from a nation that was in the midst of a political and financial collapse. The amount of greenbacks in circulation was greatly exaggerated in Britain as hard money advocates sneered at U.S. financial policy. "The Union is flooded with paper money," *The Times* declared. "It descends like snow in flakes worth half a penny apiece. Cartloads of paper cents issue daily from the Treasury, and are sown broadcast over the Federal states."[74] Union representative Andrew Dixon White made the mistake of pulling out a handful of greenbacks in a London bank before being told, "Don't offer us any of those things; we don't take them; they will never be good for anything."[75] "Why cannot a country that can raise millions within itself raise a sixpence beyond itself?" *The Economist* asked, "The reason is the terror excited in Europe by Mr Chase's policy."[76]

Although the economic legislation of early 1862 did not win over European investors, the resolution of the *Trent* crisis did enhance the standing of the North abroad. Having by all accounts backed down to British demands and abided by international law, the Lincoln administration no longer looked like the wild government committed to simultaneously waging war against the South and Britain that it had appeared to be a few months earlier. The conciliatory policy of Union statesmen during the *Trent* affair and a private meeting with lobbyist Thurlow Weed convinced American expatriate banker in London George Peabody to uphold the Union cause. "Whatever I can do, here and now for the Union cause," Peabody declared, "I will cheerfully do."[77]

Peabody's bank physically and symbolically became the nucleus of the pro-Union effort in London thereafter. Supporters of the North, ranging from British radicals such as John Bright to U.S. diplomat Charles Francis Adams to American financier Curtis Lampson, met at Peabody and Co. to acquire the latest news of the American war from the bank's new telegraph machine and to plot future pro-Union activities.[78]

---

[74] Quoted in Curtis Wilgus, "Some London *Times* Comments on Secretary Chase's Financial Administration, 1861–1864," *Mississippi Valley Historical Review*, 26 (December 1939), pp. 395–8.

[75] A. D. White, *Autobiography of Andrew D. White* (New York, 1905), I, p. 94.

[76] *The Economist*, 20 December 1862, p. 1401.

[77] *New York Times*, 23 December 1869.

[78] The transatlantic cable, which was partially funded by George Peabody, would not be in operation until after the war. A wire service from Liverpool, however, provided the bank with early notice on news from the United States before it was printed in the London press.

Peabody, a resident of London since 1837, used his connections and influence to advance the Union's cause. The Boston banker arranged meetings between Northerners and British politicians, helped Union agents plant articles in the British press, and released information from his wires to the *London American*. Peabody himself attempted to drive a wedge between Britain and the Confederacy by warning Palmerston that the Southern states sought to reopen the slave trade.[79] Peabody also became one of the few financiers in Britain to financially assist the Union when he marketed modest quantities of U.S. bonds in London.[80]

Perhaps Peabody's greatest contribution to the Union cause was also his greatest contribution to Britain. A leading philanthropist of his time, Peabody magnanimously donated £150,000 to London to construct housing for the poor in 1862.[81] This act had a political, as well as a benevolent intent. Peabody and other pro-Union supporters carefully orchestrated the timing of the donation so it could serve as a peace factor in Anglo-American relations. Although the gift was arranged in January 1862, it was publicly announced only after the smoke had settled from the *Trent* affair and *Times*' editor John Delane had promised leading coverage two months later.[82] The release of the news was very well timed. Presented while friends of the South in Parliament such as William Lindsay and John Roebuck were campaigning for the recognition of the Confederacy, the donation exemplified the benefits of Anglo-American peace— which was conditional on the maintenance of British neutrality during the Civil War. Queen Victoria awarded Peabody the Freedom of the City of London for his charity. At a London reception widely reported in the British press, Peabody articulated his hope that the donation would serve as a reminder of the Anglo-American connection:

If, by reason of the particular time at which [my donation] was made, it tended in any degree to soften asperities of feeling which had unhappily arisen between the two great nations of the Anglo-Saxon family; if it has reminded the people of both countries of their common origin and natural sympathy, I am fortunate indeed and more than repaid.[83]

---

[79] See Palmerston to Russell, 14 April 1861, Russell Papers, PRO, 30/22/21.
[80] Belmont to N.M.R. and Sons, 1 July 1862, T56/33, RA; Peabody to McCullagh, 16 May 1866, B3 F19, Peabody Papers, Essex Institute, Salem, Massachusetts; Robert van Riper, *A Life Divided: George Peabody* (London, 2000), p. 151. Unfortunately, the bank records do not reveal the amount of Union bonds that Peabody held and sold during the war.
[81] The Peabody Trust is still in operation today and provides 7,625 dwellings to the London poor.
[82] Tennant to Peabody, 26 March 1862, B195 F5, Peabody Papers.
[83] *The Times*, 11 July 1862.

Charles Francis Adams hoped that Peabody's donation would "bring forward a hint of the value of friendly relations between Europe and America."[84] Indeed, much of the British press placed the donation within the context of Anglo-American relations. "We have had a desperate family quarrel and almost come to blows," the *London Review* said of the *Trent* crisis, "Mr. Peabody, as a really wise and good relation, by a well-timed act of generosity, awakens the better sentiments that underlie so much superficial dislike, and incline both of the disputing parties to a renewal of affection."[85]

THE PROCUREMENT BATTLE IN BRITAIN

With little hope of securing financial support abroad, Union agents focused their efforts on arms purchasing in the war's early years. Fortunately for the North, pro-Union banks were more willing to advance credit to purchasing agents than they were to broker a national loan. The Barings continued to support the Union in 1862 when they trebled their advance to purchasing agent George Schuyler. With $2 million in funds provided by Barings, Schuyler provided Union armies with more than 150,000 pieces of small arms.[86] The bank also advanced $1 million for arms purchasing to Henry Sanford, the U.S. minister to Belgium.[87] Despite having adequate credit at its disposal, the Union procurement effort was not without its shortcomings. Schuyler and Sanford failed to coordinate their efforts and often doubled shipments of certain types of arms while failing to acquire any of others. Adding to the confusion were agents from different Northern states and private businessmen with government contracts. This lack of coordination often resulted in higher prices and inferior weaponry. Confederate agent James Bulloch happily reported to Richmond that upon his arrival to Britain "there were in England agents for the Federal Government as well as for several of the Northern Sates, each with large orders and abundance of ready money, and these persons, in their zeal, were actually bidding against each other,

[84] Diary of CFA, 10 July 1862, Adams Papers, Massachusetts Historical Society [microfilm].
[85] *London Review*, 29 March 1862. See also *Manchester Examiner and Times*, 27 March 1862, and *Morning Herald*, 27 March 1862.
[86] Bates to Baring, 5 October 1861, HC1.20.8, 1856–62, Letters of Joshua Bates, ING BA. See also Barings to Ward, 8 October 1861, BP. See also Carl Davis, *Arming the Union* (Port Washington, N.Y., 1973), p. 54.
[87] Joseph Fry, *Henry S. Sanford* (Reno, Nev., 1982), pp. 39–53.

thus running up the prices of arms to a figure far beyond those set down."[88]

Despite their disorganization, Union agents obtained an estimated 1,165,000 small arms in Europe in the first two years of the war. Although many were of dubious quality, these weapons helped meet the army's demands whilst Northern manufacturers converted to arms production. Moreover, these purchases were also of value in preclusive terms: every musket bought by Northern agents was one less available for Southern purchasers. Several Confederate agents, headed by Caleb Huse, searched the arsenals of Europe as early as the spring 1861 for small arms. Surplus stocks were scarce and competition between Union and Confederate agents was intense. Accordingly, several Union agents, including Sanford and Schuyler's successor, Marcellus Hartley, viewed preclusive purchases as an integral component of their missions. The Union abandoned its small arms purchasing operations in early 1863 as the production of Northern manufacturers proved capable of meeting demand.[89]

More of a threat to the Union than Confederate small arms purchases was the construction of war vessels for the South. Led by the industrious James Bulloch, Confederate naval agents arrived in Liverpool shipyards in the war's opening months to contract for warships. Union diplomats were aware of Confederate activities and, as early as the summer 1861, Henry Sanford paid British police detective Ignatius Pollacky £100 to monitor Bulloch and other Confederate agents in Liverpool.[90] Among other unscrupulous tactics, Pollacky bribed postmen to acquire information relating to Confederate activities. Charles Francis Adams was terrified of the consequences of hiring what he called "worthless people" for such delicate assignments and resented Sanford's intrusion into British affairs. "One of Mr. Seward's errors since he has been in the government," Adams bitterly disclosed in his diary, "has been the extent to which he has placed confidence in this shallow and imprudent man [Sanford]."[91] Adams' repeated protests eventually led to Pollacky's dismissal and the transfer of all Union surveillance responsibilities to

---

[88] Bulloch to Mallory, 13 August 1861, *Official Records of the Union and Confederate Navies in the War of the Rebellion*, 30 vols. (Washington D.C., 1894–1922), 2, 2, pp. 83–7. See also Morse to Seward, 26 October 1861, RG 59, T168, NA.

[89] Little has been written on Union arms purchasing abroad. The best account is provided by Davis, *Arming the Union*, pp. 51–67.

[90] Pollacky to Seward, 12 August 1861 and 12 February 1861, Seward Papers.

[91] Diary of CFA, 2 November 1861, Massachusetts Historical Society (hereafter MHS).

U.S. consuls Thomas Dudley in Liverpool and Freeman Morse in London.[92]

The American consuls assiduously tracked Confederate agents during the following year to provide evidence to Adams of vessels under construction for the South. Dudley, in particular, devoted himself to his surveillance duties and, in a high-stakes game of cat and mouse, tracked Bulloch's activities in the shipyards of Liverpool for much of the war.[93] The Union strategy was to use such evidence to petition the Foreign Office to detain vessels suspected of being built for the Confederacy, which, as a belligerent, could not purchase warships under British neutrality laws. Although the Foreign Enlistment Act, a corollary to the proclamation of neutrality issued in May 1861, ignored small arms purchases, it specifically forbade British subjects to "be concerned in the equipping, furnishing, fitting out, or arming, of any ship or vessel, with intent or in order that such ship or vessel shall be employed in the service" of a belligerent.[94]

This tactic was put to use in 1862 when Union agents identified two vessels nearing completion that were being built for the Confederacy. Although Adams' protests led to the temporary detention of the first, the *Oreto*, British courts ruled that the yet unarmed ship was not in violation of the Foreign Enlistment Act. After the court's ruling, the vessel, now renamed the *Florida* and fitted out in neutral waters following its "escape" from Liverpool, raised the Confederate flag and began its two year cruise that would result in the capture of thirty-eight Northern merchant ships. Union agents identified a second Confederate vessel under construction, the notorious ship No. 290 (the *Alabama*) of the Laird Brothers in Birkenhead, in the summer 1862. Adams fired a series of protests to Russell, contending that "the parties engaged [in contracting for the ship] are persons well known at Liverpool to be agents and officers of the insurgents in the United States."[95] Despite these repeated protests, Russell failed to act with any urgency in the matter. When British law officers finally gave their opinion that the construction of ship No. 290 may have violated the Foreign Enlistment Act and Russell sent orders to

---

[92] For more on Union espionage and intelligence, see H. C. Owsley, "H. S. Sanford and Federal Surveillance Abroad, 1861–1865," *Mississippi Valley Historical Review*, 48 (September 1961), pp. 211–28.

[93] See Brainerd Dyer, "Thomas H. Dudley," *Civil War History*, 1 (December 1955), pp. 401–13.

[94] Quoted in E. D. Adams, *Great Britain and the American Civil War* (New York, 1925), p. 116. See also *The Times*, 15 May 1861.

[95] Adams to Russell, 23 June, 22 and 24 July 1862, *FRUS*, 1862, pp. 129, 151.

temporarily detain the vessel, the *Alabama* had already left Birkenhead on a "trial run" and was safely outside of British waters.

Not surprisingly, Northerners viewed the British government's apparent complicity in the escape of the cruisers as part of a premeditated scheme to ensure the division of their nation. "The Queen's proclamation seems to be entirely disregarded," Thomas Dudley declared, "and the act of Parliament called the Foreign Enlistment Act ignored, if not a dead letter."[96] Even some Britons felt that their government had acted partially and illegally. "We can not tell you how deeply we deplore the escape and consequent piracy of the *Florida* and *Alabama*," Baring Brothers wrote to their American agent Samuel Ward, "for the sake of both countries we should be willing to do all we can in our power both to redress the injuries inflicted and to prevent their recurrence."[97] Particularly enraging to Northerners was that most of the crew of the *Alabama* were British subjects who had been recruited by Bulloch in Liverpool. As Secretary of the Navy Gideon Welles recorded in his diary, "it is pretty evident that a devastating and villainous war is to be waged on our commerce by English capital and English men under the rebel flag with the connivance of the English Government."[98]

The British government's failure to seize the *Florida* and the *Alabama*, however, resulted more from the nebulous Foreign Enlistment Act than from a premeditated strategy to divide a future rival. The act was the only British legislation regulating the outfitting of vessels for a belligerent and had never been legally interpreted before the Civil War. In theory, the language of the law appeared clear enough. However, in practice, defining a ship's "intent" and what it meant to "furnish" and "fit out" a vessel posed greater problems to British courts than the law's architects had anticipated. As we shall see in a later chapter, Confederate agents further complicated matters by finding ingenious ways to circumvent the law. Thus, even when Russell acted to prevent the release of a Confederate vessel (as in the case of the *Florida*), the law ended up on the side of the South. Simply put, the evidence required to detain a suspected Confederate vessel was available only, as E. D. Adams has noted, "after the offence had been committed and one of the belligerents injured by the violation of the law."[99]

---

[96] Dudley to Seward, 18 April 1863, RG 59, M141, NA.
[97] Baring Brothers to Ward, 28 March 1863, BP.
[98] Welles diary, 31 March 1863, in Howard Beale (ed.), *The Diary of Gideon Welles* (New York, 1960), I, p. 250.
[99] Adams, *Great Britain and the American Civil War*, p. 117.

The loopholes of the Foreign Enlistment Act allowed British leaders to avoid controversial encroachments into the normally unregulated affairs of private business. As *The Economist* said of the *Alabama* affair, "we have simply acted commercially."[100] "We have a right to make and sell. We are merchants; we sell to whoever will buy; you can buy as well as the South," Russell purportedly explained to Seward.[101] Russell was not the only one to suggest that preclusive purchasing was the best tactic to prevent future British-built *Alabamas* from raising the Confederate stars and bars. U.S. consul in London Freeman Morse had already recommended such an approach to the Secretary of State.[102] Boston businessman John Murray Forbes, a friend of Assistant Secretary of the Navy Gustavus Fox, advocated a similar plan that a Union agent should be dispatched to Britain under the guise of acting on behalf of another nation to "buy the best of the war steamers now under construction for the rebels."[103] The obvious drawback of this tactic was that Union leaders would forfeit their right to protest the sale of war vessels to the Confederacy if it became known that they were themselves doing the same. Furthermore, Britain could not be held accountable for damages caused by British-built Confederate warships in the future. Seward, it appears, was aware that preclusive purchasing would play into Britain's hands.[104] Nonetheless, the depredations of the *Alabama*—the vessel captured or sank thirty-three Northern vessels in its first six months at sea—convinced the Union statesman that drastic action, despite the unfavorable precedent that would be set, was a naval necessity.

Treasury chief Salmon Chase met with Forbes and fellow merchant William Aspinwall in a New York hotel in March 1863 to engineer a scheme for the Union to buy its way out of the predicament. The two businessmen were allocated $10 million in newly issued five-twenty bonds to be used as collateral for a loan of $5 million, preferably from Baring Brothers, to purchase or acquire a majority interest in suspected Confederate vessels.[105] The potential utility of such vessels to the North

[100] *The Economist*, 22 November 1862, p. 1292.
[101] Russell quoted in Fox to Forbes, 1 April 1863, in Sarah Forbes Hughes (ed.), *Letters and Recollections of John Murray Forbes* (Boston, 1899), II, p. 22.
[102] Neill Sanders, "Freeman Harlow Morse and the Forbes-Aspinwall Mission: An Aberration in Union Foreign Policy," *Lincoln Herald*, 80 (Spring 1978), pp. 15–25.
[103] Douglas Maynard, "The Forbes-Aspinwall Mission," *Mississippi Valley Historical Review*, 45 (June 1958), pp. 67–89.
[104] See Fox to Forbes, 19 December 1862, Hughes (ed.), *Letters and Recollections of John Murray Forbes*, I, p. 343.
[105] 204333, ING. BA.

was a secondary concern as the mission was primarily preclusive in nature. "What we want," Secretary of the Navy Gideon Welles instructed the agents, "is to prevent the rebels from getting out dangerous vessels; and if it means a necessity to buy and leave them, so be it."[106] Chase instructed the two businessmen to consult with Morse in London and Dudley in Liverpool, who were both still tracking the activities of Confederate purchasers.[107] American minister Charles Francis Adams was to be left in the dark as Morse hinted to him that Forbes and Aspinwall were in Europe to recruit foreign soldiers.[108]

Like other Union agents sent to Britain, Forbes and Aspinwall possessed both the experience and connections to facilitate their mission. Aspinwall was a prominent New York merchant and financier whom Barings had considered appointing as their American agent a decade earlier.[109] Forbes was also well-known in transatlantic finance and had obtained an emergency loan from Barings that saved the Michigan Central Railroad from insolvency during the Panic of 1857.[110] The two agents' relationship with the Barings bore fruit when they persuaded the bank to subsidize their purchasing mission upon their arrival in Britain in April 1863. The Barings were not enthusiastic about the scheme and consented to the loan on the condition that the Lincoln government would not issue letters of marque, which authorized privateering. The firm granted Forbes and Aspinwall a little more than half of what they requested, £600,000 (roughly $3 million), while taking $4 million in U.S. bonds as security.[111]

Though successful in obtaining credit, Forbes and Aspinwall had the unpredicted problem of not being able to spend the funds at their disposal. As Forbes later recalled, "so far as regarded any definite results, our mission was a failure."[112] This was largely a result of the publicity

[106] Welles to Forbes, 18 April 1863, Hughes (ed.), *Letters and Recollections of John Murray Forbes*, II, pp. 22–3.
[107] Hughes (ed.), *Letters and Recollections of John Murray Forbes*, II, pp. 4–7. The instructions were signed by Secretary of the Navy Gideon Welles.
[108] Maynard, "The Forbes-Aspinwall Mission," pp. 67–89.
[109] Bates to Ward, 6 October 1848, Ward Papers, MHS; Ralph Muriel Hidy, "Anglo-American Merchant Bankers and the Railroads of the Old Northwest, 1848–60," *Business History Review*, 34 (1960), pp. 150–69.
[110] See Hughes (ed.), *Letters and Recollections of John Murray Forbes*, I, p. 168. Forbes recalled that the loan was "on very onerous terms."
[111] Baring Brothers to Ward, 11 April 1863, BP. See also Maynard, "The Forbes-Aspinwall Mission," pp. 75–6. Barings never placed these bonds on the market. They were eventually resold to Jay Cooke. See Ellis P. Oberholtzer, *Jay Cooke* (Philadelphia, 1907), I, pp. 525–6.
[112] Quoted in Hughes (ed.), *Letters and Recollections of John Murray Forbes*, II, p. 66.

surrounding a mission that required the agents' connection with the Union to remain unknown. *The Times* reported that the two American businessmen were sent abroad to buy "up the gunboats now building in England for the rebels."[113] A Southerner living in New York explicitly informed Confederate representative James Mason that "Chase has obtained a credit of about ten millions of dollars in England and has an agent to try to purchase the vessels that are being built at Liverpool and elsewhere for the use of our Government."[114] Perhaps this advance warning explains why the Union agents found little evidence of warships contracted for the Confederacy even though several were under construction during their visit. News of the Confederates' £3 million loan brokered by the French bank Erlanger and Co. also discouraged the Union agents, who had only one-fifth of that amount at their disposal, from getting into a bidding war.[115]

It was fortunate for the Union—and the United States after the war—that Forbes and Aspinwall failed in their attempts to purchase suspected Confederate warships. The mission contradicted the diplomatic strategy of Adams and would have implicitly recognized the legal right of British shipbuilders to construct warships for a belligerent. Indeed, all of the major ships under construction for the Confederacy had already been identified by Northern agents and Adams was in the process of protesting their construction to the Foreign Office. In one case Forbes and Aspinwall considered buying the *Sumter*, a former Confederate vessel repurchased in dubious circumstances in Britain after its capture, which Adams himself had argued could not lawfully be sold to a belligerent.[116] In this sense, the Forbes-Aspinwall mission was indeed an "aberration in Union policy."[117] After learning of their intent, Adams discouraged Forbes and Aspinwall from carrying out their mission. The two agents soon abandoned their efforts. "Without embarrassing Mr. Adams by consulting him directly," Forbes and Aspinwall informed Welles, "we shall take care to do nothing, in a small way, that would interfere with the larger interests at stake."[118]

---

[113] *The Times*, 7 April 1863.

[114] Duncan to Mason, 31 March 1863, Mason Papers, Library of Congress. See also Maynard, "The Forbes-Aspinwall Mission," p. 74.

[115] Forbes and Aspinwall to Welles, 25 April 1863, Hughes (ed.), *Letters and Recollections of John Murray Forbes*, II, p. 44.

[116] Maynard, "The Forbes-Aspinwall Mission," p. 85.

[117] See Sanders, "Freeman Harlow Morse and the Forbes-Aspinwall Mission."

[118] Forbes and Aspinwall to Welles, 25 April 1863, Hughes (ed.), *Letters and Recollections of John Murray Forbes*, II, p. 44.

With the attempt to outspend the Confederacy having failed, Union statesmen resumed their strategy of protesting the construction of vessels intended for the Confederacy to the Foreign Office. Matters reached a crisis point in the summer 1863 when Union agents identified two ironclad rams under construction for the Confederacy at the Laird shipyard in Liverpool. These imposing vessels, Northerners feared, could break the blockade of the South, if not attack unprotected Northern cities such as New York and Boston. The threat that the "Laird rams" would join the Confederate navy increased when a British court invalidated the government's recent detention of the *Alexandra*, another Confederate vessel under construction in Britain, on the grounds that a ship's "intent" could not be proven from its structure alone.

Faced with the prospect of a fleet of new Confederate raiders, desperate Union diplomats turned up the pressure on British leaders. Seward hinted to Lord Lyons, the British minister in Washington, as early as February 1863 that the Lincoln cabinet would consider issuing letters of marque, which had been authorized by Congress, to protect American commerce against a British-built Confederate navy.[119] Although the 1856 Treaty of Paris had outlawed privateering, the United States was not a signatory to the accord (though Seward had attempted to sign on to the treaty in 1861 to give legitimacy to the Union blockade) and American statesmen argued that British nonenforcement of neutrality laws left them with no alternative. Russell had long warned Seward not to issue letters of marque, which would challenge British naval dominance as well as increase the likelihood of another *Trent*-like incident involving a British steamer and an overzealous Yankee captain. With the Foreign Office still unable to find a pretext to detain the Laird rams despite this threat and convincing evidence presented by the U.S. legation in the summer 1863, Adams stopped nothing short of threatening war. In a notorious letter (that Russell ironically received after he ordered the detainment of the rams), Adams informed Russell that if the rams were allowed to cruise under the Confederate flag, "it would be superfluous in me to point out to your lordship that this is war."[120]

The diplomatic pressure placed on the Palmerston government by American statesmen was matched by calls from within Britain demanding a stricter enforcement of the nation's neutrality laws. Led by William

---

[119] Seward to Adams, 19 February 1863, *FRUS*, 1863, p. 117.
[120] Adams to Russell, 5 September 1863, *FRUS*, 1863, p. 367. See also Adams to Russell, 14 August, 3 September, and 4 September 1863, *FRUS*, 1863, pp. 348, 357, 361.

Rathbone, a group of Liverpool shipowners who feared the possibility of an ocean swarming with American privateers petitioned the government to detain the rams.[121] The Union and Emancipation Society presented the government with a similar demand.[122] Goldwin Smith and Nassau Senior composed influential letters in the *Daily News* and *The Times*, respectively, that advocated detaining the rams.[123] Finally, powerful Parliamentary opposition, led by an odd grouping of MPs who had little in common but their desire to maintain Anglo-American peace, challenged the government's interpretation of the Foreign Enlistment Act in a widely reported debate in the Commons.[124] Radicals John Bright, Richard Cobden, and W. E. Forster joined pro-North Tory Thomas Baring in condemning the government's complicity in the construction of a Confederate navy and demanding an immediate tightening of the interpretation of neutrality laws. Some historians have even suggested that the decision to detain the rams was part of a farsighted plan intended to establish a precedent of a stricter definition of neutrality that would play into Britain's hand, as the world's pre-eminent naval power, in the future.[125] Indeed, Thomas Baring declared in Parliament that allowing warships to be constructed for a belligerent in the shipyards of a neutral state "may seriously affect our interests and welfare in the future."[126]

The Palmerston government eventually succumbed to these internal and external pressures and ordered the detainment of the Laird rams in early September 1863. Other suspected Confederate vessels in Britain soon met a similar fate. The decision was a pure political act, designed to placate the United States and the government's discontents at home. As Solicitor General Roundell Palmer remarked, detaining the rams was an act "of policy though not of strict law."[127] Here, paradoxically, was the problem. Although British policy regarding the construction of warships for a belligerent had changed, the law remained the same. Only a series of prolonged appeals by the British government prevented the *Alexandra* from cruising under the Confederate flag. A similar strategy had to be

---

[121] Hughes (ed.), *Letters and Recollections of John Murray Forbes*, II, pp. 91–2. See also Adams, *Great Britain and the American Civil War*, p. 142.

[122] Adams to Seward, 3 September 1863, *FRUS*, 1863, p. 356.

[123] See *The Economist*, 5 September 1863, p. 985.

[124] The Parliamentary debate was reprinted in the United States. See Thomas Baring, *The War upon American Commerce* (Boston, 1864).

[125] Crook, *The North, the South and the Powers*, p. 297; Joseph A. Fry, *Dixie Looks Abroad: The South and U.S. Foreign Relations, 1789–1973* (Baton Rouge, 2002), p. 96.

[126] *Hansard*, 3rd series, 13 May 1864, CLXXV, pp. 467–74.

[127] Quoted in Crook, *The North, the South and the Powers*, p. 325.

adopted in the case of the Laird rams after British law officers held that the government lacked the legal authority to detain the vessels soon after they were arrested. Another crisis was averted only when Palmerston decided to purchase the rams for the Royal Navy in 1864. "We are behind in iron-clads especially in rams," the Prime Minister asserted, "which would be useful for Channel service in the event of war and would tend to be peacemakers."[128] The purchasing of the Laird rams largely put the shipbuilding controversy to bed for the remainder of the war. The dispute, however, was far from resolved.

LATER FINANCIAL MISSIONS TO BRITAIN

Alongside the resolution of the *Trent* crisis, preventing the escape of the Laird rams was the crowning achievement of Union diplomacy during the war. But 1863 was not a year without Northern failures overseas. Once again, Chase sought to negotiate a loan in Britain. Union finances—thanks to the bond-selling campaign of Jay Cooke and the revenue generated from newly levied taxes—were in a relatively stable state in the spring 1863. "We have nothing to apprehend," Chase declared, "on the financial side of our affairs." The Treasury's stability, Chase assumed, would lead to the success of a Union loan in Britain that would restore the nation's reputation on European money markets. However, there were more than just financial motives for arranging a foreign loan. As Union statesmen had recognized from the war's beginning, a successful financial operation abroad could yield significant diplomatic and political benefits. The "principal" motive for securing a foreign loan, Chase asserted,

is that of exciting enquiry into the real condition of American affairs—an enquiry which cannot fail, as a I think, to result in a general conviction that all hopes and all fears that the existing rebellion will result in a dismemberment of the American Republic are alike groundless and that whatever else may happen, the good faith of the American People, signally illustrated by the twice repayment in coin of its entire National Debt, and by unvarying punctuality with which its interest on their Bonds has always been paid in like manner, will be hereafter, as heretofore scrupulously maintained.[129]

[128] Quoted in Mahin, *One War at a Time*, p. 181.
[129] Chase to Aspinwall, 30 March 1863, Chase Papers, University Publications of America (hereafter UPA) [microfilm], Library of Congress.

Chase was not the only Union statesman who recognized the diplomatic benefits of arranging a foreign loan. William Aspinwall put it more succinctly: "English sympathy is very apt to follow English Capital; this is one good political reason for placing bonds in Europe."[130] Moved by these political considerations, Chase authorized Forbes and Aspinwall to negotiate a $50 million loan with a foreign banking house, with six percent five-twenties to be issued for public subscription.[131] The modest size of this loan revealed that political and diplomatic considerations, rather than financial ones, lay behind the proposal.

Chase's hope of using a bond issue to promote the Union cause overseas was quickly dashed when British banks proved yet again unwilling to sponsor a Union loan. Although Baring Brothers granted Forbes and Aspinwall credit for their purchasing operation, the bank was unwilling to sponsor the $50 million loan. Echoing what the Rothschilds had told Belmont back in 1861, the Barings rejected the offer because of concerns about "how long the war may last and what the further wants of the Government may be."[132] The bank was also worried about "the possibility of war between this country and the United States growing out of the depredations of the *Alabama* debates."[133] Forbes and Aspinwall found no takers in London's other banks, who treated the proposal as "absurd."[134]

Paradoxically, the legislation that had improved the North's finances did little to encourage British investors. Many Britons, for example, argued that the Internal Revenue Act of 1862 would undermine the Union effort by creating social unrest—especially, as *The Times* put it, from "a people who were first moulded into a nation by the fiery indignation induced by a three penny tea-tax."[135] "We much fear," the editors of *The Economist* asserted, "that the Americans will learn that they cannot tax everything at once."[136] Concerns about the stability of the

---

[130] Aspinwall to Chase, 21 March 1863, Chase Papers, UPA.

[131] Chase to Forbes and Aspinwall, 30 March 1863, *Chase Papers*, 3, pp. 408–11.

[132] Baring Brothers to Ward, 2 April 63, BP.

[133] Forbes and Aspinwall to Chase, 25 April 1863, *Chase Papers*, 4, pp. 16–8; Baring Brothers to Ward, 2 April 1863, BP.

[134] Aspinwall to Chase, 8 and 25 April 1863, Chase Papers, UPA. Forbes and Aspinwall were also unsuccessful in their attempt to list the five-twenties on the Paris bourse. The French government was empowered to choose which securities to quote on the exchange, and Foreign Minister Eduoard de Lhuys feared that the approval of Union bonds would force the government to list the Confederate Erlanger bonds, which were then being offered in Paris. See Dayton to Seward, 26 June 1863, *FRUS*, 1863, pp. 675–6.

[135] *The Times*, 23 April 1862. See also Wilgus, "Some London *Times* Comments on Secretary Chase's Financial Administration, 1861–1864," pp. 395–8.

[136] *The Economist*, 19 July 1862, p. 787. For the skepticism of a pro-North paper, see *The Morning Star*, 12 March 1863.

dollar led Baring Brothers to inform Aspinwall that a Union loan would succeed in Britain only if it was payable in sterling.[137] The City's unanimous rejection of the Union left its mark on Chase and strengthened his resolve to finance the war at home. "I do not regret that you find European capitalists indisposed to make offers for a large loan," he informed Forbes and Aspinwall. "A domestic loan is at all times to be preferred; and, under existing circumstances, it is cheapest as well as best."[138]

While Forbes and Aspinwall were fruitlessly negotiating with British banks, Chase dispatched another financial agent to Europe to arrange a loan. Not surprisingly, Robert J. Walker soon discovered upon his arrival in Britain in April 1863 that a foreign loan was an impossibility.[139] Again, Chase was not crestfallen. Later that month he stated that "a foreign loan is... now less desirable than ever," citing the stability of the nation's finances, the success of the five-twenties at home, and the high rate of interest demanded by European capitalists.[140] Indeed, it is unlikely that Walker's mission was to find takers for a Union loan. Unlike Forbes and Aspinwall, Walker was not given specific instructions regarding the amount and rate of a loan acceptable to the government. The agent's primary objective, it appears, was to denigrate the credit of the Confederacy in order to impede sales of the new Confederate cotton bonds, issued by the French bank Erlanger and Co. in March 1863. This tactic would also be an effective way to prevent the future construction of Confederate warships in British shipyards. "If I can destroy the loan, they will break and cannot pay," Walker argued, "this would stop the building of war vessels for them and make them odious here and ruin their cause here and on the continent."[141]

Walker was not an obvious choice to send on a Union financial mission. A former Democratic senator from Mississippi and secretary of the treasury under James Polk, he had owned scores of slaves on his cotton plantation in the 1830s (he voluntarily freed them in 1838) and had been an aggressive—perhaps the most aggressive—southern expansionist of the 1840s when he advocated conquering and annexing all of Mexico.[142]

---

[137] Aspinwall to Chase, 29 April and 2 May 1863, Chase Papers, UPA.
[138] Chase to Forbes and Aspinwall, 14 May 1863, *Chase Papers*, 4, p. 31.
[139] Walker to Chase, 28 April 1863, Chase Papers, Collection No. 121, Historical Society of Pennsylvania (hereafter HSP).
[140] Chase to Samuel Hallet and Co., 25 May 1863, *Chase Papers*, 4, p. 41.
[141] Walker to Chase, 8 May 1863, Chase Papers, HSP.
[142] Walker's famous pamphlet published in 1844, *Letter of Mr. Walker, of Mississippi, Relative to the Annexation of Texas,* called for the immediate annexation of Texas. See

Despite this pro-Southern past, Walker became a staunch defender of the Union during the war and was eager to exploit his connections with British political and financial leaders for the good of his nation. Walker had been popular in Britain after his namesake Walker Tariff of 1846 greatly reduced U.S. import duties.[143] An emissary with a free trade pedigree could help counteract the unpopular protectionist reputation of the Northern states in Britain. Walker's status abroad was evinced by the warm reception given to him by Bright, Cobden, and Baring Brothers, among others, during his 1851 trip to Britain to promote bonds of the Illinois Central Railroad.[144] Walker's credentials were further enhanced by his rejection of the proslavery Lecompton constitution during his brief stint as territorial governor of Kansas in 1857. "I find that my Governorship of Kansas," he wrote upon his arrival to Britain in the spring 1863, "does me as much good here as my free trade policy of 1846."[145]

Walker employed a different approach from other Union agents to discredit the Confederacy. Unlike other propagandists, Walker did not dwell on the moral evil of slavery. This tactic was successfully used by abolitionists in Britain, other Union agents, and an estimated forty African-Americans who campaigned for the North in Britain during the war. Chief among them was Jefferson Davis' escaped coachman, William Andrew Jackson. "If there was a pro-Union figure who dominated the public debate in 1863," historian R. J. M. Blackett asserts, "it was Jackson."[146] The evangelical minister Henry Ward Beecher, popular in Britain because of his sister's novel *Uncle Tom's Cabin*, also lent his voice to the Union cause during his 1863 trip to Britain. "There is the South with her gigantic system of slavery, and there is the North with her freedom, her free soil, free labor, free speech, and her free press," Beecher declared at a public meeting in Glasgow, "and the question is, which of these two shall govern the American continent?"[147] These Union agents were assisted by and collaborated with British antislavery activists including the long-time leader of the British and Foreign

---

Frederick Merk, *Fruits of Propaganda in the Tyler Administration* (Cambridge, Mass., 1971), pp. 121–8.

[143] See *The Economist*, 2 January 1847, p. 1.

[144] See *The Economist*, 13 December 1851, p. 1372.

[145] Walker to Chase, 1 May 1863, Chase Papers, HSP. For more on Walker's political career, see James Shenton, *Robert John Walker: A Politician from Jackson to Lincoln* (New York, 1961).

[146] Blackett, *Divided Hearts*, p. 133. See also *The Times*, 23 May 1862.

[147] Henry Ward Beecher, *Speeches of Rev. Henry Ward Beecher on the American Rebellion Delivered in Great Britain in 1863* (New York, 1887), p. 83.

Anti-Slavery Society, George Thompson. These different agents and groups were brought together by a consortium of local antislavery organizations led by the London Emancipation Society and the Union and Emancipation Society of Manchester.[148] With such an organized and formidable antislavery lobby there was little need for Walker, a former slaveholder, to preach about the dark side of the Confederacy. What Walker possessed that many abolitionists lacked, however, were connections to the financial elite in Britain. Walker knew that British capitalists still regarded the Southern state repudiations of the 1840s as "the sin of all crimes." "Slavery takes the philanthropic, the sentimental and the religious classes and the people," Walker informed Chase, "but *repudiation* touches the pocket nerve and sweeps away the lenders of money."[149] Bringing repudiation back into the public view was particularly germane as the Confederate Erlanger bonds had been put up for public subscription less than a month before Walker's arrival. Walker's strategy was simple: remind British capitalists of the repudiations in Arkansas, Florida, and Mississippi in the 1840s and link Confederate President Jefferson Davis to the abominable acts. Confederate agents anticipated this attack on their nation's leader and had already attempted to disconnect his name from repudiation. John Slidell, the Confederate representative in France, penned a letter in *The Times* that claimed that Jefferson Davis had been confused with Reuben Davis, the man who Slidell alleged had led the repudiation campaign in Mississippi. "I feel confident," Slidell declared, "that Jefferson Davis never approved or justified that repudiation."[150]

In a series of pamphlets published in the summer and autumn 1863, Walker refuted Slidell's claim and connected Jefferson Davis with repudiation. "As Jefferson Davis is now at the head of a slave holding rebellion, endeavoring to destroy the Government of my country and is now engaged in selling worthless Confederate bonds in this market," Walker stated in his first pamphlet *Jefferson Davis, Repudiation, Recognition and Slavery*, "I have deemed it my duty to make this publication."[151] Walker's Davis was greedy, xenophobic, and eager to insult British bondholders after having robbed them of their investments. Not only had Davis "carried the repudiation banner" in Mississippi, but he had

[148] Blackett, *Divided Hearts*, pp. 75–88, 132–4, 186–92.
[149] Walker to Chase, 15 May 1863, Chase Papers, HSP.
[150] *The Times*, 23 March 1863.
[151] Robert J. Walker, *Jefferson Davis, Repudiation, Recognition and Slavery* (London, 1863), p. 41.

also colluded to legitimize repudiation in Arkansas.[152] Repudiation in Arkansas, Walker hoped, would particularly strike a chord in Britain as part of James Smithson's donation to the United States (the funds that established the Smithsonian Institute in Washington) had been invested in Arkansas state bonds.[153]

Walker attempted not only to malign the president of the Confederacy, but also sought to establish a pattern of corruption and immorality that plagued the Southern states as a whole. In words that recalled Alexander Trotter's writings of the 1830s, Walker held that "we are forced to the conclusion that slavery paralyzes the moral senses and would in time extinguish religion and civilization."[154] Walker repeated this theme throughout his pamphlets:

Secession, repudiation and slavery are the same in principle and had the same leaders. Jefferson Davis carried the repudiation banner in 1849, as he now does that of secession and slavery. Secession is the repudiation of law, of constitution, of country, of the flag of our forefathers, and of the Union purchased by their blood.[155]

Was Walker correct? Was Jefferson Davis responsible for repudiation in Mississippi and Arkansas? Walker's primary evidence were two letters penned by Davis during his tenure as a Mississippi senator that appeared in the London *Times* in 1849.[156] In these letters Davis condoned his state's action by asserting that the Mississippi Union Bank, which Mississippi had fronted for on the bond market, was to blame for the state's financial difficulties and it, not the state, should be held responsible for debt repayment. Even less evidence linked Davis with repudiation in Arkansas. In a speech given on the Senate floor, Davis defended the state of Arkansas and, similar to his defense of Mississippi, pointed his finger at the insolvent Real Estate Bank of the State of Arkansas. Any astute reader of Walker's pamphlets certainly would have realized that, though Davis attempted to exonerate states from the responsibility of debt repayment while in the

---

[152] Walker, *Jefferson Davis and the Repudiation of Arkansas Bonds* (London, 1863).
[153] Walker also portrayed Governor Alexander McNutt of Mississippi in a similar manner. No doubt intended to pique the interest of the world's leading bank, Walker reminded the Rothschilds what the Governor said of "Baron Rothschild": "the blood of Judas and Shylock flows in his veins."
[154] Walker to Chase, 6 November 1863, Chase Papers, HSP. See also Alexander Trotter, *Observations on the Financial Position and Credit of Such of the States of the North American Union as Have Contracted Public Debts* (London, 1839).
[155] Walker, *Jefferson Davis, Repudiation, Recognition and Slavery*, p. 41.
[156] See *The Times*, 13 July and 29 August 1849.

Senate, he could not have engineered the act as he held no political office when the three states repudiated their debts in the early 1840s. Walker also failed to mention that during Davis's unsuccessful bid to gain a seat in the state legislature in 1843, the future Confederate president parted from other Mississippi Democrats when he called for the state to pay interest on the bonds of the Planters' Bank while leaving the payment of the Union Bank bonds to the state courts. This was a moderate position somewhere in between the all-out support of repudiation by many Mississippi Democrats and the Whigs' advocacy of resumption.[157] Most astonishingly, Walker concealed the fact that he himself represented Mississippi in the U.S. Senate when the state repudiated its debt. Although Walker did not "demagogically advocate repudiation" as one historian has argued, he did little to publicly separate himself from the act in order to curry favor with the Mississippi electorate.[158]

Unfortunately for the Confederacy, it was difficult to undo the damage caused by Walker's pamphlets. "Nine out of ten [readers]," Confederate Secretary of State Judah Benjamin admitted, "will say 'Oh, if it requires so much writing and printing to prove the charge unfounded there must be a good deal of truth in it.'"[159] There is no evidence that the Confederate response, a pamphlet entitled *A Familiar Epistle* that attempted to turn the tables and accuse Walker of engineering repudiation in Mississippi, influenced the public debate regarding repudiation and the Confederacy.[160] The same could not be said for *Jefferson Davis, Repudiation, Recognition and Slavery*. Demand for Walker's pamphlets necessitated three separate printings. Publicity stunts drew further attention to the writings. Walker created somewhat of a public sensation by dropping his pamphlets on a London street from a hot-air balloon overhead. Other pamphlets were more strategically distributed: Walker personally delivered his writings to leading bankers and politicians—including a personal

---

[157] Vagn Hansen, "Jefferson Davis and the Repudiation of Mississippi Bonds: The Development of a Political Myth," *Journal of Mississippi History*, 33 (February 1971), pp. 105–32. See also Clement Eaton, *Jefferson Davis* (New York, 1977), p. 48.

[158] For the view that Walker endorsed repudiation, see Henry Cohen, *Business and Politics in America from the Age of Jackson to the Civil War: The Career Biography of W. W. Corcoran* (Westport, Conn., 1971), p. 147. For the view presented here, see Shenton, *Robert John Walker*, p. 197. In fact, Walker corresponded with Baring Brothers and worked with the bank during the restoration campaign of the 1840s.

[159] Benjamin to Hotze and McHenry, 19 September 1863, Mason Papers, Library of Congress.

[160] *An Old Acquaintance, A Familiar Epistle to Robert J. Walker* (London, 1863). This pamphlet was authored by Henry Hotze, Edwin DeLeon, and George McHenry. See also McHenry to Mason, 1 December 63, Mason Papers, LC.

meeting with William Gladstone.[161] Even the conservative *Bankers' Magazine*, a publication with a pro-Confederate bias, was convinced "that President Davis is in some degree personally responsible for the repudiation of the obligations of the State of Mississippi."[162] The popularity of the pamphlets led Walker to report to Chase that "all feel now how completely slavery and repudiation are identified and that their own hope of ever receiving anything from the repudiated states of Mississippi and Arkansas and Florida is by emancipation and the success of the Union."[163]

Indeed, the publication of *Jefferson Davis, Repudiation, Recognition and Slavery* coincided with the crash of the Confederate bonds in Europe in the summer and autumn 1863. This resulted more from the decisive Union victories at Gettysburg and Vicksburg, however, than from Walker's pamphlets. The ignominious withdrawal of John Roebuck's Parliamentary motion for the recognition of the Confederacy in July (the last time such a proposal was on the floor) further reflected the loss of confidence in the Confederate effort. Moreover, Walker was not the only pro-Northerner who linked Davis to repudiation. August Belmont returned to Europe in 1863 and continued to lobby on behalf of the Union. "The letter in the London *Times* [written by John Slidell] denying that Jefferson Davis was a leading advocate of repudiation in his State of Mississippi is the most barefaced falsehood imaginable," the banker informed Lionel de Rothschild, "Jeff Davis ran for State Senator, for Governor and for United States Senator upon the distinct issue of repudiating the bonds of the state of Mississippi."[164] In Frankfurt, as well, U.S. consul William Murphy persuaded newspaper editors to alert their readers to the fact that Jefferson Davis was "the author of repudiation in Mississippi."[165] Although events on the battlefield ultimately determined the credit of the Confederacy, the actions of three Southern

---

[161] Gladstone informed Walker that he believed the North would be unable to conquer and subdue the South. However, he claimed to sympathize with the Union and, if the North's armies would begin to win on the battlefield, "he would hasten in the most public measure to avow his convictions." See Walker to Chase, 18 July 1863, Chase Papers, HSP.

[162] *Bankers' Magazine*, December 1862, pp. 781–5.

[163] Walker to Chase, 18 July and 5 August 1863, Chase Papers, HSP. For more on Walker's mission, see Amos Taylor, "Walker's Financial Mission to London on Behalf of the North, 1863–1864," *Journal of Economic and Business History*, 3 (February 1931), pp. 296–320.

[164] Belmont to Rothschild, 14 April 1863, Belmont, *A Few Letters and Speeches of the Late Civil War*.

[165] Murphy to Seward, 10 March 1863, RG 59, Main 161, NA.

states in the early 1840s, as Walker and other Union agents made every effort to point out, contributed to the sordid standing of Confederate bonds on European stock exchanges.

EUROPEAN INVESTORS AND THE UNION

By late 1863 Union statesmen recognized that they had little chance of placing a loan in Britain and thus concentrated their financial diplomacy on thwarting Confederate efforts to secure British financial support. Continental Europe, in contrast, offered an untapped market for Union bonds. Indeed, as early as the summer 1861, August Belmont had recognized that the continent might be the best place to find takers for Union bonds.[166] Belmont's intuition would prove correct in the final two years of the war, when dealings in Union securities reached frantic levels on Dutch and German stock exchanges. Interestingly, this foreign demand preceded Union financial diplomacy, which, as we shall see, never took full advantage of the markets in continental Europe.

Robert J. Walker recognized the potential for securing financial support in Europe when he crossed the English Channel in early 1864 to meet with leading banks in Holland and Germany.[167] Following the strategy he employed to denigrate the Confederate loan in Britain, Walker distributed a new series of pamphlets across Europe entitled *American Finance and Resources* that heralded the North's economy, Chase's financial policies, and Union war-bonds. In these works Walker maintained that slavery had retarded economic growth in the South and that European textile manufacturers would benefit from the increased cotton production that would follow a Union victory and abolition. This was not a new argument as the unprofitable nature of slavery had been the central theme of one of the most widely circulated pro-Union pamphlets of the war, John Eliot Cairnes' *The Slave Power* (first published in 1862).[168] But unlike Cairnes, who attempted to "explain the real issue involved in the American contest" to British observers, Walker's sole intention was to promote Union bonds. Indeed, one of Walker's primary objectives during his European mission was to dispel

---

[166] Belmont to Chase, 15 August 1861, Belmont Papers, LC.
[167] Walker to Chase, 20 February 1864, Chase Papers, HSP.
[168] John Eliot Cairnes, *The Slave Power* (London, 1862).

the myth—which was partly spread by Confederate agents—that the Treasury paid the interest on its debt in depreciated greenbacks.[169]

Walker was not the only Northern representative promoting Union bonds on the continent. Hermann Raster, editor of the Chicago-German daily the *Illinois Staats Zeitung*, returned to his native country to drum up support for the Union cause and to find investors for Union bonds.[170] Of more importance was U.S. consul in Frankfurt William W. Murphy. Appointed to the post to replace Sam Ricker (who openly advocated the cause of the Confederacy and offered his services to Jefferson Davis once the war began),[171] Murphy was a gregarious opponent of slavery who quickly found friends on the Frankfurt bourse. He hosted patriotic parties on American holidays that served both as pro-North rallies and as ploys to market Union bonds.[172] To reach a broader audience, Murphy paid the editors of the *Neue Frankfurter Zeitung* and *L'Europe*, a French newspaper published in Frankfurt, to print columns that championed the Union cause and Union finances.[173] In the dreary months of the summer 1862, however, such propaganda yielded little result. Indeed, "American stock has so much suffered from the uncertainty about the present state of American affairs," Murphy reported, "that the principal Exchange paper of this city, the *Actioneer* (Stockholder), announces today that it will stop for a while its list of American quotations, because the latter were merely illusory."[174]

This all began to change the following year. As early as April 1863, Murphy informed Seward that Union bonds were in "great demand" as "confidence in American affairs is firmly restored." By January 1864 demand for Union bonds was "so extensive as generally to exceed the supplies in the market." Even Karl Marx fell victim to the urge to invest "in American funds" in 1864.[175] A Confederate circular of that year maintained that the Northern states "have been able to uphold their

---

[169] For the work of Confederate agents in this matter, see Murphy to Seward, 9 May 1864, RG 59, Main 161, NA. For Walker's pamphlets, see Walker, *American Finance and Resources* (London, 1863–4).

[170] Henry Adams, *Prussian-American Relations, 1775–1871* (Cleveland, 1960), pp. 84–5; Frederick Schrader, *The Germans in the Making of America* (Boston, 1924), p. 185.

[171] See Ricker to Seward, 28 May 1861; Ricker to Jefferson Davis, 20 April 1861, RG 59, Main 161, NA.

[172] See, for example, Murphy to Seward, 24 February, 25 March 1862, RG 59, Main 161, NA.

[173] Murphy to Seward, 2 and 10 March 1863, RG 59, Main 161, NA. See also White, *Autobiography of Andrew D. White*, I, p. 97.

[174] Murphy to Seward, 18 August 1862, RG 59, Main 161, NA.

[175] Niall Ferguson, *The Cash Nexus* (London, 2001), pp. 5–6.

sinking finances by the sale of large amounts of public stocks in the German markets."[176] Similar reports arrived in Washington from the U.S. minister to The Hague James Pike. "The money men of Holland have begun to buy our government securities," Pike reported in early 1863, "There have been no large operations, but each capitalist is taking a moderate sum and laying it away to wait for results."[177] A few months later Pike informed Seward that "so much are stock operators absorbed by the movement that complaints are made that everything not American is neglected."[178] By the spring 1864, Pike estimated that weekly transactions in Union bonds totaled $2 million in Amsterdam alone.[179] As *The Times* reported in July 1864, "a very large portion of the Federal debt is held in Germany and Holland, where... the quiet saving classes adopt these securities in preference to their own governments."[180]

The Times attributed the interest in U.S. bonds on the continent to the manipulative work of Union agents who preyed upon imprudent investors.[181] The publication, which notoriously misrepresented American affairs during the war, was once again mistaken. There was no coordinated attempt to market Union bonds in any nation other than Britain or France during the war. Robert J. Walker was not authorized to broker a loan and physically possessed no bonds to sell during his trip to the continent in 1864. James Pike in the Netherlands and William Murphy in Frankfurt urged Dutch and German investors to purchase Union bonds but, likewise, lacked the authority and the means to market them.

Nor did European banks sponsor a Union loan. Baring Brothers twice suggested to their long-time collaborators in American finance, the Dutch house of Hope and Co. and the French Hottinguers, the possibility of marketing Union bonds on the continent. The offers were politely declined.[182] The Rothschilds, as well, were unwilling to broker a Union loan on the continent. It appears, however, that the Rothschilds in both Frankfurt and Paris invested small amounts in Union bonds in the latter

---

[176] For Murphy's reports, see Murphy to Seward, 13 April 1863, 27 July 1863, and 2 January 1864, RG 59, Main 161, NA; Department of State to Mason, 10 October 1864, Mason Papers, LC. Confederate agents were instructed to present European capitalists with exaggerated figures of the Union debt to discourage further investment.
[177] Pike to Seward, 25 February 1863, *FRUS*, 1863, 3, p. 810.
[178] Pike to Seward, 8 April 1863, *FRUS*, 1863, 3, p. 815.
[179] Pike to Seward, 9 March 1864, *FRUS*, 1864, 3, pp. 310–11.
[180] *The Times*, 8 July 1864.
[181] *The Times*, 4 November 1863 and 12 July 1864.
[182] D. C. M. Platt, *Foreign Finance in Continental Europe and the United States* (London, 1984), pp. 149–50.

half of the war on their private account. In Frankfurt, Murphy reported that "the Rothschilds of this city are firm friends of the Union and strong opponents of slavery and they are investing largely in American stocks."[183] This support for the North and small investment in U.S. bonds, however, should not be confused with brokering a national loan for the Union. The same concerns that prevented British banks from floating a U.S. loan in London—the uncertainty of Northern victory, the threat of Anglo-American war, anxiety over Chase's policies—left continental banking houses unwilling to tie themselves to the Union.

It appears that most of the bonds marketed on the continent were originally purchased in the United States before being shipped abroad by entrepreneurs looking to profit from their resale. American banks with German connections, such as the upstart firm of J. W. Seligman and Co., exported Union bonds to Europe.[184] Groups of Union sympathizers and market speculators may have also sent representatives to the United States to purchase bonds. German investors had employed such a method while investing in American railroads in the antebellum years and a few devoted British supporters of the North, such as the London Emancipation Society leader William Evans, did the same during the war. Chase was rumored to have sold $10 million in five-twenties for a German account in New York in 1863.[185]

William Murphy placed German and Dutch bondholders into two separate categories: "private capitalists and speculators."[186] The first were individual investors willing to purchase Union bonds for long-term investment without the advice and services of a major bank. These purchases, Murphy maintained, were often the result of "sympathy for our country."[187] Indeed, many Dutch and German "private capitalists"

---

[183] Murphy to Seward, 16 September 1863, RG 59, Main 161, NA. See also *Harper's Weekly*, 25 April 1863; White, *Autobiography of Andrew D. White*, I, pp. 97–8; N.M.R. and Sons to Belmont and Co., 14 March 1862, RA; Ferguson, *The House of Rothschild*, II, p. 117. The London Rothschilds even expressed interest in purchasing U.S. bonds in 1863. See N.M.R. and Sons to Belmont and Co., 11 March 1863, RA.

[184] Barry Supple, "A Business Elite: German-Jewish Financiers in Nineteenth-Century New York," *Business History Review*, 7 (Summer 1957), pp. 143–78; Sven Beckert, *The Monied Metropolis: New York City and the Consolidation of the American Bourgeoisie, 1850–1896* (New York, 2001), pp. 123–4. Although Seligman and Co. shipped U.S. bonds to Europe, it was not on the scale that has been previously assumed. See Dolores Greenberg, "Yankee Financiers and the Establishment of Trans-Atlantic Partnerships: A Re-examination," *Business History*, 16 (January 1974), pp. 17–35.

[185] Oberholtzer, *Jay Cooke*, I, pp. 288–9.

[186] Murphy to Seward, 15 February 1864, RG 59, Main 161, NA.

[187] Murphy to Seward, 29 February 1864, RG 59, Main 161, NA.

identified with the cause of reunification and had reason to support the Union. Both nations had recently experienced or were experiencing a war of unification of sorts: the Dutch blamed the loss of Belgium in 1831 to foreign support of the insurgents and German unification was still in the works during the American war.[188] Bismarck himself was a staunch supporter of the Union cause and was rumored to have taken pleasure in German investment in U.S. securities.[189] These nations were also overwhelmingly opposed to the South's peculiar institution. A liberal government in the Netherlands abolished slavery within Dutch colonies in the summer 1862, just a few months before Lincoln issued the Emancipation Proclamation. Indeed, when news of the proclamation reached Frankfurt, Murphy reported a rise in Union bonds "evidently to be ascribed to the energetic anti-slavery proclamation of the President which has been welcomed here with universal approbation."[190] Germany and the Netherlands were also culturally connected to the North. New York City, of course, was a former Dutch colony and most of the recent Dutch emigrants to the United States had settled in northwestern states. Similarly, the overwhelming majority of the estimated 1.3 million German-Americans resided in the North and tens of thousands of them wore blue coats during the Civil War. "No one would scarcely dare in Germany to interest himself in a loan," a German newspaper wrote of the Confederate Erlanger loan, "which amount would be used for a cause against the 60,000 Germans fighting in the Union Army. The Germans cannot give money in order to allow their brethren to be beaten on the other side of the ocean."[191]

These political, ideological, and cultural motives for investing in Union bonds no doubt overlapped with the financial considerations that drove Murphy's second group, the "speculators." Like their British counterparts, European capitalists were wary of Chase's financial policies, particularly the Legal Tender Act of 1862. Dutch capitalists believed that

---

[188] A third contingent of Union bondholders, the Swiss, had also maintained their federation after a civil war in 1846. See Walker to McCulloch, 28 June 1865, AC 4831, Walker Papers, Library of Congress.

[189] See Count Otto Zu Stolberg-Wernigerode (translation), *Germany and the USA during the Era of Bismarck* (Reading, Penn., 1937), pp. 59–60.

[190] Murphy to Seward, 1 November 1862, RG 59, Main 161, NA.

[191] Quoted in Murphy to Seward, 10 March 1863, RG 59, Main 161, NA. For more on the correlation between immigration and investment in the United States, see A. J. Veenendaal, *Slow Train to Paradise: How Dutch Investment Helped Build American Railroads* (Stanford, 1996), p. 34; Lance E. Davis and Robert J. Cull, *International Capital Markets and American Economic Growth, 1820–1914* (Cambridge, 1994), p. 16.

the greenbacks were unconstitutional and repeatedly expressed their hope that the Treasury would turn to taxation, rather than the printing press, to finance the war.[192] But unlike British investors, those on the continent were willing to overlook these war-time exigencies and recognize the profit to be realized from Union securities. As Pike reported from the Netherlands, "The Dutch capitalists, unlike many of the English, have no prejudices against us, and have larger and more liberal views in regard to our resources, and believe in our ability as well as disposition to pay, than I have expected to find."[193] This confidence in the United States' ability to honor its commitments stemmed in part from a belief that the North could win the war. Not surprisingly, activity in Union bonds correlated with events on the battlefield. The dramatic Union victories in July 1863 led to increased speculation in five-twenty bonds in Amsterdam and Frankfurt. "The transactions in U.S. bonds," Murphy reported after news of the decisive Union victories at Vicksburg and Gettysburg reached Europe, "assumed, in fact, an astonishing extent."[194]

Even when Northern armies met with little success on the battlefield, however, favorable exchange rates and the large discounts at which Union bonds were quoted continued to make them an attractive investment. Five-twenties were never listed above 80 in Frankfurt after 1863 and were as low as the 40s in the summer 1864 (the bottom price in London for five-twenties was 39 on 20 August 1864, see Figure 4). These fluctuations resulted from Union military setbacks, the threat of repayment in depreciated paper, and an oversupply of securities. As Murphy reported to Washington in the summer 1864, "every steamer [from New York] brings large quantities of securities now so that the supply now sometimes exceeds the demand."[195] Offered at discounts of up to sixty percent in Europe, five-twenties in 1864 must rank as one of the all-time bargains in the history of the bond market. As Charles Francis Adams would later remark:

> shrewd as the British capitalist proverbially is, his judgment in regard to American investments had been singularly fallible. When our national bonds went a begging at a discount of sixty per cent, he transmitted them to Germany and refused to touch them himself.[196]

---

[192] Pike to Seward, 31 December 1862 and 4 February 1863, *FRUS*, 1863, 3, pp. 803–4, 807–8.
[193] Pike to Seward, 4 March 1863, *FRUS*, 1863, 3, pp. 811–12.
[194] Murphy to Seward, 27 July 1863, RG 59, Main 161, NA.
[195] Murphy to Seward, 18 April 1864, RG 59, Main 161, NA.
[196] Quoted in Wilkins, *Foreign Investment*, p. 108.

Exchange rates made Union bonds an even better deal. Since no foreign loan had been arranged, the five-twenties purchased by European investors were American issues denominated in dollars. Although nineteenth-century exchange rates were fixed to the price of gold, currency fluctuations resulted from the premium or discount at which brokers were willing to accept foreign bills of exchange.[197] Concerns about the stability of the dollar translated into foreign bills of exchange being quoted at premiums of up to forty percent in the United States during the dark days of 1864. European money, quite simply, was worth more in the United States than it was at home. Henri Hottinguer calculated that the six percent five-twenty bonds actually yielded eight and a half percent for the European investor who had ordered it from New York.[198] Indeed, Chase considered these exchange fluctuations a "danger" that provided a motive for arranging a new European loan with principal and interest payable either in pounds in London or guilders in Amsterdam.[199]

The popularity of Union securities on the continent provided the opportunity for the Treasury to obtain the foreign financial assistance that had not been forthcoming from British capitalists. "If our Government could from time to time supply some respectable banking house here with a quantity of U.S. stock," Murphy suggested, "it might be very easily sold, at any time, for a certain brokerage, and also considerably improve its value by advancing the quotations."[200] What Murphy was proposing, in effect, was to charter a German bank—in a manner similar to the new national banks created by the National Bank Act of 1863—to market Union bonds in Frankfurt. A similar proposal was sent to Chase by Frederick Kuhne, the German consul in New York and a member of the New York business partnership of Knauth, Nachod, and Kuhne, and his associate Ludwig Marx. Kuhne and Marx recommended issuing bonds with coupons payable in Europe, most likely in guilders in Amsterdam, through a "solid and mature banking house" that would act similarly to the newly chartered national banks in the North.[201] This

---

[197] For exchange rate mechanics, see L. E. Davis and J. R. T. Hughes, "A Dollar-Sterling Exchange, 1803–1895," *Economic History Review*, 13 (1960), pp. 52–78.
[198] See *The Economist*, 6 February 1864, p. 167; Aspinwall to Chase, 2 May 1863, Chase Papers, UPA; Platt, *Foreign Finance in Continental Europe and the United States*, p. 149.
[199] Chase diary, 14 September 1864, in Donald (ed.), *Inside Lincoln's Cabinet*, p. 253.
[200] Murphy to Seward, 2 January 1864, RG 59, Main 161, NA.
[201] See Chase to Cisco, 20 and 29 June 1864; Chase to Cooke, 26 June 1864; and, Chase to Fessenden, 27 August 1864, *Chase Papers*, 4, pp. 394–427. Forbes and Aspinwall had made a similar recommendation a year earlier. See Aspinwall to Chase, 5 and 8 May 1863, Chase Papers, UPA.

would facilitate the sale of Union securities in Europe as well as regulate the rate of exchange.

The dire state of the nation's finances in the summer 1864 led Chase to endorse this plan. After the dramatic victories of the preceding summer, confidence in the Union effort—particularly on Wall Street—plummeted to its low point of the war. Sales of the new ten-forty bonds (which yielded five percent interest rather than the six percent of their predecessors) stalled as Grant's campaign in Virginia yielded few results other than colossal casualty figures. Perhaps the best barometer of Wall Street's confidence in the Union cause was the gold premium. The Legal Tender Act of 1862 that established a national paper currency also created a speculative gold market where greenbacks were exchanged for gold. Events in Washington and on the battlefield influenced this "gold premium" throughout the war. After the Union defeat at Cold Harbor in June, it took $2.85 in greenbacks to purchase one dollar in gold, the worst rate of the war.[202] Further discouraging to Northern investor confidence was the likely triumph of the peace Democrats in the forthcoming November elections that even Lincoln himself predicted in August 1864. These adverse military and political developments compounded the North's financial difficulties that, in Chase's estimation, resulted from the reluctance of Congress to increase taxation, coupled with a growing trade deficit. Given the state of American financial markets, Chase had no choice but to once again attempt a foreign loan, but this time on the continent rather than in Britain. "I mean to go in for a foreign loan now," the Secretary of the Treasury informed Horace Greeley, "though it galls me."[203] However, before the plan could be implemented, long-standing political disputes with President Lincoln led Chase to resign from his post. On his way out the door, Chase advised his successor, William Fessenden, to use his plan to market bonds in Europe.[204]

---

[202] The dramatic increase in the gold premium in June 1864 was also due to the Gold Act of 17 June that prohibited speculative trading in gold futures. The act, which forced legitimate traders to turn to the black market, was repealed two weeks later. See Richard Bensel, *Yankee Leviathan: The Origins of Central State Authority in America, 1859–1877* (New York, 1990), p. 152; Jeremy Atack and Peter Passel, *A New Economic View of American History* (New York, 1994), p. 496. For the relationship between events on the battlefield and the price of gold, see Gregor Smith and R. Todd Smith, "Greenback-Gold Returns and Expectations of Resumption, 1862–1879," *Journal of Economic History*, 57 (September 1997), pp. 697–717.

[203] Chase to Greeley, 10 June 1864. *Chase Papers*, 4, p. 396; Chase to Baring Brothers, 10 June 1864, Record Group 56, Entry 29, National Archives II, College Park, Md.

[204] Chase to Fessenden, 27 August 1864. *Chase Papers*, 4, p. 427. See also Chase diary, 14 September 1864, in Donald (ed.), *Inside Lincoln's Cabinet*, p. 253.

Fessenden initially expressed interest in marketing bonds in Europe and even encouraged his predecessor to travel abroad to execute the plan.[205] This arrangement failed to materialize. However, by late 1864, Fessenden changed his mind, observing that "to effect a foreign loan would not... add much, if at all, to the whole amount of sales, unless stimulated by efforts and inducements, which our financial condition has not, as yet, called."[206] Depressed prices of Union bonds in Europe— which were still selling at less than half of their face value in Frankfurt as late as January 1865—no doubt influenced Fessenden's decision, as did reports that most European investors preferred to purchase Union bonds in dollars because of the favorable exchange rates.[207] However, the dramatic turnaround on the battlefield, namely the taking of Atlanta in September 1864, and the re-election of Lincoln two months later led to an abrupt restoration of confidence in the Union effort. Fessenden hedged that the resulting wave of patriotism would lead to increased bond sales at home. To ensure this result, he reappointed Jay Cooke as a Treasury agent (Cooke had been demoted because of allegations of profiteering). Sales of seven-thirties and newly issued five-twenties quickly picked up. With the end of the conflict in sight, Northerners took pride in the fact that they had financed their massive war effort almost entirely on their own. As Fessenden patriotically declared in December 1864, "This nation has been able, thus far, to conduct a domestic war of unparalleled magnitude and cost without appealing for aid to any foreign people."[208]

Even without a coordinated effort by the Treasury, European capitalists continued to buy Union bonds in the last months of the war. It is impossible to know the amount of Union debt held abroad as sales were never recorded by the Treasury. Post-war estimates in the North contended that German investment alone amounted to "seven or eight hundred million dollars."[209] This figure is probably exaggerated as it was given at the height of pro-German sentiment during the Franco-Prussian War. Robert J. Walker maintained that "more than one hundred and fifty millions of our securities were sold, during less than two years in Europe."[210] Uncharacteristically, Walker might have underestimated.

[205] Chase diary, 18 August 1864, in Donald (ed.), *Inside Lincoln's Cabinet*, p. 246.
[206] Quoted in Wilkins, *Foreign Investment*, p. 104. Robert Cook, " 'The Grave of All my Comforts': Williom Pitt Fessenden as Secretary of the Treasury, 1864–1865," *Civil War History*, 41 (September 1995), p. 214.
[207] See Platt, *Foreign Finance in Continental Europe and the United States, 1815–1870*, p. 149.
[208] Quoted in Wilkins, *Foreign Investment*, p. 104.
[209] This estimate is from the New York *Tribune* in 1870. See John Gazley, *American Opinion of German Unification, 1848–1871* (New York, 1926), pp. 320–2.
[210] Walker to McCulloch, 28 June 1865, AC 4831, Walker Papers, Library of Congress.

Knauth, Nachod and Kuhne estimated in 1865 that Union bonds in Europe totaled $320 million, $250 million of which were held in Holland and Germany.[211] Financial historians generally accept this figure.[212] "There is hardly a person of any means," Murphy reported from Frankfurt in February 1865, "who does not hold American Bonds and consequently is thinking of... how to advance our cause."[213]

Thus, after several unsuccessful attempts, the Union effort to obtain a foreign loan ended with Fessenden's realization that the nation could finance the war on its own. Perhaps a foreign loan could have been arranged had Union leaders recognized earlier that the investors who were willing to buy into their cause were German and Dutch, not British as they had been for much of the preceding century. But many Americans believed that the less debt that was held abroad, the better. As Heather Cox Richardson has recently illustrated, Northerners viewed early British rejections of Union loan offers as an insult to national honor that increased their determination to finance the war without European help.[214] Such views tapped into Americans' historic antagonism to foreign financial interests that had marked the Jacksonian era and would later surface during the Populist movement of the 1890s. As American financier Jay Cooke proclaimed,

We are free from foreign debt now. I count it one of the many blessings to offset the miseries of this war. I do not think it for the interest of our country that our debt should go abroad. We... better not put a whip into the hands of foreigners to punish us whenever they see fit to go to war with us.[215]

Although Union leaders preferred to keep the war debt at home, there is little question that they were prepared—indeed, at times eager—to secure the assistance of foreign capitalists. Issuing a loan on the London Stock Exchange would benefit the Union cause by strengthening the

---

[211] This estimate comes from a letter reproduced in Oberholtzer, *Jay Cooke*, I, pp. 513–15.
[212] See Wilkins, *Foreign Investment*, p. 104; Platt, *Foreign Finance in Continental Europe and the United States*, p. 151; Cleona Lewis, *America's Stake in International Investments* (Washington, D.C., 1938), pp. 54–5. John Hawgood, "The Civil War and Central Europe," in Harold Hyman (ed.), *Heard Around the World* (New York, 1969), p. 151, estimates that Union bonds in Germany amounted to $200 million. John Madden, *British Investments in the United States, 1860–1880* (New York, 1985), p. 9, claims that between $150 and $200 million of Federal securities were sold abroad, only $500,000 of which were held in Britain.
[213] Murphy to Seward, 20 February 1865, RG 59, Main 161, NA.
[214] Richardson, *The Greatest Nation of the Earth*, pp. 44, 54–5.
[215] Oberholtzer, *Jay Cooke*, I, p. 286.

nation's credit as well as extending international credibility to the cause of reunification. But leading European banks, whose support was a prerequisite to placing a large bond issue abroad, were unwilling to tie themselves to the Union government. Doubtful of the capacity of the North to restore the Union, wary of Chase's financial policies, and concerned that the war might involve nations on both sides of the Atlantic, leading European financiers—even those who sympathized with the Union—calculated that extending a loan to the North was not worth the risks that it entailed. Thus, the only financial assistance the Union received from abroad came not from the traditional means of a loan brokered by a London bank, but rather from individual bond purchases made by entrepreneurs and smaller capitalists in Frankfurt and Amsterdam.

The failure to arrange a foreign loan was in part the result of shortcomings within the Union strategy of international finance. Although Union agents, such as August Belmont, John Murray Forbes, and William H. Aspinwall, were appropriate selections who were well connected to European capitalists, the whole program of financial diplomacy was arranged on an ad hoc basis and lacked the coherence and organization necessary to woo skeptical banks across the Atlantic. Part of this was due, no doubt, to hopes that the war would end quickly and, when it did not, the initial success of the loans placed on the domestic market. But this was also the result of political rivalry within the Lincoln cabinet. The two men responsible for most international issues, Seward and Chase, were bitter political rivals, representing, respectively, the conservative and radical wings of the Republican Party. Chase even attempted to run Seward out of the government during the cabinet crisis of December 1862. There is little evidence to suggest that the two coordinated their efforts on matters of international finance and diplomacy.[216] Such cooperation could have helped as it appears that Seward was aware of the growing demand for Union bonds in Germany and Holland, via consular dispatches, long before the Secretary of the Treasury. Moreover, Union financial emissaries in Britain received little assistance from the U.S. legation and Charles Francis Adams, who apparently knew little about Chase's attempts to arrange a loan with a European banking house and harbored suspicion of the Treasury Department's envoys. Administrative

---

[216] There is no evidence of such cooperation, for instance, in the correspondence between the Treasury and the State Departments in Record Group 56, Entry 6, National Archives II, College Park, Md.

direction was also not forthcoming from the president. Although historians dispute the extent to which Lincoln orchestrated the day-to-day activities of the government, most agree that the two areas he was least involved in were finance and diplomacy.[217] Combined with the difficulties Union agents encountered in persuading European financiers to commit funds to a government embroiled in civil war, the lack of a well-conceived and well-directed policy of financial diplomacy led to the failure to place a loan on European financial markets during the war.

Fortunately for the Union, this international failure was offset by domestic success. Denied the foreign capital that the government had traditionally relied upon, Congress was forced to radically reshape the financial structure of the nation to cover the costs of the war. Legislation pertaining to currency, banking, and taxation consolidated federal power over affairs traditionally delegated to states and, in the words of one historian, provided the "blueprint for modern America."[218] The development of Wall Street during the war also portended the future. Increased trading in government bonds led to an explosion in the size and number of American investment banks and stock brokers and, not to be forgotten, necessitated the construction of a separate building in 1863 to house these transactions, the New York Stock Exchange.[219] Speculations in the "gold room" and cushy government contracts also anticipated the corruption and cronyism of the Gilded Age. All of these developments were in part a consequence of the Treasury's failure to obtain a foreign loan during the war. By war's end nearly ninety percent of the government's massive $2,677,929,000 debt was held by Americans (the percentage was even higher before the final months of the conflict).[220] Despite

---

[217] For the view that Lincoln gave Chase and Seward a free hand in conducting the affairs of their respective departments, see David Donald, *Lincoln* (New York, 1996); Frederick Blue, *Salmon P. Chase: A Life in Politics* (Kent, 1987); Phillip S. Paludan, *The Presidency of Abraham Lincoln* (Lawrence, Kan., 1994). For a more proactive Lincoln, see Monaghan, *Diplomat in Carpet Slippers*; Mahin, *One War at a Time*. For a balanced view that contends that, though Lincoln did not direct financial and diplomatic policies, he decisively intervened in important policy decisions (such as in toning down Seward's "Dispatch No. 10" and in ordering the release of Mason and Slidell during the *Trent* affair), see Richard Carwardine, *Lincoln* (London, 2003).

[218] Leonard Curry, *Blueprint for Modern America: Non-Military Legislation of the First Civil War Congress* (Nashville, 1968).

[219] See Bensel, *Yankee Leviathan*, p. 249.

[220] This estimate assumes that foreign holdings of the U.S. debt totaled $320 million. See footnotes 211–12.

these signs of American financial autonomy, this freedom from foreign debt would not last long.

Although they did not arrange a formal loan on the Treasury's behalf, foreign capitalists were far from passive observers of the Civil War. Dutch and German investment in Union bonds in the latter half of the conflict, as even Fessenden admitted, "relieved and strengthened" the "home market" during the bleak summer of 1864.[221] Across the English Channel, several British banks, led by Baring Brothers and Peabody and Co., provided political and moral, though little financial, support for the Union. Thomas Baring's advocacy of the Union in Parliament and George Peabody's well-timed donation to London served as reminders to British statesmen of the importance of the economic links between Britain and the North—links that would be severed by any attempt to meddle in the conflict.[222]

The Union effort in Europe also succeeded in minimizing European financial and material support for the Confederacy. Robert J. Walker's mission to Europe in 1863-4 tarnished the financial reputation of the Confederacy by linking Jefferson Davis to the state repudiations of the 1840s. Northern agents engaged in preclusive purchasing in Britain to prevent Southern purchasers from acquiring much needed arms for the Confederacy. Union diplomats, as well, adroitly handled the *Trent* crisis of late 1861 and the Laird rams dispute of 1863. Willing to swallow the bitter pill of bowing to British demands during the *Trent* affair yet bold enough to threaten grave consequences during the Laird rams controversy of 1863, Union diplomacy—despite its financial failures—was marked by a flexibility that the international vision of the Confederacy lacked. By maintaining peace with Britain and keeping foreign support of the Confederacy to a minimum, the Union effort overseas allowed the war to be decided by events within the nation's borders.

---

[221] Quoted in Wilkins, *Foreign Investment*, p. 104.
[222] For more on this point, see Jay Sexton, "Transatlantic Financiers and the Civil War," *American Nineteenth Century History*, 2 (Autumn 2001), pp. 29-46.

3
Confederate Finance and Diplomacy

From its inception the Confederate States of America was a nation in financial straits. Having long relied on the credit perennially advanced by banks in the North and across the Atlantic, the Southern states lacked a stable, self-sustaining financial infrastructure. Eighty-five percent of the chartered banks in the United States in 1860, issuing nearly three-quarters of the nation's domestic loans, were located north of the Mason–Dixon line.[1] Moreover, the South's largest assets—land and slaves—lacked the liquidity necessary for the economic mobilization demanded by modern war.

Accompanying this financial dependence was the South's reliance on manufactured goods from outside her borders. Northern states possessed ninety percent of the nation's prewar industrial output. Importing Yankee manufactured goods during a civil war was not an option and the Confederacy had no choice but to look across the Atlantic for the war materials and finished goods that factories at home could not adequately provide. But with the Union blockade slowly closing off access to trans-oceanic trading links, this would not be an easy task. To make matters worse, the Confederate states, having long relied on Northern and foreign merchants to arrange the exportation of cotton, possessed a mere ten serviceable merchant vessels in 1861. On paper, the Confederacy's prospects did indeed appear bleak. As the New York lawyer and shipper Caleb Cushing put it to the Confederate purchasing agent Caleb Huse before he left for Britain in 1861,

the money is all in the North; the manufactures are all in the North; the ships are all in the North; the arms and arsenals are all in the North; the arsenals of Europe are within 10 days of New York and they will be closed to the South; and the Southern ports will be blockaded. What possible chance can the South have?[2]

The chance that the Confederacy had, leaders in Richmond believed, rested in the power of cotton to compel European statesmen and financiers to side with their cause. The key commodity of the nineteenth-

---
[1] Douglass Ball, *Financial Failure and Confederate Defeat* (Urbana, 1991), p. 23.
[2] Caleb Huse, *The Supplies for the Confederate Army* (Boston, 1904), p. 14.

century Atlantic economy, Southern cotton fueled the textile industries of Europe and sustained an estimated twenty percent of the British population.[3] With this trump card in their hand, Confederate leaders were convinced that they could dictate Civil War diplomacy. Cotton, Southern statesmen held, could be a bargaining chip employed to induce British recognition of the Confederacy. With this accomplished, the commodity could reassume its traditional role as a source of foreign exchange that would provide the Confederacy with the credit needed to obtain war supplies abroad.

Confederate statesmen, however, were never able to implement a policy that used cotton to their advantage. A cotton embargo, a scheme to sell cotton at low prices to France, the issuance of cotton certificates and cotton bonds in Europe, and the direct exportation of cotton on government account all failed to improve the Confederacy's diplomatic and financial fortunes. European prejudices resulting from the sordid past of several Southern states on the financial markets and the Confederacy's system of slavery, of course, contributed to these failures. However, as we shall see, the poor statesmanship of Southern diplomats and financial agents sealed the international fate of the Confederacy.

THE FOUNDATIONS OF CONFEDERATE INTERNATIONAL POLICY

Southerners' confidence in the ability of cotton to shape international events was rooted in decades of expanding production of the commodity, but can be specifically traced back to the Panic of 1857 when the South, profiting from the steady exportation of the staple, largely escaped the financial crisis that enveloped the North. Southerners saw their avoidance of the panic as a triumph of an economy that was based on agriculture and trade rather than on finance and speculation. As *DeBow's Review*, the voice of the commercial South, declared in 1857, "the wealth of the South is permanent and real, that of the North fugitive and fictitious."[4] Absent in the South, of course, were the investment banks that were the primary victims of the financial crisis. But Southerners were nonetheless

---

[3] *The Economist*, 21 May 1853, p. 561. This estimate assumed that every worker would have three dependents. See Frank Owsley, *King Cotton Diplomacy* (Chicago, 2nd ed., 1959), pp. 8–9. Another historian estimates that 16.6 percent of Britain's population was sustained by the cotton trade and textile industry. See Ball, *Financial Failure and Confederate Defeat*, p. 66.
[4] Quoted in Robert Sobel, *Panic on Wall Street* (London, 1968), p. 111.

convinced that warehouses of cotton held more intrinsic value than banks holding securities and deposits.

What was proven in 1857, Southern fire-eaters brazenly proclaimed, would be repeated in a civil war. "King Cotton" became a rallying call and source of Southern pride in the run-up to the Civil War. The economic power of cotton soon extended itself to politics and diplomacy. Not only could the "King" shield the South from the vicissitudes of the business cycle, but it could also dictate the policies of European powers. South Carolina Senator James Henry Hammond perhaps best articulated the "King Cotton" theory in 1858:

> The South is perfectly content to go on one, two, or three years without planting a seed of cotton.... What would happen if no cotton was furnished for three years? I will not stop to depict what every one can imagine, but this is certain: England would topple headlong and carry the whole civilized world with her, save the South. No, you dare not make war on cotton. No power on earth dares to make war upon it. Cotton *is* King. Until lately the Bank of England was king, but she tried to put her screws as usual, the fall before the last, upon the cotton crop, and was utterly vanquished. The last power has been conquered. Who can doubt, that has looked at recent events, that cotton is supreme?[5]

Confederate leaders planned to employ "King Cotton" as both a carrot and a stick in the initial diplomacy of the Civil War—with the stick quickly eclipsing the carrot. On the one hand, Southern statesmen hinted to European leaders of the creation of an Atlantic free trading block, excluding, of course, the traditionally protectionist North. Yet plans to offer a maximum average tariff of twenty percent to nations willing to enter into a commercial agreement with the Confederacy—the brainchild of secessionist leader Robert Barnwell Rhett—were scuttled in early 1861 following political disputes regarding the longevity of such potential agreements. Although the prospect of a free trading Confederacy remained in the abstract throughout the war, Southern statesmen failed to extend concrete proposals of commercial alliances to European governments.

In contrast, Confederate leaders had few reservations about deploying the coercive side of their diplomatic strategy. In order to hasten European recognition of their independence, Confederate leaders slapped an export duty on cotton (which would also pay the interest on the newly issued Confederate bonds) and tacitly extended their approval to a plan to withhold cotton from Europe. This punitive side of the "King Cotton"

---

[5] Quoted in Charles Francis Adams, *Trans-Atlantic Historical Solidarity* (Oxford, 1913), p. 66.

strategy soon took center stage and overshadowed (and contradicted) the hopes of free traders such as Rhett to use reciprocal trade agreements to prompt European governments to side with the Confederacy. The so-called "cotton embargo," though never officially mandated, was adhered to by an overwhelming majority of Southern planters and merchants who believed it would induce British recognition of the Confederacy in the first year of the war. The tidal wave of cotton exports to Britain that had totaled 2,580,700 bales in 1860 was reduced to a mere trickle during the first years of the war. By 1862, only 72,000 bales of Southern cotton made its way to British ports as a result of the unofficial embargo and the tightening Union blockade.[6]

Although the embargo succeeded in limiting British imports of cotton, the overall "King Cotton" strategy made several fatal miscalculations. For one, though eighty percent of the cotton imported by Britain in 1860 was picked by slaves in the Confederacy, alternative sources had been developed in India and Egypt since the 1840s and could sustain Britain's textile industry during the crisis in America.[7] This is what would happen during the war years when seventy percent of Lancashire's cotton came from India.[8] Confederate diplomats also did not account for the surplus stocks of cotton and textiles held in British warehouses—the result of the boom years of the 1850s. Revisionist historians have even argued that the "cotton famine" experienced during the war was not a famine at all but the product of this gluttonous overproduction.[9] To support this view, historians point out that the surplus stocks of cotton held in Liverpool in 1862, the alleged hungriest year of the famine, were commensurate to those held in 1858.[10] Another indication that there was no shortage of cotton during the "famine" is that British re-exportation of the

---

[6] *The Economist*, 6 October 1866, p. 1163. See also Louis Schmidt, "The Influence of Wheat and Cotton on Anglo-American Relations during the Civil War," *Iowa Journal of History and Politics*, 16 (July 1918), p. 419.

[7] For this view, see Frenise Logan, "India—Britain's Substitute for American Cotton, 1861–1865," *Journal of Southern History*, 24 (November 1958), pp. 472–80; Peter Harnetty, "The Imperialism of Free Trade: Lancashire, India, and the Cotton Supply Question, 1861–1865," *Journal of British Studies*, 6 (November 1966), pp. 70–96; Edward Earle, "Egyptian Cotton and the American Civil War," *Political Science Quarterly*, 41 (December 1926), pp. 520–45.

[8] Hall, "The Cotton Brokers and the Development of the Liverpool Cotton Market c1800 to 1914," D.Phil. dissertation, University of Oxford, 1999, p. 28.

[9] See Eugene Bradey, "A Reconsideration of the Lancashire 'Cotton Famine,'" *Agricultural History*, 37 (July 1963), pp. 156–62; Nigel Hall, "The Liverpool Cotton Market and the American Civil War," *Northern History*, 34 (1998), pp. 149–69.

[10] D. P. Crook, *The North, the South and the Powers* (New York, 1974), p. 205.

commodity actually increased during the war.[11] As *The Economist* pointed out in late 1861, "the enormous production and the excessive exports of last year had glutted several of our most important markets... even if no American war had intervened... this year must still have been one of serious privation and of heavy loss."[12]

As they misjudged Europe's need for cotton, Confederate leaders also failed to grasp the fact that unlike their economy, which was based almost solely on one commodity, Britain and France were economically diverse nations that could endure problems in their textile industries. Indeed, the Civil War years were prosperous ones in Britain, troubles in the textile trade notwithstanding. This prosperity was at least partly a result of Britain's economic relationship with the Northern states. Although "King Corn" did not dictate British diplomacy as some historians have argued, the significant exportation of wheat and other foodstuffs from the Northern states to Britain during the war served as another reminder of the depth and diversity of the Anglo-American connection.[13] Moreover, as we have seen, leading transatlantic financiers in Britain, such as the Barings and Peabody, supported the Union during the war—largely to protect their investments and business interests in the Northern states. These financiers in London, who wielded considered political power in Westminster, demonstrated that Britain's connection to her former colonies was composed of more than cotton fibers. Finally, many in Britain resented the South's attempt to blackmail them through the cotton embargo. "The South is deliberately planning and toiling to force us into a quarrel with the North," *The Economist* warned, "and Englishmen are found ready to fall into the open trap, and help the sinister design!"[14]

Obsessed by the idea that cotton somehow made their confederation invincible, Southern statesmen overlooked the inherent shortcomings in an international strategy that was certain to hinder the Confederate effort.

---

[11] Hall, "The Cotton Brokers and the Development of the Liverpool Cotton Market c1800 to 1914," p. 64.

[12] *The Economist*, 16 November 1861, p. 1262. The historian Arthur Silver similarly states, "In actual fact had it not been for the curtailment of the cotton supply during these months [1861–3] the cotton trade would have suffered more severely than it did." See Arthur Silver, *Manchester Men and Indian Cotton, 1847–72* (Manchester, 1966), p. 158. For a reassertion of the traditional view, see David Surdam, "Cotton's Potential as Economic Weapon: The Antebellum and Wartime Markets for Cotton Textiles," *Agricultural History*, 69 (Spring 1994), pp. 122–45.

[13] Schmidt, "The Influence of Wheat and Cotton on Anglo-American Relations during the Civil War," pp. 400–39. A similar argument is made by Amos Khasigian, "Economic Factors and British Neutrality, 1861–65," *Historian*, 25 (Aug. 1963), pp. 451–65.

[14] *The Economist*, 19 October 1861, p. 1149.

While the diverse economies of Britain and France were able to survive, if not prosper, during the tumultuous war years, the singular economy of the Confederacy collapsed under the weight of its unexported cotton. After all, what had saved the South during the Panic of 1857 was not the inherent value of cotton, but the income generated from its exportation to Britain. "It is true that cotton is almost a necessity to us," the British minister to the United States Lord Lyons reported in 1860, "but it is still more necessary for them to sell it than it is for us to buy it."[15]

That the Confederate Treasury would quickly empty without the foreign exchange generated by the cotton trade would have been easy to predict in 1861. A few isolated voices in the newly created Confederate cabinet, led by Vice-President Alexander Stephens and Judah Benjamin, even recommended establishing a system of exporting and storing cotton in Britain before the Union blockade became effective. This strategy, it was argued, would establish a commercial relationship between Europeans and the Confederate Government as well as provide the Treasury with a reliable source of revenue that would be needed in the coming war. Although various leaders' commitment to this strategy would be exaggerated during the finger pointing of the postwar years, Stephens did indeed draw up a plan calling for the issuance of bonds in Europe, backed by cotton stored in Liverpool on government account. When the price of cotton rose to fifty cents per pound, Stephens proposed, the government could then sell, reserving a portion of the proceeds to handle debt repayment and pocketing the rest.[16]

Such alternative policies were soon thwarted by Jefferson Davis, Christopher Memminger, and other champions of King Cotton who were convinced that the embargo would best advance the interests of the Confederacy. Before the war began it was decided that King Cotton would be the underlying principle of the Confederate international strategy. The success of the Confederacy's first domestic loan of $15 million in the spring 1861 reassured Southern leaders that their young nation could finance what they were certain would be a quick war without the revenue generated by the cotton trade. With any luck, Confederate leaders hoped,

---

[15] Quoted in Joseph A. Fry, *Dixie Looks Abroad: The South and U.S. Foreign Relations, 1789–1973* (Baton Rouge, 2002), p. 82.

[16] For this debate within the Confederate cabinet, see Charles Hubbard, *The Burden of Confederate Diplomacy* (Knoxville, 1998), p. 25; William C. Davis, *"A Government of Our Own": The Making of the Confederacy* (New York, 1994), pp. 198–9, 203–4, 301–2; Thomas E. Schott, *Alexander H. Stephens of Georgia* (Baton Rouge, 1988), pp. 338–40, 366–7; Eli Evans, *Judah P. Benjamin: The Jewish Confederate* (New York, 1991), p. 116; Patrick Rembert, *Jefferson Davis and His Cabinet* (Baton Rouge, 1944), pp. 219–20.

Britain and France might recognize the Confederacy before the war even began. Events would soon prove otherwise. The King Cotton strategy would lead to both the diplomatic and the financial collapse of the Confederacy.

Given Confederate leaders' misreading of international affairs, it is surprising how quickly they mobilized their diplomatic efforts. In February 1861, two months before the war began, the provisional Confederate Congress appointed a three-man delegation to represent the new nation and to seek the formal recognition of European governments. Headed by fire-eater William Yancey, the emissaries were poorly selected and did little to advance the Confederacy's cause abroad. The Confederate Government unwisely entrusted its hopes of gaining recognition from the historically antislavery Palmerston government in Britain on the shoulders of Yancey, an outspoken champion of the peculiar institution and an advocate of reopening the slave trade. Indeed, it is possible that Jefferson Davis' appointment of Yancey was a shrewd political act, intent on exiling his chief political rival to Europe. Although not as extreme as Yancey, the two other members of the delegation, Pierre Rost and Dudley Mann, lacked adequate diplomatic experience and commanded little respect abroad. The newly created Confederate State Department, headed by interim Secretary of State Robert Toombs, instructed the emissaries to provide a legal and moral defense of secession in the effort to obtain recognition from Britain, followed by France, Russia, and Belgium. Although the agents were to assure European statesmen that the Confederacy would have tariffs "for mere revenue purposes, so moderate as to closely approximate free trade," the instructions they received revealed that the core of the South's diplomatic strategy was not the carrot of free trade, but the stick of the cotton embargo. Toombs advised the diplomatic team that in their quest to secure recognition, a "delicate allusion" to "the condition to which the British realm would be reduced if the supply of our staple should suddenly fail or even be considerably diminished" should be made to British Foreign Secretary Lord Russell.[17]

The Confederate emissaries arrived in Britain at the end of April along with the news of the bombardment of Fort Sumter and the beginning of the Civil War. Ironically, the Union was not represented in London at the time as Charles Francis Adams delayed his departure to attend his son's

---

[17] Toombs to Yancey, Rost, and Mann, 16 March 1861, James Richardson (ed.), *Messages and Papers of the Confederacy*, 2 vols. (Nashville, 1906), II, pp. 3–8; Owsley, *King Cotton Diplomacy*, pp. 51–86; Hubbard, *The Burden of Confederate Diplomacy*, pp. 29–47; Crook, *The North, the South and the Powers*, pp. 27–8.

wedding in Boston (a decision that provoked much criticism in the North). With Adams on the wrong side of the Atlantic and pro-Confederate MP William Gregory willing to act as an intermediary, the Confederate agents succeeded in arranging two meetings with Russell in early May 1861. The Southern emissaries presented their case to a noncommittal Russell who declined to reveal the government's position and surprised the delegates with his hostility to slavery. The Yancey team obtained little more from subsequent meetings in July with French statesmen Count de Morny and Foreign Minister Edouard Thouvenel. The Confederate representatives also failed in their attempts to arrange a loan with a European bank. George Peabody and Baring Brothers established their pro-Union policy early when they declined to even meet with Dudley Mann.[18] The Barings also rejected South Carolina's loan request at the beginning of the conflict, reminding the state's bank that since the repudiation of three Southern states in the 1840s, "there has been for several years a growing indisposition with capitalists to invest in the Bonds of Slave States."[19]

Although it would appear that these early overtures did little to reinforce the belief of an imminent pro-Confederate move by Britain or France, the Southern diplomats remained convinced that with cotton on their side it was only a matter of time before the European powers would formally recognize the Confederacy. As Yancey informed Toombs, Britain would "postpone recognition of the independence of those states as long as possible, at least until some decided advantage is obtained by them or the necessity of having cotton becomes pressing." What was needed, simply, was more time for the cotton embargo to take effect. "The question of recognition," Yancey stubbornly repeated, "must be determined by the cotton situation." The Queen's proclamation of neutrality issued on 13 May 1861, which conferred the rights of a belligerent to the Confederacy, appeared to forecast a favorable change in British policy. With the Confederate army having proven its mettle at the battle of Bull Run on 21 July, prospects for the Confederacy did indeed appear bright. Though it failed to produce immediate results, King Cotton remained the centerpiece of the Confederate international strategy.[20]

[18] *New York Times*, 23 May 1861.
[19] Baring Brothers to Waring, 15 December 1860. Baring Papers, Library of Congress [microfilm]. D. C. M. Platt, *Foreign Finance in Continental Europe and the United States, 1815–1870* (London, 1984), p. 146.
[20] Yancey, Rost, and Mann to Toombs, 21 May, 1 June, 15 July, 1 August 1861, Richardson (ed.), *Messages and Papers of the Confederacy*, II, pp. 34–54; Owsley, *King Cotton Diplomacy*, pp. 51–86; Hubbard, *The Burden of Confederate Diplomacy*, pp. 29–47.

In contrast to the poorly selected diplomatic team, purchasing agents Caleb Huse and James Bulloch proved indispensable to the Confederate effort abroad. Dispatched to Europe in the spring 1861 to provide arms and materials for the War and Navy Departments, the agents possessed the perseverance and flexibility that the Yancey–Rost–Mann team lacked. Both were well qualified for their mission: Huse, a professor at the University of Alabama, had traveled to Britain in 1859 to study arms manufacturers and Bulloch served in the U.S. Navy prior to running a New York merchant firm. Few Confederate emissaries could boast such international credentials. Two days after the bombardment of Fort Sumter, Huse was instructed to "proceed to Europe... for the purchase of ordnance, arms, equipments, and military stores." Bulloch was dispatched a few weeks later to purchase six vessels and other material for the Navy. Amazingly, neither agent was advanced the credit necessary to execute their orders. Secretary of the Navy Stephen Mallory merely directed Bulloch "to make your contracts through the intervention of some well known and established English commercial house which has the confidence of the commissioners from these States to England."[21]

Despite these vague instructions, it was not long before both agents were providing the Confederacy with much-needed arms and munitions. By mid-May Huse had contracted for 10,000 Enfield rifles from the London Armoury, a company that would provide arms for both the North and the South throughout the war. In contrast to his Union competitors who purchased the "merest rubbish in the world" that "will surely prove more dangerous to those who may venture to use them than to the troops against whom they are pointed," Huse focused on obtaining high-quality arms, specifically Enfield rifles, which would endure years of fighting. As he was well aware, lack of credit, in addition to the tightening of the blockade, might prevent the future exportation of war materials. By early 1863, Huse alone had purchased more than 130,000 long arms, 81,000 of which were Enfields.[22]

---

[21] Cooper to Huse, 15 April 1861, *Official Records of the Union and Confederate Armies in the War of the Rebellion* (hereafter *ORA*), 128 vols. (Washington, D.C., 1880–1902), 4, 1, p. 220; Mallory to Bulloch 9 May 1861, *Official Records of the Union and Confederate Navies in the War of the Rebellion* (hereafter *ORN*), 30 vols. (Washington, D.C., 1894–1922), 2, 2, pp. 64–5; Huse, *The Supplies for the Confederate Army*, p. 12; James Bulloch, *The Secret Service of the Confederate States in Europe*, 2 vols. (London, 1883), I, p. 21; Thomas Boaz, *Guns for Cotton* (Shippensburg, Pa., 1996), p. 13.

[22] Huse to Ordnance Department, 21 May 1861, ORA, 4, 1, pp. 343–6; Huse and Anderson to Walker, 11 August 1861, *ORA*, 4, 1, pp. 538–42; Samuel Thompson, *Confederate Purchasing Operations Abroad* (Chapel Hill, 1935), p. 17; Boaz, *Guns for Cotton*, p. 47.

Bulloch did for the Navy what Huse accomplished for the Army. Lacking the naval power to protect Southern ports from the Union blockade, Confederate leaders placed the onus of creating a navy almost entirely on the shoulders of Bulloch and a few of his collaborators in Britain. Confederate leaders were convinced that the acquisition of a few ironclad ships would challenge Union naval superiority and open up transatlantic trading routes. Secretary of the Navy Mallory regarded "the possession of an iron-armored ship as a matter of the first necessity. Such a vessel at this time could traverse the entire coast of the United States, prevent all blockades, and encounter, with a fair prospect of success, their entire navy." The Confederate Congress agreed and, in one of its first acts, allotted $1 million for naval purchasing abroad.[23] Although this initial allocation of funds greatly assisted Bulloch, British neutrality laws complicated the naval agent's job. While Bulloch crossed the Atlantic in May 1861, Queen Victoria issued her proclamation of neutrality that, while ignoring the exportation of small arms and munitions, specifically forbade British subjects from "equipping, furnishing, fitting out, or arming, of any ship or vessel, with intent or in order that such ship or vessel shall be employed in the service" of a belligerent. Once Bulloch was in Britain, the Liverpool solicitor F. S. Hull assured him that there were ways around the law—particularly given the law's language that appeared to differentiate between, on the one hand, arming and equipping vessels (which was forbidden) and, on the other, merely constructing them (which was not). Confident in Hull's advice, Bulloch met with shipbuilders in Birkenhead and Liverpool to contract for the creation of a Confederate navy. By August 1861, two future Confederate raiders, the *Florida* and the *Alabama*, were under construction in British shipyards. Thus began the controversy that would dominate Anglo-American relations for the next decade.[24]

The success of these early purchasing missions would not have been possible without the Confederacy's quasi-official financial depository in Europe, Fraser, Trenholm and Co. of Liverpool. The bank was the British branch of John Fraser and Co., a Charleston firm headed by George Trenholm (who would serve as Confederate secretary of the treasury in 1864–5). Prior to the war, Fraser, Trenholm was primarily a merchant

---

[23] Mallory, Navy Department Memo, *ORN*, 2, 2, pp. 70–2; Act of Confederate Congress, 10 May 1861, *ORN*, 2, 2, p. 66; Fry, *Dixie Looks Abroad*, p. 95.

[24] Bulloch to Mallory, 13 August 1861, *ORN*, 2, 2, pp. 83–7; *Times*, 15 May 1861; E. D. Adams, *Great Britain and the American Civil War* (New York, 1925), p. 116; Warren Spencer, *The Confederate Navy in Europe* (Alabama, 1983), p. 19.

bank that served as an intermediary in the booming cotton trade. The bank was far from a financial powerhouse by most estimations, but, by 1860, could proudly lay claim to being Liverpool's fourth largest importer of cotton. When war broke out in April 1861, it was never a question which side the firm would support. Charles Prioleau, the head of the Liverpool bank, was a South Carolinian who had long attempted to free the South from, as he viewed it, the economic hegemony of the North. The Civil War certainly provided this opportunity and the bank's New York branch was hastily relocated to Nassau where it could assist in the firm's blockade-running ventures. Fraser, Trenholm was so intimately connected to the Southern states that the five ships in its Liverpool–Charleston line sailed under the Confederate flag once the war began. The firm's connection to the Confederacy was made explicit in late 1861 when Jefferson Davis authorized the Treasury Department to use it as a foreign depository.[25]

Under Prioleau's sympathetic leadership, the firm underwrote the activities of Confederate purchasing agents abroad. Bulloch could not have contracted for the *Florida* and the *Alabama* without the firm's advances while he waited for funds to arrive from the Treasury in Richmond. As Bulloch would later write, "It is an unquestionable fact that the Confederate Government had great financial difficulties to meet, and the 'depositories' in England were often under heavy advance." The credit provided by Fraser, Trenholm, however, was not simply given to Confederate agents. In theory, the Confederate Treasury was to remit to Fraser, Trenholm, in either specie or a bill of exchange, the amount expended in Europe by shipping it to Liverpool, or by depositing it at John Fraser and Co. in Charleston. In practice, however, Confederate remittances never kept pace with expenditures in Britain. Hard currency was difficult to come by in the South after most states and banks suspended specie payments in the winter 1860–1. Gold obtained by the Treasury from the $15 million loan of 1861 helped—some £120,000 was sent to Liverpool in the spring 1861—but was clearly not a long-term solution. Likewise, bills of exchange were in short supply in the Confederacy. Without the cotton trade to generate new ones, existing bills (which were often held by Southern banks and merchants) were soon quoted at a high premium, making it difficult for the Confederate Treasury to purchase them for remittance to Fraser, Trenholm.[26]

---

[25] Ball, *Financial Failure and Confederate Defeat*, p. 71.
[26] Bulloch, *The Secret Service of the Confederate States in Europe*, I, p. 53; Stephen Wise, *Lifeline of the Confederacy* (Columbia, S.C., 1988), p. 47; Boaz, *Guns for Cotton*, p. 12; Spencer, *The Confederate Navy in Europe*, p. 5; Thompson, *Confederate Purchasing*

Confederate Finance and Diplomacy

As the war dragged on, it became clear that this haphazard system of international finance was not sufficient to cover the Confederacy's overseas expenditures. By the summer and autumn 1862, the Confederacy's account at Fraser, Trenholm had been severely overdrafted and the firm had no choice but to limit the letters of credit it issued to Southern agents. Purchasing operations were put on hold as Confederate agents were unable to meet their obligations without fresh advances from Fraser, Trenholm. Mallory informed Bulloch that "the exchange of the country is nearly exhausted and can only be procured in very small amounts... I am seriously apprehensive that the Treasury Department will fail to meet your demands."[27]

The Confederacy's financial quandary largely resulted from the failure to integrate its domestic and international financial policies. The so-called "produce loans" of 1861–2 allowed Southerners, who were inveterately short on cash, to pledge their cotton, tobacco, and other crops in exchange for Confederate Government bonds. The scheme was not entirely successful—many planters sold their cotton on the black market after having received its value in bonds—but it did provide the government with an estimated 400,000 bales of cotton by August 1862. Though a far cry from the 2.6 million bales exported by the Southern states in 1860, the cotton held by the Confederate Government was a substantial, though unemployed, asset. The price of cotton dramatically increased as a result of the cotton embargo and the Union blockade. By 1862, cotton averaged seventeen pence per pound, nearly triple the price in 1860. With the Treasury short on gold, the logical move, it appeared, was to establish a currency based on "white gold" in Europe. As the naval agent James North recommended to Mallory, "If I had Confederate bonds or authority to pledge cotton on the faith of the Government, backed with the signature of our minister out here, I think I might raise money and on much more favorable terms than you can in the Confederacy. The work is in rapid progress and it will be much to be deplored if it should all fail for the want of money."[28]

Operations Abroad, p. 49; Ball, *Financial Failure and Confederate Defeat*, pp. 72–3. For bills of exchange, see Judith Fenner, "Confederate Finances Abroad," Ph.D. dissertation, Rice University, 1969.

[27] Mallory to Bulloch, 20 September 1862, *ORN*, 2, 2, pp. 269–71.

[28] North to Mallory, 2 September 1862, *ORN*, 2, 2, pp. 258–60. See also Richard Todd, *Confederate Finance* (Georgia, 1954), pp. 30–42; Lester, *Confederate Finance and Purchasing in Great Britain* (Charlottesville, 1975), p. 18; Thompson, *Confederate Purchasing Operations Abroad*, p. 50; Hall, "The Liverpool Cotton Market and the American Civil War," pp. 149–69.

But inflexible Confederate leaders were reluctant to scrap the King Cotton strategy before it had been given the time they believed it required to succeed. The appointment of permanent representatives to Europe to replace the Yancey team in November 1861 certainly did not portend a change in strategy. The Confederacy's new envoys, James Mason and John Slidell, were both devout champions of King Cotton diplomacy. Although they boasted more foreign relations experience than their predecessors (Mason had served on the Foreign Relations Committee while a senator and Slidell had negotiated with the Mexican government in the 1840s), neither possessed a favorable reputation abroad. "Appointing Mr Mason is really astounding," the London *Daily Star* declared, "[he] is the author of the worst law that is on the Statute book of any nation—the Fugitive Slave Law."[29] Indeed, it is partly reflective of Mason and Slidell's diplomatic acumen that the closest they came to inducing a pro-Confederate move by the British government was when they were locked up in a Northern jail during the *Trent* crisis in December 1861.

Mason and Slidell's initial activities in Europe upon being released by the Lincoln administration after the *Trent* imbroglio, however, did appear to hold promise. In Britain, Mason collaborated with a consortium of pro-Confederate politicians including William Lindsay, John Roebuck, and Lord Campbell. This "powerful Southern lobby," as one historian has dubbed it, campaigned in Parliament in the spring 1862 to establish the illegality of the Union blockade.[30] This high-level lobbying was matched by a public opinion campaign, spearheaded by Liverpudlian James Spence and, to a lesser extent, Mason. Under the ruse of the Confederate States Aid Association and the Liverpool Southern Club (later consolidated into the Southern Independence Association), Spence and other pro-Confederate Britons arranged partisan public meetings, organized petitions, and promoted Southern victories on the battlefield in the British press. This propaganda campaign was largely concentrated in Lancashire where, by the summer 1862, most textile mills were operating at a reduced capacity and unemployment reached staggering proportions. Although the recent scholarship of R. J. M. Blackett has invalidated the revisionist argument that the British working class, particularly in Lancashire, unanimously supported the Confederacy, it is clear that the South did have some friends in all classes of British society, many of whom were eager to campaign for its recognition. All of this pro-

---

[29] *Daily Star*, 14 January 1862.
[30] Owsley, *King Cotton Diplomacy*, pp. 154–202.

Confederate activity—limited though it was—appeared to confirm to Confederate leaders that the King Cotton strategy was finally paying its dividends.[31]

A pro-Confederate policy seemed to be foreshadowed by the British Government's decision to adopt a loose interpretation of its neutrality laws and allow British-built cruisers to fall into Confederate hands in the spring 1862. As we have seen, James Bulloch contracted for the construction of several warships shortly after his arrival in Liverpool in 1861. A year later, after eluding Union spies and having scraped together enough funds from the coffers of Fraser, Trenholm, two Confederate ships were ready to set sail. To avoid violating the Foreign Enlistment Act, Bulloch arranged for these ships to be armed and outfitted outside of British waters. As he later described it,

It was necessary first, to build or buy a ship, and to disguise or omit the semblance of equipment for purposes of war.... When everything was ready, it was no easy matter to so combine movements that ship and tender, sailing from different ports, should meet at the appointed rendez vous; and then, after the meeting, there was always much difficulty and many obstacles to the safe and speedy transfer of stores and the completion of the armament.[32]

---

[31] British sympathies during the Civil War, particularly of the working class in Lancashire, have been the subject of much historical debate. The traditional view, articulated by contemporaries such as John Stuart Mill and Karl Marx as well as early twentieth-century historians such as E. D. Adams, held that class affiliation largely determined British sympathies. The aristocracy and upper middle class, the argument went, identified with the gentlemanly and conservative Confederacy, while professionals, Dissenters, and the working class advocated the cause of the free-labor North. The interpretation of a working class that placed antislavery conviction ahead of economic self-interest came under intense attack beginning with an article by Royden Harrison in 1957. The revisionist view that the working class, specifically the cotton operatives of Lancashire, supported the Confederacy was most fully presented by Mary Ellison in her 1972 work *Support for Secession*. This view immediately drew criticism from Philip Foner, who reasserted the traditional interpretation. R. J. M. Blackett's masterfully researched *Divided Hearts* will do much to end this debate. While acknowledging the substantial support the Confederacy received from the aristocracy, ministers of the Church of England, and the merchant community of Liverpool, Blackett documents significant support for the Union among Dissenters, radicals, and trade union leaders. The picture remains muddled for the working class, though Blackett makes a convincing case that "even in Lancashire...the friends of the Union carried the day" (pp. 211–2). See E. D. Adams, *Great Britain and the American Civil War* (New York, 1925); Royden Harrison, "British Labour and the Confederacy: A Note on the Southern Sympathies of Some British Working Class Journals and Leaders during the American Civil War," *International Review of Social History*, 2 (1957), pp. 78–105; Mary Ellison, *Support for Secession: Lancashire and the American Civil War* (Chicago, 1972); Philip Foner, *British Labor and the American Civil War* (New York, 1981); R. J. M. Blackett, *Divided Hearts: Britain and the American Civil War* (Baton Rouge, 2001).

[32] Bulloch, *The Secret Service of the Confederate States in Europe*, I, pp. 23–4.

Whether this subterfuge was legal would be intensely debated for the next decade.[33] Whether the British Government was aware of the ultimate purpose of the vessels would be debated as well. What was clear was that Lord Russell disregarded the repeated protests of U.S. diplomats and failed to prevent the ships from sailing, ultimately under the Confederate flag. Clandestinely armed in neutral waters, the Confederacy's new cruisers, christened the *Florida* and the *Alabama*, quickly altered the naval complexion of the war. The two elusive raiders would capture or destroy more than one hundred Union merchant vessels during the war.

The propagandist Henry Hotze made certain that these Confederate achievements did not go unnoticed. A Swiss-born Alabaman, Hotze was appointed the Confederate Commercial Agent (a misnomer as he had nothing to do with commerce) in November 1861. The State Department directed Hotze to "impress upon the public mind abroad the ability of the Confederate States to maintain their independence" while exposing the "tyranny" of the Lincoln administration. In a matter of weeks, the twenty-six-year-old Hotze managed to get his pro-South columns published in the influential *Times* and *Morning Post*. A few months later, the Confederate agent reported to Richmond that he had succeeded in persuading no less than seven leading London journalists to advocate the Confederate cause in their reporting. "I have thus the opportunity," Hotze explained, "of multiplying myself, so to speak, to an almost unlimited extent." Hotze proved to be just as capable at behind-the-scenes politicking as he was at providing slanted copy for London newspapers. At a dinner party at the home of pro-Confederate Lord Campbell, Hotze convinced Chancellor of the Exchequer William Gladstone that not only would the South emerge from the conflict victorious, but also that the southern half of each border state would join the Confederacy. What Gladstone recorded in his journal as "a most interesting conversation" was one of the few times a Confederate agent met with a legitimate policy-maker in Britain.[34]

---

[33] Bulloch believed that he had complied with the Foreign Enlistment Act. He would later write, "If you think the object really was to build a ship in obedience to an order, and in compliance with a contract, leaving it to those who bought it to make what use they thought fit of it, then it appears to me that the Foreign Enlistment Act has not been in any degree broken." Bulloch, *The Secret Service of the Confederate States in Europe*, I, p. 335.

[34] Hotze to Hunter, 14 November 1861, Hotze to Benjamin, 26 September 1862, Hotze Papers, Library of Congress (hereafter LC); H. C. G. Mathew (ed.), *The Gladstone Diaries* (Oxford, 1978), vol. 6, 30 July 1862. See also Peter Parish, "Gladstone and America," in Peter Jagger, *Gladstone* (London, 1998).

Hotze was not content with merely contributing to the London press and established his own pro-Confederate publication, the *Index*, in May 1862. Ironically, the office of the *Index* was separated by only a tobacco shop from the headquarters of its pro-North rival on Fleet Street, the *London American*. "Happily," one British observer remarked in the *Saturday Review*, "the weapons with which the contest in this quarter is carried on are such as may be used without danger or impediment to the travelers along that crowded thoroughfare."[35] Subtitled "A Weekly Journal of Politics, Literature, and News," the *Index* cogently stated its object in its first issue:

> Here, over a dominion the size of twenty kingdoms, there exists a Government now in the second year of its existence, appointed by the formal action of the Legislature of each of the Confederate States, and in each of them sanctioned by a vote of the people—maintaining in the field an army of more than 300,000 men—upheld by many millions of people, with a self-sacrifice, a devotion, and a unanimity rarely equaled in modern history, and sustaining law, order, freedom of speech and freedom of the press throughout its wide domain. As a question of fact, is this a Government or is it not? Once admitted to be such, it is then the bounden duty of other Powers to acknowledge and recognize the fact.[36]

In addition to this fundamental appeal, the *Index* advanced several other arguments as to why Britain should recognize the independence of the Confederacy. Delineating one of the strongest connections between the South and Britain, the *Index* heralded the Confederacy's commitment to free trade and assailed the Union's protectionist Morrill Tariff. Similarly intended to parallel a popular Victorian political doctrine, the *Index* argued that the Southern states were fighting for self-determination, not slavery. To its blue-blooded readership, the publication stressed the aristocratic links between the English nobility and the Southern gentleman. "The South," the *Index* asserted, "has been proud of its closer affinity of blood to the British parent stock, than the North, with its mongrel compound of the surplus population of all the world."[37] Targeting MPs from northern electorates and middle-class capitalists, the *Index* closely covered the deepening cotton famine. Each issue contained exaggerated updates of the scarcity of the cotton supply while sentimentally reporting the plight of both Lancashire mill owners and their operatives. Alternative sources of cotton, most notably in India, the *Index* alleged, were "destined only to disappointment."[38] In reporting the actual war,

---

[35] *Saturday Review*, 2 August 1862. [36] *Index*, 1 May 1862.
[37] *Index*, 15 May 1862. [38] *Index*, 10 Jul 1862.

the *Index* trumpeted Confederate victories and celebrated the heroics of Robert E. Lee and Stonewall Jackson, both sentimental favorites in Britain.

But not all was good for Hotze and the Confederacy in what appeared to be the promising autumn 1862. Even with the modest circulation of 2,300, Hotze was unable to fund his weekly publication and his frequent pleas for more money fell upon deaf ears in Richmond. The Confederacy's financial problems, as we have seen, were not restricted to the *Index*. The naval purchasing agent James North wrote back to Richmond "that anything can be done in this country if you only have money, and without it you can do nothing." Bulloch echoed this sentiment, informing Mallory that he "could extend operations to any extent and for every kind of supplies, if sure that means have been devised for getting funds over here with certainty even a year hence." If the cotton embargo did not yield immediate results in the form of recognition or British intervention, Southern statesmen would have no choice but to reformulate their financial and diplomatic strategies.[39]

THE CITY, THE BRITISH CABINET, AND THE INTERVENTION CRISIS OF 1862

King Cotton diplomacy was on trial in the autumn 1862 when the Palmerston cabinet twice considered intervening in the Civil War, most likely by joining France in extending an offer of mediation to the warring sides. Though not an outright recognition of the Confederacy's independence, mediation was a policy favorable to the South as it would seek peace—which, given the success of Confederate armies at the time, would almost certainly result in the separation of the North and South. Gladstone hinted at a pro-Confederate change of policy in a speech delivered in Newcastle in October: "There is no doubt that Jefferson Davis and other leaders of the South have made an army; they are making, it appears, a navy; and they have made what is more than either—they have made a nation."[40]

Historians have long attempted to explain the motives behind this brief activist phase of British policy during the war. Humanitarian concerns

---

[39] North to Mallory, 27 January 1862, *ORN*, 2, 2, p. 138; Bulloch to Mallory, 15 November 1862, *ORN*, 2, 2, p. 297. "London Expenditures of the Confederate Secret Service," *American Historical Review*, 35 (July 1930), pp. 814–22.

[40] *The Times*, 8 October 1862.

growing from the appalling bloodshed of the war moved many to support British intervention in the hope that such a move would bring a negotiated peace, even at the price of a new slaveholding Confederacy.[41] Not all, of course, were motivated by altruism. Many British leaders, Palmerston in particular, recognized the benefit of dividing a future rival and feared that if Britain remained on the sidelines, the ambitious Louis Napoleon might take advantage of the situation in North America (as he was doing with his venture in Mexico). The "cotton famine" in Lancashire and other economic disruptions caused by the war also account for the shift in British policy. With nearly half of the cotton operatives in Lancashire unemployed and seeking relief in the autumn 1862, the so-called "cotton famine" was at its height when the cabinet considered intervention.[42] Economic interests in London also pressed for British mediation in the American conflict. Ironically, the thrust of this pressure originated not only from the cotton merchants, mill owners, and textile operatives targeted by the King Cotton strategy, but also from a group of capitalists in the City. Led by the Rothschilds and publicized in the pages of *The Economist*, influential British capitalists argued in the summer and autumn 1862 that the time had arrived for Britain to intervene to end the war.

It is important to note that the Rothschilds, whose holdings of Southern state securities were minimal and were only tangentially involved in the cotton trade, did not financially nor politically support the Confederacy. Rothschild records clearly reveal the firm's disdain for slavery.[43] Nor, despite the popular myth, did the bank loan money to the Confederacy during the war.[44] The Rothschilds' support for British intervention stemmed from their belief that the North would be unable to forcibly restore the Union. It was an accepted military axiom of the nineteenth century—a lesson ascertained in part from the American War of Independence—that when a large, organized body of people was determined to break away from a state, there was little that could be done to prevent

---

[41] This view is often attributed to Gladstone. See Parish, "Gladstone and America."
[42] Owsley, *King Cotton Diplomacy*, p. 142.
[43] See N.M.R. and Sons to Belmont, 7 May, 9 July 1861, Rothschild Archive (hereafter RA), London.
[44] There is no evidence in the Rothschild Archive to support the myth that the bank lent money to the Confederacy. In fact, in only one instance did the firm broker (not to be confused with purchase) a sale of Confederate bonds. This brokerage was for only $6,000 worth of Confederate bonds and was made on behalf of Joseph Deynood on 30 September 1864. This sole instance pales in comparison to the hundreds of thousands of dollars worth of Union bonds that the bank brokered in the same period. See American Stock Books, RA.

it. "The forcible re-incorporation of the seceding states," *The Economist* declared soon after the war erupted, "is about as hopeless a scheme as it is unwise an aim."[45] If Southern independence was a *fait accompli*, then why not call for British mediation to put an end to the unnecessary bloodshed and disruption of transatlantic trade and finance? The Rothschilds, despite the lobbying of their American agent August Belmont to uphold the cause of the Union, used this line of reasoning as early as September 1861. "It has been the impression here for some time past," the bank argued,

> that the South would not submit to be forced to reenter the Union, but we are not without hope that the Federal Government will before long see the evil of prosecuting so destructive a war for an object so uncertain in its attainment as in the result, and that by foreign mediation or otherwise some arrangement may be effected.[46]

The significance of this response to the war was that humanitarianism became a motive for foreign intervention, rather than for support of the North. The moral issue of slavery did not enter the equation, as the Lincoln government had not yet pronounced emancipation as a war aim. Consequently, the Rothschilds could write with integrity that "we abhor slavery here more than we like cotton" and still call for British intervention.[47]

The Rothschilds' advocacy of British mediation in the American conflict was also a result of the views of their relations in Paris. Similar to the London house, the French Rothschilds were skeptical of the North's ability to restore the Union by force. The pro-Southern views of Salomon de Rothschild are partly to explain. A son of James de Rothschild (head of the Paris bank), Salomon visited the Southern states during the secession winter of 1860–1 where he was swept up in the romanticism of the Confederate cause. He wrote home to Paris that the tariff, not slavery, was at the heart of the dispute and that it was in the interest of humanity for the bank to recognize the independence of the Confederacy to help prevent pointless bloodshed.[48] Salomon's pro-Southern arguments portended the friendly overtures made by the Paris Rothschilds to the Confederacy in the war's first years. Collaborating with the French

---

[45] *The Economist*, 6 July 1861, p. 731.
[46] N.M.R. and Sons to Belmont and Co., 24 September 1861, RA.
[47] N.M.R. and Sons to Belmont and Co., 9 July 1861, RA.
[48] Salomon de Rothschild to N.M.R. and Sons (Paris), 28 April 1861 in Sigmund Diamond (ed.), *A Casual View of America: The Home Letters of Salomon de Rothschild, 1859–1861* (London, 1962).

consul in Richmond, the Rothschilds negotiated with Richmond officials to repossess commodities that the firm purchased before the war but, because of the blockade, were being held by the Confederate government.[49] Later, the firm met with Confederate emissary John Slidell in 1862 and gave orders for the purchase of 20,000 bales of cotton from the Richmond government.[50] Implicit in these dealings was the recognition of the Confederate government as the legitimate arbiter of economic dealings occurring within the Southern states and a disregard for the Union blockade. As the London house informed Belmont, "our Paris friends... are largely concerned in the South."[51]

Given these portents, it was not surprising that the London Rothschilds privately urged British leaders to intervene to end the conflict in America as early as August 1862. This timing was not by accident: Atlantic trade was depressed, the long-anticipated cotton famine appeared to be on the immediate horizon, and international instability resulting from the Civil War had forced the bank to suspend its profitable importation of bullion from America.[52] A string of Union defeats on the battlefield gave the bank the pretext in August to ask Belmont "whether the difficulties of the Federals will incline them towards peace on terms that would be likely to be successful."[53] Such terms, the Rothschilds recognized, might include the permanent separation of North and South. From an undisclosed source, the bankers also believed that an offer of mediation from Britain would be acceptable to the Union government.[54]

The Rothschilds were not alone in the financial community in supporting British intervention in the summer and autumn 1862. As early as June, *The Economist* argued that the time had arrived for the "friendly interposition" of the European powers.[55] Walter Bagehot, the publication's editor, had long believed that the forcible reunion of the United States was impossible and therefore the devastation the war caused, in both humanitarian and economic regards, was pointless. "Who can say,"

---

[49] Hubbard, *The Burden of Confederate Diplomacy*, pp. 154–5. Much to the Rothschilds' chagrin, the tobacco was not recovered until after the war.
[50] Slidell to Hunter, 26 September 1862, Richardson (ed.), *Messages and Papers of the Confederacy*, II, pp. 187–90.
[51] N.M.R. and Sons to Belmont and Co., 31 October 1862, RA.
[52] N.M.R. and Sons to August Belmont and Co., 29 November 1861 and 3 January 1862, RA.
[53] N.M.R. and Sons to Belmont and Co., 12 August 1862, RA.
[54] N.M.R. and Sons to Belmont and Co., 20 August 1862, RA.
[55] *The Economist*, 14 June 1862, p. 646. See also Michael Churchman, "Walter Bagehot and the American Civil War," *The Dublin Review*, 56 (1965), pp. 377–93.

Bagehot asked in a column in *The Economist*, "that the Confederates have not made good their claim to be considered as a people who have won their independence and are able to maintain it, and deserve to have it recognised?"[56]

This position, Bagehot contended, was not proslavery. An independent, slaveholding Confederacy would lack the power to expand its territory. If left alone in a limited area, the peculiar institution would prove to be economically unsustainable and would soon wither away. If anything, Bagehot argued, an independent South would strengthen Britain's relations with the United States as the two nations would cooperate to enforce the abolition of the slave trade and to confine the territorially ambitious Confederacy.[57] Regardless of what the future held, foreign mediation had nothing to do with slavery, as the Lincoln administration had still not proclaimed abolition as a war aim in the summer 1862. What mediation was about, *The Economist* made clear, was preventing the economic disaster that would result from the continued shortage of cotton and disruption in Atlantic trade. Bagehot argued that the war's adverse effects on the British economy gave Britain the right to intervene in the conflict. "We participate in the ruin that is going on," Bagehot opined, "we have, therefore, a right to speak and to be heard."[58] *The Economist* continued to call for British mediation and possible recognition of the Confederacy throughout the autumn 1862.[59]

Circumstantial evidence suggests that the advocacy of British intervention by the Rothschilds and *The Economist* was a factor that led the Palmerston cabinet to consider a more active American policy in the autumn 1862. Those in the cabinet who endorsed intervention, Foreign Secretary John Russell and Chancellor of the Exchequer William Gladstone, did not do so until September 1862 at the earliest.[60] Both were lobbied to intervene in the conflict by capitalists in the City. Lionel de Rothschild, who was an old ally and confidant of Russell's since the campaign for Jewish emancipation in the 1840s, pressed the Foreign Secretary to extend an offer of mediation to the warring states in America. It is possible that Russell used his connections with Lionel as a way to informally test the American reaction to British mediation in 1862. In the weeks preceding the cabinet's discussions on intervention, the Roths-

---

[56] *The Economist*, 20 September 1862, p. 1038.
[57] *The Economist*, 15 February 1862, p. 171.
[58] *The Economist*, 14 June 1862, p. 646.
[59] *The Economist*, 30 August, 20 September 1862.
[60] Jones, *Union in Peril*, pp. 159–61.

childs twice asked Belmont, who was in correspondence with Lincoln, to intimate to the President "that if he should be desirous of availing of the services of the European Powers for bringing about pacific arrangements, your friends would be happy to take charge of his message."[61] Likewise, Bagehot had promoted his views on the American war to Gladstone, going so far as to send the Chancellor a copy of an article he composed on the topic.[62] Whether all of this led Russell and Gladstone to support intervention is somewhat of a moot point. What is clear is that by September 1862 influential voices in both the City and in Westminster were calling for British action to end the war in America.

Contingent military and political events in the United States strengthened the argument for intervention. Lee's invasion of Maryland in September 1862 demonstrated the Confederacy's capacity to conduct an offensive war in Northern territory. Paradoxically, the subsequent Union victory at Antietam reinforced the humanitarian argument for intervention. British observers viewed the Union victory not as a decisive shift in the tide of the conflict, but rather as a Confederate setback that would only strengthen the North's resolve to continue to wage its futile war.[63] Moreover, Lincoln's pronouncement of the Emancipation Proclamation, though it would ultimately galvanize support for the Union in Europe, was initially viewed in Britain as a desperate call for a slave insurrection to weaken the Confederacy from within.[64] Convinced that the time was right for British mediation, Russell and Gladstone pressed for action in a series of memoranda and cabinet meetings in early October. This attempt did not materialize into the desired offer of mediation. Still believing that intervention was the appropriate course of action, Russell and Gladstone seized an offer for joint mediation extended by Napoleon in early November to reintroduce intervention in the American war to the cabinet.

As in October, the prointervention faction of the cabinet faced the opposition of Secretary for War Sir George Cornewall Lewis. Convinced that an offer of mediation was a recipe for disaster, Lewis argued against British diplomatic action in a memorandum distributed to the cabinet prior to its meeting. Although an offer of mediation might be extended

---

[61] N.M.R. and Sons to August Belmont and Co., 26 August 1862, RA.

[62] Bagehot to Gladstone, 30 September 1861, Gladstone Papers, Add. Mss. 44,397, British Library.

[63] Jones, *Union in Peril*, p. 8.

[64] Richard Heckman, "British Press Reaction to the Emancipation Proclamation," *Lincoln Herald*, 77 (Winter 1969), pp. 150–3. See also Jones, *Union in Peril*, pp. 159–61.

with good intentions, Lewis maintained, it would be destined for failure. The Secretary for War focused on the practical and logistical difficulties of mediation: Would the North agree to such an offer? What nations would arbitrate the dispute? What would prevent the arbitrating nations from descending into a conflict of their own in their attempts to protect their interests in the settlement? How could European statesmen, who were largely ignorant of American affairs, settle a dispute that the Americans themselves had not been able to resolve despite decades of attempted compromises? All of these considerations, Lewis maintained, were cogent reasons for Britain not to embroil herself in the war. Persuaded by Lewis's arguments, Palmerston and the majority of the cabinet rejected Napoleon's offer for joint mediation. The British cabinet would never again seriously consider a pro-Confederate policy.[65]

"Has it come to this?" the *Index* asked, "Is England, or the English Cabinet, afraid of the Northern States?"[66] The answer was, though few in Britain would openly admit it, yes. Having been bloodied in 1776 and again in 1812, British leaders were disinclined to provoke what they viewed as the unpredictable and wild diplomacy of the democratic masses in the United States by attempting to intervene in the Civil War. British intervention of any kind, it was feared, would lead to a war with the North where the colossal Union army would easily take Canada. Britons even feared that the North's new ironclad vessels would be formidable foes to their vastly superior, yet wooden, navy. Implicit in these worries of war was the concern that reckless diplomacy would ruin the prosperity of the Atlantic economy. Attempts to act as mediators between North and South could lose Britain her most important trading partner, devastate her merchant marine, and close one of the most profitable markets to British investors. The possible procurement of cotton—for it was far from a guarantee that a proposal of mediation would lead to the resumption of the cotton trade—was clearly not worth the risk of an Anglo-American war. The cotton shortage in Lancashire was simply the lesser of two economic evils. As the London *Times* argued, "it would be cheaper to keep all Lancashire on turtle and venison than to plunge into a desperate war with the Northern States of America."[67] Indeed, the Rothschilds

---

[65] Sir George Cornwall Lewis, "Recognition of the Independence of the Southern States of the North American Union," 7 November 1862, Gladstone Papers, Add. Mss. 44,595, Vol. 510, British Library. For more detail on Lewis and the argument against intervention, see Jones, *Union in Peril*, pp. 181–230.

[66] *Index*, 20 November 1862.

[67] Quoted in Fry, *Dixie Looks Abroad*, p. 82.

eventually reversed their position on intervention upon learning of the North's probable reaction from Belmont. "It is certain that any intervention on the part of England or France," Belmont informed the bank, "would only result in a protracted war with the United States...the injury done to British commerce and industry would be tenfold greater than the supply of cotton for two years to come."[68] British statesmen came to a similar conclusion. As Lewis stated in somewhat Shakespearean language, it was

> Better to endure the ills we have,
> Than fly to others which we know not of.[69]

Unaware of the secret meetings in Westminster, however, Confederate statesmen remained convinced that the cotton situation would force Britain to act on their behalf. Even after the London press reported that the Palmerston cabinet had declined Napoleon's offer for joint mediation, Mason informed Benjamin that "the cotton famine still continues to extend herself with apparently gigantic strides...which must lead to some change in the attitude of England."[70] Likewise, Slidell reassured Richmond that "France will act alone" if Britain refused to move.[71] But however confident the Confederate emissaries remained in the power of cotton to produce diplomatic results, they could no longer overlook the financial problems that were caused to a large extent by the cotton embargo. Even if the European powers were still considering intervention (which they were not), it was clear that no such move was likely to come in the immediate future. There was no way around it, the Confederacy needed to address its financial problems.

COTTON FINANCE AND THE ERLANGER LOAN

How to address these problems was another matter. Marketing the Confederate Treasury bonds in Britain that were offered domestically held little promise. Although Confederate bonds bore the high rate of

---

[68] Belmont to N.M.R. and Sons, 5 July 1862, RA.

[69] Lewis, "Recognition of the Independence of the Southern States of the North American Union," Gladstone Papers, Add. Mss. 44,595, Vol. 510. These words are a variation of those spoken by Hamlet in the "To be, or not to be" soliloquy in Act 3, scene I. See Jones, *Union in Peril*, p. 266.

[70] Mason to Benjamin, 11 December 1862, *ORN*, 2, 3, pp. 618–19. See also Hubbard, *The Burden of Confederate Diplomacy*, p. 137.

[71] Quoted in Owsley, *King Cotton Diplomacy*, p. 358.

eight percent, they did not lure British investors away from their government consols that yielded only three percent. Upon learning of the first Confederate bond issue of $15 million in the spring 1861, *The Times* maintained that "it has nothing to recommend it to European consideration."[72] *The Economist* agreed, informing its readers "that the South is poor; we know that its credit is worth nothing," before advising British investors to "lend at lower rates to old and recognised states."[73] The specter of the repudiation of three future Confederate states in the 1840s and the likely inability of the young nation to develop an adequate tax system to service its debt made British investors wary of Confederate securities.

Given the views of British capitalists, it is not surprising that early attempts to market Confederate Treasury bonds in Britain met with little success. The Confederate agent Major Ferguson took $1 million worth abroad in 1862 and a further $2 million were sent to Fraser, Trenholm in October 1862. Despite their high interest rate, no takers could be found and Mallory directed Bulloch to return the bonds to the Confederacy if they remained unsold. A similar fate met the $2 million in bonds brought across the Atlantic by Norman Walker in late 1862. Intended to back the purchasing operations of Caleb Huse, the bonds could not be sold and Huse had to wait for a shipment of cotton to bail him out of financial straits in February 1863. Matters were similar on the continent. Although Confederate Treasury bonds were officially listed on the Amsterdam Stock Exchange (a recognition that the Confederacy could never obtain, even with the Erlanger bonds, on the London Stock Exchange), the securities attracted little interest and were never quoted above half of their face value. This low demand was not surprising considering that Dutch investors rarely received interest payments on their bonds during the war—particularly after 1863 when all available resources went to pay coupons of the Erlanger cotton bonds, which Confederate statesmen hedged would bring their nation financial and political recognition. In all, several million dollars worth of Confederate Treasury bonds were sent to Europe, few of which were sold at prices above half of their face value.[74] The bonds that Confederate agents managed to dispose of ended

---

[72] *The Times*, 10 April 1861.
[73] *The Economist*, 24 August 1861, p. 927 and 9 August 1862, p. 869.
[74] The value of Confederate Treasury bonds sent to Europe is not known. Platt cites Baring records that claim there were $100 million in Britain by 1864. See Platt, *Foreign Finance on the Continent and in the United States*, p. 151. This is likely an exaggeration. Fenner (Gentry) contends that $14,050,000 in Confederate bonds were sent abroad during

up heavily depreciated and were hawked across the markets by speculators.[75]

British capitalists' lack of confidence in Confederate bonds, coupled with the failure of the cotton embargo to induce British recognition, led Southern statesmen to reconsider their strategy of withholding cotton from Europe. Without the nation's vast reserves of "white gold" to back its bond issues abroad, it was apparent that few investors were willing to take the risk of purchasing Confederate securities. As Mason and pro-Confederate MP William Lindsay asserted, "the present state of affairs do not admit of the ordinary mode of raising money on loan, and consequently cotton must be looked to as the representative of security." The shortage of cotton in Europe had dramatically increased the price of the commodity. Before the war, American cotton sold at $6\frac{1}{4}$ pence per pound in Liverpool; by 1862, the price had skyrocketed to $17\frac{1}{4}$ pence per pound, and two years later, it stood at an astonishing $27\frac{1}{2}$ pence per pound.[76]

Demanding such a high price abroad, there seemed to be little justification for continuing the unsuccessful cotton embargo when Confederate agents in Britain were desperate for funds. Though slow to realize that their valuable commodity could be used as collateral for a foreign loan, Confederate leaders, led by newly appointed Secretary of State Judah Benjamin, began to abandon their strategy of withholding cotton from Europe in 1862. Indeed, as early as January 1862, Benjamin attempted to arrange a $1 million loan, with cotton to serve as collateral, from Baring Brothers' New Orleans agent E. J. Forstall. A few months later, Benjamin attempted to use the precious commodity as a diplomatic ace up his sleeve when he instructed Slidell to offer both 100,000 bales of cotton at a low price and the prospect of a free trade agreement to the French government. Benjamin's hope was that Confederate–French commercial cooperation would be an initial step toward the recognition of the Confederacy and, more importantly, would lead Napoleon to deploy part of his fleet near the Southern coast to protect French commercial

the war. See Fenner, "Confederate Finances Abroad." John Slidell put the figure at a mere $6 million in early 1863. See Owsley, *King Cotton Diplomacy*, p. 368.

[75] This paragraph draws from Mallory to Bulloch, *ORN*, 2, 2, p. 339; Gorgas to Seddon, *ORA*, 3, 2, p. 227; Mason to Confederate States Commission, 5 February 1863, *ORN*, 2, 3, pp. 675–7; Ball, *Financial Failure and Confederate Defeat*, p. 75; Platt, *Foreign Finance on the Continent and in the United States*, p. 151. For an economic view, see Marc Weidenmier, "The Politics of Selective Default: The Foreign Debts of the Confederate States of America," Claremont Colleges Working Papers.

[76] Hall, "The Liverpool Cotton Market and the American Civil War," pp. 149–69.

interests. Although the French government and the pro-Union Barings predictably declined to enter into such machinations, Benjamin's offers marked a clear change in the South's financial and diplomatic thinking.[77]

This change was further evidenced in a series of cotton certificate schemes undertaken by Confederate agents in 1862. Confederate officials in Richmond authorized George Sanders to issue some $1.5 million in certificates (or warrants as they were often called) that were redeemable in cotton to finance the creation of an Anglo-Confederate mail line in July 1862. Setting a price for the cotton, however, proved to be a stumbling block and Mason soon directed Sanders back to Richmond to negotiate the specifics for future cotton warrant proposals. While Sanders embarked on the long transatlantic journey, the South's pressing financial needs forced Mason to endorse the plan of naval agent George Sinclair to issue £60,000 in cotton certificates, arranged by William Lindsay's financial firm, to underwrite the contract for a Confederate vessel under construction in Glasgow. The one unappealing provision to the certificates—a provision that would plague all Confederate cotton warrants and bonds during the war—was that they were redeemable only in the American South. The Confederacy could not guarantee cotton certificate holders cargo space on blockade-runners, such space being limited and generally already contracted out. British investors, consequently, would have to provide for the shipment of the cotton through the blockade on their own, a process that, though not impossible, was expensive and involved considerable risk. Despite this drawback, the "Sinclair bonds" were quickly taken up by a small group of British investors, many of whom expressed interest in future issues.[78]

The success of the Sinclair scheme illustrated the potential for cotton-backed warrants and bonds to provide Confederate agents with the funds they required in Britain. As Mason put it, "Cotton, as the property of the government, will always be in Europe a sure basis of credit, so sure as to

---

[77] Memo of meeting between Mason, Lindsay, and Huggins, *ORN*, 2, 3, p. 595; Benjamin to Forstall, 17 January 1862, *ORA*, 4, 1, pp. 845–6; Hubbard, *The Burden of Confederate Diplomacy*, pp. 87–101; Owsley, *King Cotton Diplomacy*, pp. 303–4.

[78] Mason to Benjamin, 18 September 1862, *ORN*, 2, 3, pp. 529–32; Dept. of State to Benjamin, 28 October 1862, *ORN*, 2, 3, pp. 579–80; Mason to Confederate States Commission, 5 February 1863, *ORN*, 2, 3, pp. 675–7; Memminger to Mason, 24 October 1862, Mason Papers, LC; Adams, *Great Britain and the American Civil War*, II, pp. 156–7; Hubbard, *The Burden of Confederate Diplomacy*, pp. 126–7; Thompson, *Confederate Purchasing Operations Abroad*, pp. 52–4; Owsley, *King Cotton Diplomacy*, pp. 363–5; Wise, *Lifeline of the Confederacy*, p. 95; Spencer, *The Confederate Navy in Europe*, pp. 89–91; Lester, *Confederate Finance and Purchasing in Great Britain*, pp. 18–21. For a preserved cotton warrant, see vol. 3, Mason Papers, LC.

engage money on better terms than any other form of credit."[79] By the end of October 1862, the new method of raising funds in Europe through the sale of cotton certificates received the endorsement of Secretary of the Treasury Christopher Memminger.[80] With the new financial strategy quickly coming into being, it was clear that the Confederate government needed to take steps to organize and coordinate the marketing of the various bonds and cotton certificates in Britain. By February 1863, Slidell estimated that $6 million in Treasury bonds and $3 million in cotton certificates were held or being offered abroad.[81] Matters were further complicated when the Navy Department dispatched another purchasing agent, Matthew Maury, in December 1862 with the authority to issue cotton certificates to finance his operations.[82] As Bulloch recognized, "sending bonds to different parties did not work satisfactorily.... [Confederate agents] became practically competitors one with the other."[83]

The burden of managing this cacophonous fundraising system fell on the shoulders of the Englishman James Spence. Author of the widely circulated pro-South pamphlet *The American Union* and of numerous letters defending the rebellion in the London *Times*, Spence was the Confederacy's staunchest ally abroad and was at the center of nearly every pro-Confederate organization in Britain. Leaders in Richmond, therefore, did not hesitate to enlist Spence's services when he offered to help manage the Confederacy's finances in Britain in the summer 1862. Spence was soon managing the various cotton certificates and Confederate Treasury bonds that Southern leaders attempted to place in British markets. The array of certificates and bonds that Confederate officials directed Spence to market certainly did not make his job easy. Nor did Memminger's desire for him to first sell the Treasury bonds (not backed by cotton) that had been shipped to Britain in the preceding months. The Treasury was so desperate to rid itself of the bonds that Spence was instructed to sell up to $5 million worth, "even at 50 cents" on the dollar. Predictably, Spence found no takers for the Confederacy's junk bonds. Cotton certificates held more promise, but Spence was discouraged from arranging any new sales in December 1862 when Mason informed him

---

[79] Mason to Benjamin, 5 February 1863, *ORN*, 2, 3, p. 675–7.
[80] Memminger to Mallory, 30 October 1862, *ORN*, 2, 2, p. 287.
[81] Owsley, *King Cotton Diplomacy*, p. 368.
[82] Maury to Bob, 21 April 1863, Mathew Maury Papers, Library of Congress. See also Mason to Benjamin, 10 December 1862, *ORN*, 2, 3, p. 617–8.
[83] Bulloch, *The Secret Service of the Confederate States in Europe*, I, p. 222.

that negotiations were underway to arrange a large loan backed by cotton.[84]

It was through this new cotton loan that Confederate statesmen hoped that King Cotton would finally be employed to their advantage. Although the appointment of Spence as financial agent was a necessary step toward organizing the Confederacy's chaotic finances abroad, matters would be simplified by brokering one large, cotton-backed loan rather than marketing multiple issues of cotton certificates that competed against one another and Treasury bonds that failed to attract even the wildest speculators. Furthermore, a proper national loan, if successfully marketed and managed, offered the political advantage of legitimizing the South's independence. If Westminster refused to recognize the Confederacy, perhaps the City, through subscribing to such a loan, would.

Although the idea of a foreign loan appealed to nearly every Confederate statesman, the amount of such a loan and the bank through which it should be arranged was the source of much controversy in the winter 1862–3. Mason supported plans to issue warrants, convertible into cotton at the fixed price of four pence per pound, through the British firm of William Lindsay and Co. The bank was a known entity, having brokered the Sinclair bonds the previous autumn, and Lindsay's willingness to support the South in Parliament was an additional attraction. So eager was Lindsay to assist the Confederacy (and to profit from its struggle) that he offered his services to Mason, suggesting that cotton warrants be issued in several small installments of £100,000 to £200,000 so as not to flood the market. When the certificates had been successfully placed, Lindsay argued, the Confederacy would finally establish itself in the eyes of European capitalists and "the Government would have the advantage of whatever premium they might attain in its subsequent issues."[85]

While Mason and Lindsay were fine-tuning their proposal, John Slidell was busy arranging a much larger loan through the Paris house of Emile Erlanger and Co. Like Lindsay, Erlanger had offered his services unsolicited to the Confederacy. Unlike Lindsay who proposed to offer small amounts of cotton certificates, however, Erlanger wanted to

---

[84] Mason to Confederate States Commission, 5 February 1863, *ORN*, 2, 3, pp. 675–7; Spence to Mason, 28 April 1862, *ORN*, 2, 3, pp. 402–5; Mallory to Bulloch, 20 September 1862, *ORN*, 2, 2, pp. 269–71; Memminger to Mason, 24 October 1862, Mason Papers, LC; Spence to Mason, 21 December 1862, Mason Papers, LC; Blackett, *Divided Hearts*, p. 140; Frank Hughes, "Liverpool and the Confederate States," M.Phil. dissertation, Keele University, 1998, pp. 112–13.

[85] Mason to Benjamin, 4 November 1862, *ORN*, 2, 3, pp. 593–6.

issue £5 million in bonds across Europe that could be, but did not have to be, redeemed in cotton at a fixed price. In contrast to Lindsay's cotton certificates, these cotton bonds would bear eight percent interest per annum until they were exchanged for cotton. Erlanger and his Southern allies argued that this arrangement, far more typical of nineteenth-century government loans, would extend political credibility to the Confederacy.[86] Slidell was quickly sold on the proposal, emphasizing in a letter to Richmond the political advantages that would result from "one of the most extensive and responsible houses in Europe" siding with the Southern cause. Erlanger, Slidell believed, was a trusted confidant of Napoleon himself and a loan arranged through his house would be a political, as well as a financial, coup.[87] Though a respectable bank, the Erlangers were far from the leaders of finance in the 1860s, trailing firms such as the Rothschilds, Barings, Hottinguers, and Hope and Co. in terms of both financial might and political pull. Indeed, it has been suggested by more than one historian that Slidell's personal ties with Erlanger, who would marry Slidell's daughter a year after the loan was arranged, influenced his views of the bank.[88]

Beneath Slidell's zeal for Erlanger was a loan proposal that nearly every Confederate statesman believed was too harsh to accept. Erlanger would profit immensely from a contract that gave him all proceeds above 70 percent of the bonds' face value in addition to a 5 percent commission and a 1 percent fee for handling the sinking fund (a mechanism that annually retired 1/40 of the bonds).[89] All of these figures meant that even if the loan was placed at par—a very unlikely prospect for the bonds of an unrecognized, partially occupied confederation fighting off a colossal invading army—the Confederacy would net only £3,300,000 out of the £5,000,000.[90] The "volunteer bankers of the Confederacy," Mason wrote, "had driven a hard bargain."[91] Given these onerous terms, it is not surprising that Confederate officials rejected the loan proposal when three of Erlanger's agents arrived in Richmond in late 1862. However,

---

[86] See A. Collie to Fraser, Trenholm and Co., 11 December 1862, Fraser, Trenholm Papers, Library of Congress [microfilm]; *Bankers' Magazine*, May 1863, p. 394.

[87] Slidell to Benjamin, 1 December 1862, Richardson (ed.), *Messages and Papers of the Confederacy*, II, pp. 339–41.

[88] Owsley, *King Cotton Diplomacy*, p. 165; Hubbard, *The Burden of Confederate Diplomacy*, p. 132; Ball, *Financial Failure and Confederate Defeat*, p. 76.

[89] Slidell, Huse, and Erlanger to Mason, 28 October 1862, *ORN*, 2, 3, pp. 568–72.

[90] See Owsley, *King Cotton Diplomacy*, p. 370.

[91] Quoted in Thompson, *Confederate Purchasing Operations Abroad*, p. 50.

after Erlanger revised the contract, the Confederate cabinet and congress extended its approval to the scheme in late January 1863.

The final terms of the contract were an improvement on the loan's initial provisions. The amount of the loan was reduced to £3 million (from £5 million), the Confederacy was granted the first 77 percent of the issue (rather than the first 70 percent) and the bonds were to bear seven (rather than eight) percent interest. Convertibility into cotton was set at six pence per pound. Despite these modest improvements, many leading Confederate statesmen still questioned the Erlanger loan. Mason and Spence opposed the scheme, confident that, though smaller, the Lindsay offer would eventually bring in the required revenue while avoiding the exorbitant commission guaranteed to Erlanger. Charles Prioleau was convinced that Erlanger sought to supplant Fraser, Trenholm as the Confederacy's financial agency in Europe in order to profit from the naiveté of inexperienced Confederate representatives. "This man Erlanger is a dangerous one," the Liverpool banker asserted, "I judge him to be ambitious, selfish, daring and unscrupulous.... It is apparent to me that he desires to become a general agent of the government and keep them always in debt to him and to secure for himself the profit of future loans for which his appetite has been whetted."[92] That Erlanger was more concerned with his profits than with assisting the South is now apparent. New evidence reveals that even as he brokered a loan for the Confederacy, Erlanger purchased Union bonds in Frankfurt, which he accurately identified as a safer long-term investment.[93]

Given the opposition to Erlanger's offer, it is perhaps surprising that Confederate leaders agreed to enter into the scheme. However, it should not be forgotten how desperate the Confederacy was for funds in 1862–3. The British firms that had entered into contracts with Southern purchasers were pressing for remittance and, in some instances, threatening legal action. Naval agents James Bulloch and James North defaulted on payments and were left to fend for themselves.[94] In light of the dire state of Confederate finances abroad, the terms of the Erlanger loan, which guaranteed funds in advance, did not seem quite so severe.[95] The Lindsay proposal would not have provided immediate cash and, as Slidell pointed

---

[92] Quoted in Hughes, "Liverpool and the Confederacy," p. 256.
[93] For Erlanger and Union bonds, see Murphy to Seward, 20 January 1863, RG 59, Main 161, National Archives.
[94] Bulloch to North, 17 March 1863, *ORN*, 2, 2, p. 375.
[95] Spence to Mason, 13 March 1863, Mason Papers, LC.

out, actually offered cotton at a lower price than did the Erlanger plan (four pence per pound as opposed to six pence per pound).

At the heart of the Confederate decision to enter into the Erlanger loan, however, was the belief that the successful flotation of a national loan would demonstrate the confidence of European capitalists in the South's cause and would prompt Britain and France to reconsider their decision not to recognize the Confederacy. As Benjamin informed Slidell, only after the "political advantages likely to be derived from the loan" had been considered did the cabinet decide to accept Erlanger's proposal.[96] What the cotton embargo failed to provide, Southerners hoped, the Erlanger loan would deliver. The Erlanger loan, therefore, was as much of a political and diplomatic operation as it was a financial one.

It certainly appeared that this gamble would pay off when the loan was first issued to the public on 19 March 1863. Offered at ninety percent of their face value, the bonds were made available in Amsterdam, Frankfurt, and Paris through Erlanger's agencies, in Liverpool through Fraser, Trenholm, and in London through Erlanger's associates, J. H. Schröder and Co. Aided by an aggressive advertising campaign in Europe's leading journals (including the London *Times*), the initial interest in the cotton bonds surprised even the most optimistic Confederates. By the end of the day, the bonds were selling at a premium of four and one-half percent, having been oversubscribed by a factor of five.[97] Slidell boasted that the success of the loan constituted the "financial recognition of our independence," while Mason confidently concluded that "cotton is king at last."[98] Even *The Economist*, a publication that generally opposed Confederate financial schemes, found it "startling that the Confederates should be able to borrow money in Europe while the Federal Government has been unable to obtain a shilling from that usually liberal and enterprising quarter."[99]

This optimism, however, soon proved to be premature. Despite the loan's promising beginning, it was destined for failure so long as the war continued. As *The Economist* put it, there were several "gambling elements" to the loan that frightened off long-term investors.[100] First among these was the fine print at the bottom of the placards advertizing the loan

---

[96] Benjamin to Slidell, 15 January 1863, Richardson (ed.), *Messages and Papers of the Confederacy*, II, pp. 405–8.
[97] Mason to Benjamin, 30 March 1863, *ORN*, 2, 3, pp. 730–1.
[98] Slidell to Benjamin, 21 March 1863, *ORN*, 2, 3, pp. 718–20; Mason to Benjamin, 30 March 1863, *ORN*, 2, 3, pp. 730–1; Owsley, *King Cotton Diplomacy*, p. 376
[99] *The Economist*, 21 March 1863, p. 309.
[100] Ibid.

that informed bondholders that, like the Sinclair certificates of 1862, the bonds were redeemable in cotton only within the Confederacy. To make matters worse, the cotton would not be made available at a port on the Atlantic coast but was only guaranteed to be delivered within ten miles of a railroad station or a navigable river somewhere within the Confederacy! In order to exchange an Erlanger bond for cotton, a British investor would have to run the blockade to get to the Confederacy, provide for the transport of the cotton from the nation's interior to a port, and, finally, break the blockade a second time to sell the cotton in Liverpool.

Erlanger and Schröder attempted to remove this barrier to investment in the cotton bonds by establishing the European Trading Company, a blockade-running line for Erlanger bondholders. The company's main vessel, the *Denbigh*, was a success, completing 73 round trips (Mobile to Havana) before running aground in May 1865.[101] Plans of other bondholders to construct blockade-running steamers, however, were less fruitful and were abandoned after being deemed "financially unsound."[102] Even if the potential profits of selling the cotton at a high price in Liverpool would cover the shipping and insuring costs required to obtain it, as one historian has argued, there is little question that this aspect of the loan was a significant disincentive to potential investors in Confederate bonds.[103]

The difficulties in exchanging the bonds for cotton were compounded by developments in the war when the loan was issued in 1863. Although a Union victory was far from inevitable at this point, it was by then clear that the blockade was tightening and that Northern forces were engulfing Southern ports. So desperate was the Confederacy to prevent its resources from being used by its enemies that retreating Southern armies burned reserves of cotton rather than allow them to be seized by Union forces. This tactic did little to impart confidence to investors hoping to redeem their bonds in cotton. "The order of Mr. Memminger, directing the burning of cotton in imminent danger of capture produced an anxious flutter" on cotton bond quotations, Henry Hotze informed Benjamin.[104] Finally, it should not be forgotten that by the time the Erlanger bonds

---

[101] Richard Roberts, *Schröders: Merchants and Bankers* (Basingstoke, 1992), p. 68. See also McRae to Memminger, 2 October 1863, *ORA*, 4, 2, pp. 980–1.

[102] *The Economist*, 7 May 1864, p. 577.

[103] For the view that the value of cotton in Liverpool compensated for the risk involved in redeeming a cotton bond in the South, see Ball, *Financial Failure and Confederate Defeat*, p. 77.

[104] Hotze to Benjamin, 27 August 1863, *ORN*, 2, 3, pp. 875–81.

were offered, Lincoln had issued the Emancipation Proclamation and the war took on the dimension of antislavery versus defenders of slavery. Few capitalists in traditionally antislavery Britain, who had historically avoided the bonds of slave states before the war, were eager to side with the slaveholding Confederacy.

That all of these factors would lead to the failure of the cotton bonds, however, was not apparent, at least on the surface, after the loan's successful first day. However, had Confederate agents and their bankers in Britain possessed more experience, they might have realized that the loan's promising beginning was far from a financial recognition of the South's independence (Schröder and Co. and Fraser, Trenholm had never before issued bonds on behalf of a government).[105] For starters, it was standard for a new government loan to be oversubscribed on its first day. An investor wanting ten bonds would often subscribe for thirty to ensure he would acquire the amount desired.[106] Moreover, it appears that Confederate agents overlooked exactly who was buying the bonds. In the Rothschilds' estimation, the loan was "of so speculative a nature that it was very likely to attract all wild speculators."[107] Erlanger bondholders were clearly interested in the Confederate loan only as a speculation in cotton, not because they sought to politically assist the Confederacy or because they thought the loan a good long-term investment.

The character of Erlanger bondholders soon became an issue when the bonds fell to 86 (four below the issue price) in the first week of April. If the loan continued to decline, Confederate statesmen worried, the entire operation could collapse if capricious investors opted to forfeit their down payment on the bonds (the 15 percent paid up front) rather than meet the next installment that was due in a few weeks. "This aspect of the new loan demands earnest consideration," James Spence anxiously wrote to Mason, "If it breaks down it will not only do the utmost political injury but will be disastrous in the effect on any other mode of raising money."[108] Drastic action, it appeared, was required to salvage the entire scheme.

What exactly to do, however, was another question. In an emergency meeting of Confederate agents and bankers, the potential courses of action were vigorously debated. Spence was convinced that the bonds

---

[105] Roberts, *Schröders*, p. 66.
[106] Judith Gentry, "A Confederate Success in Europe: The Erlanger Loan," *Journal of Southern History*, 36 (May 1970), pp. 157–88.
[107] N.M.R. and Sons to August Belmont and Co., 24 March 1863, RA.
[108] Spence to Mason, 4 April 1863, Mason Papers, LC.

had been quoted too high when they were issued and recommended withdrawing a third of the bonds from the market until investor confidence was restored and demand increased.[109] Erlanger argued that the sag in the bonds was a result of the activities of Union agents who he alleged were spreading false rumors about the loan in order to "bear" the market. Confronted with such opposition, Erlanger held, Confederate agents must take matters into their own hands and "bull" the market by repurchasing the sagging bonds in order to drive prices back up. Erlanger's argument won the day, and between 7 and 24 April, Confederate agents bought back £1,517,000—more than half of the issue—of the bonds they had just sold.[110]

Whether the repurchasing of Erlanger bonds was an appropriate decision has been the subject of much controversy. Historians traditionally argued that the effort was unnecessary and precipitate, given that the bonds had only slipped to 86. Furthermore, it is not clear why Confederate statesmen were so afraid that bondholders would default on their impending payment. Erlanger's interest in keeping the bonds' price as high as possible (it should be recalled that the French banker was guaranteed all above 77), it has been alleged, explains why he pressed Confederate agents to bull the market. Unsuspecting Confederate agents, the argument goes, foolishly accepted the banker's advice and unknowingly increased his immense profits.[111] It has even been alleged that Erlanger himself was a large holder of the bonds and that he engineered the whole repurchasing scheme merely to dump his bonds on the Confederacy at a high price (all the while, earning his commission).[112]

More recent historians have been kinder to Erlanger and the management of the loan. Judith Gentry contends that the buyback scheme was a necessary move that saved the loan. The effort to bull the market, she points out, raised the bonds above the issue price (from 86 to $91\frac{1}{2}$) and ensured that wary capitalists did not abandon their investment. The money spent on "bulling" the market was not entirely wasted as many of the repurchased bonds were used as currency in future purchasing

---

[109] Spence to Mason, 9 May 1863, Mason Papers, LC.

[110] For this meeting, see "Memorandum of meeting at Erlanger & Co.," 4 June 1863; Mason to Erlanger and Co., 24 April 1863, RG 365, Entry 323, National Archives (hereafter NA).

[111] For this view, see Lester, *Confederate Finance and Purchasing in Great Britain*, pp. 38–47; Owsley, *King Cotton Diplomacy*, pp. 403–4; Todd, *Confederate Finance*, pp. 183–4; and Thompson, *Confederate Purchasing Operations Abroad*, pp. 64–5.

[112] John C. Schwab, *The Confederate States of America* (New York, 1901), p. 35. See also McRae to Erlanger, 13 June 1863, RG 365, Entry 319, NA.

operations. In all, Gentry calculates that the Confederacy realized £1,759,894 from the Erlanger loan, a much larger figure than those of previous scholars. Given the dismal state of Confederate finances at the time, Gentry argues, the Erlanger episode was a "success."[113]

Although it is important to acknowledge that the options available to Confederate policy-makers were severely limited, it is a stretch to label the operation a "success." The mismanagement of the loan and its depreciating bonds discouraged future investment in Confederate securities and contributed to the South's long-term financial troubles abroad. The decision to have the Confederate government enter the market to firm up the sagging bonds, as one Southern agent maintained, was "in direct contravention of the stipulations of the contract, and defeats the purposes for which the Loan was contracted."[114] Nor did the buy-back scheme yield lasting results. Following the decisive Union victories at Gettysburg and Vicksburg in the summer 1863, the Confederate bonds began to steadily depreciate once again.[115] From then on, interest in the bonds was confined to venture capitalists and cotton brokers willing to take on a risky investment. Charles Prioleau conceded as early as May 1863 that "the Confederate Cotton Loan is I regret to say, so far, a failure as a source of revenue" while Bulloch maintained in his memoirs that the supply of funds realized from the loan was "never very large."[116] Erlanger funds only temporarily relieved the pressure on Confederate purchasing agents. It was not long, as we shall see, before proceeds from the loan were exhausted and the desperate Confederacy was forced, yet again, to find new means of raising funds in Europe. But with Erlanger bonds plummeting on European stock exchanges, it would be even more difficult to persuade European capitalists to loan money to the Confederacy.

In political terms as well, there can be little question that the Erlanger loan was a dismal failure. Intended to demonstrate European capitalists'

---

[113] Gentry, "A Confederate Success in Europe: The Erlanger Loan," pp. 157–88. For lower estimates of the proceeds realized from the Erlanger loan, see Owsley, *King Cotton Diplomacy*, pp. 380–2; Todd, *Confederate Finance*, p. 184; Thompson, *Confederate Purchasing Operations Abroad*, p. 64; and, Schwab, *The Confederate States*, p. 42.

[114] McRae to Erlanger, 13 June 1863, RG 365, Entry 319, NA.

[115] For the view that the Confederate defeats at Gettysburg and Vicksburg constituted a "turning point" in cotton bond quotations, see William Brown and Richard Burdekan, "Turning Points in the U.S. Civil War: A British Perspective," *Journal of Economic History*, 60 (March 2000), pp. 216–31.

[116] Prioleau quoted in Hughes, "Liverpool and the Confederate States," p. 252; Bulloch, *The Secret Service of the Confederate States in Europe*, II, p. 418. See also Mallory to Bulloch, 29 August 1863, *ORN*, 2, 2, p. 484.

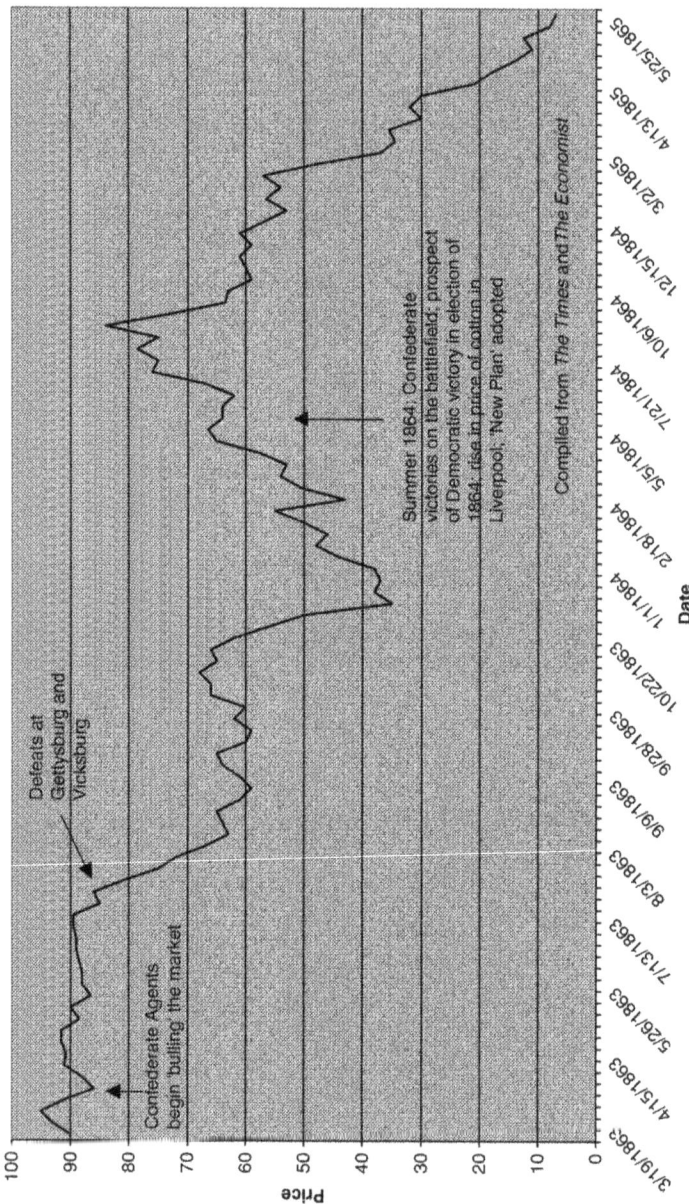

Figure 5   Confederate Erlanger Bonds in London, 1863–1865

confidence in the Confederate Government, the depreciating bonds soon became a yardstick used by Union diplomats to measure declining confidence in the Confederacy abroad. "We may at length conclude," Henry Adams wrote to his brother when the Erlanger bonds fell to forty in December 1863, "that the opinion among capitalists is fairly become that the chances are against the independence of the rebels."[117] The ruling elite in Europe, who were allegedly close confidants of Erlanger, showed no signs of being impressed by the scheme. In retrospect, there can be little doubt that the Confederacy should have gone with the Lindsay proposal rather than that of Erlanger. Not only would a smaller initial offering of cotton certificates have met with greater success on the financial markets, but Lindsay's status and influence as an MP would have also extended more political credibility to the Confederacy. Decisions taken in London, not Paris, determined European policy towards the American conflict.

The political failing of the Erlanger scheme was also evinced in the loan's bondholders. Leaders in Richmond predicted that politically and financially influential persons would buy into the cotton loan and demonstrate widespread support for the Confederacy to the British Government. Although British investors took up most of the £3 million loan, the London Rothschilds "did not hear of any respectable people having anything to do with it.... We ourselves have been quite neutral and have had nothing to do with it."[118] Historians have erred in accepting a list of Erlanger bondholders propagated by John Bigelow, the U.S. consul in Paris.[119] Bigelow clearly intended to slander those who had sympathized with the South during the war when he circulated a specious list of

---

[117] Henry Adams to Charles Francis Adams, Jr., 11 December 1863, in Worthington Chauncey Ford (ed.), *A Cycle of Adams letters, 1861–1865* (London, 1921), II, p. 109. See also Benjamin Moran, *The Journal of Benjamin Moran, 1857–1865*, 2 vols. (Chicago, 1948–9), II, pp. 1137, 1142, 1195, 1249, 1301.

[118] N.M.R. and Sons to August Belmont and Co., 24 March 1863, RA.

[119] Lester, *Confederate Finance and Purchasing in Great Britain*, p. 209, lists principle holders of the Erlanger loan. He offers no evidence, however, to validate the names on the list. Lester cites John Bigelow, *Lest We Forget: Gladstone, Morley and the Confederate Cotton Loan of 1863* (New York, 1905). See also *The Morning Star*, 5 October 1865. A similar list can be found in the *New York Times*, 9 December 1865. This list is also unreliable. In it William Gladstone is presumed to be a cotton bondholder because a W. R. Gladstone is listed and since "no such person known; must be Rt. Hon. W.E. Gladstone." The *NYT* editors even question some of the names on the list (some of which are misspelled). Another purported list of Erlanger bondholders in Britain is, in fact, a roll call of the Southern Independence Association. See Court of Commissioners of Alabama Claims, *A Partial List of the Southern Bond-Holders in Great Britain during the War of the Rebellion* (Washington, D.C., 1885).

cotton bondholders in 1905 that included William Gladstone, John Delane (editor of the *Times*), Evelyn Ashley (secretary to Lord Palmerston), and J. S. Gilliat (a director of the Bank of England). Gladstone, Delane, and Ashley publicly denied the accusation, convincing even the skeptical Charles Francis Adams that they had nothing to do with the bonds.[120] J. S. Gilliat was almost certainly confused with J. K. Gilliat, head of a London firm that accepted £250,000 in Erlanger bonds for repayment of a Confederate debt.[121] Indeed, it appears that a significant portion of the bonds wound up in the hands of the Confederacy's prior creditors as debt repayment. Isaac, Campbell and Co. was likewise given £150,000 in bonds to settle a Confederate debt.[122] Other bondholders were merchants and cotton brokers, most often in Liverpool (such as the Southern expatriate H. O. Brewer who held $50,000 in Erlanger bonds), who purchased the bonds as a speculation in cotton or, in the words of a Union diplomat, "principally as a means of giving shape and a seeming security against claims to the Confederates already existing or contracted for."[123]

Whoever the bondholders were—and it is unlikely it will ever be completely known—it is clear that they did not constitute the powerful pro-Confederate lobby that statesmen in Richmond had predicted. Far from being outspoken proponents of the Confederacy, Erlanger bondholders were notoriously secretive of their identity, due, no doubt, to their indirect connection with slavery. As a frustrated William Seward noted, "It is regretted that the holders of this loan are so uncommunicative in regard to their names and their social and political position.... the information so carefully withheld might be useful in enlightening us as to the real state of British opinion in regard to our international affairs."[124]

Most of the Confederate bondholders in Europe remained anonymous after the war, preferring to accept their losses rather than to fight for repayment either from a Confederate government that no longer existed

---

[120] *The Morning Star*, 5 October 1865. For Gladstone, see Mathew (ed.), *The Gladstone Diaries*, vol. 6, 4 October 1865, p. 388; and *The Times*, 6 October 1865. See also Adams to Seward, 5 October 1865, *Foreign Relations of the United States* (hereafter *FRUS*) (Washington, D.C., 1861–5). Adams wrote, "Mr. Gladstone and Mr. Evelyn Ashley disavow all association with it very properly. I presume the insertion of their names must have been a mistake."

[121] Owsley, *King Cotton Diplomacy*, p. 382.

[122] McRae to Memminger, 9 July 1863, RG 365, Entry 319, NA.

[123] Dayton to Seward, 27 March 1863, *FRUS*. For Brewer and some names of other Erlanger bondholders, see RG 365, Entry 323, "Records Relating to the Erlanger Loan," NA.

[124] Seward to Adams, 4 November 1865, *FRUS*, 1865, 1, pp. 628–9.

or from its vanquisher in Washington. "Having re-established their authority over the Southern States by the sacrifice of several hundreds of thousands of lives and several thousands of millions of dollars," one British financier wrote after the war, "it could hardly be expected that the United States would agree to repay to aliens the loans they subscribed to support these violations of United States jurisdiction."[125] Nonetheless, a group of Confederate bondholders in Britain,[126] assisted by the American financier in London James McHenry, drafted a plan in 1866 to recover their lost investments. Recognizing that the federal assumption of Confederate debts was not likely to occur, the bondholders offered their services to the U.S. Treasury in brokering a £20 million loan earmarked for the reconstruction of the Southern states—a proposal that must have appealed to some Republican leaders who were frustrated at the lack of investment in the South after the war. The catch to this otherwise attractive proposal was that Erlanger bondholders would get to subscribe to the loan at discounts of up to fifty percent. McHenry thought that this was a fair price for the government to pay to restore the "public credit of the Southern states." Seward and Secretary of the Treasury Hugh McCulloch thought otherwise, agreeing that the scheme did not "deserve consideration on the part of the government of the United States."[127]

Having failed to recover their holdings through legitimate means, several Erlanger bondholders resorted to chicanery on the money markets to salvage what they could of their investments. Bondholders spread rumors on the London Stock Exchange that as part of the resolution of the *Alabama* claims the United States would assume Confederate debts in Britain. Confederate cotton bonds were then dumped on gullible investors at inflated prices.[128] It is puzzling that anyone would have fallen for this ploy as U.S. diplomats had long made it clear that Confederate debts would be repudiated, and *The Economist* warned investors "not to allow themselves to be misled into buying the bonds at their present price under the impression that there is even so much as the faintest chance of their ever being redeemed."[129] Moreover, section four of the Fourteenth Amendment (passed by Congress in 1866 and ratified by the states two

---

[125] J. Barr Robertson, *The Confederate Debt and Private Southern Debts* (London, 1884), p. 13.
[126] These British cotton bondholders were Sir Provo Wallis, E. Morgan, Francis Phillips, C. M. T. Weston, W. M. Morgan, and F. Harvey.
[127] Ex. Doc. No. 95, 39th Congress, 1st Session, pp. 1–6; McCulloch to Johnson, 10 April 1866, McCulloch Papers, Library of Congress.
[128] *The Investor's Monthly Manual* (report in *The Economist*), 30 January 1869, p. 26.
[129] *The Economist*, 23 April 1870, p. 513.

years later) explicitly declared all Confederate debts "illegal and void." As Erlanger's grandson would later state, Confederate bonds were then "good only for papering walls."[130] Hopefully, Erlanger and other holders of Confederate bonds did not plaster their homes with cotton bonds as, now that the Confederacy has been dead for a century and a half, Erlanger bonds are quoted at $2,000 on exchanges at Civil War memorabilia stores.[131]

THE "NEW PLAN" AND LAST EFFORTS

Bad news seemed to come in bunches for the Confederacy. While the Erlanger loan began its ignominious decline, Confederate naval purchasing was dealt a decisive blow by the British Government. Like the cotton bond scheme, this failure seemed to follow what was thought would be certain success. Following the release of the *Florida* and the *Alabama* in 1862, Confederate agents contracted for the construction of several more vessels in British shipyards. Aided by proceeds from the sale of cotton certificates and Erlanger bonds, a small fleet was nearing completion in 1863. Matthew Maury purchased the *Rappahannock* from the British navy (which was unaware that he was a Confederate agent) and oversaw the construction of the *Georgia* in Dumbarton. James North contracted for a large warship, the so-called "Scottish Sea Monster," with a firm in Glasgow. As a gift to the Confederacy, Fraser, Trenholm financed the construction of the *Alexandra*, a small gunboat built by William Miller and Sons in Liverpool. At the center of this nascent navy were two rams constructed by the Laird brothers in Liverpool, the builders of the *Alabama*. Heavily armed iron-clad warships that boasted a ram beneath the bow designed for piercing the wooden ships that blockaded the Southern coast, the "Laird rams" were to be the flagships of the new Confederate fleet that optimistic Southerners hoped would change the course of the war by the year's end.

Whether these vessels could have influenced the outcome of the war was a question forever left to Civil War buffs when the Palmerston ministry tightened its interpretation of the Foreign Enlistment Act and detained vessels being constructed for the Confederacy in Britain in the summer and autumn 1863. Bulloch's ingenious subterfuge of arming

---

[130] Quoted in Roberts, *Schröders*, p. 69.
[131] Boaz, *Guns for Cotton*, pp. 70–3.

Confederate warships outside of British waters no longer provided British statesmen, who were under tremendous pressure from Union diplomats, with an excuse to turn a blind eye to Southern activities. Of the vessels under construction for the Confederacy in 1863, only the *Georgia* saw action under the rebel flag. The others were either detained by British authorities or sold to other nations once Confederate agents realized that they would not be allowed to leave British ports (this explains why North's "Scottish Sea Monster" ended up in the Danish navy in 1864). A bitter Bulloch would later write that "the neutrality of England was practiced in a way to give great advantages to the United States."[132]

Thus, the year that began with Confederate hopes of British intervention ended in complete disaster by the autumn 1863. Naval agents packed their bags to head to France as it became clear that they were no longer welcome in Britain. On the financial front, the funds provided by the Erlanger loan and from the sale of various cotton certificates were quickly exhausted and Confederate agents were again begging for credit in their dispatches. Diplomatically, the Confederacy was further away from British recognition than it had ever been in its brief existence. A Parliamentary motion calling for the recognition of the Confederacy engineered by Lindsay and fellow MP John Roebuck was ignominiously withdrawn in July 1863. To add insult to injury, Russell refused to officially receive Mason as the representative of a sovereign state in the Foreign Office. "Under these circumstances," Benjamin informed Mason, "your continued residence is neither conducive to the interests nor consistent with the dignity of this government."[133] Mason soon left Britain for the continent, leaving the friends of the South in London to fend for themselves. Accompanying these failures was the news from across the Atlantic of the decisive Union victories at Vicksburg and Gettysburg. The tide of the war, both at home and abroad, had shifted.

The Confederate agents who remained in Britain, however, attempted to pick up the pieces of their shattered diplomatic and financial strategy in 1864. The financial situation was particularly alarming. Already unable to redeem a warrant issued by Fraser, Trenholm for £300,000 the previous summer, the newly appointed Confederate financial agent in Europe Colin McRae reported in February 1864 that Southern purchasers had overdrafted the proceeds of the Erlanger loan by more than

---

[132] Bulloch, *The Secret Service of the Confederate States in Europe*, I, p. 358.
[133] Benjamin to Mason, 4 August 1863, *ORN*, 2, III, pp. 852–3.

£200,000.¹³⁴ This shortage of funds was exacerbated by the fact that agents from different government bureaus competed for the same pieces of a rapidly shrinking pie. To make matters worse, private contractors sent by state governments determined to provide for their troops arrived in Britain to obtain supplies for the Confederacy. Often paid a commission of the total value of their purchases, these contractors had a vested interest in "hawking their contracts... to the highest bidder." "Such exhibitions are very damaging to our credit," McRae declared, "as they create the impression among capitalists and all prudent men that a government which is so reckless of its means is not likely to achieve its independence against such fearful odds."[135]

This lack of organization left the Confederacy particularly vulnerable to profit-gouging middlemen who charged excessive commissions and handling charges for their services. One of McRae's first acts as financial agent was to investigate Caleb Huse's dealings with the London firm Isaac, Campbell and Co. After an inquiry that exposed various jealousies and rivalries existing between Confederate agents and bureaus, McRae discovered that, unbeknownst to Huse, Isaac, Campbell and Co. had kept a double set of ledgers to legitimate their overcharging. The firm's practices, which included price hikes of up to twenty percent on top of their already high commission charges, McRae wrote, could "be characterized by no other term than that of fraudulent."[136] Indeed, the firm had a history of shady practices, having been investigated by the British Government for allegedly attempting to bribe a government official with £500 to secure a contract during the Crimean War. Though few firms were as unscrupulous as Isaac, Campbell and Co., many British businesses overcharged Confederate agents as a quasi-insurance policy for the risk they took in dealing with a government that might not be around long enough to fulfill its obligations. This was particularly the case with blockade-running firms who, in addition to overcharging for cargo space, preferred to pack their vessels with luxury goods that would reap the highest prices in the South rather than consign their cargo to the government for military supplies.[137]

The inability of the Confederate government to implement an efficient system of obtaining funds and supplies in Europe led some Southern states to take matters into their own hands. Virginia and Alabama

[134] Charles Davis, *Colin J. McRae: Confederate Financial Agent* (Alabama, 1961), p. 47.
[135] McRae to Memminger, 7 October 1863, *ORA*, 4, 2, pp. 982–5.
[136] McRae to Seddon, 4 July 1864, *ORA*, 4, 3, pp. 525–9.
[137] For more, see Wise, *Lifeline of the Confederacy*.

marketed their state bonds abroad even while Richmond attempted to sell cotton certificates and Erlanger bonds. So desperate were these states to establish their financial probity in the eyes of British capitalists that they both expended considerable resources to ship specie coin through the blockade to meet interest payments due to foreign creditors. The exigencies of war soon made this unfeasible. Virginia defaulted on its interest payments in the summer 1862, while Alabama amazingly continued to ship gold to Britain until January 1865.[138] These efforts, however, did little to reassure skeptical investors who, for obvious reasons, were disinclined to grant credit to states partially occupied by invading Union armies. The adjacent bond graph illustrates the low standing of Virginia six percent bonds offered in London during the war.

With unsecured state bonds not commanding interest on British markets, North Carolina Governor Zebulon Vance stole a page from the Confederate government's marketing book and issued $1.5 million in bonds redeemable in cotton at the low price of four pence per pound—a price that undercut the six pence per pound offered by Erlanger bonds. John White and Thomas M. Crossan were dispatched to Britain in 1863 and soon arranged for the issue to be marketed through the Manchester and County Bank. Vance hoped that White would "not be asked to go any lower than 75 cents upon the dollar and have strong hopes that you can sell at 85 or 90."[139] Although Vance would have been disappointed at the discounts that the bonds were eventually quoted, the scheme was a relative success and the state soon had in its possession the *Advance*, a blockade-runner in which to transport the supplies obtained in Britain back to North Carolina.[140]

Despite the success of North Carolina's fund-raising efforts in Britain, state-sponsored cotton certificates were clearly not the answer to the Confederacy's financial problems. The plethora of agents, purchasers, and financial schemes in Britain led to confusion, competition, and inefficiency. What was needed was better organization and collaboration, in a word, centralization. With the cotton embargo, the marketing of Treasury bonds, and the issuance of cotton certificates and Erlanger bonds having all failed to provide the Confederacy with a reliable source

---

[138] B. U. Ratchford, *American State Debts* (Durham, N.C., 1941), p. 155.

[139] Vance to White, 15 Nov 1862, in Frontis Johnston (ed.), *The Papers of Zebulon Baird Vance* (Raleigh, 1963), pp. 361–3.

[140] For more, see Wise, *Lifeline of the Confederacy*, p. 105; Mira Wilkins, *The History of Foreign Investment in the United States to 1914* (Cambridge, Mass., 1989), p. 103; Leland H. Jenks, *The Migration of British Capital to 1875* (London, 1927), pp. 421–5.

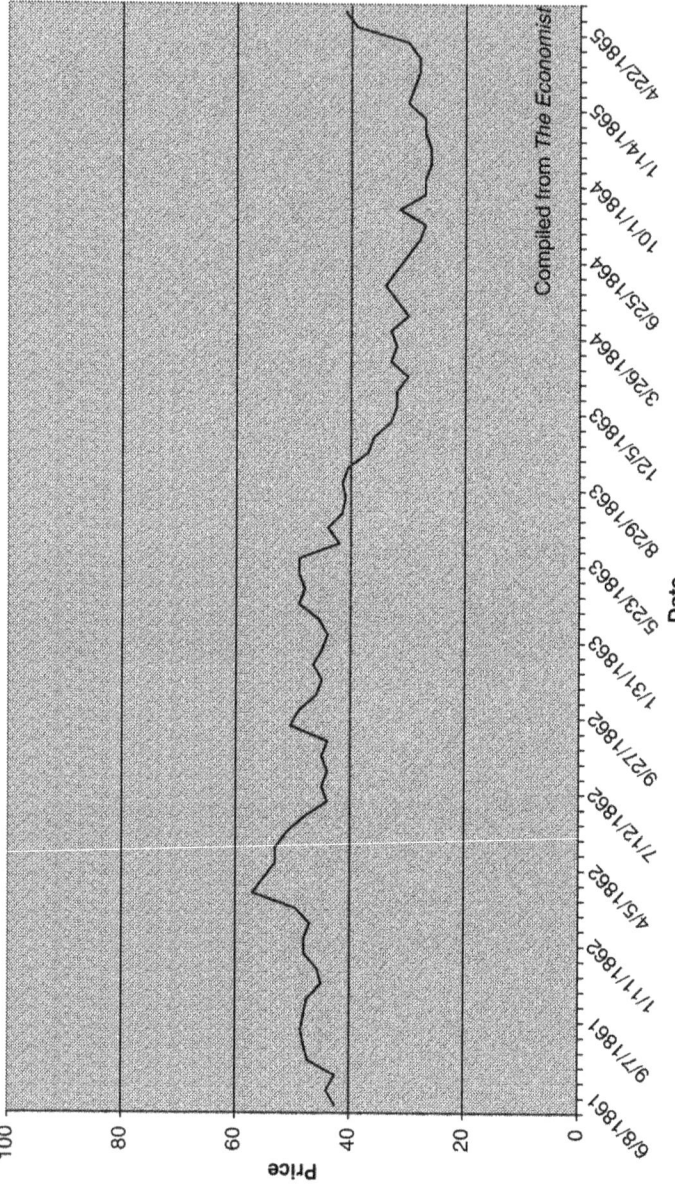

Figure 6 Virginia 6% Bonds in London, 1861–1865

of revenue, centralization meant the systematic exportation of cotton on government account. "Why does not the government take the subject of the blockade-running entirely into its own hands?" McRae asked. "Not a bale of cotton should be allowed to come out of the country nor a pound of merchandise go in except on government account."[141]

In an October 1863 dispatch to Treasury Secretary Memminger, McRae urged Richmond to centralize its operations abroad by adopting a series of new policies. First, he urged the government to abolish the system where purchasing agents received a percentage of their total contracts as payment. To bring coherence to purchasing operations, McRae next recommended that the Navy and War Departments designate one chief agent to coordinate the activity of its other agents and to liaise with a Treasury agent who, similarly, would possess powers plenipotentiary. Only when this new structure was in place, McRae maintained, could the government benefit from a nationalized system of blockade-running. The government could then require all outgoing blockade-runners to carry cotton pledged for sale in Britain. The price of valuable commodities could be set by officials in Richmond, who would also ensure that "no cotton, tobacco, or naval stores should be allowed to leave the country except on Government account or for account of holders of produce bonds, and none but the same parties should be allowed to import."[142]

All of these recommendations amounted to a revolutionary departure from the laissez-faire, states' rights political ideology that was the bedrock of the Confederacy. Forbidding individuals from engaging in commercial transactions without government approval was more of an infringement of individual rights than anything attempted by Republican politicians in the run-up to the Civil War. Similar to other aspects of state formation in the Confederacy, the exigencies of war led to dramatic changes in the scope of central authority and regulation.[143] As Jefferson Davis put it, "the condition of the contest demands that the Confederate States should call into requisition whatever resources of men and money they have for the support of their cause."[144] Nearly every Confederate

---

[141] Quoted in Owsley, *King Cotton Diplomacy*, p. 387.

[142] McRae to Memminger, 7 October 1863, *ORA*, 4, 2, pp. 982–5. See also Ball, *Financial Failure and Confederate Defeat*, pp. 96–9.

[143] For a discussion of this theme, see Richard Bensel, *Yankee Leviathan: The Origins of Central State Authority in America, 1859–1877* (New York, 1990), pp. 94–237.

[144] Jefferson Davis to the House of Representatives, 20 December 1864, *ORA*, 4, 3, pp. 948–53.

emissary in Britain, led by James Mason, Henry Hotze, and James Bulloch, echoed McRae's call for the implementation of a centralized financial and purchasing program. The Confederate Congress was also surprisingly quick to extend its approbation to the so-called "New Plan" in a bill passed on 6 February 1864. The new regulation forbade the importation of luxury goods, prohibited the private exportation of cotton without presidential approval, and, most importantly, reserved half of the cargo space of all blockade-runners for the Confederate government.[145] All of the theorizing about the diplomatic and financial potential of King Cotton that had led to a series of doomed machinations was finally reduced to the simple trading of cotton for guns.

There was one hurdle to be overcome before the new plan could be successfully implemented: shipping. Simply put, the Confederacy needed vessels to run the blockade. In the decades before the war, the Southern states relied almost entirely on Yankee and European merchants to carry their cotton across the Atlantic. When war broke out in 1861, the Confederate government possessed a mere ten serviceable steamships.[146] Although it would seem clear that the government needed to acquire more merchant vessels, Confederate leaders made little effort to do so in the war's first years. This was a result of both Southerners' confidence in the power of King Cotton to yield diplomatic results and the prevailing laissez-faire views of political economy. In the war's early years, however, it appeared that this hands-off strategy of allowing private interests to monopolize blockade-running would work. The transnational firm of John Fraser and Co. (Charleston, S.C.) and Fraser, Trenholm and Co. (Liverpool) was the leading blockade-running firm in 1861–3. Using its newly established agency in Nassau as a staging point, the firm's fleet took advantage of the porous blockade and profited immensely from government contracts and, most of all, from cotton exports to Liverpool. Crew members of blockade-runners received large bounties and a few successful runs could pay for a new ship.

It was not long before competitors entered the business. In the South various companies, led by the Importing and Exporting Company of South Carolina and the Chicora Importing and Exporting Co., were formed both out of patriotism and the profit motive. To encourage more blockade-running while sharing in on the profits of its competitors,

---

[145] "Regulations upon the Foreign Commerce of the Confederate States," in Richardson (ed.), *Messages and Papers of the Confederacy*, I, pp. 417–20.
[146] Wise, *Lifeline of the Confederacy*, p. 26.

John Fraser and Co. was a large shareholder of many of these joint-stock blockade-running firms. On the other side of the Atlantic, Confederate agents encouraged British entrepreneurs to form similar ventures. Mayor of Hull Zachariah Pearson committed his shipping company to running the blockade, and Edward Lawrence of Liverpool established the Anglo-Confederate Trading Company. A recent study has found that more than half of the tonnage of blockade-running vessels was underwritten by Liverpudlians.[147] The heart of the cotton trade before the war, Liverpool became a bastion of pro-Confederate sympathy and business during the war.[148]

However profitable these ventures were for Southern and British entrepreneurs, by 1863 it was apparent that the arrangement was not advantageous to the Confederacy as a whole. The debt-ridden Confederate Government could not afford the excessive commissions and freight charges of these companies. More importantly, private companies could not be relied on to import the military supplies needed by Southern armies as they preferred to pack their cargoes with luxury items that would demand the highest price at public auctions. Creating a government-owned fleet of blockade-runners seemed to be the only viable solution. Proponents of this idea could point to the few precedents that occurred earlier in the war when the government took shipping into its own hands. In the autumn 1861, James Bulloch purchased a merchant ship, the *Fingal*, to transport war supplies obtained in Europe. The first government vessel to successfully run the blockade, the *Fingal* brought some £48,702 worth of goods to the Confederacy.[149] The Ordnance Department copied Bulloch's technique in the winter 1862–3 when Caleb Huse purchased three steamers to transport the guns and munitions he acquired in Britain to the Confederacy.[150]

These ventures illustrated the potential for the government to eliminate expensive and inefficient middlemen from the Confederacy's international commerce. The passage of the new shipping regulations in the Confederate congress was accompanied by an aggressive attempt to

---

[147] Neil Ashcroft, "'Uncertain and Unexpected Vicissitudes': British Maritime Enterprise and the American Civil War, 1856 to 1870," Ph.D. dissertation, University of Hull, 1999, p. 175.

[148] For more on Liverpool during the war, see John Pelzer, "Liverpool and the American Civil War," *History Today*, 40 (March, 1990), pp. 46–52.

[149] For Bulloch's recollection of this episode, see Bulloch, *The Secret Service of the Confederate States in Europe*, I, p. 110.

[150] Wise, *Lifeline of the Confederacy*, p. 96.

construct a government-owned merchant fleet. McRae turned first to Fraser, Trenholm for help in creating this new fleet. Having curtailed its blockade-running in 1863 because of increased competition and the tightening of the blockade, the Liverpool bank jumped at the opportunity to assist the Confederacy and to profit from so doing. Fraser, Trenholm agreed to finance the construction of eight runners that would be owned and operated by the firm until imports of cotton covered the expenses of the vessels plus a twenty percent commission fee. "I am sure that we cannot employ our capital better," Charles Prioleau disclosed, "or render a greater service to the government than this."[151] McRae did not stop with the Fraser, Trenholm contract. Using Erlanger bonds that had been repurchased by Confederate agents in April 1863 as collateral, McRae entered into a second deal with the London firm of J. K. Gilliat and Co. for the construction of a further six vessels. It would take time, the winter of 1864–5 at the earliest, for this fourteen-ship fleet to be completed. In the meantime, McRae extended short-term contracts with William Crenshaw and Alexander Collie, a Richmond merchant and British shipper, who had built four steamers for the Confederacy in a mixed private–public venture the previous year.[152]

Thus, after decades of failed commercial conventions, a few decisive actions by McRae and the Confederate Congress laid the foundations for a merchant marine owned and operated by Southerners. Even before the new ships were serviceable, the "New Plan" of nationalized blockade-running of cotton to Britain appeared to meet with success. By July, McRae wrote to Richmond that "our credit begins to grow stronger, and by proper management will soon be available for all of our wants."[153] Jefferson Davis proudly informed congress that the new plan "put an end to a wasteful and ruinous contract system."[154] The perception that the Confederacy was finally organizing its finances and backing its operations with sales of "white gold" contributed to a resurgence in quotations of Erlanger cotton bonds. Quoted as low as thirty-six in December 1863, the promise of a blockade-running fleet that could redeem cotton bonds, combined with a precipitous increase in the price

---

[151] Quoted in Hughes, "Liverpool and the Confederacy," p. 200.
[152] McRae to Seddon, 4 July 1864, *ORA*, 4, 3, pp. 525–9; Mallory to Bulloch, 22 February 1863, *ORN*, 2, 2, p. 368. See also Wise, *Lifeline of the Confederacy*, pp. 148–9.
[153] McRae to Seddon, 4 July 1864, *ORA*, 4, 3, pp. 525–9.
[154] Jefferson Davis to the House of Representatives, 20 December 1864, *ORA*, 4, 3, pp. 948–53.

of cotton in Liverpool, helped raise the bonds to eighty-four in September 1864.[155]

This apparent improvement in the finances of the Confederacy, however, was deceptive. Although the new plan promised a system of finance in Europe based on the exportation of cotton, this ambitious scheme was never realized during the war. The rise in commercial and investor confidence in the Confederacy in the summer 1864 was probably more a result of the stalling of Grant's invasion in Virginia and the possibility of a Democratic victory in the 1864 elections than it was a product of McRae's new plan of finance. The historian Stephen Wise has shown that up to 12 August 1864, only 1,672 bales of cotton went to McRae for the credit of the Treasury while more than twice that amount went to private contractors to pay off old contracts.[156] The Treasury Department also worried that "our means are being absorbed in the purchase of steamers that may not come into active service until the present exigency has passed."[157] Records of Confederate Secretary of the Treasury George Trenholm reveal that between 4 July and 2 November 1864 only 10,412 bales of cotton were shipped out on government account.[158] Compared to preceding years, this was a significant amount that would earn top dollar in Liverpool. However, 10,000 bales of cotton were not enough to alter the state of the Confederacy's finances. In the end, the new plan was too little, too late.

The same could be said of James Bulloch's ambitious attempt to continue the Confederate naval construction program in France in the latter half of the war. After the British Government tightened its interpretation of its neutrality laws in 1863, Bulloch and his minions relocated across the channel. France was selected after Napoleon assured the Confederate emissary John Slidell that his government would make no attempt to impede naval construction.[159] Further enticing to Confederate naval agents was the vague French neutrality act that, like its British counterpart, invited loose interpretation. As in Britain, there was not a shortage of contractors willing to enter into profitable contracts with the

---

[155] For the increase in cotton bond quotations in the summer 1864, see Marc Weidemier, "The Market for Confederate Cotton Bonds," *Explorations in Economic History*, 37 (January 2000), pp. 76–97; Brown and Burdekan, "Turning Points in the U.S. Civil War: A British Perspective," pp. 216–31.
[156] Wise, *Lifeline of the Confederacy*, p. 151.
[157] Trenholm to Seddon, 12 August 1864, *ORA*, 4, 3, pp. 587–9.
[158] MSS 20,039, Trenholm Papers, Library of Congress.
[159] Slidell to Benjamin, 28 October 1862, Richardson (ed.), *Messages and Papers of the Confederacy*, 1, p. 348.

Confederacy. A French shipbuilder, Lucien Arman, approached Bulloch in April 1863 with an offer to construct warships for the South at his Bordeaux shipyard. Similar to a year earlier in Britain, a Confederate fleet was in the making in France by the winter of 1863–4. In all, Southern agents contracted for four wooden corvettes and two ironclad rams that, it was hoped, would replace the detained Laird rams. With assurances from the emperor himself that no move would be made to enforce neutrality laws, little effort was made to conceal the intent of these vessels and the careful subterfuge of arming the ships in neutral waters was scrapped in favor of quick construction. "Magazines and shell-rooms were placed in each," Bulloch later recalled, "and all the bolls, traverses and gear required for mounting the guns were provided" in the shipyard.[160]

Predictably, Union representatives John Bigelow and William Dayton caught wind of the Confederate shipbuilding effort and sent off protests to the French government. The Union case received a shot in the arm when an employee of Arman's shipbuilding company stole incriminating papers and forwarded them to Dayton. Having already irritated American statesmen with his imperial venture in Mexico, Napoleon was not eager to further provoke the United States and ordered the detainment of the ships in February and May 1864. Knowing that their ships would soon be confiscated, Confederate agents sold their half-constructed vessels to the highest bidder. None of the ships constructed in France would fire at a Northern vessel and only one would raise the Confederate stars and bars. But in a fitting epilogue to the Confederate effort abroad, the *Stonewall* arrived in American waters in May 1865 only to learn that the Southern states had already surrendered.[161]

With the Confederate international effort on the verge of collapse, Southern leaders reluctantly opted to play their only remaining card in a desperate attempt to procure the support of European powers. In late 1864 Benjamin persuaded Jefferson Davis and the rest of the cabinet that the South's last hope for diplomatic progress was to offer to abolish slavery in exchange for European recognition. Davis appointed Duncan Kenner, a leading Louisiana planter and politician, to inform Mason and Slidell that the Confederacy was prepared to consider emancipating the slaves if it would yield immediate diplomatic results.[162]

[160] Bulloch, *The Secret Service of the Confederate States*, II. p. 288.
[161] For more on the Confederate naval program in France, see Spencer, *The Confederate Navy in Europe*, pp. 147–76. See also Peter Parish, *The American Civil War* (London, 1975), p. 445.
[162] Benjamin to Slidell, 27 December 1864, ORN, 2, 3, pp. 1253–6.

The so-called Kenner mission was entirely secret and never received the approbation of either the Confederate Congress or the Southern people. If it had succeeded, it is doubtful that Southerners would have held up their end of the bargain. Indeed, Article I, Section 9 of the Confederate Constitution explicitly forbade the formation of any law "denying or impairing the right of property in negro slaves."[163] Like the last-minute decision to allow slaves into the Confederate army, the Kenner mission provoked determined opposition. Many opposed the initiative for the obvious reason that, if slavery was destroyed, there was little justification for continuing to fight. So paranoid were Confederate statesmen about the threat to slavery from the outside world that Benjamin had removed James Spence from his post of financial agent in 1863 when he attempted to distance the Confederacy from slavery in his efforts to garner British support for the South (Spence's duties were later assumed by Colin McRae).[164] Mason was opposed to the emancipation strategy, adamant that slavery had little to do with the South's diplomatic failures. Indeed, the British cabinet had barely discussed slavery during its deliberations on intervention in the autumn 1862. It was not slavery, but a series of other considerations—fear of war with the North, the logistical difficulties of arranging an international coalition to mediate in the conflict, and the lack of any graspable economic or strategic benefit that would result from intervention—that had forestalled a pro-Confederate move by the Palmerston government.

Despite the reservations of leading Confederate statesmen, the Kenner mission went forward in March 1865. Slidell presented the offer to Napoleon in Paris, who held that "he had never taken [slavery] into consideration" in his views on the Confederacy. French intervention was out of the question, the emperor held, unless Britain could be persuaded to act jointly. Kenner and Mason crossed the channel hoping that this last effort would finally produce the diplomatic result that had eluded the Confederacy for four years. However, like Napoleon, Palmerston maintained that slavery had never been the roadblock to recognition and made it clear that the military situation in America made it unpropitious for the implementation of a pro-Confederate policy.[165] The last

---

[163] Constitution of the Confederate States, Article I, Section 9, Richardson (ed.), *Messages and Papers of the Confederacy*, I. p. 43.

[164] Benjamin to Hotze, 9 January 1864, Bigelow Papers, B18, F5, New York Public Library.

[165] Mason to Benjamin, 31 March 1865, *ORN*, 2, 3, pp. 1270–1.

card had been played and, once again, Confederate diplomacy had failed.[166]

These final diplomatic efforts were accompanied by a last ditch attempt to salvage the Confederacy's finances. Although McRae's plan of exporting cotton for cash had shown promise, the advances of Union forces made it impossible to continue this strategy. The fall of Charleston and Wilmington in early 1865 closed the Confederacy's last operational ports. Lacking the means to get cotton out of the confederacy, a foreign loan was the only way that Confederate purchasing operations could continue. Fortunately for the South, such an offer was on the table. A French financier, allegedly acting on behalf of a consortium of European bankers, approached newly appointed Secretary of the Treasury George Trenholm (the head partner of Fraser, Trenholm and Co.) in late 1864 with an offer to arrange a £15 million loan bearing seven percent interest.[167] Like the Erlanger scheme of 1863, the loan would be convertible into cotton at a fixed price. Further appealing to the Confederacy was the promise that £500,000 would be advanced to Southern agents in Europe once the contract was signed. Trenholm urged Jefferson Davis to endorse the proposal, arguing that the loan would "restore the value of the currency" and "relieve the pressure upon our finances."[168]

The bankrupt Confederate government had no choice but to accept the offer and Trenholm authorized Duncan Kenner to agree to the loan before his departure.[169] Having learned a lesson from the Erlanger debacle, Kenner was instructed to issue the loan to the public at seventy percent of its face value. However, by the time Kenner arrived in Paris in March 1865, even the riskiest speculators knew better than to broker a loan to a nation on the verge of collapse. The £15 million loan was never realized and the Confederacy ended the war deeply in debt in Europe. The twin diplomatic and financial failings of the Kenner mission provide a fitting denouement to the Confederate effort in Europe.

---

[166] For more on the Kenner mission, see Craig Bauer, "The Last Effort: The Secret Mission of the Confederate Diplomat, Duncan F. Kenner," *Louisiana History*, 22 (Winter 1981), pp. 67–95.

[167] It is not known exactly whom this agent, Comte Berle de Channigry, represented. It is possible that he had connections with Erlanger and Schröder. The two banks extended a similar proposal to the Confederacy in June 1864. See Bouris to Memminger, 11 June 1864, Trenholm Papers, LC.

[168] Trenholm to Davis, 15 December 1864, Trenholm Papers, LC.

[169] Treasury to Kenner, 4 January 1865, Trenholm Papers, LC.

Historians have traditionally been quick to criticize a Confederate diplomatic strategy that failed to obtain the support of foreign powers. As one scholar recently asserted, "the misguided commitment to King Cotton diplomacy burdened the Confederate diplomatic effort" from its inception.[170] Curiously, this criticism has not been extended to the South's overseas financial operations. Scholars have generally applauded the efforts of Confederate financial and purchasing agents. The Erlanger loan has been labeled a "success" while generations of scholars have pointed to James Bulloch and Colin McRae as the South's most capable agents abroad. Indeed, despite the Union blockade and the South's poor credit in Europe, Confederate agents succeeded in acquiring an estimated $200 million worth of supplies in Europe during the war.[171] These arms and supplies were essential in sustaining the Confederate effort through four years of war.

These accomplishments of the Confederate financial and commercial effort abroad, however, should not be viewed uncritically. Although the South could not have lasted as long as it did without the materials and funds obtained in Europe (particularly in Britain), what is most notable about the Confederacy's international effort is not what it provided, but what it did not. Despite possessing a near monopoly of the world's supply of cotton in 1861, Confederate statesmen were unable to implement a policy that used the commodity to their advantage. Furthermore, the procurement of funds and arms, despite the exceptional efforts of a few envoys and the generous advances of Fraser, Trenholm and Co., never kept pace with the demands of the South's armies. This was partly a result of European financiers' predominantly pejorative view of Confederacy. None of the titans of transatlantic finance—the Barings, Rothschilds, Peabody, Hope and Co.—were prepared to jeopardize their historic relations with the U.S. Government and Northern states and railroads in order to advance funds to a slaveholding republic, notorious for the financial infidelities of three of its states in the 1840s.

However, the shortcomings of the Confederate financial and commercial effort abroad were also a result of the South's ill-conceived diplomatic strategy. That the diplomatic and financial fortunes of the South were inextricably linked would be quickly and devastatingly illustrated by the ill-fated cotton embargo. The "King Cotton" strategy of 1861-2

---

[170] Hubbard, *The Burden of Confederate Diplomacy*, p. 177.
[171] For this figure, see Lester, *Confederate Finance and Purchasing in Great Britain*, p. 199; and, Boaz, *Guns for Cotton*, p. 68.

prevented the South from establishing a coherent plan of international finance from the war's beginning. Without cotton to dangle in front of British capitalists, Confederate statesmen lacked any effective means of courting creditors and obtaining supplies in Europe. The cotton certificate and bond schemes of 1862–3, although a step in the right direction, also proved insufficient because of mismanagement and the excessive risk demanded of potential investors. The political benefits that Southern statesmen believed would accompany the issuance of the Erlanger loan never came to fruition as few influential investors publicly connected themselves with the Confederacy.

In hindsight, there is little doubt that the Confederacy should have implemented at the beginning of the war the policy it eventually adopted in 1864 of exporting cotton on government account as its primary means of fundraising abroad. Such a tactic would have greatly extended the purchasing power of agents in Britain and would have cultivated commercial links between the Confederate Government and European states that the cotton embargo never allowed to develop. As James Bulloch reflected twenty years after Lee's surrender at Appomattox,

> If 200,000 bales of cotton could have been shipped to Liverpool during the first year of the war, the financial position of the Confederate States would no doubt have been infinitely strengthened, and the first armies might have been put into the field in such a state of efficiency, as regards clothing and equipment, as to have greatly affected the results of the struggle.[172]

Indeed, it is possible to imagine an alternative Confederate international strategy based on the exportation of cotton and its storage in Britain on government account. If shrewdly managed, Confederate agents could have manipulated the cotton market to obtain maximum revenue from the precious commodity.[173] Moreover, such a scheme could have yielded political, as well as financial, benefits. The Palmerston government might have been more willing to negotiate with Confederate emissaries if the emissaries possessed a bargaining chip that they were willing to offer to Britain—ideally accompanied by a free trade agreement—in exchange for diplomatic or financial support. Britain would have then been reliant not just on cotton, but on the Confederate government's supply of cotton. As Bulloch suggested during the war, "If we

---

[172] Bulloch, *The Secret Service of the Confederate States in Europe*, I, p. 103. See also Surdam, "Cotton's Potential as Economic Weapon," p. 145.

[173] For a discussion of this possibility, see Ashcroft, "Uncertain and Unexpected Vicissitudes," pp. 67–9.

could accumulate a considerable supply here, the Government through its mercantile agent would not only rule the market, but important political influences might be brought to bear."[174] Although it is true that the glutted cotton market and the prudence of British statesmen would have no doubt moderated the potential of this alternative strategy, there can be little question that it would have given the Confederacy its best chance of financial and diplomatic success.

That such a policy was not implemented until it was too late testifies to the persistence of a flawed understanding of international finance and politics held by key Southern policy-makers. The failure of Confederate statesmen to develop a sound international strategy contributed in no small way to the South's defeat.

---

[174] Quoted in Bulloch, *The Secret Service of the Confederate States in Europe*, II, p. 224.

4
"Were it not for our Debt," 1865–1873

"Half the public bodies in America want to borrow English capital, and more than half the enterprises," *The Economist* observed in 1872, "and nothing forbids this but the unsettled Alabama difficulty."[1] Few historians have followed *The Economist's* lead in connecting the apparently distinct *Alabama* claims with American efforts to attract foreign investment after the Civil War. Scholars have traditionally focused on how national pride, Canadian independence, and the personalities of American and British statesmen contributed to and hindered efforts to settle the Anglo-American dispute regarding British compensation to the United States for damages inflicted by the *Alabama* and other British-built Confederate cruisers during the Civil War. The work of Allan Nevins and Adrian Cook, to name but two historians, has delineated the contours of the *Alabama* debate and explored how the dispute related to the broader geopolitical strategies of Britain and the United States in the nineteenth century.[2]

There is, however, another story to be told in relation to the *Alabama* claims. This story involves the interlocking relationship between finance and diplomacy. More specifically, it shall be seen that the United States' need for cheap foreign capital to refinance its massive national debt at a lower rate of interest influenced its relations with Britain in the years after the Civil War. Indeed, the Treasury's desire to market low-interest bonds abroad were so intertwined with the diplomatic attempts to resolve the *Alabama* controversy that it is impossible to view either in isolation. Not only did financial considerations shape U.S. policy, but financial leaders, motivated by obvious self-interest, were key players in the diplomacy of 1869–72. These financiers operated on both sides of the Atlantic and were instrumental in bringing about a resolution to the *Alabama* dispute. The benefits of the conciliatory policy pushed by the financial lobby became clear in 1871 and 1873 when the U.S. Treasury, working in connection

[1] *The Economist*, 18 May 1872, p. 605.
[2] The standard works on the *Alabama* claims remain Adrian Cook, *The* Alabama *Claims: American Politics and Anglo-American Relations, 1865–1872* (Ithaca, 1975); and Allan Nevins, *Hamilton Fish: The Inner History of the Grant Administration* (New York, 1939).

with the consortium of elite London bankers who had helped resolve the *Alabama* claims, placed low-interest bonds in Europe to fund the debt contracted during the Civil War.

THE RECOVERY CAMPAIGN IN EUROPE

Before the United States attempted to arrange a foreign loan or resolve the *Alabama* claims, the State and Treasury Departments collaborated in an effort to "recover," or more aptly to claim, Confederate property in Europe. American leaders argued that since the rebellion had been illegal, all property of the Confederacy was unlawfully acquired and belonged to the United States. Denying the legal existence of the Confederate Government—instead of merely asserting the right to Confederate property by right of conquest—dovetailed with the then U.S. strategy in the *Alabama* dispute that held that Britain's proclamation of neutrality had been an unlawful recognition of Confederate belligerence and, implicitly, the Confederate government. Beneath this legal ruse lay the straightforward desire to profit from the seizure of ex-Confederate property while exacting revenge on those who had supported the rebellion.

Not surprisingly, early efforts focused on the European financial agency of the Confederacy, the Liverpool bank of Fraser, Trenholm and Co. In the months following Lee's surrender at Appomattox, the U.S. consul in Liverpool Thomas Dudley continued his campaign against the Confederacy when he sought to "recover" a shipment of cotton from the Confederate government received by the firm after the end of the war. In the case *U.S. vs. Prioleau*, British courts upheld U.S. claims for £20,000 (the value of the cotton) on the grounds that Fraser, Trenholm had received the Confederate property after the war. Though a victory in the short-term, this ruling established the unfavorable precedent that the United States could lay claim to property only if the transaction occurred after the war. As Dudley put it, "a sale made before the rebellion was put down is good, or at least that it will be so held in the courts of this country."[3]

This ruling did not deter leaders in Washington from continuing the recovery campaign in Europe. In January 1867 Secretary of State William

---

[3] Quoted in Carvel Painter, "The Recovery of Confederate Property and Other Assets Abroad, 1865-1873," Ph.D. dissertation, American University, 1973, p. 132. See also Ex. Doc. No. 304, 40th Congress, 2nd Session.

Seward appointed former attorney general and commissioner to China Caleb Cushing "to act as counsel in the matter of certain suits now pending" in Britain.[4] Cushing, who coordinated the campaign from his office in Washington, believed that "the courts have generally erred because of their looking at the cases before them from an English point of view instead of as they should have, an American one."[5] Determined to file more recovery suits and press the American point of view, Cushing and Treasury agent H. B. Titus soon established a network of agents in Britain to locate Confederate property in return for a commission of "a sum not to exceed one-fourth part of such net amount as may be received by the Government." Lured by the promise of windfall profits, it was not long before British entrepreneurs were offering their services to the U.S. Government. Predictably, these self-appointed U.S. agents had little in mind other than quick, easy money. One agent who was promised £150,000 for his services even had a police record in London as "a professional swindler."[6]

Cushing's refusal to travel to London to orchestrate the campaign and the unreliable character of many U.S. agents soon led to problems. Promises of $30 million of recoverable property in Europe set unreasonable expectations that could never be met. Furthermore, a lack of communication between U.S. consuls Dudley and Freeman Morse (in London) led to disaster in 1866-7 when the latter made an unauthorized out-of-court settlement with Fraser, Trenholm. Under the agreement, the Liverpool bank was to sell its assets, keeping the first £150,000 (its claims on the Confederacy) and handing the rest to the U.S. Treasury. Dudley was convinced that these terms were too lenient and pressed forward with his own suit against the firm despite it being a violation of the Morse agreement. Seward soon intervened in the dispute by voiding Morse's settlement and, in collaboration with Cushing and Treasury Secretary Hugh McCulloch, drew up plans for a new agreement with the ex-Confederacy's bankers. Any hopes for a large pecuniary reward, however, came to an end in May 1867 when Fraser, Trenholm, crippled by legal fees and debts from the war, declared bankruptcy.[7]

---

[4] Seward to Cushing, 12 January 1867, Cushing Papers, Box 293, Library of Congress (hereafter LC).
[5] Cushing to Seward, 26 October 1865, Cushing Papers, Box 296, LC.
[6] Painter, "The Recovery of Confederate Property," p. 346.
[7] For this sorry episode, see Ex. Doc. No. 63, 39th Congress, 2nd Session; Ex. Doc. No. 304, 40th Congress, 2nd Session; Stephen Wise, *Lifeline of the Confederacy* (Columbia, S.C., 1988), pp. 222-4. Eventually, the two sides came to a compromise agreement in 1870.

Other U.S. attempts to recover Confederate property in Europe met a similar fate. A suit against the French shipbuilder Lucien Arman derailed when French courts dismissed incriminating documents from the proceedings on the grounds that they had been stolen by one of Arman's employees and represented a "breach of faith."[8] Back in Britain, attempts to seize assets held by the former Confederate financial agent Colin McRae, who absconded to Honduras where he would remain for the rest of his life, were stymied by a British court ruling that maintained that the United States had no legal claim to the "property which has been voluntarily contributed to, or acquired by, the insurrecting government."[9]

This ruling, combined with flagging interest in tracking down holders of ex-Confederate property who when found were often bankrupt, led the incoming Grant administration to largely abandon recovery operations. "I have reluctantly come to the accord," U.S. agent L. Chandler conceded in 1868, "of the impossibility of bringing the proceedings for the recovery of Confederate property in England to a satisfactory conclusion productive of pecuniary results."[10] Incoming Secretary of State Hamilton Fish agreed, stating that "it is desirable to be rid of the pending litigation if the point of honor be maintained."[11] "About all that this near decade-long activity accomplished," its historian concludes, "was to demonstrate an assortment of human frailties ranging between jealous backbiting and a denial by some of the involved that 'a public office is a public trust.'"[12] The campaign also had an unintended side effect: angering British business interests who either had dealt with the Confederacy during the war or were falsely accused of holding Confederate property by unscrupulous U.S. agents. The whole scheme seemed to confirm the view abroad, particularly prevalent during radical Reconstruction, that the sectional struggle was far from resolved and that Northern vengeance precluded a return to business as usual in the Atlantic economy.

THE NATIONAL DEBT AND THE *ALABAMA* CLAIMS

Alienating British capitalists was not a good idea considering the financial predicament the U.S. Government found itself in after the Civil War.

---

[8] Cushing to Williams, 2 December 1872, Cushing Papers, LC.
[9] Quoted in Painter, "The Recovery of Confederate Property," p. 403.
[10] Chandler to Dudley, 6 April 1868, Entry 319, RG 365, National Archives.
[11] Fish Diary, 20 January 1870, Fish Papers, LC.
[12] Painter, "The Recovery of Confederate Property," p. 444.

With all of the attention given to the political and social aspects of Reconstruction, it is often forgotten that the nation faced an equally daunting financial crisis in the years after the Civil War. In October 1865, Secretary of the Treasury Hugh McCulloch announced that the national debt stood at $2.8 billion. The previous high mark for the debt prior to the Civil War years occurred in 1815 when war with Britain placed the nation $127 million in the red. Of immediate concern to McCulloch in 1865 was that half of the Treasury's outstanding issues were to mature in three years or less.[13] Moreover, the overwhelming majority of the debt was contracted at high interest rates in the popular wartime issues of the seven-thirties (three-year notes bearing 7.3 percent) and five-twenties (six percent bonds callable between five and twenty years). With high war taxes already the source of political controversy, it made clear fiscal and political sense for the Treasury to take advantage of the Union victory by refinancing its debt at a lower rate of interest. "Taking a five per cent loan instead of a six per cent loan," Civil War financier and Treasury agent Jay Cooke advised McCulloch in December 1865, "would in effect surrender to the government one-sixth of the annual interest in lieu of taxation."[14]

Looking to execute such a refunding operation abroad also made clear financial sense. With ninety percent of the national debt held at home, it was feared that American bondholders would be reluctant to exchange their seven-thirties and five-twenties for lower-yielding securities. In contrast, British consols bore a mere three percent interest. Consequently, it was hoped that European capitalists, particularly those in Britain, might be tempted by a relatively high-yielding U.S. loan, but one that was more secure than the wartime issues that had met with little success abroad. The high standing and historic connections of European banks to the United States was also an incentive for arranging a foreign loan. Although the war years had witnessed an explosion in the size and number of investment banks and brokerage firms on Wall Street, the world's leading banks remained in Europe, principally in London. There were no better houses than the Rothschilds or Baring Brothers to help the United States fund its $2.8 billion debt at a lower rate of interest.

Placing a new loan abroad had another, more important pecuniary advantage to the United States: injecting gold into the nation's monetary

[13] Henrietta Larson, *Jay Cooke* (Cambridge, Mass., 1936), p. 208.
[14] Cooke quoted in Ellis Paxson Oberholtzer, *Jay Cooke*, 2 vols. (Philadelphia, 1907), II, p. 9. See also Belmont to N.M.R. and Sons, 12 May 65, T56/210, Rothschild Archive (hereafter RA), London; Larson, *Jay Cooke*, p. 208.

system. Following the suspension of specie payments in December 1861, the Treasury printed some $450 million of "greenbacks," paper notes not tied to the price of gold, to help finance the war. Even when implemented during the financial exigencies of the war years, the creation of the greenbacks met with much opposition from those who believed that paper money would lead to ruinous inflation, not to mention violating the sanctity of gold. Thus, with the war over and government expenditure rapidly on the decline, Republican leaders and Northeastern financial interests (who as creditors stood to gain from a tight currency) pressed for the retirement of the greenbacks and a resumption of specie payments.

There were two general ways that this could happen: currency contraction or an increase in the gold supply, both of which sought to bring devalued greenbacks back to par with gold. Congress, under intense pressure from McCulloch, committed the nation to the first of these options in an 1866 law that called for $10 million in greenbacks to be refunded in six months with an option for an additional $4 million each month thereafter.[15] Currency contraction, however, was a painful process to debtors and small farmers, and it was not long before opportunistic Democrats and genuinely aggrieved Westerners were applying political pressure to end McCulloch's policy (which led to the repeal of the contraction policy in early 1868). A foreign influx of gold, consequently, could mitigate the effects of contraction whilst helping to bring greenbacks back to par. Although a foreign loan was a short-term solution—as the loan plus interest eventually would have to be returned to Europe—it could clearly assist the Treasury and the Republican Party in their quest to enact a quick return of specie payments.[16]

Thus, in the year following the conclusion of the war, several unofficial overtures were made to European banks by the Treasury and, as European bankers sensed the United States' intentions, vice versa. The American financier in Paris J. D. Curtis offered his services to McCulloch in placing a $500 million loan in Paris, Amsterdam, and Frankfurt.[17] Both the Rothschilds and Baring Brothers were asked by their American agents whether they had any interest in brokering a new U.S. loan in Britain. "We think the 5% Bonds of the US, principal and interest payable in

---

[15] Margaret Meyers, *A Financial History of the United States* (New York, 1970), pp. 174–96; Robert Sharkey, *Money, Class, and Party: An Economic Study of Civil War and Reconstruction* (Baltimore, 1959), pp. 56–80.

[16] For this motive for a foreign loan, see George Boutwell, *Reminiscences of Sixty Years in Public Affairs*, 2 vols. (New York, 1902), II, p. 144.

[17] Bigelow to McCulloch, 9 March 1866, McCulloch Papers, LC.

London," the Rothschild agent in New York August Belmont wrote to his London superiors, "will attract the attention of your capitalists and would like very much to know what you think of them."[18] Entrusted by the Lincoln administration during the war to seek foreign financial assistance, there can be little doubt that Belmont's approach was given with the knowledge and support of the Treasury.

For a variety of reasons, these plans never made it off the drawing board. It appears that McCulloch himself did not support giving priority to a new loan to the foreign capitalists who had rejected loan offers during the Civil War when financiers on Wall Street had stood by the nation throughout its trial. McCulloch preferred the debt to be a "home" one, agreeing with Jay Cooke that "if it is held by our own people there is no annual loss of wealth from the collection and payment of interest."[19] McCulloch's views were no doubt influenced by the cool reaction of financiers across the Atlantic to a possible low-interest U.S. loan. Part of the apprehension in Europe was the product of political concerns. Although the Union had been restored, the nation's political and social problems did not exactly make the United States a safe destination for capital. The great questions of Reconstruction—what to do with former Confederate states and leaders, what rights would the emancipated slaves be granted, who would control the process—all threatened the stability of the nation and frightened off European capitalists. As Britain knew firsthand, repaying a debt was not simple, and domestic political disputes would only complicate the already difficult task.

If the political situation was not promising, the financial portents of placing a U.S. loan abroad were also discouraging. The Panic of 1866 in London, which witnessed the failure of one of the City's largest banks in Overend, Gurney and Co., certainly did not put British capitalists in the mood for a risky venture. Low quotations of five-twenty bonds on the London Stock Exchange also did not inspire confidence that a new American issue, at a lower rate of interest, would prove successful. As the Rothschilds informed Belmont, "there should be a rise of from 5 to 6 points upon the present price of 5/20 Bonds" as a precondition to offering a new issue abroad.[20] The high premium of gold and the

---

[18] Baring Brothers to Ward, 10 Feb 1866, Baring Papers (hereafter BP), LC [microfilm]; Belmont to N.M.R. and Sons, 19 Jan 1866, T57/4, RA.

[19] Quoted in Mira Wilkins, *The History of Foreign Investment in the United States to 1914* (Cambridge, Mass., 1989), p. 110.

[20] N.M.R. and Sons to Belmont, 6 February 1866, RA. See also Baring Brothers to Ward, 20 September 1866, BP.

prolonged suspension of specie payments in the United States also made new fixed-income bonds a risky investment for European financiers. "I am no finance doctor," Thomas Baring wrote to the Boston businessman John Murray Forbes, "but is seems to me that the greatest evil which ought to be avoided is an increase of the paper currency."[21] Indeed, five-twenty bond quotations in London were inversely linked to the gold premium in New York throughout the 1860s: when the gold premium went up (bringing greenbacks further from par with gold), U.S. bonds went down.[22] All of these factors led European financiers to hold a wait-and-see attitude before committing themselves to a new U.S. loan. As the London *Bankers' Magazine* put it in 1866, "our attitude towards America should, financially speaking, be that of non-intervention or neutrality."[23]

While financiers in the City remained uninterested in U.S. Government securities, capitalists in Germany and Holland proved more willing to invest in them in the immediate postwar years. As one German observed, "There was hardly an investor in South Germany who did not buy United States bonds."[24] This continued the trend from the war years when the Amsterdam and Frankfurt exchanges were the only markets for Union bonds in Europe. The low price of five-twenty bonds, which at times led to an annual yield of ten to fifteen percent, was clearly an incentive to German and Dutch risk takers. However, even as increased demand led to higher prices, U.S. bonds continued to be purchased in Amsterdam and Frankfurt. The U.S. consul in Frankfurt William Murphy reported in March 1866 that demand for U.S. bonds led five-twenty quotations to be one and one-half percent higher in Frankfurt than in New York and declared a year later that the five-twenties' "superiority over all other Government's Stocks has been acknowledged by the European Capitalists."[25] It is widely accepted that the majority of the $700 million in U.S. federal bonds abroad in 1868—the largest

---

[21] Thomas Baring to J. M. Forbes, 4 February 1865, in Sarah Hughes (ed.), *Letters and Recollections of John Murray Forbes* (New York, 1899), II, pp. 131–2.
[22] See Levi Morton to McCulloch, 20 Nov 1866, McCulloch Papers, LC.
[23] *Bankers' Magazine*, vol. 26 (March 1866), pp. 217–21. *The Economist* came to a similar conclusion: "The proper course, therefore, is to watch carefully and patiently the gradual progress of events in this new and strange scene.... A financial problem, equally interesting and equally important, has perhaps never been presented to the civilised world." See *The Economist*, 12 August 1865, pp. 968–9.
[24] Quoted in Stanley Chapman, *The Rise of Merchant Banking* (London, 1984), p. 46.
[25] Murphy to Seward, 19 March 1866, 24 June 1867, General Records of the Department of State, RG 59, National Archives.

foreign indebtedness of the U.S. Government in its history up to that point—were held in German and Dutch hands.[26]

The importance of German and Dutch investment in this period, however, should not be exaggerated. The Treasury had not arranged a new refunding loan and the bonds purchased were the high-interest Civil War issues that had made their way across the Atlantic. If anything, these investments might have hurt the United States as the bonds were often purchased at large discounts and gold had to be sent abroad to meet the interest payments. On the other hand, German and Dutch investments helped revive flagging European interest in U.S. securities and suggested that a proper refunding loan might yet meet with success. Indeed, demand for five-twenties in Germany led the London Rothschilds to broker large sales of U.S. bonds and strengthened federal securities on the London Stock Exchange.[27] Moreover, European investors' interest in refunding the U.S. debt must have increased when Secretary of State William Seward and his wily representative Samuel Ruggles led an international effort at the Paris monetary convention of 1867 to regulate currency markets as well as establish an international gold standard.[28]

Any hopes the Treasury held of arranging a foreign loan, however, were dashed by the political turmoil of 1868. The impeachment of Andrew Johnson convinced many European capitalists that the American political system was inherently unstable and that the crisis of the Union was yet to be resolved. Harris Fahnestock, a correspondent of Jay Cooke, declared that the financial "effect [of impeachment] abroad is so pernicious" while *The Economist* advised the United States to abolish its constitution and adopt Britain's parliamentary system.[29] Of more concern to European capitalists was the agitation in the United States concerning the repayment of the five-twenty bonds. Appalled at the debilitating effects of currency contraction, several Westerners in Congress called for the repayment of five-twenty bonds in greenbacks. Such a policy, it was argued, would diminish the pains of contraction to debtors and small farmers, help pay down the massive national debt, and wrestle political and economic power away from the creditors and financial

---

[26] See Wilkins, *Foreign Investment*, pp. 109-10; D. C. M. Platt, *Foreign Finance in Continental Europe and the United States, 1815-1870* (London, 1984), p. 151; John Madden, *British Investments in the United States, 1860-1880* (New York, 1985), p. 400.

[27] N.M.R. and Sons to Belmont, 15 May 1866, RA; *The Economist*, 17 October 1868, p. 1198.

[28] For the Paris monetary conference, see Ernest Paolino, *The Foundations of the American Empire: William H. Seward and U.S. Foreign Policy* (Ithaca, 1973), pp. 76-104.

[29] *The Economist*, 18 January 1868, 32; Larson, *Jay Cooke*, p. 231.

interests of the Northeast. The so-called "Pendleton Plan," the namesake of Ohio Democrat George Pendleton, gathered momentum in 1867 and was incorporated into the Democratic Party's platform in the 1868 convention, much to the chagrin of Democratic Chairman August Belmont.[30] Other leaders of both parties called for an end to currency contraction (which occurred early in 1868), while extreme voices demanded the printing of more greenbacks and the permanent abandonment of a hard-money system.[31]

European financiers, who had long regarded gold as sacrosanct, were united in their denunciation of such schemes. In their eyes, plans to repay the debt in depreciated paper were commensurate to an outright repudiation of the U.S. Government's obligations to its creditors. "If the public debt of the United States is to be repudiated," the *Bankers' Magazine* asked, "where, it may well be asked, will repudiation stop?"[32] Even those sympathetic to the United States did not hesitate to condemn repayment of the debt in greenbacks. John Stuart Mill, who had stood by the Union in the darkest years of the Civil War, begged Americans to resist the urge to "repudiate" their debt in a letter reproduced in *The Nation* after the 1868 Democratic convention.[33] To Mill, the Pendleton Plan "would...be one of the heaviest blows that could be given to the reputation of popular governments, and to the morality and civilization of the human race." Mill was concerned with more than economic theory, although the infallibility of the gold standard was certainly on his mind.[34] As the political thinker was all too aware, the repudiation of the American debt would give ammunition to the opponents of democracy and reform in Britain who lost no opportunity to connect the failings of the United States to the shortcomings of democracy. As Mill acknowledged, "the charge against democracy of being a return to barbarism would be made out, if its effect were to be the public repudiation of pecuniary engagements." Indeed, a letter printed in *The Economist* had already claimed

---

[30] The Democratic platform called for debt repayment in "lawful money," which at the time included greenbacks, and advocated "one currency for the government and the people, the laborer and the officeholder...the producer and the bondholder." For more, see Belmont to N.M.R. and Sons, 7 February 1868, T57/90, RA; Sharkey, *Money, Class, and Party*, pp. 120-1; Irving Katz, *August Belmont: A Political Biography* (New York, 1968), p. 173.

[31] For the Anti-Contraction Bill, see Sharkey, *Money, Class, and Party*, pp. 107-15.

[32] *Bankers' Magazine*, vol. 28 (April 1868), pp. 385-8.

[33] *The Nation*, vol. 7, 15 October 1868, pp. 308-9.

[34] It was a common belief in the mid-nineteenth century, the historian Robert Sharkey argues, "that the Almighty had ordained the use of gold and silver as money." Sharkey, *Money, Class, and Party*, p. 60.

that "the tendency to repudiation" was most likely to occur in states "where universal suffrage holds sway."[35] Whatever the Pendleton Plan and other schemes for using paper money to repay the debt meant for the future of democracy in Britain, it was clear that they deterred European investors from purchasing U.S. bonds and closed the possibility to the Treasury of brokering a low-interest loan abroad. "The United States will ruin their European credit if they pay in paper," *The Economist* avowed, "for no one who lends to them hereafter will ever know what he will receive."[36]

Fortunately for those in the United States who sought to attract foreign investment, Ulysses S. Grant and the Republican Party offered a hard-money alternative in the election of 1868. As one Republican senator told Jay Cooke, "it would be a good investment for you" to support the Grant campaign.[37] The Republican platform was unequivocally pro-gold, declaring that "the national honor requires the payment of the public indebtedness in the uttermost good faith to all creditors at home and abroad."[38] "It is all that the Bondholders can expect," Democratic Chairman, but obviously pro-gold, August Belmont informed the Rothschilds, "and is directly opposed to the impractical and unfair proposition of Pendleton and his Western friends."[39] Indeed, U.S. bonds rallied on the London Stock Exchange as it became clear that Grant would prevail in the upcoming elections and that a business-friendly administration would protect the interests of financiers in and out of the United States.[40] As Barings informed their American correspondents in October, the likely outcome of the upcoming election "has produced a favourable effect on five-twenties."[41]

Upon his election, Grant did not disappoint the financial community. "The payment of the debt, principal and interest, as well as the return to a specie basis," the newly elected president declared, "must be provided for."[42] Such words were music to the ears of European financiers searching for a profitable and safe outlet for their capital. The conservative

---

[35] *The Economist*, 5 September 1868, p. 1023.
[36] *The Economist*, 26 October 1867, p. 1213.
[37] Quoted in Larson, *Jay Cooke*, p. 202. Cooke took this advice when he contributed $20,000 to the Republican campaign. See Eric Foner, *Reconstruction: America's Unfinished Revolution, 1863–1877* (New York, 1988), p. 341.
[38] Quoted in Sharkey, *Money, Class, and Party*, 122.
[39] Belmont to N.M.R. and Sons, 22 May 1868, T57/104, RA.
[40] See *The Economist*, 17 October 1868, 1198.
[41] Baring Brothers to Ward, 17 October 1868, BP.
[42] Quoted in Boutwell, *Reminiscences of Sixty Years in Public Affairs*, II, p. 228.

Rothschilds were so confident in Grant's intentions that they ordered Belmont to purchase $100,000 in five-twenties even before he took office.[43] This soon proved a wise investment. The administration's first act was to sign into the law the Public Credit Act, which pledged the Treasury to refund its obligations in coin and called for a quick resumption of specie payments. It was also not long before Hamilton Fish, the new secretary of state, sought to regain the support of overseas investors when he initiated a correspondence with Britain and European states with the aim of establishing "a common unit and standard on an international gold coinage."[44] Such actions immediately improved the financial standing of the United States overseas. *The Economist* pronounced that among nations only Britain was a more reliable debtor than the United States.[45] A congressional report in 1869 estimated that foreign investment had increased to the unprecedented figure of $1.5 billion, two-thirds of which was placed in federal bonds.[46]

The new secretary of the treasury, former Massachusetts governor George Boutwell, sought to take advantage of the popularity of U.S. securities overseas. Though a radical Republican and ringleader of the effort to impeach Andrew Johnson, Boutwell was a financial conservative who, in the words of Hans Trefousse, was "fanatically devoted to reducing the national debt and establishing a hard currency."[47] Not surprisingly, Boutwell advocated issuing a low-interest loan in Europe to achieve both of these ends. Even before being named secretary of the treasury, Boutwell had led a Congressional effort in 1868 to make new issues of U.S. bonds "payable, principal and interest, at the option of the takers, either in the United States, or in London, Paris, or Frankfort." Although this effort failed when Congress could not agree on the particulars of a bill to refund the debt, Boutwell remained committed to brokering a foreign loan when he accepted Grant's invitation to the cabinet in early 1869.[48]

[43] Belmont to N.M.R. and Sons, 26 February 1869, T58/3, RA.
[44] Hamilton Fish, "Circular on Gold Standard," 11 June 1870, *Foreign Relations of the United States* (hereafter *FRUS*), 1870, pp. 240-6.
[45] *The Economist*, 30 October 1869, pp. 1277-8. See also *The Economist*, 16 January and 27 February 1869, pp. 69, 244.
[46] "Report of the Special Commissioner of the Revenue upon the Industry, Trade, Commerce, &c. of the United States for the Year 1869," United States House of Representatives, Ex. Doc. No. 27, 41st Congress, 2nd session. This report is reproduced in full in Mira Wilkins (ed.), *Foreign Investments in the United States: Department of Commerce and Department of Treasury Estimates* (New York, 1977).
[47] Hans Trefousse, *The Radical Republicans* (New York, 1969), p. 448.
[48] See Boutwell, *Reminiscences of Sixty Years in Public Affairs*, II, pp. 141, 183. See also *The Economist*, 30 October 1869, pp. 1277-8.

With the improvement of the United States' financial standing abroad and the gold premium rapidly declining, it appeared that such an operation might succeed.

But just as the financial and monetary roadblocks to placing a refunding loan abroad were removed, a more threatening diplomatic one appeared when relations with Britain soured in the spring 1869. Tense Anglo-American relations were not altogether new as the two nations had been at odds since the Civil War. Northerners felt betrayed by British leaders who considered intervening in the conflict, publicly pronounced their support for the South (the main culprit here was William Gladstone), and allowed Confederate raiders to be constructed in British shipyards. The shipbuilding issue, generally referred to as the *Alabama* dispute after the most notorious British-built Confederate raider, became the focus of Northern anger after the war. The narrative of the escape of the *Alabama* from the Laird shipyard seemed to confirm Northern accusations of active British support for the South and complicity in the rebellion. The material damage inflicted by the British-built raiders was also significant: hundreds of American ships were sunk or captured during the war and a further 750 were transferred to foreign flags or mothballed because of the threat and to increasing insurance premiums.[49]

Hence, before the war was even over, U.S. statesmen made it clear that they expected to be compensated for the damages inflicted by Confederate cruisers that they argued were constructed in violation of Britain's neutrality laws. It was in this spirit that Charles Francis Adams composed a note outlining the American position to Foreign Secretary Lord Russell in May 1865. Russell, however, refused to accept liability for the depredations of the *Alabama* and responded by proposing that the two governments establish a joint commission to hear the claims of both Americans and Britons for the loss of property during the war. But since Britain had adequately enforced her neutrality laws, the Foreign Secretary maintained, the so-called *Alabama* claims should not be permitted before such a commission, leaving only the claims of British subjects to be considered. "Wonderful liberality!" a disgusted Adams proclaimed.[50]

The situation reversed itself a year later when the United States rejected a British plan to resolve the *Alabama* dispute. Conservative

---

[49] Cook, *The* Alabama *Claims*, p. 15.
[50] Quoted in Martin Duberman, *Charles Francis Adams, 1807–1886* (Boston, 1961), p. 324.

Foreign Secretary Lord Stanley revived the idea of a joint commission, but, unlike his predecessors, acknowledged that the *Alabama* claims could be presented before the commission. The only conditions that Stanley placed upon such a commission were that both nations should agree upon the issues to be discussed before it sat and that Britain's proclamation of neutrality should not be put before the arbitrators. The latter point, however, was unacceptable to Secretary of State Seward. Issued in May 1861, the proclamation of neutrality conferred belligerent rights to both the North and South and governed British actions during the war. Northerners argued that Britain had issued the proclamation precipitately and believed that it had encouraged the South to continue its struggle by giving the impression that British diplomatic recognition of the Confederacy was forthcoming. As Seward declared, the proclamation was "unnecessary, ungracious, unfriendly, irritating and injurious."[51] Only by putting the proclamation before the proposed commission, Seward argued, could the full extent of British transgressions during the war be understood. But to Stanley and other British statesmen, it was inappropriate to question Britain's right to confer the status of belligerency to a group of rebels in a civil war in front of an international commission. To do so would compromise British sovereignty and honor and establish a dangerous precedent.

Thus, by early 1867, a solution to the *Alabama* controversy appeared as far away as it was in 1865. It is clear, as historians have pointed out, that the United States missed an opportunity to put the issue to rest when Seward rejected Stanley's proposal.[52] However, it should not be forgotten that there was little incentive for Seward to compromise in 1867. In contrast to the later years of the dispute, there was not a pressing financial inducement to resolve the *Alabama* controversy as the Treasury had no plans for placing a loan abroad. On the contrary, there were motives for keeping the dispute unsettled. It is likely that Seward expected the British to yield even more in the future. More importantly, by leaving the dispute unresolved, Seward left open the possibility of British territorial cession as compensation for the *Alabama* claims. The architect of the purchase of Alaska and the failed scheme to acquire the Danish West Indies, Seward was an expansionist who had long advocated the annexation of Canada. Indeed, in 1866 the Secretary of State dispatched propagandists to north of the border to whip up support for Canadian

---

[51] Quoted in Cook, *The* Alabama *Claims*, p. 41.
[52] For this view, see Cook, *The* Alabama *Claims*, 42.

entry into the United States.[53] As Charles Francis Adams observed, "Mr. Seward's thirst for more land seems insatiable."[54]

If Seward's intention was to get territory out of the *Alabama* dispute, he changed his mind by late 1868 when he proposed the establishment of a joint commission to settle the outstanding claims between the two nations. Significantly, Seward dropped his previous demand that the proposed commission have the authority to consider the recognition of Confederate belligerency in May 1861. Reverdy Johnson, Adams' successor at the U.S. legation in London, and Lord Stanley quickly drafted the details for the creation of the commission that was signed in January 1869 by Johnson and Lord Clarendon (who regained his post as foreign secretary after the Liberal victory in the general election of 1868). The ill-fated Johnson–Clarendon agreement called for the establishment of a joint Anglo-American claims convention, much like that held in London in the 1850s, which would hear all claims by American citizens against the British Government and by British subjects against the U.S. Government. These claims would be submitted to a five-person commission consisting of two Americans, two Britons, and one arbitrator.

Though a fair means of resolving international claims, the Johnson–Clarendon agreement fatally erred in not granting special consideration to the *Alabama* issue. Under the settlement, grievances of British subjects against the U.S. Government would be treated equally to the claims of Americans against the British Government regarding the *Alabama*. Particularly infuriating to Americans was the prospect of British holders of defaulted Confederate bonds and owners of captured blockade-runners seeking compensation from the federal government. Moreover, the Johnson–Clarendon treaty offered no redress of national honor to the United States. Under the terms of the agreement, Britain was under no obligation to admit wrongdoing or apologize for the *Alabama* affair and was bound only to compensate individual ship-owners affected by British-built Confederate cruisers as opposed to the United States as a whole. Thus, the Johnson–Clarendon agreement reduced a diplomatic issue involving violations of neutrality laws into a series of individual claims. Finally, the apparatus of Johnson–Clarendon was insufficient. In the

---

[53] For more on Canadian independence/annexation and the *Alabama* claims, see Doris Dashew, "The Story of an Illusion: The Plan to Trade the *Alabama* Claims for Canada," *Civil War History*, 15 (December 1969), pp. 332–48.

[54] Quoted in Cook, *The Alabama Claims*, 41. For more on Seward's Canadian desires during this time, see Martin Duberman, *Charles Francis Adams, 1807–1886* (Boston, 1961), pp. 329–30.

likely case of a split vote between the American and British representatives, an arbitrator would be chosen by lot to break the tie. Although a last-minute amendment to the treaty provided for arbitration on certain issues (primarily the *Alabama* claims) by a foreign head of state, the gambling element of the agreement was, as one historian put it, "ridiculous."[55] The lame-duck Johnson administration pocketed the treaty and left ratification for incoming President Grant and his secretary of state, New Yorker Hamilton Fish.

While Grant and Fish formulated their foreign policy and assessed the Johnson–Clarendon agreement, the Senate, led by Foreign Relations chairman Charles Sumner, took action. In a notorious speech delivered on 13 April 1869, Sumner vociferously denounced the Johnson–Clarendon agreement for failing to remove "the massive grievance under which our country suffered for years." Sumner argued that the treaty failed to adequately provide the nation with redress for the wrongs committed by Britain during the war. The Massachusetts senator scoffed at the prospect of Britain not having to apologize for her alleged pro-Confederate actions and at the possibility of British subjects who had purchased Confederate bonds or run the blockade receiving compensation from U.S. taxpayers.

Sumner's opposition to Johnson–Clarendon, however, did not end there. The Senate veteran reasserted the old accusation that Britain's proclamation of neutrality was conferred illegally and without it "no rebel ship could have been built in England ... nor could any munitions of war have been furnished" to the Confederacy. In addition to providing compensation to those ship-owners directly affected by the *Alabama*, Sumner argued that any future resolution to the *Alabama* claims should also include redress for so-called "national" or indirect damages. Such damages included increased insurance premiums, the transfer of much of the American merchant marine to foreign flags and the cost of pursuing Confederate vessels during the war. Most amazingly, Sumner maintained that British material and moral support given to the South enabled the Confederacy to continue its struggle and that "through British intervention, the war was doubled in duration." Since the Confederacy would have collapsed without British support in the summer 1863, Sumner contended, Britain might be "justly liable for the additional expenditure

---

[55] For the shortcomings of the Johnson–Clarendon agreement, see Cook, *The* Alabama *Claims*, pp. 69–76; David Donald, *Charles Sumner and the Rights of Man* (New York, 1970), p. 366.

to which our country is doomed." In other words, fair compensation for the *Alabama* claims might be for Britain to assume the U.S. debt contracted after the battle of Gettysburg—or some $2 billion! Such harsh demands only increased the calls of expansionists for the British cession of Canada as compensation for the *Alabama* claims. Indeed, Sumner's biographer has suggested that, similar to Seward's rejection of the Stanley offer in 1867, the desire to annex Canada lay behind his speech.[56] Whatever his intentions, Sumner's speech led the Senate to reject the Johnson–Clarendon agreement by a vote of 54 to 1 and placed Anglo-American relations in their tensest state since the war.[57]

Unfortunately for Secretary of the Treasury Boutwell, the consequences of Sumner's speech were not limited to an escalation of diplomatic tensions with Britain. U.S. bonds, recently bolstered by the Public Credit Act, dropped by ten percent on the London Stock Exchange in the weeks following the Senate's rejection of the Johnson–Clarendon treaty.[58] "Mr. Sumner's speech," Barings wrote to one of their New York correspondents, "doubtless had something to do with this."[59] A few days later, *The Nation* reported that "millions after millions of five-twenties were thrown upon the [European] market in headlong haste."[60] Sumner's speech had such a prejudicial effect upon Anglo-American financial relations that when the Bank of England raised its discount rate in May 1869, many on Wall Street ascribed the action "to the unfriendly feeling produced by the *Alabama* controversy."[61] Although it is unlikely that Sumner's speech dictated the actions of the Bank of England, it is clear that it precluded Boutwell from placing a low-interest loan in Europe. Barings advised their American agent that "if it is the policy of the Secretary of the Treasury to increase the currency of the Bonds in Europe, the Washington Cabinet will naturally be reluctant to provoke a serious discussion" with Britain along the lines of Sumner's

---

[56] Donald, *Charles Sumner and the Rights of Man*, p. 391.

[57] For Sumner's speech, see Charles Sumner, *The Alabama Claims, Speech against the Ratification of the Johnson-Clarendon Treaty* (London, 1869). See also Donald, *Charles Sumner and the Rights of Man*, pp. 374–86; Cook, *The* Alabama *Claims*, pp. 74–98; Nevins, *Hamilton Fish*, p. 152.

[58] U.S. five-twenties were quoted at 85 ⅝ on 10 April 1869 (*The Economist*, 10 April 1869, p. 415); Barings wrote on 8 May 1869 that five-twenties were as low as 76 ½ . See Baring Brothers to Duncan, Sherman and Co., 8 May 1869, BP.

[59] Baring Brothers to Duncan, Sherman and Co., 8 May 1869, BP. *The Economist* (1 May 1869, p. 501) declared that Sumner's speech "caused an almost uninterrupted decline in prices."

[60] *The Nation*, vol. 9, 12 August 1869, p. 124.

[61] *The Nation*, vol. 8, 3 June 1869, p. 428.

"Were it not for our Debt," 1865–1873 207

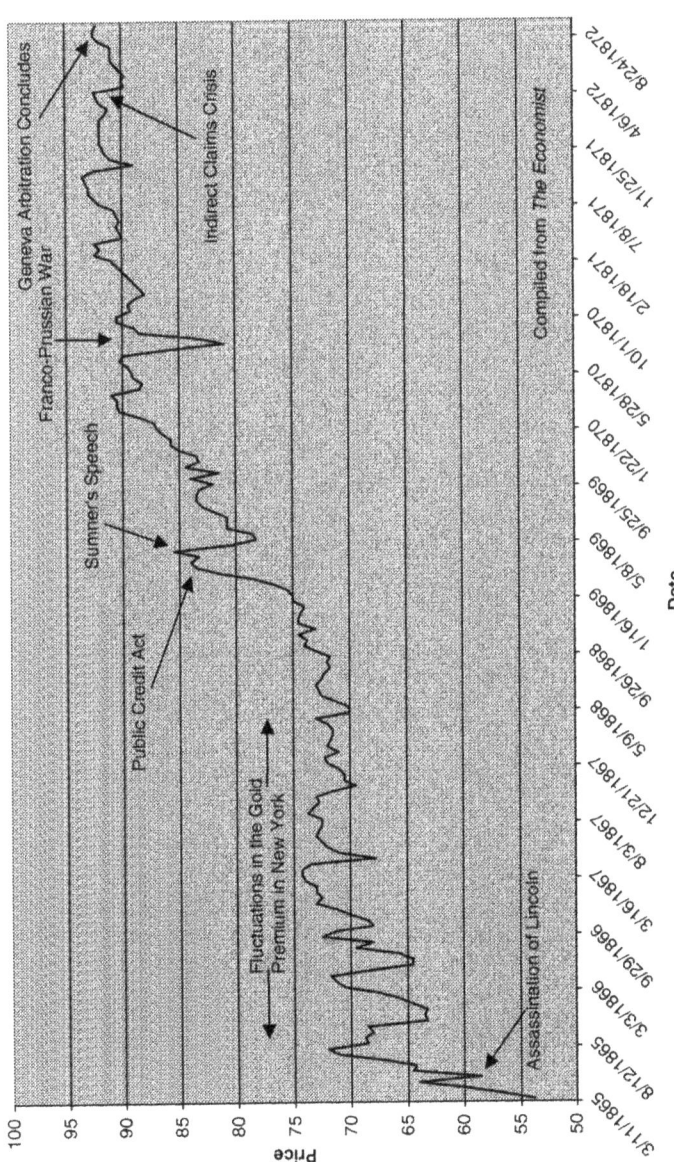

Figure 7 U.S. 5-20 Bonds in London, 1865–1872

speech.⁶² The connection between finance and diplomacy that would do much to determine the course of the *Alabama* claims had been made apparent. As *The Nation* put it, "We are, in short, put upon our good behavior towards other countries... it is no doubt unpleasant to be thus obliged to count in advance the cost of every shift in our foreign policy."⁶³

Given the financial repercussions of Sumner's speech, it is not surprising that it was a group of elite international bankers who made the first attempts to reopen talks on the *Alabama* dispute. With stocks tumbling, wary capitalists withdrawing their investments, and merchants being denied short-term credit, financial leaders on both sides of the Atlantic quickly recognized the economic imperative of reconciling Anglo-American differences and resolving the *Alabama* controversy. Just days after Sumner's speech, August Belmont privately advised Lionel de Rothschild to appeal to Foreign Secretary Lord Clarendon to deploy a "special ambassador" to Washington with authority to settle the *Alabama* issue. Belmont reminded Rothschild of how Lord Ashburton's mission to the United States in 1842 "had a most salutary effect and settled the knotty question of the North Eastern boundary." The Ashburton example was an appropriate one for Belmont to invoke as it illustrated the ability of banker-diplomats to resolve international disputes that had befuddled the State Department and Foreign Office. The 1842 treaty, it should be recalled, was successfully negotiated by Lord Ashburton, the former head of Baring Brothers, and Secretary of State Daniel Webster, a legal and financial consultant who had long been on Barings' payroll.⁶⁴

Canadian financier Sir John Rose put a similar plan to Secretary of State Fish in the summer 1869. A partner in the London branch of Levi Morton's Wall Street bank (Morton, Bliss and Co.), Rose was an experienced politician and diplomat who, in addition to serving as the first finance minister in Canada, had been the British representative on the 1863 commission that settled claims of British companies south of the 49th parallel after the Oregon Treaty. Like Belmont, Rose cited the Ashburton mission in his discussions with Fish and suggested possible British envoys who might best settle the current crisis.⁶⁵ Although Fish

---

⁶² Baring Brothers to Ward, 14 August 1869, BP.
⁶³ *The Nation*, vol. 9, 12 August 1869, p. 124.
⁶⁴ Belmont to N.M.R. and Sons, 16 April 1869, T58/8, RA. See also Belmont to N.M.R. and Sons, 28 April 1869, RA.
⁶⁵ The names mentioned were the Duke of Argyll, John Bright, Lord Granville, and Sir Henry Bulwer. See Fish Diary, 11 July 1869, Fish Papers, LC.

was receptive to Rose's overture, it was deemed unpropitious to proceed with such a plan while Anglo-American relations remained tense so soon after Sumner's speech. Fish encouraged Rose, however, to present his plan to British leaders upon his return to London.[66]

Although Rose's proposal may have been premature, the international setting a year later was more conducive to the settlement of the *Alabama* claims. On the British side of the Atlantic, the whole dispute was beginning to become more than just a diplomatic nuisance. The precedent of lax neutrality laws terrified British statesmen as Franco-Prussian rivalry threatened to involve Britain in a European war. Indeed, after the outbreak of the Franco-Prussian War in July 1870 and Russia's attempt to militarize the Black Sea that November, Undersecretary in the Foreign Office Lord Tenterden called it "a matter of national exigency" to settle the *Alabama* dispute.[67] American diplomats did not waste the opportunity to push Britain into a favorable settlement. Fish bluntly informed the British minister to Washington Sir Edward Thornton that "if England became involved [in the Franco-Prussian War], it would be impossible to prevent retaliation, and the ocean would swarm with 'Alabamas.'"[68] In their attempt to avoid entanglement in the Franco-Prussian War and an ocean swarming with *Alabamas*, British leaders tightened their nebulous neutrality laws in August 1870. Fish interpreted this action, which American statesmen had long called for, as "itself a practical admission of the inefficiency of their former enactments & of their fault in not having provided the means of discharging their international obligations towards us."[69] The turmoil in Europe thus made British leaders willing to make concessions to the United States and led them to acknowledge—albeit indirectly—that they may bear some responsibility for the destruction caused by the *Alabama* during the Civil War. "I do not pretend in this state of things on the continent of Europe," Foreign Secretary Lord Granville disclosed to Thornton in October 1870, "that I should not like to make all things snug on your side of the water."[70]

[66] For Rose's meeting with Fish, see Fish Diary, 11 July 1869, Fish Papers, LC; Nevins, *Hamilton Fish*, p. 213; J. C. Bancroft Davis, *Mr. Fish and the* Alabama *Claims* (Boston, 1893), p. 44; Cook, *The Alabama Claims*, p. 118.
[67] "Relations with the United States," Confidential Memorandum by Lord Tenterden, 21 November 1870, FO 5/1331, Public Records Office (hereafter PRO).
[68] Fish Diary, 24 March 1870, Fish Papers, LC.
[69] Fish Diary, 11 September 1870, Fish Papers, LC.
[70] Quoted in Maureen Robson, "The *Alabama* Claims and the Anglo-American Reconciliation, 1865–1871," *Canadian Historical Review*, 42 (March 1961), pp. 1–22. See also C. P. Stacey, "Britain's Withdrawal from North America, 1864–1871," *Canadian Historical Review*, 36 (September 1955), pp. 185–98.

For their part, American leaders also became more willing to compromise. Grant removed John Lothrop Motley, an ally of Charles Sumner who shared his extreme views on the *Alabama* issue, from his post as U.S. minister to London in June 1870. Although this was done to exact revenge on Sumner for his opposition to the administration's scheme to annex Santo Domingo, the appointment of Robert Schneck, a railroad executive with British connections, portended conciliatory Anglo-American relations. More importantly, American statesmen dropped their demand for British withdrawal from Canada, which it was hoped would open the door to annexation, as a prerequisite for talks on the *Alabama* claims. Although Fish and Boutwell, like most nineteenth-century Americans, believed that the United States would eventually annex Canada, neither was willing to jeopardize peaceful relations with Britain to expedite this end.[71] Furthermore, Fish and Boutwell doubted both the desire of Canadians to join the United States and the Treasury's ability to finance forcible annexation. The two statesmen thus checked Grant's appetite for Canada during cabinet meetings in 1870. As Boutwell stated to Grant, the *Alabama* claims "cannot properly be connected with the question of Canadian Independence & it is important to have them settled before the next Presidential Elections."[72] In another instance, Grant brazenly declared that "were it not for our debt," he hoped "Congress would declare war with Gt. Britain ... take Canada, & wipe out her commerce." Boutwell and Fish shook their heads, before the Treasury Secretary advised the President to "wait until the funding bill has passed."[73]

It was the passage of this funding bill that firmly committed the Grant administration to resolving the *Alabama* dispute. As we have seen, the Treasury had sought to restructure its massive debt at a lower rate of interest, preferably through a new loan placed in Europe, since the end of the Civil War. Boutwell had openly advocated such a plan for several years, and Fish had been informed that Baring Brothers thought favorably of a four and a half percent loan in Britain as early as October 1869.[74]

---

[71] For Boutwell's temporary interest in connecting British withdrawal from Canada to a resolution of the *Alabama* dispute, see Boutwell to Grant, 29 July 1870, *The Papers of Ulysses S. Grant* (Carbondale, 1967–2000), vol. 20, p. 256.

[72] Fish Diary, 30 November 1870, Fish Papers, LC.

[73] Fish Diary, 22 March 1870, Fish Papers, LC. For more on the end of U.S. hopes to annex Canada, see Robson, "The *Alabama* Claims and the Anglo-American Reconciliation, 1865–1871," p. 5; and Dashew, "The Story of an Illusion: The Plan to Trade the *Alabama* Claims for Canada," p. 345.

[74] Aspinwall to Fish, 11 October 1869, Fish Papers, LC. See also Baring Brothers to Ward, 27 November 1869, BP.

Without congressional approval, however, the Treasury lacked the authority to place a new loan abroad. This obstacle was removed on 14 July 1870 when Congress passed the "Act for Funding the Public Debt." Drafted by Boutwell, this bill authorized a "funded loan," to be placed both at home and abroad, to convert $1.5 billion of six percent five-twenties into varying amounts of five, four and a half, and, ultimately, four percent Treasury bonds.[75]

Boutwell's hope of placing the new loan abroad, however, lasted exactly twenty-four hours as the Franco-Prussian War erupted the day after the passage of the bill. "If the war continues any length of time," *The Economist* stated, "the prospect of funding the American debt at a much lower rate of interest, with two such borrowers as France and Germany out of the market, must be postponed for a pretty long period."[76] Indeed, quotations in London of the old six percent U.S. bonds dropped from 90 to 81 after the war broke out because of German investors liquidating their American holdings.[77] "No one borrows," a European correspondent informed Fish. "United States Bonds fell to 25 per cent below par. Other American securities were wholly unsaleable, and European securities were from 20 to 50 per cent lower than ever before."[78] With Germans dumping their six percents, it was certain that they would not be interested in a new five percent loan. The only alternative to funding the entire debt at home, Boutwell soon recognized, was to place part of the new loan in Britain. But with the *Alabama* dispute unresolved, British financiers did little to encourage the Secretary of the Treasury to make such an attempt. A prominent London banker bluntly informed Boutwell "that the unsettled condition of the Alabama Claims interfered with the funding of the Public Debt."[79] Thus, before the funded loan could be placed on the London Stock Exchange, the *Alabama* dispute needed to be resolved.

---

[75] For the text of the funded bill, see *The Economist*, 16 July 1870, p. 893. See also Boutwell, *Reminiscences of Sixty Years in Public Affairs*, II, pp. 137–43, 183. The act called for $1.5 billion of sixes to be converted into $200 million in fives (payable after 10 years), $300 million in four and a halves (payable after 15 years), and $1 billion in fours (payable in 30 years).

[76] *The Economist*, 23 July 1870, p. 914.

[77] *The Economist*, 23 July 1870, p. 914. See also *The Nation*, vol. 11, 11 August 1870, pp. 84–5; Belmont to N.M.R. and Sons, 20 July 1870, T58/68, RA.

[78] Webster to Fish, 28 February 1871, Fish Papers, LC.

[79] Fish Diary, 9 December 1870, Fish Papers, LC. The banker, it turns out, was Sir John Rose.

THE TREATY OF WASHINGTON AND THE FUNDED LOAN

Canadian banking magnate Sir John Rose was certainly aware of the United States' dilemma and sought to use it to entice British leaders to take the initiative to resolve the *Alabama* dispute. In a confidential memorandum circulated to the British cabinet in November 1870, Rose maintained that the United States' desire for foreign capital necessitated a resolution to the *Alabama* affair and made the Grant administration likely to back off the extreme demands made by Sumner the previous year. "The United States' Government," Rose argued,

> are most anxious to effect a conversion of their debt in Europe into one bearing a lower rate of interest; and they are sensible of the reluctance of capitalists to consider it until the American demands are put in a shape for amicable adjustment. The reduction of the national burdens by means of such a conversion, has been a leading idea with the President and his party; on the accomplishment of which they in a great measure base their hopes of re-election in 1872.[80]

Rose reiterated his earlier proposal that, with both nations now desiring a settlement, Britain should send "some intermediate agency" to Washington. This unofficial envoy would not resolve the controversy but would arrange for the creation of a joint commission, composed of an equal number of American and British representatives, to settle all outstanding diplomatic disputes between the two nations. Such disagreements included not only the *Alabama* claims, but also the disputed fisheries off the Canadian shore, ownership of San Juan Island in the Puget Sound, navigation rights on the St. Lawrence River, and new international copyright agreements.

The idea of a wide-ranging joint commission to settle all Anglo-American disputes was not new. Lord Tenterden had made a similar recommendation in a cabinet memorandum a few days earlier, and Hamilton Fish had expressed his desire to "settle all the questions pending between the countries at once" in a September 1870 meeting with Thornton.[81] With both sides in general agreement, the Gladstone ministry opted to act on Rose's proposal and deploy a special minister to Washington to arrange for the establishment of a joint commission. The belief that the United States' need for cheap foreign capital would make American statesmen

---

[80] "Memorandum by Sir John Rose" Confidential, 5 December 1870, FO 5/1331, PRO.
[81] For Tenterden, see "Relations with the United States," Confidential Memorandum by Lord Tenterden, 21 Nov. 70, FO 5/1331, PRO. For Fish, see Fish Diary, 26 Sep 1870, Fish Papers, LC; Cook, *The* Alabama *Claims*, p. 140; Nevins, *Hamilton Fish*, p. 426.

likely to compromise was the primary factor that led the British cabinet to take this first step. As Granville stated in his endorsement of Rose's plan to Gladstone, "a pet object with Grant is to reduce the rate of interest from six to four and a half per cent and that [Grant] is aware this cannot be done without a fair settlement of old scores with England."[82]

While deciding whom to send on this delicate mission, it struck Granville "that Sir John Rose might be usefully employed in the way indicated by his confidential instructions."[83] The rest of the cabinet agreed and the Canadian financier received instructions for his negotiations with the United States on 19 December 1870.[84] There is little doubt that Rose was the appropriate choice to send on the mission to Washington. He was well acquainted with the nuances of the *Alabama* dispute, trusted by leaders on both sides of the Atlantic, and could use his Canadian connections to pose as a third-party arbitrator. Indeed, Rose himself had prepared the groundwork for a special mission to the United States, not only through his memo to the British cabinet, but also by confidentially informing Fish and Grant the previous month "that the British Cabinet is disposed to enter upon a negotiation."[85]

It is surprising, however, that Gladstone and Granville were apparently oblivious to the secondary object that Rose pursued during his diplomatic mission to Washington: securing the appointment for his bank of brokering the U.S. funded loan in Europe. Serving as the financial agent for a government loan was the most lucrative and respected function of nineteenth-century investment banks. It should come as little surprise, therefore, that Rose and his New York partner, Levi Morton, lobbied to secure the contract from the Grant administration once it became known that the Treasury sought to place part of the loan abroad. Thus, Rose clearly had his eyes fixed on more than resolving the *Alabama* dispute during his secret mission to the United States. Indeed, on Rose's very first day in Washington, he met with Boutwell with whom he mutually agreed "that some means might now be devised of settling all points of the controversy" in order to facilitate the Treasury's funding plans abroad.[86]

---

[82] Granville to Gladstone, 22 November 1870. Gladstone Papers, vol. LXXXII, Add. Ms. 44,167. British Library.
[83] Granville to Thornton, 17 December 1870, FO 362/1, Granville Papers, PRO.
[84] Granville to Rose, 19 Dec 1870, FO 5/1298. Tenterden urged Granville not to give Rose too much freedom of action on his mission. See Tenterden to Granville, 19 December 1870, FO 5/1298, PRO.
[85] Fish Diary, 9 December 1870, Fish Papers, LC.
[86] Rose to Granville, 10 January 1871, FO 5/1298, PRO.

Though shocking to modern observers, it is unlikely that this overlapping of personal, financial interests with diplomacy detrimentally influenced Rose's negotiations with Fish in January 1871. Rose certainly did not compromise Britain's interests in his desire to resolve the dispute in order to secure his appointment for brokering the funded loan. Negotiations with Fish concerning the establishment of the proposed joint commission were far from smooth, often lasting until as late as three in the morning.[87] Sumner's power and influence in the Senate made Fish reluctant to yield to Britain's positions as articulated by Rose. Despite Fish's intransigence, Rose got the upper hand in the negotiations. The Canadian financier refused to back down to Fish's demands that Britain admit wrongdoing in the *Alabama* affair before the commission met and forced the Secretary of State to accept his ultimatum that Britain would not accept "any foregone condition for payment of money" to compensate the United States.[88] Nor did Rose flinch when Sumner absurdly demanded that "as a condition precedent to any negotiation, Great Britain must withdraw her flag from this hemisphere."[89] If anything, Rose's connections with the Treasury helped lay the foundation for a settlement by reminding American statesmen of the financial necessity of putting the *Alabama* controversy to rest. Moreover, Rose's partner, Levi Morton, helped his cause by outlining the benefits of resolving the *Alabama* dispute to his friend Ulysses Grant, whose support was obviously crucial to the success of Rose's mission.[90] The United States' need for cheap capital to refinance its debt necessitated diplomatic compromise, and Rose and Morton lost no opportunity to make this point to the Grant administration.[91]

Fish's concessions in the negotiations with Rose illustrate how much the Grant administration was willing to yield in order to open the financial markets of London to a U.S. loan. Less than two years after the leading Republican in the Senate had demanded enormous reparation payments from Britain (if not the cession of Canada), a Republican administration consented to Britain's demands that Canadian independence was out of the question and that the joint commission would

---

[87] Ibid.; Davis, *Mr. Fish and the* Alabama *Claims*, p. 59.
[88] Rose to Granville, 27 January 1871, FO 5/1298, PRO; Fish Diary, 30 January 1871, Fish Papers, LC.
[89] Rose to Granville, 21 January 1871, FO 5/1298, PRO.
[90] Rose to Granville, 10 January 1871, FO 5/1298, PRO.
[91] For the details of the Rose–Fish negotiations, see Robert Carlton Clark, "The Diplomatic Mission of Sir John Rose, 1871," *Pacific Quarterly Review*, 27 (July 1936), pp. 227–42. See also Cook, *The* Alabama *Claims*, p. 163.

commence its deliberations without Britain admitting liability for the depredations of the *Alabama*. Although Fish and Grant could rightly argue that these concessions did not compromise national interests or honor (as it was by now clear that Canadians wanted nothing of annexation and that it was likely that the commission would hold Britain accountable in some degree for the *Alabama* claims), Sumner and his allies predictably cried foul and opposed the creation of the joint commission under the terms agreed to by Fish and Rose. Eager to begin its refunding operation and aware of the economic fallout that was certain to follow another failed attempt to resolve the *Alabama* dispute, however, the Grant cabinet agreed to the plan despite the disapproval of discontented Republicans.[92] Each nation quickly appointed their five-member negotiating team and on 24 February 1871 the joint commission first met. "We are taking several bites out of that big cherry," Granville wrote to John Bright, "reconciliation with the states."[93]

British statesmen matched Fish's willingness to compromise during the two months of intense but gentlemanly negotiations that culminated in the Treaty of Washington (signed in May 1871). Gladstone and Granville reluctantly ordered the abandonment of efforts to acquire compensation for Fenian raids into Canada launched from south of the border and allowed American access to Canadian fisheries in exchange for a payment agreed upon by a future international commission. The Liberal statesmen also agreed to draw up the so-called "due diligence" neutrality regulations that required both nations to use due diligence in future to prevent another *Alabama* dispute over the construction of vessels in the shipyards of a neutral state. Finally, the treaty included the long-sought after expression of British regret for the escape of the *Alabama* and other vessels bound for the Confederacy.[94] Although these were all significant concessions, there is no reason to expect that Britain would have made them were it not for Fish's willingness to resolve Anglo-American differences as exemplified in his earlier negotiations with Rose. In the end, the Treaty of Washington was, as much in nineteenth-century Anglo-American diplomatic relations, the product of mutual compromise.

---

[92] For Sumner's views, see Donald, *Charles Sumner and the Rights of Man*, pp. 484–8.
[93] Quoted in Robson, "The *Alabama* Claims and the Anglo-American Reconciliation, 1865–1871," p. 22.
[94] For British compromises during the treaty negotiations, see, Campbell, *The Transformation of American Foreign Relations*, pp. 31–4.

These mutual compromises led to a curious diplomatic achievement that managed to lay the foundations for the Anglo-American rapprochement of the late-nineteenth century while glossing over a few persistent disagreements.[95] On the successful side, the agreement pre-empted future border controversies when it referred the San Juan Island issue to arbitration (which awarded the island to the United States a year later). The treaty also opened binational waterways, namely the St. Lawrence River, to both nations for perpetuity and referred routine claims arising out of the Civil War (apart from the *Alabama* claims) to a joint claims convention modeled after that of the 1850s. However, as the Webster–Ashburton Treaty of 1842 sidestepped the Oregon dispute, the Treaty of Washington left some of the prickliest issues unresolved.[96] The agreement reached on the fishery dispute aroused anger on both sides and the issue would remain contentious through the 1880s.[97] More important was the unsettled state of the *Alabama* claims. Although the "due diligence" agreement provided the basis to judge British action (or inaction) during the war, the *Alabama* issue remained unresolved as the commissioners opted to refer the controversy to international arbitration after each nation was given the opportunity to compile and compose a case to present before a tribunal in Geneva the following year. It was presumed and hoped that this arbitration would be an uneventful success, demonstrating the benefits of international cooperation and negotiation. Events, as we shall see, would prove otherwise.

Despite these inadequate provisions, it should be recognized that the treaty succeeded in one of its central aims: enticing British capitalists to participate in the Treasury's refunding plans. The two nations' commitment to resolve their differences through peaceful negotiation restored the confidence of cautious banks and investors who had feared that the *Alabama* dispute would lead to war. The renewed interest of British capitalists in U.S. securities that followed an easing of Anglo-American tensions led the Grant administration to make preparations for issuing the low-interest funded loan abroad. Indeed, on the very day that the cabinet accepted Rose's proposal for the creation of the joint commission

---

[95] For the text of the Treaty of Washington, see William Malloy, *Treaties, Conventions, International Acts, Protocols and Agreements between the United States of America and Other Powers* (Washington, 1910), vol. 1, pp. 700–16.

[96] Charles Campbell thus labels the Treaty of Washington a "quasi settlement." Charles Campbell, *The Transformation of American Foreign Relations, 1865–1900* (New York, 1976), pp. 25–49.

[97] For the fishery dispute, see Campbell, *The Transformation of American Foreign Relations*, pp. 31–2, 123–32.

that would ultimately draft the Treaty of Washington, Boutwell announced his intentions to go ahead with a foreign loan. It is certain that Boutwell's "reasons to believe he will be able to do so" originated from his discussions with Rose and Morton.[98] Rose was so confident that his London firm would be chosen to broker the funded issue that he declined Granville's offer for a place on the British high commission in Washington so that he could devote his full attention to "bringing out the new United States Loan in London," which was tentatively set for 6 March 1871.[99]

If Rose thought that he had secured the Treasury's appointment to bring out the loan, he must have been sorely disappointed when Boutwell decided to offer the agency for the first $200 million, five percent funded loan to "everybody."[100] Specifically, the Treasury jointly offered the loan to five London banks: the British houses of Baring Brothers and the Rothschilds, and three lesser known American firms in London, Morton, Rose and Co., Jay Cooke and Co., and J. S. Morgan and Co. (formerly George Peabody and Co. and soon to become J. P. Morgan and Co.). It is not surprising that Boutwell did this considering that long-time Republican benefactor Jay Cooke actively lobbied for the appointment while the established and reputable Barings and Rothschilds expressed interest in the Treasury's plan. After all, Morton, Rose and Co. was a relative unknown in international finance, having just established a London house in 1869 (the New York parent firm of Morton, Bliss and Co. was itself only founded in 1863). Although the Barings and Rothschilds were not accustomed to sharing the profits of a government loan with each other, let alone with lesser known American banks, both houses recognized the significance of Boutwell's offer. With the Treasury deciding to issue only $200 million, $1.3 billion in future funded loans remained to be placed on the market, and it was doubtful that a future agency would be granted to a bank who had been unwilling to participate in the first issue.

The number of banks brokering the funded loan, however, soon proved problematic. Despite the newly operational transatlantic telegraph, Boutwell struggled to coordinate the actions of five banks in London from his office in Washington. Before the loan had even been issued to the public, the Rothschilds admitted that the operation "takes

[98] Fish Diary, 24 January 1871, Fish Papers, LC. See also Nevins, *Hamilton Fish*, p. 442.
[99] Rose to Granville, 9 February 1871, FO 5/1298, PRO. Rose also was concerned that his "connection with a banking firm which has interests in the United States might be urged in opposition to the propriety of my selection."
[100] Oberholtzer, *Jay Cooke*, II, p. 270.

up more of our time and trouble than we are likely to be compensated for."[101] Of more concern was the possibility that the loan would meet with little success in a London market flooded with railroad issues offering up to eight percent and a promising new French loan.[102] The Rothschilds confessed "that in recommending the Exchange of the old 6% for the new 5% bonds to our friends we are at a loss to find an argument in its favour."[103] The loan did not get off to a promising start when the Rothschilds received only one application for $10,000 in the four days after the announcement of the loan on 10 March 1871.[104]

The whole operation began to unravel when Boutwell, anxious to quickly procure subscribers to the loan, extended invitations to several more banks to assist in its placement. Already reluctant to share profits with four competitors, the Barings and Rothschilds were appalled when the Treasury asked American financier Henry Clews, who they viewed as an "unfit association," to join the banking consortium.[105] The final straw occurred when Boutwell considered offering $10 million of the loan to a Russian bank that the Rothschilds had never heard of.[106] On 21 March 1871 the Rothschilds backed out of the scheme and Baring Brothers followed soon thereafter.[107] Having lost the support of the world's two largest banks, the first funded loan appeared to be on the verge of collapse. By late April the loan was a complete failure in Europe and had attracted only $53 million in total. This partial success was in itself deceiving as the majority of the buyers had been national banks in the United States who were required by law to hold federal bonds as reserves.[108]

The early failure of the funded loan threatened to tarnish the financial standing of the United States as well as yield unfavorable political consequences. Without a successful low-interest loan in hand, the

[101] N.M.R. and Sons to Belmont, 2 March 1871, RA.
[102] For the competition between the U.S. and French loans, see *The Economist*, 18 March 1871, p. 311.
[103] N.M.R. and Sons to Belmont, 28 February and 10 March 1871, RA. See also *The Nation*, vol. 11, 27 October 1870, pp. 273–4.
[104] N.M.R. and Sons to Belmont, 14 March 1871, RA.
[105] Thomas Baring to Ward, 4 March 1871, BP. See also N.M.R. and Sons to Belmont, 7 March 1871, RA.
[106] N.M.R. and Sons to Belmont, 23 May 1871, RA.
[107] N.M.R. and Sons to Belmont, 21 March 1871, RA; Baring Brothers to Ward, 8 April 71, BP.
[108] For the initial failure of the loan, see *The Economist*, 22 April 1871, p. 480. "The loan goes very slow," Belmont reported, "the whole subscription, thus far, only amounting to 20 millions... the refusal of yourselves and Barings to join, will probably cause the arrangement to fall through." Belmont to N.M.R. and Sons, 24 March 1871, T58/96, RA. See also Belmont to N.M.R. and Sons, 31 March 1871, T58/97, RA.

Grant administration would have little to show for the compromises made during the *Alabama* talks the previous winter and would invite renewed attacks from the Sumnerian quarter of Congress. Consequently, Boutwell took two significant steps in the summer 1871 to save the funded loan after the withdrawal of the Rothschilds and Barings. First, the Treasury secretary arranged for interest payments on the new bonds to be payable in gold in London. Having interest payable only in the United States was an obvious disincentive to foreign investors who had to pay a fee to a broker to arrange for the conversion of their coupons into gold. Interest payable in Europe would provide the motive for holders of the old six percent five-twenties to convert their bonds into the new five percents that had not existed when the loan was first issued. Indeed, the Rothschilds and other British capitalists had repeatedly urged Boutwell to do this before issuing the loan back in March.[109]

Making interest on government bonds payable abroad, however, was a politically sensitive issue. The Senate Finance Committee and several prominent congressmen opposed this policy because of the belief that such a plan was a "national degradation" that would drain the nation's gold supply only to enrich foreign financiers.[110] This powerful lobby had blocked two previous attempts—led by Boutwell in 1868 and 1870—to make U.S. bonds payable overseas. Thus, Boutwell had to finesse his way around this opposition by making interest on the new bonds payable in checks of the U.S. Treasurer, which did not require congressional approval. Though not specie coin, Treasurer's checks were accepted by banks around the world where they stood "as good as gold." "My object," Boutwell later recalled, "was to make the loan more acceptable in Europe."[111] In August 1871 the Treasury opened an office on Lombard Street to arrange for interest on the new five percent bonds to be paid in this manner. "The feeling in the City," *The Economist* reported, "is entirely favourable to the success of the experiment."[112]

---

[109] See, for example, Belmont to N.M.R. and Sons, 14 March 1870, T58/52, RA. "No provision has been made for the payment of the coupons in Europe," stated *The Economist*, and this "will militate against the success of the loan." *The Economist*, 11 March 1871, p. 311.

[110] For this view, see Murray, "Shall a Great Nation Go Abroad to Pay its Interest?" *New York Daily Times*, 7 March ? (TIF, p.v.59), New York Public Library; Belmont to N.M.R. and Sons, 9 January 1872, T58/115, RA. See also Boutwell, *Reminiscences of Sixty Years in Public Affairs*, II, pp. 141.

[111] Boutwell, *Reminiscences of Sixty Years in Public Affairs*, II, pp. 141-2.

[112] *The Economist*, 19 August 1871, p. 999. By 1900, seventy-seven percent of all interest payments on U.S. bonds were paid by Treasurer's check. See Boutwell, *Reminiscences of Sixty Years in Public Affairs*, II, pp. 141-2.

Second, with the consortium of banks commissioned to place the loan in disarray, Boutwell imparted exclusive authority to Philadelphia financier Jay Cooke to broker the loan.[113] The most prominent banker in the United States, Cooke had been the financial hero of the Civil War when he succeeded in placing loan after loan even in the darkest hours of the conflict. The appointment of an agent with exclusive authority was far more typical of nineteenth-century government loans and avoided the inevitable wrangling and competing that had accompanied the previous joint appointment. Furthermore, Cooke's bank had recently opened a London branch, with former Secretary of the Treasury Hugh McCulloch as its resident partner. Cooke's promotion infuriated Levi Morton and Sir John Rose, who already felt snubbed by the Treasury, and led Morton, Rose and Co. to withdraw their name from the banking consortium.[114] Unfazed by the third defection in the loan's short life, Cooke organized a large European syndicate under his command (which ironically included the former Confederate bankers in Paris, Erlanger and Co.) to sell the new five percent bonds. Within a matter of days, Cooke and his associates placed $75 million of the loan in Europe, primarily in Britain.[115] By August 1871 *The Economist* declared that the loan "has been successful" and that the United States represented "the leading foreign state which borrows in our markets."[116] In all, Boutwell later estimated that $134 million out of the $200 million loan was sold abroad, principally in Britain.[117]

The success of the first funded loan in Europe had implications greater than merely refinancing $200 million of the public debt at a lower rate of interest. For the first time in the history of the United States, an American bank placed a U.S. Government loan in Europe. Not only had an American firm successfully entered into the territory of the world's leading banks, but it had done so with what was at that point the largest foreign loan in American history. Grant expressed his pleasure

---

[113] Boutwell, *Reminiscences of Sixty Years in Public Affairs*, II, pp. 183–202; Oberholtzer, *Jay Cooke*, II, pp. 275–9.

[114] Robert McElroy, *Levi Parsons Morton: Banker, Diplomat and Statesman* (New York, 1930), p. 52.

[115] *Bankers' Magazine*, vol. 32 (January 1872), pp. 5–6; Larson, *Jay Cooke*, pp. 317–27; Platt, *Foreign Finance in Continental Europe and the United States, 1815–1870*, p. 154. The U.S. Treasury sent agents William Richardson and John Bigelow to Europe with the new bonds safely held in a state-of-the-art "iron safe, manufactured expressly for the occasion." See *The Economist*, 1 July 1871, p 784.

[116] *The Economist*, 19 August 1871, p. 999.

[117] Boutwell, *Reminiscences of Sixty Years in Public Affairs*, II, p. 187.

to a partner of Jay Cooke and Co. that the loan "was established without the aid or co-operation of certain firms who have heretofore assumed that nothing could be done without them" and "that the prestige of success was attached to American agents rather than to the Barings and Rothschilds."[118] Levi Morton likewise acknowledged Cooke's success and admitted that it "will put Jay Cooke & Co. head and shoulders above any American house in Europe, and make them the peers of the proudest European houses."[119] The development of American finance and investment banking that began during the Civil War years appeared to finally bring Wall Street to par with the City of London.

The financial independence of the United States, however, should not be exaggerated. Although it was an American bank that orchestrated the placement of the funded loan, it was British gold that ultimately led to its success. Moreover, the prominence of Jay Cooke and Co. would prove ephemeral as the bank collapsed less than two years later during the Panic of 1873. Nonetheless, by late 1871 American finances in general and Jay Cooke and Co. specifically enjoyed an unprecedented standing in Britain. "It may be said that with the exception of England," the ultra-conservative *Bankers' Magazine* opined, "no nation stands higher in respect of public credit than the United States."[120] There was even talk that Cooke would replace the Barings as the overseas agent of the U.S. Government (this in fact occurred later in the year).

Such demonstrations and acknowledgments of American financial autonomy led the traditional London banking powers to fear they might be cornered out of the market for brokering U.S. loans altogether. Thus, the Rothschilds decided to team up with Jay Cooke in January 1872 to form a new syndicate to market the remaining $500 million five percent bonds and $300 million four and a half percents authorized by the Funded Act of 1870.[121] The two banks soon sent their proposal to Boutwell and began preparations for the issuance of the second funded loan in Europe in less than a year.

---

[118] Granted quoted in Oberholtzer, *Jay Cooke*, II, p. 283.
[119] McElroy, *Levi Parsons Morton*, p. 53. See also *The Economist*, 23 December 1871, p. 1566.
[120] *Bankers' Magazine*, vol. 31, September 1871, pp. 789–91.
[121] Belmont to N.M.R. and Sons, 9 and 19 January 1871, T58/115, RA; Oberholtzer, *Jay Cooke*, II, p. 288; Larson, *Jay Cooke*, p. 360. It is often suggested that Jay Cooke's bank would have survived the Panic of 1873 had this proposal been accepted by the Treasury. See Oberholtzer, *Jay Cooke*, II, p. 288; Larson, *Jay Cooke*, p. 360.

THE "INDIRECT CLAIMS" CRISIS

Ambitious plans for marketing $800 million in low-interest bonds in Europe had to be put on hold when the cantankerous *Alabama* issue threatened to divide Britain and the United States yet again in January 1872. At issue this time was the last chapter of the United States' case to be presented before the arbitrators in Geneva. Authored by Assistant Secretary of State J. C. Bancroft Davis, the U.S. case included claims for the so-called "indirect" or national damages inflicted upon the United States by the *Alabama* and other British-built Confederate cruisers. These indirect claims, first articulated by Charles Sumner in his Senate speech in 1869, included damages to the U.S. merchant marines from increased insurance costs and transference to foreign flags, the cost of pursuing Confederate vessels, and the alleged prolongation of the war. "The Tribunal will see," the case read,

> that, after the battle of Gettysburg, the offensive operations of the insurgents were conducted only at sea, through the cruisers; and observing that the war was prolonged for that purpose, will be able to determine whether Great Britain ought not, in equity, to reimburse the United States the expenses thereby entailed upon them.[122]

British statesmen were enraged upon reading American demands for compensation for the indirect damages of the *Alabama*. Granville estimated that if the Geneva tribunal ruled in favor of the United States the costs might amount to $4.5 billion.[123] "We must be insane," Gladstone declared in the Commons in February 1872, "to accede to demands which no nation with a spark of honor or spirit left could submit to even at the point of death."[124] But it was not only the potential cost of the indirect claims that angered British leaders, who argued that U.S. representatives had tacitly agreed not to put forward the indirect claims during the Treaty of Washington deliberations. Although the treaty did not explicitly forbid claims for indirect damages, British commissioners had consistently and outspokenly opposed their inclusion, a position that the Americans appeared to accept through their silent acquiescence. Indeed, it has been suggested by more than one historian that Fish and other American statesmen similarly came away from the Washington

---

[122] United States, *The Case of the United States to be Laid before the Tribunal of Arbitration* (London, 1872), p. 479.
[123] Nevins, *Hamilton Fish*, p. 524.
[124] Quoted in Duberman, *Charles Francis Adams*, p. 348.

negotiations with the understanding that Britain would not accept indirect claims in the Geneva arbitration. Faced with the powerful opposition of Sumner, however, the administration had allowed the misperception to prevail in the Senate in order to secure congressional approval of the Treaty of Washington.[125] What began as a ploy to save the treaty soon became its bane. With British leaders demanding the withdrawal of the indirect claims, the Grant administration, politically constrained and never eager to bow to a British demand, dug in its heels. Thus, by January 1872, the two nations were once again in diplomatic deadlock about how to resolve the *Alabama* dispute.

Predictably, the indirect claims crisis jolted financial markets on both sides of the Atlantic. Similar to the panic that followed Sumner's speech in 1869, U.S. securities, particularly railroad stock, plummeted on the London Stock Exchange as investors feared the escalation of the dispute. "The sensitive imagination of some persons on the Stock Exchange," *The Economist* reported, "has assumed that the probable failure of the Alabama arbitration will probably lead to war between this country and America."[126] The financial situation, however, was not without its advantages. Boutwell ordered the $12 million U.S. account at the Bank of England to be expended on retiring depressed five-twenties on the London market.[127] Similarly, in a textbook stock operation, Morton, Rose and Co. used inside information that the dispute would not soon be resolved to sell short during the panic.[128]

Apart from the short-term profits of such operations, however, it was clear to American statesmen and financiers that the unresolved state of the *Alabama* issue was not in the nation's economic interests. Once again, the seemingly endless diplomatic dispute blocked foreign investment and obstructed international trade. After successfully selling short, Rose became more cautious about conducting transatlantic business and investing in American securities. "We ... must take in sail immediately and keep under double reefed canvas till the storm blows over," the Canadian banker informed partner Levi Morton, "we must be very watchful as to prolonged commitments in the way of credits."[129] More

---

[125] Cook, *The* Alabama *Claims*, pp. 212–14; Nevins, *Hamilton Fish*, p. 486.
[126] *The Economist*, 10 February 1872, p. 161. See also N.M.R. and Sons to Belmont, 30 January 1872, RA; Rose to Morton, 27 January 1872, Morton Papers, New York Public Library (hereafter NYPL).
[127] Boutwell, *Reminiscences of Sixty Years in Public Affairs*, II, p. 202.
[128] Rose to Morton, 27 January 1872, Morton Papers, NYPL.
[129] Rose to Morton, 3 February 1872, Morton Papers, NYPL.

significantly, the indirect claims interfered with the Treasury's plans to place a second funded loan in Europe. The Rothschilds, who planned to issue the new loan, argued that "the uncertainty about the relations between the two countries must throw back all [of the Americans'] financial operations in respect to the reduction of the interest on their Debt and to the loans they are desirous of introducing."[130]

Given the financial consequences of the crisis, it is not surprising that Sir John Rose and Levi Morton were once again in the middle of attempts to find a compromise to the dispute. Acting as conduits between the two governments, Rose and Morton cabled potential compromises to each other before floating their ideas to Fish in Washington and Granville in London.[131] Unlike their involvement during the creation of the joint commission in January 1871, however, the bankers were not neutral third-party arbitrators. Both believed that the United States had misinterpreted the Treaty of Washington, which they argued did not permit the inclusion of indirect claims in the U.S. case. As Morton bluntly informed Fish, "we are in the wrong in the interpretation we put upon the Treaty."[132]

The depressed state of American securities in Britain, particularly the railroad shares that Morton, Rose and Co. were attempting to market, no doubt contributed to Morton's reading of the treaty. "This misunderstanding," the Wall Street banker contended, "is costing this Country almost daily more than any amount we could possibly expect to receive, even if England would agree to refer the question of consequential damages."[133] However financially sensible Morton's view was, Fish refused to let Britain dictate how the United States interpreted the treaty and how it chose to present its case. "I hope that they do not expect on the other side to tell us how we must present our side of the 'case,'" the Secretary of State replied to Morton, "they cannot be litigant—counsel for their opponent—and judge all at once."[134] With the normally con-

[130] N.M.R. and Sons to Belmont, 13 February 1872, RA.
[131] For example, see Morton to Fish, 4 May 1872, Morton Papers, NYPL; Rose to Morton (wired to Fish), 27 April 72, Fish Papers, LC; Fish to Morton, 14 February and 30 March 1872, Morton Papers, NYPL; Rose to Morton, 3 February and 11 May 1872, Morton Papers, NYPL. In one instance, Morton proposed to abandon the Geneva arbitration and instead have Britain pay the United States a lump sum of $12 to $15 million. Fish declined, claiming only £10 million would suffice. See Fish to Morton, 18 February 1872, Morton Papers, NYPL; Fish Diary, 2 February 1872, Fish Papers, LC; Cook, *The Alabama Claims*, p. 219.
[132] Morton to Fish, 28 February 1872, Fish Papers, LC.
[133] Morton to Fish, 28 February 1872, Fish Papers, LC.
[134] Fish to Morton, 18 February 1872, Morton Papers, NYPL.

ciliatory Fish reluctant to yield and Granville threatening British withdrawal from the Geneva arbitration in April 1872, the *Alabama* dispute once again threatened Anglo-American peace.

Fortunately, British statesmen put a compromise on the table before negotiations were formally broken off. In May, the Gladstone cabinet drafted a supplemental article to the treaty that bound both nations never to seek indirect damages for violations of neutrality in the future in exchange for U.S. withdrawal of the indirect claims at Geneva. As the traditionally neutral nation, such an agreement was clearly in the United States' long-term interests. The supplemental article also provided British leaders with the assurance they required that they would not be held liable for the indirect damages of the *Alabama*. The genesis of this compromise is unclear, though it is possible that financiers were once again behind the diplomatic scenes as Lionel de Rothschild suggested the plan to Granville and Gladstone.[135] The one problem with this scheme was that it required congressional approval before it could be formally introduced into the treaty. Aware as always of the radical contingent in congress, the Grant administration was not eager to place an amendment to the treaty before the Senate.

Incorporating the supplemental article into the treaty, however, appeared to be the administration's last chance to resolve the *Alabama* dispute. In Westminster, Lord Russell called upon the House of Lords to demand British withdrawal from the Geneva arbitration scheduled for 15 June. Once again, Secretary of the Treasury Boutwell led the effort within the Grant cabinet to avoid the diplomatic and financial fallout of an escalation of the *Alabama* dispute. In a confidential note to Fish, Boutwell advocated withdrawal of the indirect claims in exchange for the agreement "that a neutral nation is not legally liable to a belligerent for consequential damages."[136] Similarly, the Secretary of the Treasury privately pressed Grant to yield on the indirect claims after a cabinet meeting.[137] There can be little doubt that the Treasury's refunding operation in Europe was the motive for Boutwell's actions. The financial lobby was also at work. Morton used "every influence to induce the Government to accept the English modification" while Jay Cooke lobbied

---

[135] August Belmont had floated this idea to Rothschild, who agreed to sound it out on the British cabinet. See N.M.R. and Sons to Belmont, 14 March and 27 May 1872, RA. Adrian Cook contends that Attorney-General George Williams came up with the idea during a cabinet meeting in April 1872. See Cook, *The* Alabama *Claims*, p. 223.
[136] Boutwell to Fish, 9 May 1872, Fish Papers, LC.
[137] Boutwell, *Reminiscences of Sixty Years in Public Affairs*, II, pp. 200–1.

his political allies Carl Schurz and Vice-President Schuyler Colfax to do the same.[138]

The Grant administration was certainly in a position to be swayed by pressure from the financial community. Fish had never been an advocate of the indirect claims and Grant desired a settlement to the *Alabama* dispute before his re-election campaign got underway. The administration's interest in the supplemental article no doubt increased when Grant's long-time associate Horace Porter, who corresponded with Morton on the *Alabama* issue, reported that the Senate would likely ratify the alterations to the treaty.[139] Pressure from financial interests paid off when the administration opted to put the issue before the Senate on 26 May. After inserting some minor changes to the language of the British proposal, the Senate resoundingly extended their approval to the supplemental article by a vote of 43 to 8. As a Philadelphia banker wrote to Morton the next day, "if it had not been for the efforts of Sir John Rose and yourself I feel assured that the Treaty would have proved a failure."[140]

Such praise proved premature when the Gladstone ministry, despite a plea from Queen Victoria to do otherwise, rejected the amended supplemental article. In the eyes of British cabinet members, the Senate's alterations to the treaty were not the innocuous word changes that the Americans claimed. British statesmen argued that the amended supplemental article broadened the treaty to shield the United States from anticipated Canadian compensation claims for Fenian raids launched from south of the border.[141] Unless the United States accepted the supplemental article as written in Britain, the Geneva arbitration appeared dead. Having already "backed down" once, Belmont informed Lionel de Rothschild, the Senate would not consider the supplemental article a second time.[142]

Backing down a second time was not necessary as the Grant administration had one card left to play. Prior to the supplemental article episode, Boutwell had convinced Fish to give Charles Francis Adams, the head of the American legal team at the Geneva arbitration, authority to make an

---

[138] Rose to Morton, 11 May 1870, Morton Papers, NYPL; Cook, *The* Alabama *Claims*, p. 242. Fish also encouraged Morton to garner support for the supplemental article. See Fish Diary, 27 April 1872, Fish Papers, LC.
[139] Horace Porter to Morton, 6 May 1872, Morton Papers, NYPL.
[140] Childs to Morton, 27 May 1872, Morton Papers, NYPL.
[141] For more, see Cook, *The* Alabama *Claims*, pp. 231–2; Nevins, *Hamilton Fish*, p. 545.
[142] Belmont to N.M.R. and Sons, 31 May 1872, T58/128, RA.

informal pledge to British representatives that he would not seek indirect damages. As Adams had already pronounced his opposition to the indirect claims to prominent Britons, it was presumed that the British legal team would treat seriously this unofficial offer. Working through back channels would also save the United States from the embarrassment of having to revise its case under British pressure. After meeting with Boutwell in a New York hotel in April 1872, Adams recorded in his diary "that the Administration has become alarmed at the prospect of losing the Treaty, and is ready to retreat but do not know how to strike out a way." Boutwell and Fish, Adams accurately recognized, planned to make him "the mule to carry so heavy a burden on their account."[143] Adams did not have to act as the Grant administration's "mule" when he reached London in early May as it appeared that the supplemental article that the Senate was then considering would settle the issue. However, after the British rejection of the Senate's alterations to the treaty, Adams came to the "conclusion that I must cut this now if I can."[144]

In a series of dramatic last-minute diplomatic maneuvers, Adams, working with fellow U.S. representative J. C. Bancroft Davis, saved the Geneva arbitration in June 1872. The veteran diplomats persuaded Alexander Cockburn, the head of the British legal team at Geneva, not to call for a postponement in the arbitration (which, with elections in both nations pending, would likely lead to the reopening of the *Alabama* controversy). In exchange, Adams and Davis, along with British representative Lord Tenterden, arranged for the arbitrators to issue a statement that precluded the indirect claims from consideration during the tribunal. "These claims do not constitute," the statement asserted, "good foundation for an award of compensation or computation of damages between nations."[145] Leaders in London and Washington, relieved to have the situation informally but adequately solved, quickly endorsed the arbitrators' decision to disregard the indirect claims. The *Alabama* dispute was settled by the end of the summer when the Geneva arbitrators ruled that Britain was liable for the direct damages inflicted upon American vessels by the *Alabama*, the *Florida*, and partially for those of the *Shenandoah*. British compensation was set at $15.5 million—ironically the amount of the Confederate Erlanger loan of 1863 largely subscribed to

---

[143] Charles Francis Adams (hereafter CFA) diary, 22 April 1872, Massachusetts Historical Society [microfilm]. See also Duberman, *Charles Francis Adams*, p. 360.
[144] CFA diary, 15 June 1872.
[145] Quoted in Nevins, *Hamilton Fish*, p. 550.

by British investors—and, appropriately, Morton, Rose and Co. and Jay Cooke and Co jointly handled the transfer of funds.

Although the shrewd diplomacy that led to the Geneva arbitrators' statement ultimately ended the indirect claims crisis, the role of the financial lobby in resolving the dispute should not be understated. It is significant that it was Boutwell, with Fish's consent, who empowered Adams to informally resolve the dispute. As in the run-up to the Treaty of Washington, the Secretary of the Treasury sought to place low-interest bonds on the London market and labored behind-the-scenes to make this possible. Indeed, had Boutwell not persuaded the administration to grant Adams the authority to settle the controversy by informally withdrawing the indirect claims, it is probable that Britain would have withdrawn from the Geneva arbitration, thereby reopening the *Alabama* dispute and escalating Anglo-American tensions. Moreover, private financiers in London and New York had an obvious interest in stabilizing Anglo-American relations and worked unremittingly to that end. The constant pressure applied by the Treasury and investment banks clearly left its mark on Fish and Grant. "The Commercial and Moneyed interests," Fish would later recall, "made more embarrassments during the whole discussion [than did] the threatened withdrawal of G.B. from the arbitration."[146] Nor were the efforts of financiers unnoticed at the time. Sir John Rose was promoted to Baronet for his role in facilitating a resolution to the *Alabama* dispute.[147] "While the Ministers are to be praised for their success," *The Times* maintained after the resolution of the indirect claims matter, "the public ought to recognize also the great services done in this long and vexatious negotiation by two gentlemen not directly connected with either government... Sir John Rose, of London, and Mr. L.P. Morton, of New York."[148]

Similar to the joint commission in 1871, the settlement in Geneva opened the door to the London Stock Exchange for low-interest U.S. bonds. As before, Boutwell opted to offer the agency to several leading houses in London. In January 1873, two "super syndicates," the Rothschilds and Cooke on the one hand and Barings, Morton, and Morgan on the other, submitted competing proposals to the Treasury to issue $300 million in five percent bonds. Desiring to satisfy political allies Cooke and Morton, who were both active in the Republican Party, and coveting the

---

[146] Fish to Boutwell, 10 February 1880, Fish Papers, LC. This citation was brought to my attention in Cook, *The* Alabama *Claims*, p. 241.

[147] *New York Evening Post*, 14 September 1872.

[148] Quoted in McElroy, *Levi Parsons Morton*, p. 68.

backing of both the Rothschilds and Barings, Grant proposed "that the two unite."[149]

The two banking consortiums reluctantly agreed and began accepting subscriptions to the loan in February 1873. As with the first funded loan, early sales of the five percent bonds sagged, a fact Jay Cooke attributed to the "miserable jealousies" of the Rothschilds and Barings.[150] Although the difficulties brought on by firms competing for profits hindered the operation, the slow sales of the second funded loan were more a result of the gathering financial storm than of old jealousies. Indeed, the Panic of 1873—the financial thunderbolt that would destroy Jay Cooke and Co. in September and initiate the longest economic depression in American history—first struck in Vienna in May. Witness to the most cataclysmic financial crash of the latter half of the nineteenth century, the year 1873 was not a good one for the Treasury to place the largest issuance abroad in its history. Sales of the second funded bonds continued to sag after the panic and the loan was not fully absorbed for three years.[151]

THE FINANCE OF RECONSTRUCTION AND DEVELOPMENT

The federal government was not the only American body seeking foreign investment in the decade after the Civil War. States and railroads, in addition to mining companies and banks, all hoped to expand in the predicted postwar boom with the help of European capital. The impoverished states of the former Confederacy required outside investment to rebuild after the devastating war and to modernize their economies. Plans to obtain European capital increased when Republicans, eager to transform the region from its plantation antecedents into a diversified economy connected by railroads, took control of state legislatures during radical Reconstruction. With Northern and European investment, it was hoped, economic development could complement and assist the political and social reconstruction of the South.[152] Similarly, railroad executives planned to lay track across the continental United States,

[149] Fish Diary, 21 January 1873, Fish Papers, LC; Belmont to N.M.R. and Sons, 23 January 1873, T58/134, RA.
[150] Quoted in Oberholtzer, *Jay Cooke*, II, p. 372.
[151] For more on the 1873 funded loan, see Larson, *Jay Cooke*, p. 395; Platt, *Foreign Finance in Continental Europe and the United States, 1815-1870*, p. 154; Jean Strouse, *Morgan: American Financier* (London, 1999), pp. 149-50.
[152] For an elucidation of these themes, see Mark Summers, *Railroads, Reconstruction, and the Gospel of Prosperity: Aid under the Radical Republicans, 1865-1877* (Princeton, 1984).

thus connecting ports on the Pacific to the farms of the Midwest and the manufacturers of the Northeast. However, as both Southern states and Yankee railroad entrepreneurs would soon discover, attracting European capital was not an easy prospect.

The prevailing belief in Europe that the ex-Confederacy was in a state of physical ruin, political chaos and embroiled in racial strife certainly did not assist Southern states in their effort to market bonds abroad. "The degree of ruin, destitution in the Southern states," a correspondent of *The Economist* reported in September 1865, "surpasses anything that had been imagined."[153] This theme of devastation and material want repeatedly appears in the correspondence of American agents to their superiors in banks in London. It is little wonder that the Rothschilds steered clear of Southern state bonds after Belmont reported in 1867 that "the condition of the Southern States is most deplorable" and predicted that "a conflict between the two races [would be] almost impossible to avoid."[154]

Such beliefs tipped the scales against Southern states, which were already discriminated against on the financial markets because of the repudiations of the 1840s. As it hampered the efforts of Confederate agents to broker a foreign loan during the war, the financial infidelities of Mississippi, Florida, and Arkansas some three decades earlier remained in the minds of European investors. As *The Economist* unequivocally stated, European money markets would remain closed to "those which have repudiated their debts."[155] Indeed, far from considering lending more money to the South, disavowed holders of the old repudiated Mississippi bonds, led by the Rothschilds, organized themselves to apply pressure to the new Republican state legislature to honor the state's previous commitments.[156]

Financial plans of the reconstructing Southern states were also thwarted by the racism of many European financiers. Although European capitalists (particularly those in Britain) had been reluctant to invest in slave states in the antebellum years, they were far from progressive in their views of the newly emancipated slaves. August Belmont even regretted that the war amounted to little more than "a bloody struggle of 4 years for

---

[153] *The Economist*, 16 September 1865, pp. 1113–14.
[154] Belmont to N.M.R. and Sons, 31 December 1867, T57/84, RA. Baring Brothers held similar views. See Baring Brothers to Ward, 13 October 1865, BP.
[155] *The Economist*, 13 January 1872, p. 35.
[156] Belmont to N.M.R. and Sons, 24 December 1869, T58/39; N.M.R. and Sons to Belmont, 9 April 1872, RA.

the sake of a miserable set of Negroes."[157] The inability of the South to return cotton production to its prewar level was attributed to "the unwillingness of the blacks to work," while the British press warned investors to stay away from the "swindling bonds" placed on the market by allegedly African-American-led state legislatures.[158] It was not an uncommon view in Europe that corrupt black legislatures were attempting to fleece European investors with large bond issues (primarily marketed in 1868–71) that they never intended to repay. The Republican's tenuous grasp of power also did little to reassure skeptical investors abroad. Such themes resonated in James Pike's popular 1873 polemic *The Prostrate State*, which exposed financial corruption in the Republican South Carolina legislature and attributed it almost exclusively to blacks. The former U.S. minister to The Hague who developed close relationships with Europe's leading capitalists during the war, Pike's work (which was translated into Dutch in 1874) helped define European attitudes toward Southern state bonds.[159]

All of these factors led bonds of Southern states during Reconstruction to be quoted at deep discounts in Europe. Figure 8 illustrates the low financial standing of Southern states by comparing quotations of comparable Virginia and Massachusetts state bonds, both bearing five percent interest with coupons payable in London, after the war. "It is hard to imagine," *The Times* said of Southern securities in 1871, "any Englishman of sense investing in them."[160] Even those bearing eight percent interest found few takers. But despite their sordid standing, B. U. Ratchford's estimate that only $12 million worth of Southern state bonds were sold abroad during Reconstruction (1865–77) might be too low.[161] An 1869 congressional report claimed that the foreign indebtedness of Virginia, Louisiana, and Alabama alone amounted to more than $14 million.[162] As Mira Wilkins suggests, total

---

[157] Belmont to N.M.R. and Sons, 12 December 1865, T56/243, RA.

[158] Belmont to N.M.R. and Sons, 24 December 1867, T57/82, RA; Reginald McGrane, *Foreign Bondholders and American State Debts* (New York, 1935), p. 283.

[159] See A. J. Veenendaal, *Slow Train to Paradise: How Dutch Investment Helped Build American Railroads* (Stanford, 1996), p. 47. For more on James Pike's *The Prostrate State*, see Foner, *Reconstruction*, pp. 525–6.

[160] Quoted in McGrane, *Foreign Bondholders*, p. 347.

[161] B. U. Ratchford, *American State Debts* (Durham, N.C., 1941), pp. 165–80.

[162] "Report of the Special Commissioner of the Revenue upon the Industry, Trade, Commerce, &c. of the United States for the Year 1869," United States House of Representatives, Ex. Doc. No. 27, 41st Congress, 2nd session. This report is reproduced in full in Wilkins (ed.), *Foreign Investments in the United States*.

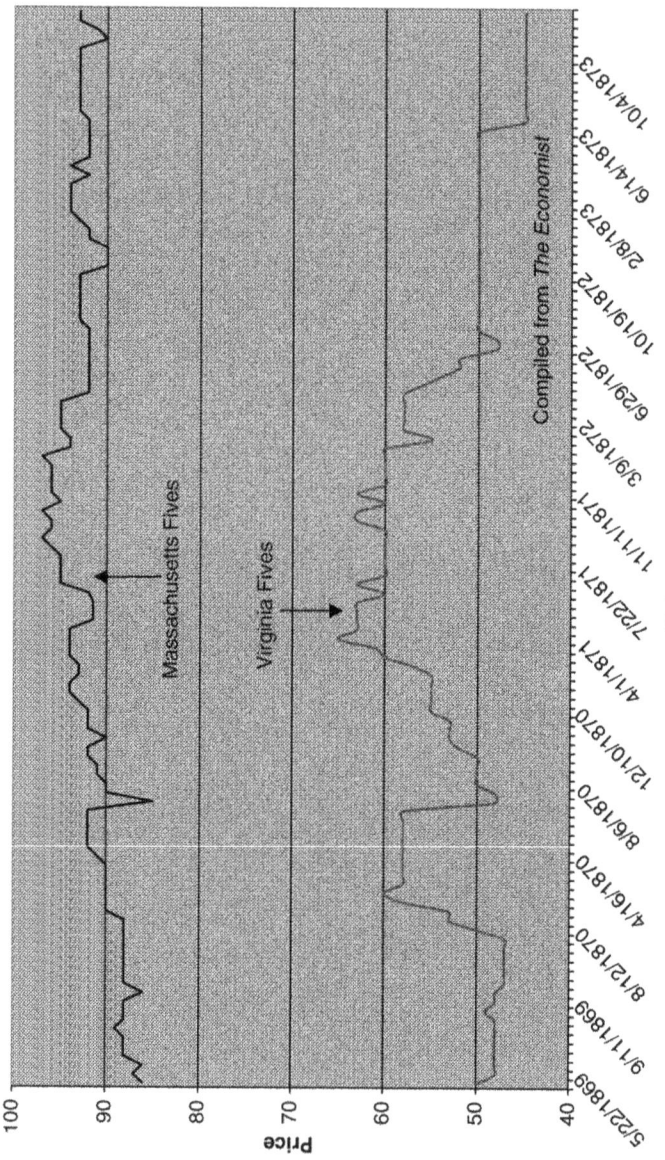

Figure 8 Massachusetts and Virginia 5% Bonds in London, 1869–1873

state foreign indebtedness (of both North and South) increased to a total of nearly $93 million by 1874.

Although it is unclear how much Europeans invested in Southern state bonds, it is certain that those who did were not rewarded. Reminiscent of the late 1830s, several Southern states overextended themselves in their zeal to back railroad construction and other development schemes. When the bubble burst in 1873 and infant railroad companies went bust, the states that had backed them also became victims of the panic. One by one, Southern states stopped interest payments. By 1874, nine of the former eleven states of the Confederacy were in default (Alabama, Arkansas, Florida, Georgia, Louisiana, North Carolina, South Carolina, Tennessee, and Virginia). In all, Wilkins estimates that American states, primarily those in the South, defaulted on $54.2 million in debt after the Panic of 1873.[163] The failure of the Republican state governments to deliver on their promises of economic prosperity, fueled by outside investment for railroad construction, hastened the demise of the Republican Party in the South and lent political capital to opportunistic Democrats who seized the moment to connect the economic turmoil with the race issue.[164] Once redeemed, Democratic-led state legislatures in the South refused to honor the "bayonet bonds" they associated with black and carpetbag legislators.[165] Some redeemed states went as far as to amend their state constitutions to forbid the resumption of Reconstruction era debts. The outstanding foreign indebtedness of several Southern states would remain a contentious issue well into the twentieth century, particularly when European states found themselves deeply indebted to American capitalists after the Great War.[166]

Northern entrepreneurs and railroad tycoons hoped that European wariness of Southern state bonds would translate into more foreign investment for their projects. Jay Cooke, whose firm was the financial agent of several Northern railroads after the war, labeled the South "a land of whiskey and bowie knives" and urged Europeans to invest their capital in "the great Northwest, where there are no heart-burnings, Ku Klux or carpet-baggers."[167] Indeed, the outlook appeared bright for American railroad companies seeking European capital after the war.

[163] Wilkins, *Foreign Investment*, pp. 111–13.
[164] Summers, *Railroads, Reconstruction, and the Gospel of Prosperity*, p. 290.
[165] McGrane, *Foreign Bondholders*, p. 347; Summers, *Railroads, Reconstruction, and the Gospel of Prosperity*, pp. 296–7.
[166] See Max Winkler, *Foreign Bonds: An Autopsy* (Philadelphia, 1933).
[167] Quoted in Oberholtzer, *Jay Cooke*, II, pp. 85, 174.

Sir Morton Peto, a prominent MP and banker, toured the United States in 1865 and, in his subsequent book *The Resources and Prospects of America*, concluded that U.S. railroads were a safe and profitable investment.[168]

It was not long, however, before agents of American railroads in Europe had problems of their own. The Panic of 1866 hit British firms associated with railroads the hardest, leading Peto's house, which was associated with the Atlantic and Great Western Railroad, to go belly-up. Moreover, as the repudiation of three states in the 1840s tarnished the bonds of Southern states as a whole, the disastrous experience of investors with the Atlantic and Great Western and the Erie Railroad shaped British views of American railroads. Bonds and shares of these two lines were immensely popular in Britain after the war. It is estimated that $50 million out of the Erie's $70 million capital stock and one-third of the Atlantic and Great Western's funded debt were held in Britain.[169] After the Atlantic and Great Western came under the control of the Erie and Jay Gould in 1868, the two lines became synonymous in Europe.

Heavily invested in these railroads, it is not surprising that British investors took particular interest when stories of widespread corruption in the management of the companies broke.[170] As Pike's *The Prostrate State* did much to define European attitudes to the finances of Southern states, the investigative reports of Charles Francis Adams, Jr., who was well-known in Britain from his father's days in London as U.S. minister, on the scandalous management of the Erie helped shape British views of American railroads. Published in 1871, *Chapters of Erie* exposed to British capitalists the great "Erie Wars" of the 1860s, which witnessed the corrupt triumvirate of Daniel Drew, "Jubilee" Jim Fisk, and Jay Gould wrestle control of the line from Cornelius Vanderbilt by, amongst other shady methods, fraudulently issuing stock to acquire a majority stake in the company. Dubbed a "swindler" by *The Economist*, Jay Gould did little to win over British investors when he infamously predicted that "there will be icicles in Hell when Erie common pays a dividend" (actually, it

---

[168] Sir Morton Peto, *The Resources and Prospects of America* (London, 1866), p. 307. Peto's views were no doubt influenced by his association with James McHenry and the Atlantic and Great Western.

[169] Platt, *Foreign Finance in Continental Europe and the United States, 1815 to 1870*, p. 153; Dorothy Adler, *British Investment in American Railways, 1834–1898* (Charlottesville, 1970), pp. 107–18.

[170] For the extent of railroad corruption in this period, see Richard White, "Information, Markets, and Corruption: Transcontinental Railroads in the Gilded Age," *Journal of American History*, 90 (June 2003), pp. 19–43.

would only be until 1942).[171] Jay Gould, *The Economist* asserted, "induces English investors to demand eight, nine and ten per cent for their loan to American railways, instead of the six per cent which they would otherwise be content."[172] Matters were little better with the Atlantic and Great Western. After bringing down Peto's bank in 1866, Britons wondered if the railroad even existed or whether it was a line on paper only.[173] These scandals soon left their mark on British investors who lost an estimated £10 to £20 million in the two railroads.[174] By 1874, Erie shares were quoted at twenty-seven percent of par in London and twenty-two percent in Amsterdam.[175] Nor was the damage confined to these two lines. "One great lesson to be drawn from all this," the *Bankers' Magazine* observed, "[is] that the English public should refrain, as much as possible, from making investments in American railway shares."[176]

The Rothschilds, always conservative with American investments, certainly agreed with the *Bankers' Magazine* that American railroads were a risky enterprise. The bank refused Belmont's offer to negotiate a loan for the Union Pacific Railroad in 1867 because of fears that it would turn into another Atlantic and Great Western (the Union Pacific, of course, would soon have troubles of its own with the Crédit Mobilier scandal). Although Belmont was himself a victim of the Erie wars and sued Gould and Fisk for their illegal creation of 58,000 shares of stock, the long-time American agent of the Rothschilds threatened to dissolve his partnership with the London bank because of their reluctance to accept his advice on investment opportunities. Belmont was so desperate to secure Rothschild backing that he offered to lower his commission charge from one-quarter to one-eighth of a percent. This tactic met with little result as the Rothschilds, and for that matter most leading British houses, remained skeptical of the new American railroad lines that sought foreign capital in the years after the Civil War.[177]

[171] *The Economist*, 13 January 1872, p. 35. Gould quoted in Veenendaal, *Slow Train to Paradise*, p. 120.
[172] *The Economist*, 4 January 1873, p. 4.
[173] See, *The Economist*, 2 March 1867, p. 232.
[174] Adler, *British Investment in American Railways*, p. 119.
[175] Veenendaal, *Slow Train to Paradise*, p. 120.
[176] *Bankers' Magazine*, vol. 29 (November 1869), p. 1120. See also *The Nation*, vol. 10, 5 May 1870, p. 282.
[177] For the Rothschilds' reluctance to invest in American railroad securities during this period, see Belmont to N.M.R. and Sons, 2 February 1866, T57/7; 14 June 1867, T57/65; 10 December 1867, T57/81; 24 December 1869, T58/39; 3 December 1870, T57/70, RA. See also Adler, *British Investment in American Railways*, pp. 94–101; Wilkins, *Foreign Investment*, p. 110.

Despite the skepticism of leading banks, American railroads did succeed in attracting European capital in the decade following the Civil War. The foreign indebtedness of American railroads, which before 1870 was primarily Dutch and German, multiplied from $100 million in 1866, to $243 million in 1869 and to $390 million in 1874.[178] After the furor over the Erie scandal died down, British capitalists became more willing to invest in American railways. From 1870 to 1874, roughly seventy percent of all railroad securities issued in London were American.[179] Even a Southern railroad, the Atlanta and Chattanooga, was able to enlist the services of European banks (appropriately, the former agents of the Confederacy, Erlanger and Co. in Paris and J. H. Schröder and Co. in London).[180] Although recent scholarship has de-emphasized the role of foreign capital in the construction of the nearly 40,000 miles of track laid during the Reconstruction era, it is clear that in terms of aggregate investment, American railroads had never before received such assistance from financiers across the Atlantic.[181]

It was in this context of widespread, though not speculative, European investment in American railroads that Jay Cooke agreed to become the financial agent of the Northern Pacific Railroad in 1869. Like the transcontinental Union Pacific, the Northern Pacific sought to connect the old northwest with the new northwest, thus opening the envisaged China trade, via American ports on the Pacific, to the rest of the country. It is "an inexhaustible gold mine," an agent of the line informed Cooke, "there is no mistake about it."[182] Cooke gambled that European capitalists would view the new line in the same light when, realizing that American financial markets were flooded with new railroad issues, he opted to place $50 million of the $80 million high-yielding 7.3 percent bonds the railroad required in Europe.[183] Attracting Europe's leading

---

[178] Wilkins, *Foreign Investment*, p. 110. For slightly lower estimates, see Platt, *Foreign Finance in Continental Europe and the United States, 1815 to 1870*, p. 161.

[179] Wilkins, *Foreign Investment*, p. 115. The London Stock Exchange listed 43 new U.S. railroad securities from 1872 to 1873, compared with only seven from 1868 to 1869. The story was similar in Amsterdam where twenty-four new American railroad securities were listed in 1872, compared with only three in 1869. See Veenendaal, *Slow Train to Paradise*, p. 167.

[180] *The Economist*, 21 August 1869, p. 993.

[181] For the view that foreign investment was not crucial to the development of American railroads during the postwar years, see Platt, *Foreign Finance in Continental Europe and the United States, 1815 to 1870*, p. 162; Madden, *British Investments in the United States*, pp. 73–5.

[182] Quoted in Oberholtzer, *Jay Cooke*, II, p. 120.

[183] Oberholtzer, *Jay Cooke*, II, p. 226.

banking houses to the scheme, however, did not go according to plan. Cooke first targeted the Rothschilds to join him in placing the Northern Pacific's bonds on the London market. Despite the American financier's attempts to "influence those old money bags and make them understand what America is and what is the capacity of the West," the Rothschilds declined to commit themselves to the enterprise unless the federal government guaranteed the railroad's bonds.[184] Such an agreement—even in the prevailing atmosphere of corruption, bribery, and cronyism that pervaded Washington—could not be made, and it soon became clear to Cooke that the Rothschilds had little interest in the Northern Pacific.

Cooke's subsequent attempts to secure the backing of other European banks fared little better. A short-lived contract with Frankfurt financier Moritz Budge in 1870 dissolved after attempts to attract German investment failed. Negotiations with another German firm, Bischolffsheim and Goldschmidt, came to nothing and a tentative agreement with the Union Bank of Vienna was abrogated after Austrian representatives inspected the construction of the railroad in 1871. It was not long before Cooke admitted that "I would not again undertake such a job for all the money in the world."[185] These rejections of Cooke, who it should be recalled was the pre-eminent American financier at the time, illustrate the growing shrewdness of European banks and investors in regard to American railroads by 1870. Having fallen victim to the aggressive marketing tactics of the Atlantic and Great Western, European capitalists had learned their lesson. The Northern Pacific was soon dubbed "the banana belt," a derisive reference to the pamphlets and investment circulars that falsely depicted the land owned by the railroad as ideal for the growing of fruit. Nor did German investors fall for Cooke's ploy of naming a town on the line after Otto von Bismarck (Bismarck, North Dakota). Confronted with an increasingly skeptical financial press in Europe, Cooke could not hide delays in the construction of the line and the mismanagement of the railroad (Cooke was forced to sack the railroad's president in 1871).

Unable to secure the backing of a European bank, Cooke, despite the warnings from his partners to do otherwise, recklessly issued Northern Pacific bonds through the London branch of his own bank. Predictably, sales were sluggish. Former Secretary of the Treasury Hugh McCulloch, Cooke's resident partner in London, could only sell an eighth of the initial £4 million in bonds that Cooke hoped would ignite European

---

[184] Quoted in Larson, *Jay Cooke*, pp. 263-7.
[185] Quoted in Larson, *Jay Cooke*, p. 302.

interest in the railroad. By 1872, the Northern Pacific was nearly $2 million in debt, with little prospect of attracting further investment. Final attempts to place a new issue in Europe, ironically bearing a lower rate of interest in order to impart the impression that the railroad was prospering, failed in 1873. As one German investor put it, "even if signed by an angel of Heaven," an American railroad bond "would not sell" in 1873.[186]

Thus, by September 1873, the fate of Jay Cooke and Co.—largely through the bank's failure to attract European capital for the Northern Pacific Railroad—had been sealed. Cooke's firm, of course, was not alone in being connected with a rickety railroad on the verge of collapse. Indeed, the failure of Jay Cooke and Co. on 18 September 1873 was preceded by the closure of two firms associated with bankrupt railroads: the New York Warehouse and Security Co. on 8 September 1873 (creditor to the Mississippi, Kentucky, and Texas Railroad) and Kenyon, Cox and Co. fives days later (creditor to the Canada Southern Railroad). Nor can the responsibility for the Panic of 1873 be placed exclusively on the shoulders of Jay Cooke and Co. As economic historians have pointed out, the financial storm in New York in September 1873 was preceded by a panic in Vienna that May, the partial repudiation of the Spanish debt, and a general collapse in the confidence of South American government bonds.[187]

But like the bankruptcy of the Ohio Life and Trust Co. in 1857 or the Knickerbocker Trust in 1907, there is little doubt that the failure of Jay Cooke and Co. precipitated the Panic of 1873. The most respectable house in the United States and the bank that had largely been responsible for the success of government loans during the Civil War, the closing of the doors of Cooke and Co. sent tremors through not only Wall Street, but the whole of the nation. Contemporaries, from August Belmont to the *Bankers' Magazine*, pointed their fingers at the speculation in railroad securities, particularly Cooke's involvement with the Northern Pacific, as the cause of the panic.[188] Wary capitalists pulled their investments out of feeble railroad companies following the collapse of Jay Cooke and Co., leading to the failure of more railroads and banks alike. The day following

---

[186] See Oberholtzer, *Jay Cooke*, II, pp. 384, 418; Larson, *Jay Cooke*, p. 361.

[187] For the historiography of the Panic of 1873, see Elmus Wicker, *Banking Panics of the Gilded Age* (Cambridge, 2000), p. 17.

[188] Belmont to N.M.R. and Sons, 19 September 1873, T58/148, RA; *Bankers' Magazine*, vol. 33 (October 1873), pp. 917–19. "The proximate cause of the difficulties," the *Bankers' Magazine* reported, "appears to be the large absorption of capital in railway enterprises."

Cooke's failure, more than thirty houses in New York and Philadelphia, including the prominent firm of Fisk and Hatch, suspended payments.[189] For the first time in its history, the New York Stock Exchange closed its doors in the hope of containing the panic. The consequences of the panic on Wall Street were not confined to the United States. Of the fifty-five American railroads listed on the Amsterdam exchange, thirty were in default after the panic. In all, Mira Wilkins estimates that of the $390 million of American railroad bonds and shares held abroad in December 1874, $148 million (or thirty-eight percent) were in default.[190] Contemporary publications put the figure at up to sixty-five percent, contributing to the atmosphere of panic that forced sound American railroads to abandon plans to attract foreign capital. "United States Railway investments," a London financial journal only mildly exaggerated in 1874, "are only another term for total loss of interest and most serious depreciation of capital value."[191]

The postwar years were thus not altogether good ones for the states and railroads that sought European investment. Although capital flowed westward across the Atlantic during this period, it did not come cheaply or reliably. European skepticism of American state and railroad securities, combined with the financially friendly policies of successive Republican administrations in Washington, led foreign capitalists to increasingly favor U.S. Treasury bonds. As the congressional report on foreign investment in 1869 illustrated, the federal government was the beneficiary of two-thirds of the total foreign investment in the United States. Not since before the boom in state securities in the early 1830s had the federal government been the largest beneficiary of foreign investment.[192] Given the size and significance of the U.S. Government's foreign indebtedness, it is not surprising that financial and diplomatic issues were inextricably intertwined during this period.

The Treaty of Washington and the peaceful resolution of the *Alabama* claims opened a new chapter in the history of Anglo-American relations. Although minor irritants such as American access to Canadian fisheries would resurface, the more dangerous disputes between the two nations

---

[189] Oberholtzer, *Jay Cooke*, II, p. 428; Wicker, *Banking Panics of the Gilded Age*, p. 4. Wicker finds that there were a total of 101 bank suspensions in 1873, thirty-seven of which were in New York.
[190] Wilkins, *Foreign Investment*, p. 121.
[191] Quoted in White, "Information, Markets, and Corruption," p. 28.
[192] For more on this point, see Wilkins, *Foreign Investment*, p. 111.

were resolved by the summer 1872. Just as important as the removal of these cankers was the manner in which it had been done. Peaceful negotiations, both formal and informal, marked the discussions concerning the *Alabama* dispute. As Hamilton Fish opined, "I trust it will not be considered vain to give expression to the belief that the treaty [of Washington] inaugurates a new era in the relations of the two governments, and possibly even beyond that in the mode of settlement of grave questions between great Powers."[193] Scholars have traditionally concurred with Fish's interpretation that the Treaty of Washington and the Geneva arbitration were watersheds both in Anglo-American relations and in the settlement of international controversies. Indeed, it is difficult to dispute Roy Jenkins' recent claim that "the settlement not only was the greatest nineteenth-century triumph of rational internationalism over shortsighted jingoism, but also marked the breakpoint between the previous hundred years of Anglo-American strain and the subsequent century... of two world wars fought in alliance."[194]

It would be a mistake, however, to attribute the beginning of the Anglo-American rapprochement to the clairvoyance of statesmen in Washington and London. As we have seen, leaders in both countries viewed the *Alabama* issue through a lens specific to their short-term national interests. Although Gladstone and other Liberals sought to establish an ethical foreign policy marked by international agreements and arbitrations, a settlement with the United States, as Granville made clear, was also desired in order to erase the precedent of loose neutrality laws to prevent the construction of future *Alabamas* in Yankee shipyards during a European war. In order to obtain this objective, British leaders were willing to back away from demanding compensation for American-backed Fenian raids into Canada, agree to the "due diligence" clause governing the actions of neutral states, and take the unprecedented step of compensating the United States for the depredations of the *Alabama*.

In the United States, the Grant administration viewed the *Alabama* claims in relation to its desire to fund the national debt through a foreign loan. The Treasury's desire to market a low-interest loan on the London Stock Exchange was a powerful incentive for settling the *Alabama* dispute. In order to achieve this financial goal, the Grant administration was willing to back away from the extreme demands articulated by Charles Sumner in 1869 and to make the concessions necessary to ensure a

[193] Quoted in Nevins, *Hamilton Fish*, p. 494.
[194] Roy Jenkins, *Gladstone: A Biography* (New York, 1995), p. 356.

diplomatic settlement with Britain. Prompted by the intermediary efforts of transatlantic financiers, such as Sir John Rose, Levi Morton, and Lionel de Rothschild, who had their own motives for preserving Anglo-American peace, the United States and Britain avoided a war that many in both nations feared inevitable. "Were it not for our [the United States'] debt," as Grant himself proclaimed, the *Alabama* dispute might have had a different ending, jeopardizing the future "special relationship" of the proceeding centuries.[195]

The long-term strategic and diplomatic significance of the Anglo-American settlements of the early 1870s has also obscured the financial implications of the resolution of the *Alabama* dispute. Diplomatic compromises enabled the U.S. Treasury to refund hundreds of millions of dollars of its debt at a lower rate of interest. Although the influx of European gold into the Treasury's vaults was not enough for Boutwell to enact a return to specie payments (especially when sales of the second funded loan stalled in 1873), future foreign loans, modeled after those of 1871 and 1873, bolstered U.S. gold supplies and, as economic historians have recently emphasized, paved the way to resumption in 1879.[196] Furthermore, the settlement of the *Alabama* claims helped restore European confidence in American securities.[197] As the Rothschilds acknowledged, the resolution of the *Alabama* dispute was significant "not only in promoting the friendly understanding of the two Governments, but also the prosperity and activity of the intercourse between the two countries."[198] The peak years of foreign investment in the United States waited in the near future.[199]

---

[195] For Grant's quote, see Fish Diary, 22 March 1870, Fish Papers, LC.
[196] See Wilkins, *Foreign Investment*, p. 184; Jeremy Atack and Peter Passell, *A New Economic View of American History* (New York, 1994), pp. 497–8.
[197] See, for example, *Bankers' Magazine*, vol. 31, September 1871, pp. 789–91.
[198] N.M.R. and Sons to Belmont, 7 June 1872, RA.
[199] Foreign investment in the United States exploded after 1873 until the outbreak of war in Europe in 1914. Mira Wilkins estimates that foreign investment grew from $1.5 billion in 1875 to $3 billion in 1889 and to $7.1 billion in 1914. See Wilkins, *Foreign Investment*, p. 147.

Conclusion

George Peabody, the founder of the American investment bank in London that would later evolve into J. P. Morgan's financial empire, died in 1869. Though a resident of London since 1837, Peabody never lost his American identity and requested that his remains be buried in his home state of Massachusetts ("Danvers—Danvers, don't forget" were his last words). Indebted to Peabody for his philanthropic acts, the British Government shipped the banker's remains across the Atlantic as a gesture of appreciation in the new, foreboding warship HMS *Monarch*. "First and best service possible for *Monarch*, bring home body Peabody," a young Andrew Carnegie anonymously cabled the British cabinet. At the funeral arranged by J. P. Morgan, British and American soldiers marched in step behind Peabody's remains. Back in London, the American banker received the ultimate honors of a headstone in Westminster Abbey and a statue outside the Royal Stock Exchange.[1]

As Peabody's life and death attests, transatlantic financiers functioned, in Lord Ashburton's words, "as messengers of peace" in Anglo-American relations during the mid-nineteenth century. Acting as intermediaries between statesmen on both sides of the Atlantic, financiers lobbied politicians, floated compromises, and recommended conciliatory policies. Financial interests, however, were not always relegated to behind-the-scenes activity. From the Webster–Ashburton Treaty to the Joint Claims Convention to the preliminary talks of the Treaty of Washington, transatlantic financiers served as special emissaries who were granted diplomatic authority by leaders in Washington and London. Indeed, there were few diplomatic disputes and negotiations of importance in the era that London-based financiers did not play a role in resolving or diffusing.

The intervention of the international financial lobby, of course, would have amounted to little had they not possessed political leverage and had their arguments not resonated with American and British statesmen. The financial and commercial interdependence of the two nations made war nearly unthinkable to leaders on both sides of the Atlantic. Although national honor and territorial desires inflamed passions and periodically

---

[1] This account of Peabody's funeral draws from Ron Chernow, *The House of Morgan* (London, 1990), p. 15; and Robert van Riper, *A Life Divided: George Peabody* (London, 2000), pp. 7–12.

brought the two nations to the brink of conflict, the economic imperative for peace trumped these motives for war. This was particularly true on the American side. Going to war with Britain, one American remarked in the 1850s, would be "like breaking your neighbor's windows with doubloons."[2] The United States' need for foreign investment in particular made American statesmen think twice before twisting the British lion's tail. The threat of war, as Figure 9 illustrates, was the most significant determinant of the price of U.S. Treasury bonds in London. Crashes in U.S. bonds in London were most often the result of unfavorable political and diplomatic developments. The coming of the Civil War, the *Trent* crisis, the likelihood of a Union defeat in the summer 1864 (most likely from a Democratic victory in the impending elections), and Charles Sumner's speech on the *Alabama* claims all led U.S. bonds to plummet in London. "Political circumstances," *The Economist* maintained in 1860, "are the most influential in determining the price of the funds."[3] Although a nationalistic foreign policy might result in more territory or prestige, it would lead to a cessation in the flow of capital from Europe that was so vital to the U.S. Government, various states, and railroad and canal companies.

The contingency of the diplomatic disputes of the era further highlighted the connection between finance and foreign relations. Nearly every Anglo-American dispute of this period occurred at a time when the U.S. Government—not just the United States in general—was in need of foreign capital. The Webster–Ashburton Treaty negotiations of 1842 coincided with an economic depression that resulted in government deficits and led the Treasury to seek a foreign loan at the same time. The latter stages of the Oregon dispute in 1846 occurred just as the Mexican War erupted—a war that would lead the Polk administration to place U.S. bonds on the London market. British demands during the *Trent* crisis in 1861 reached the United States days after Secretary of the Treasury Salmon P. Chase issued his annual report that called for borrowing to comprise ninety percent of the government's receipts for the coming fiscal year (though, it should be added, no foreign loan was being contemplated at the time). Finally, the diplomatic imbroglio that followed Sumner's provocative speech on the *Alabama* issue in 1869

---

[2] Quoted in Kenneth Bourne, *Britain and the Balance of Power in North America, 1815–1908* (London, 1967), p. 411.

[3] *The Economist*, 27 October 1860, p. 1174. See also, Niall Ferguson, *The Cash Nexus* (London, 2001), pp. 290–6.

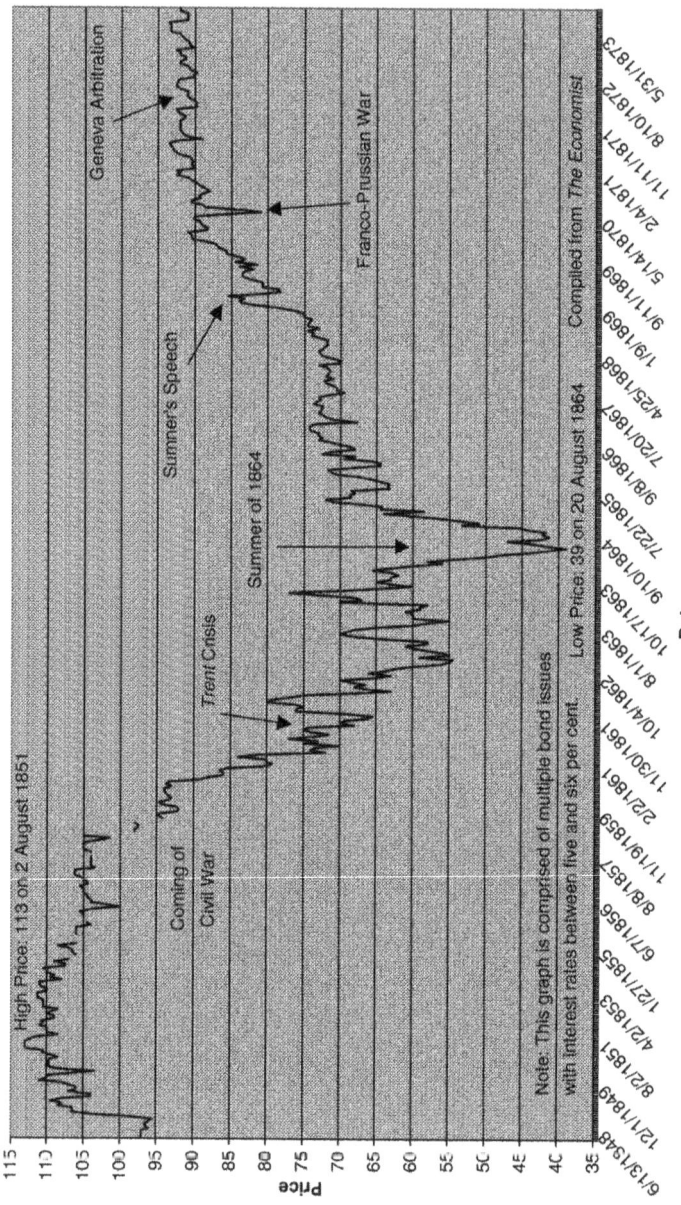

Figure 9 U.S. Bonds in London, 1848–1873

occurred weeks after a new Republican administration committed itself to restructuring the massive national debt at a lower rate of interest—preferably, because of the need to increase gold supplies in order to facilitate the resumption of specie payments, through a loan issued on the London Stock Exchange. The remarkable contingency of the nation's financial needs and its diplomatic disputes strengthened the case for conciliation while reminding American statesmen of the financial implications of their policies. Contingent circumstances and the nation's need for foreign investment, however, did not always lead to conciliatory foreign policies. The revolutions of 1848, for example, led to a boom in U.S. Treasury bonds in Europe in the late 1840s and early 1850s—bonds that were used to pay for the Mexican War. Overall, however, financial considerations tempered American diplomacy and, in particular, laid the groundwork for peaceful Anglo-American relations.

This did not necessarily translate, it should be stated, into thorough and far-sighted diplomatic agreements. Financial exigency often led American statesmen to negotiate settlements that satisfied the short-term need to reassure investors that peace would be maintained but failed to resolve long-term disputes. Such was the case in the Webster–Ashburton negotiations when the two diplomats nimbly avoided the Oregon question and glossed over differences such as impressment; the nebulous Clayton–Bulwer Treaty failed to settle the Anglo-American rivalry in Central America; and, the Treaty of Washington remained unclear on the thorny issue of whether indirect claims would be allowed at the Geneva arbitration. These treaties testify to American officials' desire to reap the rewards of Anglo-American accord without openly addressing the most contentious issues between the two nations. Unfortunately, the United States could not have the best of both worlds and each of these agreements' respective shortcomings would continue to poison Anglo-American relations after their signing, not to mention blocking foreign investment.

Heir to the political and economic philosophies of Alexander Hamilton, the Whig and Republican parties were the strongest advocates of attracting foreign investment in mid-nineteenth-century politics. This was primarily the result of the two parties' desire to promote the development of the nation's economy and infrastructure. Thus, Whigs and Republicans attempted to nurture economic—and consequently diplomatic—relations with Britain, which they believed were essential to American prosperity. Statesmen such as Daniel Webster and Hamilton Fish (who was named after Alexander Hamilton) exemplified the

Whig/Republican attitude toward Britain. Both were committed to American economic development—Webster even worked for a British bank to achieve this goal—and were unwilling to sacrifice the nation's economic and financial interests for strips of remote territory or the nebulous notion of national honor.

Territory and national honor, of course, were very important matters to Democrats. Following the lead of their Anglophobic archetype Andrew Jackson, the Democrats were hardly eager to make diplomatic or territorial concessions in order to secure British investment. Polk's demands during the Oregon dispute and the Ostend Manifesto of 1854, for example, strained Anglo-American relations and, in the process, made European investors think twice before buying American securities. But, despite their nationalistic rhetoric and zeal to expand the nation's territory, the Democrats were not entirely aloof to the nation's financial needs. The efforts of Robert J. Walker and William Corcoran to market Treasury bonds in Europe in 1848 demonstrated that when in need of capital the Democrats, like their Whig adversaries, were willing to look across the Atlantic for assistance. Likewise, it was chairman of the Democratic National Committee August Belmont who sailed to Britain in the first year of the Civil War to arrange a foreign loan. However, the Democrats' greatest contribution to promoting foreign investment was accidental. Democratic policies such as Jackson's veto of the Maysville Road, Polk's refusal to sign a river and harbor improvements bill, and opposition to the federal backing of railroads in the 1850s had the unintended and paradoxical effect of leading state governments and, to a lesser extent, private corporations to seek foreign capital. Thus, both the 1830s and 1850s—years when the Democrats largely controlled the presidency and congress—were decades that witnessed dramatic increases in the nation's foreign indebtedness, particularly that of states.

European capital did not flow westward, however, when American leaders—Democratic and Republican, Northern and Southern—had their greatest need for foreign investment: 1861–5. This was not the result of a lack of effort. Both the Union and the Confederacy incorporated attempts to attract foreign capital into their larger international strategies. Both, for the most part, failed. "Prudent Englishmen," the *Bankers' Magazine* declared in 1862, "will have as little as possible to do either with the money matters of the North or South."[4] This was not altogether true. By the end of the war, $320 million in Union bonds—roughly twelve

---

[4] *Bankers' Magazine*, December 1862, pp. 781–5.

percent of the national debt—was held abroad, primarily by Dutch and German capitalists. European investment in Union bonds relieved the home market during the bleak summer of 1864 and portended the boom in U.S. securities overseas in the decade following the war. Nonetheless, Union efforts to arrange a foreign loan during the war can be labeled nothing other than a failure. Despite repeated attempts, Union statesmen could not persuade British banks, who doubted both the potential of Northern armies to forcibly restore the Union and the ability of the Treasury to redeem its ballooning debt, to buy into their cause.

Confederate financial diplomacy, as well, failed to deliver on its objectives of procuring the funds and political support of Europe's financial class. The "King Cotton" strategy of 1861-2 effectively prevented the Confederacy from implementing a coherent policy of international finance until it was too late. When Southern agents finally succeeded in floating the only foreign loan of the war, the Erlanger scheme of 1863, mismanagement bungled the operation and contributed to its demise. With Erlanger bonds plummeting, Confederate agents were unable to broker another loan in Europe. Moreover, the Erlanger loan failed to attract the high-profile, politically active investors whom Southern leaders had presumed would buy the cotton bonds and lobby for British recognition of the Confederacy thereafter. In retrospect, it is clear that the Confederacy should have implemented the policy it adopted in 1864 of exporting cotton on government account from the war's beginning, particularly when the Union blockade was porous in 1861-2. By attempting to economically blackmail Britain during the cotton embargo and then placing themselves at the mercy of European financiers who were disinclined to invest in a slaveholding, unrecognized nation notorious for financial infidelities during the 1840s, Southern financial statesmanship must bear some responsibility for the collapse of the Confederacy.

Although leading European banks distanced themselves from the slaveholding Confederacy (if not supported the Union), they were the target of much slander and opprobrium after the war. Both Baring Brothers and George Peabody and Co. were falsely accused of selling Confederate bonds.[5] Apart from initial ambivalence, these two firms were some of the Union's staunchest supporters in Europe who campaigned for the preservation of British neutrality.[6] Neither bank, of course, was an

---

[5] Ward to Baring Brothers, 22 September 1871, Baring Papers, Library of Congress [microfilm]; Van Riper, *A Life Divided*, p. 12.

[6] For the banks' rebuttals, see *The Times*, 26 June 1871 and *The New York Times*, 23 December 1869.

unconditional ally of the Union. Both firms declined offers to broker a U.S. loan in Europe during the war. Furthermore, a leading partner of Baring Brothers, Russell Sturgis, supported the Confederacy. Although Sturgis' sympathies did not influence the policies of the firm, the bank would pay for his disloyalty later when Secretary of the Treasury John Sherman refused to invite Barings to broker the funded loans of 1875-9 after Sturgis became the bank's head (Thomas Baring died in 1873).[7]

The Rothschilds were more often the targets of slander after the war. The bank was ridiculously blamed for orchestrating the outbreak of the war in order to profit from the sale of both Confederate and Union war bonds. These attacks were originally launched by Union veterans' groups and have been reasserted in more recent times in the poetry of Ezra Pound and the popular writings of present-day conspiracy theorists.[8] August Belmont's conspicuous role as chairman of the Democratic National Committee, his financial contributions to the presidential campaign of George McClellan in 1864, and his connections with a powerful Jewish bank are largely to blame.[9] "The question before the country is," the Chicago *Tribune* asked in September 1864, "will we have a dishonorable peace, in order to enrich Belmont, the Rothschilds, and the whole tribe of Jews, who have been buying up Confederate bonds, or an honorable peace won by Grant and Sherman at the cannon's mouth?"[10]

There is little need to refute these allegations here. It is hoped that the research presented in the preceding pages provides a reliable account of the actions and sympathies of European financiers during the Civil War. What is significant is that these attacks on European capitalists were not restricted to a few extremists. Indeed, throughout the nineteenth century foreign financiers were the targets of repeated condemnations from American leaders and journalists. Jacksonian policies such as eliminating the national debt, striking down the charter of the Bank of the United States, and rejecting government-sponsored internal improvement programs were the results, in part, of the fear that centralized financial institutions and policies would enrich European capitalists at the expense of the average American.

---

[7] Mira Wilkins, *The History of Foreign Investment in the United States to 1914* (Cambridge, Mass., 1989), p. 720, footnote 162.

[8] Ezra Pound, "Canto XLVI." For conspiracy theories about the Rothschilds and the Civil War, see Jim Marrs, *Rule by Secrecy* (New York, 2000).

[9] Belmont contributed over $25,000 to McClellan's campaign. See David Black, *The King of Fifth Avenue* (New York, 1981), p. 253.

[10] Quoted in Rudolf Glanz, "The Rothschild Legend in America," *Jewish Social Studies*, 19 (1957), pp. 3–28.

American suspicion of foreign financiers increased after the Civil War. Nationalists claimed that Secretary of the Treasury George Boutwell's effort to negotiate a foreign loan to restructure the national debt at a lower rate of interest was "designed by an English Gentleman and parasitical financier and financial correspondent of the Barings in London."[11] Similarly, culpability for the "Crime of 1873," a congressional act that demonetized silver, rested on the shoulders of Englishman Ernest Seyd, who was accused of doling out $500,000 in bribes to force the measure through congress.[12] Not all of the concerns about the power and influence of foreign financiers were groundless. In 1868 British investors established the Corporation of Foreign Bondholders (incorporated in 1873), which, often collaborating with its Dutch and German counterparts, sought to protect the interests of holders of foreign bonds. Not surprisingly, issues relating to American securities were among the group's principal concerns. The Council's first report in 1874 explored ways to get defaulting American railroads and states to resume payment on their debts after the Panic of 1873.[13]

These fears of the "monied aristocracy" in Europe (as Andrew Jackson called it) illustrate the ambivalent views Americans held toward foreign financiers. On the one hand, foreign capital was essential to the nation's economic growth and to financing the government debt. When in financial exigency, American leaders—even those of the Democratic Party— did not hesitate to seek help from abroad. On the other hand, many Americans believed that foreign financiers posed a threat to their republican institutions and that their power must be checked. As the nineteenth century progressed, state legislatures, particularly those in the South and West, passed laws restricting foreign ownership of land and corporate stock. Appeals for such laws were often couched in crude conspiracy theories accompanied by xenophobic and, at times, anti-Semitic rhetoric.[14] This dark underbelly of American nationalistic thinking would

[11] Smith to Grant, 2 June 1871, Boutwell Papers, Library of Congress.
[12] George Boutwell, *Reminiscences of Sixty Years in Public Affairs* (New York, 1902), II, p. 153; Irwin Unger, *The Greenback Era: A Social and Political History of American Finance, 1865–1879* (Princeton, 1964), p. 339.
[13] For the Council of Foreign Bondholders, see Wilkins, *Foreign Investment*, p. 121; A. J. Veenendaal, *Slow Train to Paradise: How Dutch Investment Helped Build American Railroads* (Stanford, 1996), pp. 55, 82–111; *The Economist*, 25 November 1871; *Bankers' Magazine*, vol. 32, February 1872, p. 76.
[14] For the reaction to foreign investment, see Wilkins, *Foreign Investment*, pp. 557–69; Lance E. Davis and Robert J. Cull, *International Capital Markets and American Economic Growth, 1820–1914* (Cambridge, 1994), pp. 50–5; Edward P. Crapol, *America for Americans: Economic Nationalism and Anglophobia in the Late Nineteenth Century* (Westport, Conn.,

climax in the 1890s and tarnish the Populist movement that, with its calls for government regulations to protect Americans from the excesses of big business, has been viewed as one of the peak moments of democratic participation in American history.[15]

The Populists and their predecessors, however, exaggerated the power of foreign capitalists. Although it is clear that foreign investment dramatically increased during the mid-nineteenth century and that foreign financiers did wield considerable influence in American politics and diplomacy, European capitalists were far from the ubiquitous agents who corrupted republican democracy that the Populists claimed. The inability of European creditors of Arkansas, Florida, and Mississippi to recover their investments demonstrates that foreign financiers were not the puppet-masters of American politicians (attempts to compel Mississippi to redeem its debt did not end until the Supreme Court dismissed a case of foreign creditors in 1934).[16] Moreover, the evidence suggests that leading British banks were disinclined to intervene in domestic affairs in order to avoid charges of meddling in American politics. "It is very important that we should not in any way interfere in the Elections," Joshua Bates informed Thomas Wren Ward during the restoration campaign of the 1840s, "we must not shame our case by doing that which we are bound not to do or, rather, that we have no right to do."[17]

If European financiers were not the masters of American politicians, their financial dominance in the United States was in the decline as well by 1873. That the United States could survive without much foreign financial assistance was demonstrated during the Civil War. Although the amount of government debt abroad increased by a factor of twelve between 1853 and 1865 ($27 million to $320 million), in proportional terms, it declined considerably (45 percent of the national debt in 1853 to 12 percent in 1865). The unwillingness of European capitalists to buy into the Union cause directly contributed to the creation and

---

1973); Roger V. Clements, "British Investment and American Legislative Restrictions in the Trans-Mississippi West, 1880–1900," *Mississippi Valley Historical Review*, 42 (1955), pp. 207–28. For anti-Semitism, see the quotes of Governor Alexander McNutt in A Member of the Boston Bar, *An Account of the Origin of the Mississippi Doctrine of Repudiation* (Boston, 1842); and Glanz, "The Rothschild Legend in America," p. 6.

[15] For this view of the Populists, see Lawrence Goodwyn, *Democratic Promise: The Populist Moment in America* (New York, 1976). For a more critical view, see Richard Hofstadter, *The Age of Reform: From Bryan to FDR* (New York, 1955).

[16] Wilkins, *Foreign Investment*, p. 609.

[17] Bates to Ward, 4 November 1844, Thomas Wren Ward Papers, Massachusetts Historical Society.

development of modern Wall Street. American banks and brokerage firms multiplied in size and number as a result of the increased trading in Union bonds. The average daily exchange of the New York Clearing House totaled $19,269,520 in 1861; ten years later it amounted to $105,964,277.[18] The lunch counter, an early facilitator of the American appetite for fast food, was developed around the New York Stock Exchange for bond traders on the go during the Civil War. "The vast influx of bonds, and bondholders, into the country's financial markets," business historian John Steele Gordon contends, "transformed Wall Street almost overnight."[19] The emergence of the financial center of New York is perhaps the price that European capitalists—particularly those in London—paid for their "prudence" during the Civil War.[20]

In the 1840s George Peabody predicted from his London bank that he would soon "see the resources of the [the United States] so developed as to make it independent of the world, and of this Island in particular."[21] Ten years later his junior partner J. S. Morgan prophesied that "the wonderful increase of capital in the United States" would mean that the United States would "no longer have to watch with solicitude the rate on Threadneedle Street." Morgan took an initial step to attaining this goal when his firm of J. S. Morgan and Co. (formally George Peabody and Co.) became the first American bank to sponsor a loan for a European government when it did so for France in 1870.[22] What J. S. started his son, J. P., would help finish.

Portents of American financial autonomy were also evinced in the changing of the guard in the U.S. financial agency in Europe. Baring Brothers, apart from a brief period in the late 1830s and early 1840s, had long served as the overseas agents of the U.S. Government. This changed forever in 1871 when the U.S. Government appointed Jay Cooke and Co. to serve as its agents. The U.S. Navy similarly transferred its overseas business to Clews, Habicht and Co. This was done not out of

---

[18] *The Economist*, 19 October 1872.
[19] John Steele Gordon, *The Great Game: A History of Wall Street* (London, 1990), pp. 95–7.
[20] For the development of an American "bourgeoisie" class that accompanied this growing financial independence, see Sven Beckert, *The Monied Metropolis: New York City and the Consolidation of the American Bourgeoisie, 1850–1896* (New York, 2001).
[21] Peabody to Unknown, estimated 1840–5, Peabody Papers, B197 F1, Essex Institute, Salem, Mass.
[22] Quoted in Jean Strouse, *Morgan: American Financier* (London, 1999), pp. 130, 140. For the beginnings of American foreign investment, see Davis and Cull, *International Capital Markets*, pp. 79–107.

dissatisfaction with Barings, the Navy Department maintained, "but is the result solely of the opinion entertained by the department that the establishment in London of respectable houses of purely American origin and character makes it in every sense becoming and desirable that the government business should be entrusted to someone of them."[23] "The days were past," Barings' historian Philip Zeigler maintains, "when a British bank could represent the American government in London."[24] Ironically, both Jay Cooke and Co. and Clews, Habicht failed during the Panic of 1873. The agencies were then transferred to another American firm in London, Morton, Rose and Co.

One must be careful not to take the financial autonomy of the United States in 1873 too far. The panic of that year illustrated that the nation, particularly its decentralized banking system, was still vulnerable to vicissitudes in the business cycle. Moreover, the peak years of foreign investment lay ahead. By 1914 the United States was the world's greatest debtor nation, owing more than $7 billion to foreign capitalists. However, unlike the years of this study, the overwhelming majority of this debt was private (placed in railroads, mining companies, manufacturing, etc.). Indeed, the amount of public debt (that is the debt of the national, state, and municipal bodies) held abroad rapidly declined after 1873. The federal government's foreign indebtedness, for example, remarkably dropped from its nineteenth-century high of $1 billion in 1869 to less than $10 million in 1899.[25] Particularly after the Treasury resumed specie payments in 1879, attracting foreign investment became less of a concern of American statesmen.

But in the mid-nineteenth century, the relationship between the United States and European financiers was central to American foreign relations. Obtaining foreign capital was a significant policy objective, particularly during the Civil War when both the Union and the Confederacy sought the financial and political support of overseas capitalists. Furthermore, the need to attract foreign investment often influenced American diplomatic relations with Britain. This was particularly the case during the border controversies of the 1840s, the Central American settlement of 1850, and the *Alabama* imbroglio after the war. Finally, the United States' foreign indebtedness and the prominence of leading

---

[23] Navy Department to Baring Brothers, 15 May 1871, BP.
[24] Philip Zeigler, *The Sixth Great Power: Barings, 1765–1929* (London, 1988), p. 215.
[25] See Wilkins, *Foreign Investment*, p. 147.

banking houses in London extended considerable political and diplomatic leverage to transatlantic financiers who became important actors in Anglo-American relations. Although the United States was an expansionist power in the mid-nineteenth century, it was also a debtor nation, connected to Britain and Europe by the bonds of finance. Any conception of American foreign relations that does not consider these links is incomplete.

BIBLIOGRAPHY

MANUSCRIPT AND ARCHIVAL SOURCES

Adams, Charles Francis, Diary, Letterbook, and Reminisces of his Trip to England, 1861–2, Massachusetts Historical Society (microfilm).
Bates, Joshua, Diary and Letterbook, ING. Barings' Archives (Baring Brothers Bank), London.
Baring Brothers, Papers and Records, Library of Congress, Washington, D.C. (microfilm).
Baring, Thomas, Letterbook, ING. Barings' Archives (Baring Brothers Bank), London.
Belmont, August, Miscellaneous Papers, Library of Congress, Washington, D.C.
Bigelow, John, Papers, New York Public Library.
Bright, John, Papers, British Library, London.
Brown Brothers and Co., Papers and Records, New York Public Library.
Boutwell, George, Papers, Library of Congress, Washington, D.C.
Chase, Salmon P., Papers, Historical Society of Pennsylvania, Philadelphia.
——, Papers, Library of Congress, Washington, D.C.
——, Papers, University Publications of America, Library of Congress, Washington, D.C. (microfilm).
Clayton, John M., Papers, Library of Congress, Washington, D.C.
Cobden, Richard, Papers, British Library, London.
Colfax, Schuyler, Papers, Library of Congress, Washington, D.C.
Corcoran, William, Papers, Library of Congress, Washington, D.C.
Cushing, Caleb, Papers, Library of Congress, Washington, D.C.
Disraeli, Benjamin, Papers, Bodleian Library, Oxford.
Fraser, Trenholm and Co., Business Records, Library of Congress, Washington, D.C. (microfilm).
Gladstone, William E., Papers, British Library, London.
Granville, Earl, Papers, Public Records Office, Kew, England.
Great Britain, FO 5/1298, Conferences at Washington, Public Records Office, Kew, England.
——, FO 5/1331, Case of the Alabama, Public Records Office, Kew, England.
Hotze, Henry, Papers and Letter Book, Library of Congress, Washington, D.C.
Kenner, Duncan, Papers, Library of Congress, Washington, D.C.
Lincoln, Abraham, Papers, Library of Congress, Washington, D.C.
Mason, James M., Papers, Library of Congress, Washington, D.C.
Maury, Matthew, Papers, Library of Congress, Washington, D.C.
McCulloch, Hugh, Papers, Library of Congress, Washington, D.C.

Moran, Benjamin, Diary, Volumes 8–18, 1860–7, Library of Congress, Washington, D.C.
Morgan, J. S., Papers, The Morgan Library, New York.
Morton, Levi, Papers, New York Public Library.
N. M. Rothschilds and Sons, Papers and Records, Rothschild Archive, London.
Peabody, George, Papers, Franklin Library, Peabody Essex Institute, Salem, Massachusetts.
——, Papers, Library of Congress, Washington, D.C.
Russell, Lord John, Papers, Public Record Office, Kew.
Seward, William, Papers, Rush Rhees Library, University of Rochester, Rochester, New York (microfilm).
Taylor, Zachary, Papers, Library of Congress, Washington, D.C.
Trenholm, George, Papers, Library of Congress, Washington, D.C.
United States, Record Group 59, General Records of the Department of Treasury, National Archives, Washington, D.C.
——, Record Group 59, General Records of the Department of State, National Archives, Washington, D.C.
——, Record Group 76, Records of Boundary and Claims Commissions and Arbitrations, 1716–1979, National Archives, Washington, D.C.
——, Record Group 365, Treasury Department Collection of Confederate Records, 1833–1878, National Archives, Washington, D.C.
Walker, Robert J., Papers, Library of Congress, Washington, D.C.
Ward, Samuel, Papers, New York Public Library.
Ward, Thomas Wren, Papers, Massachusetts Historical Society, Boston.
Weed, Thurlow, Papers, Library of Congress, Washington, D.C.

U.S. Congressional Documents
   Ex. Doc. No. 63, 39th Congress, 2nd session.
   Ex. Doc. No. 304, 40th Congress, 2nd session.
   Ex. Doc. No. 27, 41st Congress, 2nd session.
   House Report No. 296, 27th Congress, 3rd session, vol. 4, pp. 1–15.
   House Doc. No. 197, 27th Congress, 3rd session, pp. 1–6.
   Senate Doc. 18, 26th Congress, 1st session, vol. 2, pp. 1–2.

PUBLISHED PRIMARY SOURCES

A Disciple of the Washington School, *Oregon: The Cost, and the Consequences* (Philadelphia, 1846).
A Member of the Boston Bar, *An Account of the Origin of the Mississippi Doctrine of Repudiation* (Boston, 1842).
A Northern Man, *The Diplomatic Year: Being a Review of Mr. Seward's Foreign Correspondence of 1862* (Philadelphia: John Campbell, 1863).

An Anglo-American, *American Securities* (London: Mann Nephews, 1860).
An Old Acquaintance, *A Familiar Epistle to Robert J. Walker* (London, 1863).
Adams, Henry, *The Education of Henry Adams* (New York: Penguin, 1995).
American Historical Review, "London Expenditures of the Confederate Secret Service," 35 (July 1930), 814–22.
Baker, George (ed.), *The Works of William H. Seward*, 5 vols. (Boston: Houghton Mifflin, 1884).
Baring, Thomas, *The War upon American Commerce* (Boston, 1864).
Barr, Robertson, J., *The Confederate Debt and Private Southern Debts* (London: Waterlow and Sons, 1884).
Beale, Howard (ed.), *The Diary of Gideon Welles* (New York: W. W. Norton, 1960).
Beckett, Ian F. W., *The American Civil War: The War Correspondents* (London: Alan Sutton, 1993).
Beecher, Henry Ward, *Speeches of Rev. Henry Ward Beecher on the American Rebellion Delivered in Great Britain in 1863* (New York: Frank F. Lovell and Co., 1887).
Belmont, August, *A Few Letters and Speeches of the Late Civil War* (New York: Privately Printed, 1870).
——, *Letters, Speeches and Addresses* (New York: Privately Printed, 1890).
Bigelow, John, *Retrospections of an Active Life*, 5 vols. (New York: Baker and Taylor, 1909–13).
Bleser, Carol (ed.), *Secret and Sacred: The Diaries of James Henry Hammond, a Southern Slaveholder* (London: Oxford University Press, 1988).
Bourne, Kenneth, and D. Cameron Watt (eds.), *British Documents on Foreign Affairs: Reports and Papers from the Foreign Office Confidential Print*, vols. 5–6 (Bethesda, Md.: University Publications of America, 1986).
Boutwell, George, *Reminiscences of Sixty Years in Public Affairs*, 2 vols. (New York, 1902).
Bright, John, *War with Russia* (London: New Broad Street, 1854).
——, *Speeches of John Bright, MP, on the American Question* (Boston: Little, Brown and Co., 1865).
——, *The Diaries of John Bright* (London: Cassell and Co., 1930).
Brogan, Hugh, The Times *Reports the American Civil War* (London: Times Books, 1975).
Bulloch, James, *The Secret Service of the Confederate States in Europe* (London: Richard Bentley, 1883).
Cairnes, John Eliot, *The Slave Power* (London, 1862).
Court of Commissioners of Alabama Claims, *A Partial List of the Southern Bond-Holders in Great Britain during the War of the Rebellion* (Washington: Gibson Bros., 1885).
Davis, Bancroft, *Mr. Fish and the* Alabama *Claims* (Boston, 1893).

Diamond, Sigmund (ed.), *A Casual View of America: The Home Letters of Salomon de Rothschild, 1859–1861* (London: Cresset Press, 1962).
Donald, David (ed.), *Inside Lincoln's Cabinet: The Civil War Diaries of Salmon P. Chase* (New York: Longmans, Green, 1954).
Ford, Worthington Chauncey (ed.), *A Cycle of Adams Letters, 1861–1865*, 2 vols. (Boston: Houghton Mifflin, 1920).
Hansard, Thomas C. (ed.), *Hansard's Parliamentary Debates* (London: Wyman, 1830–91).
Hassard, J. R. G., *Life of the Most Reverend John Hughes* (New York: Appleton, 1866).
Hay, Melba P. (ed.), *The Papers of Henry Clay*, 11 vols. (Lexington: University Press of Kentucky, 1991).
Henderson, Gavin (ed.), "Southern Designs on Cuba, 1854–1857, and Some European Observations," *Journal of Southern History*, 5 (August 1939), pp. 371–85.
Holland, Sir Henry, *Recollections of a Past Life* (London: Longmans, Green, 1972).
Hoole, Stanley (ed.), *Confederate Foreign Agent: The European Diary of Major Edward C. Anderson* (Alabama: Confederate Publishing, 1976).
Hughes, Sarah Forbes (ed.), *Letters and Recollections of John Murray Forbes*, 2 vols. (Boston: Houghton Mifflin, 1899).
Huse, Caleb, *The Supplies for the Confederate Army* (Boston, 1904).
Johnston, Frontis (ed.), *The Papers of Zebulon Baird Vance* (Raleigh, 1963).
Malloy, William, *Treaties, Conventions, International Acts, Protocols and Agreements between the United States of America and Other Powers* (Washington, 1910).
Massachusetts Historical Society, *Proceedings XLV* (1912).
Mathew, H. C. G. (ed.), *The Gladstone Diaries* (Oxford: Clarendon, 1978).
Meriwether, Robert (ed.), *The Papers of John C. Calhoun*, 25 vols. (South Carolina: University of South Carolina Press, 1959).
Moran, Benjamin, *The Journal of Benjamin Moran, 1857–1865*, 2 vols. (Chicago: University of Chicago Press, 1948–9).
Niven, John (ed.), *The Salmon P. Chase Papers*, 5 vols. (Kent, Ohio: Kent State University Press, 1993–8).
O'Brien, D. P. (ed.) *The Correspondence of Lord Overstone*, 3 vols. (Cambridge: Cambridge University Press, 1971).
Peto, Sir Morton, *The Resources and Prospects of America* (London, 1866).
Richardson, James (ed.), *Compilations of Messages and Papers of the Confederacy, Including Diplomatic Correspondence, 1861–1865*, 2 vols. (Nashville: United States Publishing, 1906).
——, *A Compilation of the Messages and Papers of the Presidents, 1789–1897*, vol. 6 (Washington, D.C.: 1917–25), pp. 2580–1.

Sanders, Elisabeth (ed.), *Harriet Martineau in the London* Daily News (London: Garland, 1994).
Seward, Frederick, *Seward at Washington as Senator and Secretary of State: A Memoir of His Life, with Selections from His Letters*, 3 vols. (New York: Derby and Miller, 1891).
Seward, William, *The Diplomatic History of the War for the Union* (Boston: Houghton Mifflin, 1884).
Shewmaker, Kenneth (ed.), *The Papers of Daniel Webster: Diplomatic Papers*, 2 vols. (London: University Press of New England, 1983–7).
Sideman, Bell (ed.), *Europe Looks at the Civil War* (New York: Collier Press, 1962).
Simon, John Y. (ed.), *The Papers of Ulysses S. Grant*, 24 vols. (Carbondale: Southern Illinois University Press, 1967–2000).
Smith, Sydney, *Letters on American Debts* (London, 1844).
Stephen, Leslie, *The Times on the American War* (New York: William Abott, 1915).
Sumner, Charles, *The Alabama Claims, Speech Against the Ratification of the Johnson-Clarendon Treaty* (London, 1869).
Train, George Francis, *Train's Union Speeches* (London: John Adams Knight, 1862).
——, *Thirty Speeches in Two Weeks in all parts of Kansas* (Leavenworth: Prescott and Hume, 1867).
——, *My Life in Many States and in Foreign Lands* (New York: D. Appleton, 1902).
Trotter, Alexander, *Observations on the Financial Position and Credit of Such of the States of the North American Union as Have Contracted Public Debts* (London, 1839).
United States, *Congressional Globe*.
——, *The Case of the United States to be Laid before the Tribunal of Arbitration* (London: Richard Bentley and Son, 1872).
——, Department of the Army, *Official Records of the Union and Confederate Armies in the War of the Rebellion*, 128 vols. (Washington, D.C., 1894–1927).
——, Department of the Navy, *Official Records of the Union and Confederate Navies in the War of the Rebellion*, 30 vols. (Washington, D.C., 1894–1927).
——, Department of State, *Foreign Relations of the United States* (Washington, 1865–1873).
Walker, Robert J., *Jefferson Davis, Repudiation, Recognition and Slavery* (London, 1863).
——, *Jefferson Davis and the Repudiation of Arkansas Bonds* (London, 1863).
——, *American Finance and Resources* (London, 1863–4).
Weed, Thurlow, *Letters From Europe and the West Indies* (Albany: Weed, Parsons, 1866).

Weed, Thurlow, "The Late George Peabody: A Vindication of His Course During the War," *New York Times*, December 23, 1869.

——, *Life of Thurlow Weed including His Autobiography and a Memoir* (New York: Houghton Mifflin, 1883).

White, Andrew D., *Autobiography of Andrew D. White* (New York: The Century Co., 1922).

Wilkins, Mira (ed.), *Foreign Investments in the United States: Department of Commerce and Department of Treasury Estimates* (New York: Arno Press, 1977).

Wiltse, Charles (ed.), *The Papers of Daniel Webster: Personal Correspondence*, 7 vols. (London: University Press of New England, 1974–86).

——, *The Papers of Daniel Webster: Speeches and Formal Writings*, 2 vols. (London: University Press of New England, 1986).

NEWSPAPERS AND MAGAZINES

The Daily Richmond Examiner
The Index
The Times
The London American
The London Herald
The New York Times
The New York Evening Post
The Saturday Review
The Morning Star
The Nation
Bankers' Magazine
The Economist
The Daily News
London Review
The Investor's Monthly Manual
North American Review
Westminster Review
The Nation

PUBLISHED SECONDARY WORKS

Adams, Charles Francis Jr., *Charles Francis Adams* (Boston: Houghton Mifflin, 1900).

——, *Trans-Atlantic Historical Solidarity* (Oxford: Clarendon Press, 1913).

Adams, E. D., *British Interests and Activities in Texas, 1838–1846* (Baltimore: Johns Hopkins Press, 1910).

―――, *Great Britain and the American Civil War*, 2 vols. (New York: Longmans, Green, 1925)
Adams, Henry, *Prussian-American Relations, 1775–1871* (Western Reserve University, 1960).
Adler, Dorothy, *British Investment in American Railways: 1834–1898* (Charlottesville: University Press of Virginia, 1970).
Allen, H. C., *Great Britain and the United States: A History of Anglo-American Relations, 1783–1952* (London: Odhams Press, 1954).
―――, *The Anglo-American Relationship since 1783* (London, 1959).
―――, "Civil War, Reconstruction and Great Britain," in Harold Hyman (ed.), *Heard Round the World* (New York: Knopf, 1969).
Atack, Jeremy, and Peter Passel, *A New Economic View of American History* (New York: Norton, 1994).
Ball, Douglas, *Financial Failure and Confederate Defeat* (Urbana: University of Illinois Press, 1991).
Bauer, Craig, "The Last Effort: The Secret Mission of the Confederate Diplomat, Duncan F. Kenner," *Louisiana History*, 22 (Winter 1981), pp. 67–95.
Bauer, K. Jack, *Zachary Taylor: Soldier, Planter, Statesman of the Old Southwest* (Baton Rouge: Louisiana State University Press, 1985).
Baylen, Joseph, "Dr. John M" Clintock: Union Propagandist, 1860–1864," *Civil War History*, 5 (June, 1959), pp. 133–45.
Beckert, Sven, *The Monied Metropolis: New York City and the Consolidation of the American Bourgeoisie, 1850–1896* (Cambridge: Cambridge University Press, 2001).
Beloff, Max, "Historical Revision No. CXVIII: Great Britain and the American Civil War," *History*, 37 (February 1952), pp. 40–8.
Belohlavek, John, *"Let the Eagle Soar!": The Foreign Policy of Andrew Jackson* (Lincoln, Neb.: University of Nebraska Press, 1985).
―――, "Economic Interest Groups and the Formation of Foreign Policy in the Early Republic," *Journal of the Early Republic*, 14 (Winter 1994), pp. 476–85.
Bemis, Samuel Flagg, *A Diplomatic History of the United States* (New York: Holt, Rinehard and Winston, 1955).
Bensel, Richard, *Yankee Leviathan: The Origins of Central State Authority in America, 1859–1877* (New York: Cambridge University Press, 1990).
Beringer, Richard E., Herman Hattaway, Archer Jones, and William N. Still, Jr., *Why the South Lost the Civil War* (Athens: University of Georgia Press, 1986).
Berwanger, Eugene, *The British Foreign Service and the American Civil War* (Lexington: University of Kentucky Press, 1994).
Bigelow, John, *Lest We Forget: Gladstone, Morley and the Confederate Cotton Loan of 1863* (New York, 1905).
Binder, Frederick M., *James Buchanan and the American Empire* (London: Associated University Press, 1994).

Black, David, *The King of Fifth Avenue: The Fortunes of August Belmont* (New York: Dial Press, 1981).

Blackett, R. J. M., *Divided Hearts: Britain and the American Civil War* (Baton Rouge: Louisiana State University Press, 2001).

Blumenthal, Henry, "Confederate Diplomacy: Popular Notions and International Realities," *Journal of Southern History*, 32 (May 1966), pp. 151–71.

Boaz, Thomas, *Guns for Cotton* (Shippensburg, Pa., 1996).

Bourne, Kenneth, "British Preparations for War with the North, 1861–1862," *English Historical Review*, 76 (October 1961), pp. 600–32.

———, *Britain and the Balance of Power in North America, 1815–1908* (London, Aberdeen Press, 1967).

———, *The Foreign Policy of Victorian England, 1830–1902* (Oxford: Clarendon Press, 1970).

Bradey, Eugene, "A Reconsideration of the Lancashire 'Cotton Famine,'" *Agricultural History*, 37 (July 1963), pp. 156–62.

Brauer, Kinley, *Cotton Versus Conscience: Massachusetts Whig Politics and Southwestern Expansion, 1843–1848* (Lexington: University of Kentucky Press, 1967).

———, "British Mediation and the American Civil War: A Reconsideration," *Journal of Southern History*, 38 (February 1972), pp. 49–64.

———, "The Slavery Problem in the Diplomacy of the American Civil War," *Pacific Historical Review*, 46 (1977), pp. 439–69.

———, "Diplomacy of American Expansionism, 1821–1860," in William Becker and Samuel Wells (eds.), *Economics and World Power* (New York, 1984).

———, "The United States and British Imperial Expansion, 1815–1860," *Diplomatic History*, 12 (Winter 1988), pp. 19–37.

———, "The Need for a Synthesis of American Foreign Relations, 1815–1861," *Journal of the Early Republic*, 14 (Winter 1994), pp. 467–76.

———, "The Great American Desert Revisited: Recent Literature and Prospects for the Study of American Foreign Relations, 1815–1860," in Michael J. Hogan (ed.), *Paths to Power: The Historiography of American Foreign Relations to 1941* (Cambridge, 2000), pp. 49, 77.

Briggs, Asa, *Victorian People: A Reassessment of Persons and Themes, 1851–1867* (Chicago: University of Chicago Press, 1955).

Brown, Charles H., *Agents of Manifest Destiny: The Lives and Times of the Filibusters* (Chapel Hill: University of North Carolina Press, 1980).

Brown, William, and Richard Burdekan, "Turning Points in the U.S. Civil War: A British Perspective," *Journal of Economic History*, 60 (March 2000), pp. 216–31.

Buck, Norman, *Anglo-American Trade, 1800–1850* (New Haven: Yale University Press, 1925).

Burns, Richard, *Guide to American Foreign Relations since 1700* (Oxford, 1983), p. 293.

Cain, P. J., and A. G. Hopkins, *British Imperialism: Innovation and Expansion, 1688–1914* (London: Longman Group, 1993).

Callahan, James Morton, *The Diplomatic History of the Southern Confederacy* (Baltimore: Johns Hopkins Press, 1901).

Campbell, Charles, *From Revolution to Rapprochement: The United States and Great Britain, 1783–1900* (New York: Wiley, 1974).

——, *The Transformation of American Foreign Relations, 1865–1900* (New York: Harper and Row, 1976).

Campbell, Duncan A., *English Public Opinion and the American Civil War* (London: Royal Historical Society, 2003).

Carey, Robert, *Daniel Webster as an Economist* (New York: AMS Press, 1966).

Carwardine, Richard, *Transatlantic Revivalism: Popular Evangelicalism in Britain and America, 1790–1865* (London: Greenwood Press, 1978).

——, *Evangelicals and Politics in Antebellum America* (New Haven: Yale University Press, 1993).

——, *Lincoln* (London: Longmans, 2003).

Case, Lynn M., and Warren F. Spencer, *The United States and France: Civil War Diplomacy* (Philadelphia: University of Pennsylvania Press, 1970).

Chaffin, Tom, "Sons of Washington: Narciso Lopez, Filibustering, and U.S. Nationalism, 1848–1851," *Journal of the Early Republic* 15 (Spring 1995), pp. 79–108.

——, *Fatal Glory: Narciso Lopez and the First Clandestine U.S. War against Cuba* (Baton Rouge: Louisiana State University Press, 1996).

Chapman, Stanley, *The Rise of Merchant Banking* (London: George Allen and Unwin, 1984).

Chernow, Ron, *The House of Morgan* (London: Simon and Schuster, 1990).

Churchman, Michael, "Walter Bagehot and the American Civil War," *Dublin Review*, 56 (1965), pp. 377–93.

Clark, Robert Carlton, "The Diplomatic Mission of Sir John Rose, 1871," *Pacific Quarterly Review*, 27 (July 1936), pp. 227–42.

Clayton, Lawrence A., "The Nicaragua Canal in the Nineteenth Century: Prelude to American Empire in the Caribbean," *Journal of Latin American Studies*, 19 (November 1987), pp. 323–52.

Clements, Roger V., "British Investment and American Legislative Restrictions in the Trans-Mississippi West, 1880–1900," *Mississippi Valley Historical Review*, 42 (1955), pp. 207–28.

Cohen, Henry, *Business and Politics in America from the Age of Jackson to the Civil War: The Career Biography of W. W. Corcoran* (Westport, Conn.: Greenwood, 1971).

Cook, Adrian, *The Alabama Claims: American Politics and Anglo-American Relations, 1865–1872* (Ithaca: Cornell University Press, 1975).

Cook, Robert, "'The Grave of All My Comforts': William Pitt Fessenden as Secretary of the Treasury, 1864–65," *Civil War History*, 41 (September 1995).

Crawford, Martin, *The Anglo-American Crisis of the Mid-Nineteenth Century: The Times and America, 1850–1862* (London: University of Georgia Press, 1987).

Crapol, Edward, *America for Americans: Economic Nationalism and Anglophobia in the Late Nineteenth Century* (Westport, Conn., 1973).

——, "The Foreign Policy of Anti-Slavery, 1833–1846," in Lloyd Gardner (ed.), *Redefining the Past: Essays in Diplomatic History in Honor of William Appleman Williams* (Oregon: Oregon State University Press, 1986), pp. 85–103.

——, "John Tyler and the Pursuit of National Destiny," *Journal of the Early Republic*, 17 (Fall 1997), pp. 467–91

——, "Coming to Terms with Empire: The Historiography of Late Nineteenth-Century American Foreign Relations," in Michael J. Hogan (ed.), *Paths to Power: The Historiography of American Foreign Relations to 1941* (Cambridge: Cambridge University Press, 2000) pp. 79–116.

Crook, D. P., *The North, the South, and the Powers, 1861–1865* (New York: Wiley, 1974).

Cullop, Charles P., *Confederate Propaganda in Europe, 1861–1865* (Coral Gables, Fla.: University of Miami Press, 1969).

Currie, A.W., "British Attitudes toward Investment in North American Railroads," *Business History Review*, 34 (1960), pp. 194–215.

Curry, Leonard, *Blueprint for Modern America: Non-Military Legislation of the First Civil War Congress* (Nashville: Vanderbilt University Press, 1968).

Dashew, Doris, "The Story of an Illusion: The Plan to Trade the *Alabama* Claims for Canada," *Civil War History*, 15 (December 1969), pp. 332–48.

Davis, Carl, *Arming the Union* (Port Washington, N.Y.: Kennikat Press, 1973).

Davis, Charles, *Colin J. McRae: Confederate Financial Agent* (Tuscaloosa: University of Alabama Press, 1961).

Davis, Lance E., and Robert Cull, "International Capital Movements, Domestic Capital Markets, and American Economic Growth, 1820–1914," in Stanley Engerman and Robert Gallman (eds.), *The Cambridge Economic History of the United States: The Long Nineteenth Century* (Cambridge: Cambridge University Press, 1996–2000), pp. 733–812.

——, and ——, *International Capital Markets and American Economic Growth, 1820–1914* (Cambridge: Cambridge University Press, 1994).

Donald, David, *Charles Sumner and the Rights of Man* (New York: Knopf, 1970).

——, *Lincoln* (New York, 1996).

Duberman, Martin, *Charles Francis Adams, 1807–1886* (Stanford: Stanford University Press, 1960).

Dyer, Brainerd, "Thomas H. Dudley," *Civil War History*, 1 (December 1955), pp. 401–13.

Dykstra, David, *The Shifting Balance of Power: American-British Diplomacy in North America, 1842–1848* (Lanham, Md.: University Press of America, 1999).

Earle, Edward, "Egyptian Cotton and the American Civil War," *Political Science Quarterly*, 41 (December 1926), pp. 520–45.

Eaton, Clement, *Jefferson Davis* (New York: Free Press, 1977).
Ellison, Mary, *Support for Secession: Lancashire and the American Civil War* (Chicago, 1972).
Ellsworth, Edward W., "Anglo-American Affairs in October of 1862," *Lincoln Herald*, 66 (Summer 66), pp. 89–96.
English, William, "Understanding the Costs of Sovereign Default: American State Debts in the 1840s," *American Economic Review*, 86 (March 1996), pp. 259–75.
Evans, Eli N., *Judah P. Benjamin: The Jewish Confederate* (New York: Free Press, 1988).
Fehrenbacher, Don, *The Slaveholding Republic: An Account of the United States Government's Relations to Slavery* (New York: Oxford University Press, 2001).
Ferguson, Niall, *The World's Banker: The History of the House of Rothschild* (London: Weidenfeld and Nicolson, 1996).
———, *The Cash Nexus: Money and Power in the Modern World, 1700–2000* (London: Penguin Press, 2001).
Ferris, Norman, *Desperate Diplomacy: William H. Seward's Foreign Policy, 1861* (Knoxville: University of Tennessee Press, 1976).
———, *The Trent Affair: A Diplomatic Crisis* (Knoxville: University of Tennessee Press, 1977).
Fladeland, Betty, *Men and Brothers: Anglo-American Antislavery Cooperation* (Urbana: University of Illinois Press, 1972).
Foner, Eric, *Reconstruction: America's Unfinished Revolution, 1863–1877* (New York: Harper and Row, 1988).
Foner, Philip S., *British Labor and the American Civil War* (New York: Holmes and Meier, 1981).
Fry, Joseph, *Henry S. Sanford* (Reno, Nev.: University of Nevada Press, 1982).
———, *Dixie Looks Abroad: The South and U.S. Foreign Relations, 1789–1973* (Baton Rouge: Louisiana State University Press, 2002)
Gallagher, Jack, and Ronald Robinson, "The Imperialism of Free Trade," *Economic History Review*, 6 (1953).
Gentry, Judith, "A Confederate Success in Europe: The Erlanger Loan," *Journal of Southern History*, 36 (May 1970), pp. 157–88.
Ginzberg, Eli, "The Economics of British Neutrality during the American Civil War," *Agricultural History*, 10 (October 1936), pp. 147–56.
Glanz, Rudolf, "The Rothschild Legend in America," *Jewish Social Studies*, 19 (1957), pp. 3–28.
Gordon, John Steele, *Hamilton's Blessing: The Extraordinary Life and Times of Our National Debt* (New York: Penguin Press, 1997).
———, *The Great Game: A History of Wall Street* (London: Orion, 1999).
Graebner, Norman, *Empire on the Pacific* (New York: Ronald Press, 1955).
———, "European Interventionism and the Crisis of 1862," *Journal of the Illinois State Historical Society*, 69 (February, 1976), pp. 35–45.

Grant, Alfred, *The American Civil War and the British Press* (Jefferson, N.C.: Scarecrow Press, 2000).

Gribble, Francis, *What America Owes Europe* (London: Hurst and Blackett, 1932).

Hall, Nigel, "The Liverpool Cotton Market and the American Civil War," *Northern History*, 34 (1998), pp. 149–69.

Hammond, Bray, *Banks and Politics in America from the Revolution to the Civil War* (Princeton: Princeton University Press, 1957).

Hansen, Vagn, "Jefferson Davis and the Repudiation of Mississippi Bonds: The Development of a Political Myth," *Journal of Mississippi History*, 33 (February 1971), pp. 105–32.

Harnetty, Peter, "The Imperialism of Free Trade: Lancashire, India, and the Cotton Supply Question, 1861–1865," *Journal of British Studies*, 6 (November 1966), pp. 70–96.

Harrison, Royden, "British Labour and the Confederacy: A Note on the Southern Sympathies of Some British Working Class Journals and Leaders during the American Civil War," *International Review of Social History*, 2 (1957), pp. 78–105.

———, *Before the Socialists: Studies in Labour and Politics, 1861–1881* (London: Routledge Press, 1965).

Harvie, Christopher, *The Lights of Liberalism: University Liberals and the Challenge of Democracy 1860–86* (London: Allen Lane, 1976).

Haynes, Sam W., "Anglophobia and the Annexation of Texas: The Quest for National Security," in Haynes and Christopher Morris (eds.), *Manifest Destiny and Empire: American Antebellum Expansionism* (Arlington, Tex.: Texas A&M University Press Consortium, 1997).

Heckman, Richard, "British Press Reaction to the Emancipation Proclamation," *Lincoln Herald*, 77 (Winter 1969), pp. 150–3.

Henderson, Conway, "The Anglo-American Treaty of 1862 in Civil War Diplomacy," *Civil War History*, 15 (December 1969), pp. 308–19.

Hernon, Joseph, "British Sympathies in the American Civil War: A Reconsideration," *Journal of Southern History*, 33 (August 1967), pp. 356–67.

Hidy, Murial Emmie, *George Peabody Merchant and Financier, 1829–1854* (New York: Arno Press, 1978).

Hidy, Ralph, "The Organization and Functions of Anglo-American Merchant Bankers, 1815–60," *Journal of Economic History*, 1 (1941), pp. 53–66.

———, *The House of Baring in American Trade and Finance* (Cambridge, Mass.: Harvard University Press, 1949).

———, "Anglo-American Merchant Bankers and the Railroads of the Old Northwest, 1848–60," *Business History Review*, 34 (1960), pp. 150–69.

Hietala, Thomas, *Manifest Design: Anxious Aggrandizement in Late Jacksonian America* (Ithaca: Cornell University Press, 1985).

Holt, Michael, *The Rise and Fall of the American Whig Party: Jacksonian Politics and the Onset of the Civil War* (New York: Oxford University Press, 1999).

Horseman, Reginald, *Race and Manifest Destiny* (Cambridge, Mass.: Harvard University Press, 1981).
Howe, Daniel Walker, *The Political Culture of the American Whigs* (Chicago: University of Chicago Press, 1979).
Hoyt, Edwin, *The House of Morgan* (London: Frederick Muller, 1968).
Hubbard, Charles, *The Burden of Confederate Diplomacy* (Knoxville: University of Tennessee Press, 1998).
Huston, James, "Western Grains and the Panic of 1857," *Agricultural History*, 57 (1983), pp. 14–32.
———, *The Panic of 1857 and the Coming of the Civil War* (Baton Rouge: Louisiana State University Press, 1987).
Hyman, Harold (ed.), *Heard Round the World: The Impact Abroad of the Civil War* (New York: Knopf, 1968).
Jenkins, Brian, *Fenians and Anglo-American Relations during Reconstruction* (Ithaca: Cornell University Press, 1969).
———, *Britain and the War for the Union*, 2 vols. (London: McGill-Queen's University Press, 1974–80).
Jenkins, Roy, *Gladstone: A Biography* (London: Papermac, 1995).
Jenks, Leland Hamilton, *The Migration of British Capital to 1875* (London: Alfred A. Knopf, 1927).
Jones, Howard, *To the Webster-Ashburton Treaty: A Study in Anglo-American Relations, 1783–1843* (Chapel Hill: University of North Carolina Press, 1977).
———, *The Union in Peril: The Crisis of British Intervention in the Civil War* (Chapel Hill: University of North Carolina Press, 1992).
———, *Abraham Lincoln and a New Birth of Freedom: The Union and Slavery in the Diplomacy of the Civil War* (Lincoln, Neb.: University of Nebraska Press, 1999).
———, and Donald Rakestraw, *Prologue to Manifest Destiny: Anglo-American Relations in the 1840s* (Wilmington, Delaware: SR Books, 1997).
Jones, Robert, "Long Live the King?" *Agricultural History*, 37 (July 1963), pp. 166–9.
Jones, Wilbur D., *The American Problem in British Diplomacy, 1841–1861* (London: Macmillan, 1974).
Jordan, Donaldson, and Edwin Pratt, *Europe and the American Civil War* (New York: Houghton Mifflin, 1931).
Kaplan, Lawrence, "Introduction," *Journal of the Early Republic*, 14 (Winter 1994), pp. 453–7.
Katz, Irving, *August Belmont* (New York: Columbia University Press, 1968).
Khasigian, Amos, "Economic Factors and British Neutrality, 1861–1865," *Historian*, 25 (August 1963), pp. 451–65.
LaFeber, Walter, *The New Empire* (Ithaca: Cornell Universtiy Press, 1963).
———, *The American Age* (New York: W. W. Norton, 1994).

LaFeber, Walter, *The Search for Opportunity* (Cambridge: Cambridge University Press, 1995).

Larson, Henrietta, *Jay Cooke: Private Banker* (Cambridge, Mass.: Harvard University Press, 1936).

Leffler, Melvyn, "The Origins of Republican War Debt: An Open Door Interpretation Policy, 1921–1923," *Journal of American History*, 59 (December 1972), pp. 585–601.

Lester, Richard, *Confederate Finance and Purchasing in Great Britain* (Charlottesville: University Press of Virginia, 1975).

Logan, Frenise, "India—Britain's Substitute for American Cotton, 1861–1865," *Journal of Southern History*, 24 (November 1958), pp. 472–80.

Logan, Kevin, "The *Bee-Hive* Newspaper and British Working Class Attitudes toward the American Civil War," *Civil War History*, 22 (December 1976), pp. 337–48.

Longmate, Norman, *The Hungry Mills: The Story of the Lancashire Cotton Famine, 1861–1865* (London: Maurice Temple Smith, 1978).

Lorimer, Douglas, "The Role of Anti-Slavery Sentiment in English Reactions to the American Civil War," *Historical Journal*, 19 (June 1976), pp. 405–20.

McElroy, Robert, *Levi Parsons Morton: Banker, Diplomat and Statesman* (New York: G. P. Putnam's Sons, 1930).

McGrane, Reginald, *Foreign Bondholders and American State Debts* (New York: Macmillan, 1933).

———, "Some Aspects of American State Debts of the Forties," *American Historical Review*, 38 (July 1933), pp. 673–86.

McPherson, James, *Battle Cry of Freedom: The Civil War Era* (New York: Oxford University Press, 1988).

Madden, John, *British Investments in the United States, 1860–1880* (New York: Garland, 1985).

Maier Charles, "Marking Time: The Historiography of International Relations," in Michael Kammen (ed.), *The Past Before Us: Contemporary Historical Writing in the United States* (Ithaca: Cornell University Press, 1980), pp. 355–87.

Mahin, Dean, *One War at a Time: The International Dimensions of the American Civil War* (Washington, D.C.: Brassy's Press, 1999).

Martin, Thomas P., "The Upper Mississippi Valley in Anglo-American Anti-Slavery and Free Trade Relations: 1837–1842," *Mississippi Valley Historical Review*, 15 (September 1928), pp. 204–20.

———, "Free Trade and the Oregon Question, 1842–1846," in Arthur H. Cole, A. L. Dunham, and N. S. B. Gras (eds.), *Facts and Factors in Economic History: Articles by Former Students of Edwin Francis Gay* (Cambridge, Mass.: Harvard University Press, 1932), pp. 470–91.

———, "Cotton and Wheat in Anglo-American Trade and Politics, 1846–1852," *Journal of Southern History*, 1 (August 1935), pp. 293–319.

Maurer, Oscar, "'Punch' on Slavery and Civil War in America, 1841–1865," *Victorian Studies*, 1 (September 1957), pp. 5–28.
May, Robert E., *The Southern Dream of a Caribbean Empire, 1854–1861* (Baton Rouge: Louisiana State University Press, 1973).
—— (ed.), *The Union, the Confederacy, and the Atlantic Rim* (Indiana: Purdue University Press, 1995).
——, *Manifest Destiny's Underworld: Filibustering in Antebellum America* (Chapel Hill: University of North Carolina Press, 2002).
Maynard, Douglas, "The Forbes-Aspinwall Mission," *Mississippi Valley Historical Review*, 45 (June 1958), pp. 67–89.
Merk, Frederick, *Manifest Destiny and Mission and American History* (New York: Alfred A. Knopf, 1963).
——, *The Oregon Question* (Cambridge, Mass: Harvard University Press, 1967).
——, *Fruits of Propaganda in the Tyler Administration* (Cambridge, Mass: Harvard University Press, 1971).
Merli, Frank, and Theodore Wilson, "The British Cabinet and the Confederacy," *Maryland Historical Magazine*, 65 (Fall 1970), pp. 239–62.
Meyers, Margaret, *A Financial History of the United States* (New York: Columbia University Press, 1970).
Milne, A. Taylor, "The Lyons-Seward Treaty of 1862," *American Historical Review*, 38 (April 1933), pp. 511–25.
Monaghan, Jay, *Diplomat in Carpet Slippers: Abraham Lincoln Deals with Foreign Affairs* (New York: Bobbs-Merrill, 1945).
Morrison, Michael, "Westward the Curse of Empire: Texas Annexation and the American Whig Party," *Journal of the Early Republic*, 10 (1990), pp. 221–49.
——, *Slavery and the American West: The Eclipse of Manifest Destiny and the Coming of the Civil War* (Chapel Hill: University of North Carolina Press, 1997).
Nevins, Allan, *Hamilton Fish: The Inner History of the Grant Administration* (New York: Dodd, Mead, 1939).
Nicholas, H. G., *Britain and the United States* (London: Chatto and Windus, 1963).
Niven, John, *Salmon P. Chase* (New York: Oxford University Press, 1995).
Oates, Stephen, "Henry Hotze: Confederate Agent Abroad," *Historian*, 27 (February 1965), pp. 131–54.
Oberholtzer, Ellis P., *Jay Cooke*, 2 vols. (Philadelphia: George W. Jacobs, 1907).
Officer, Lawrence, "The Floating Dollar in the Greenback Period: A Test of Theories of Exchange-Rate Determinism," *Journal of Economic History*, 41 (September 1981), pp. 629–50.
Orbell, John, *Barings and the United States: Two Hundred Years of History* (London: Barings).

Owsley, Frank, and Harriet Chappell Owsley, *King Cotton Diplomacy: Foreign Relations of the Confederate States of America* (Chicago: University of Chicago Press, 2nd ed., 1959).

Owsley, H. C., "H.S. Sanford and Federal Surveillance Abroad, 1861–1865," *Mississippi Valley Historical Review*, 48 (September 1961), pp. 211–28.

Paludan, Philip Shaw, *"A People's Contest": The Union and Civil War, 1861–1865* (New York: Harper and Row, 1988).

———, *The Presidency of Abraham Lincoln* (Lawrence: University of Kansas Press, 1994).

Paolino, Ernest, *The Foundations of the American Empire* (Ithaca: Cornell University Press, 1973).

Parish, Peter, *The American Civil War* (London: Eyre Methuen, 1975).

———, "Gladstone and America," in Peter Jagger, *Gladstone* (London: Hambledon Press, 1998).

Parker, Franklin, *George Peabody: A Biography* (Nashville: Vanderbilt University Press, 1971).

Pelzer, John, "Liverpool and the American Civil War," *History Today*, 40 (March, 1990), pp. 46–52.

Perkins, Bradford, *"The Tragedy of American Diplomacy*: Twenty-Five Years After," *Reviews in American History*, 12 (March 1984).

———, *The Creation of a Republican Empire, 1776–1865* (Cambridge: Cambridge University Press, 1993).

Platt, D. C. M., *Finance, Trade, and Politics in British Foreign Policy, 1815–1914* (Oxford: Clarendon Press, 1968).

———, *Foreign Finance in Continental Europe and the United States, 1815–1870* (London: G. Allen and Unwin, 1984).

Pletcher, David M., *The Awkward Years: American Foreign Relations under Garfield and Arthur* (Columbia, Mo.: University of Missouri Press, 1962).

———, *The Diplomacy of Annexation* (Columbia, Mo.: University of Missouri Press, 1973).

———, "Rhetoric and Results: A Pragmatic View of American Economic Expansionism, 1865–1898," *Diplomatic History* 5 (Spring 1981), pp. 93–104.

———, *The Diplomacy of Trade and Investment* (Columbia, Mo.: University of Missouri Press, 1998).

———, *The Diplomacy of Involvement: American Economic Expansion across the Pacific, 1784–1900* (Columbia, Mo.: University of Missouri Press, 2001).

Potter, J., "Atlantic Economy, 1815–60: The U.S.A. and the Industrial Revolution in Britain," in L. S. Pressnell (ed.), *Studies in the Industrial Revolution* (London, 1970).

Rakestraw, Donald, *For Honor or Destiny: The Anglo-American Crisis over the Oregon Territory* (New York: P. Lang, 1995).

Ratchford, B. U., *American State Debts* (Durham, N.C.: Duke University Press, 1941).

Rembert, Patrick, *Jefferson Davis and His Cabinet* (Baton Rouge: University of Louisiana Press, 1944).
Remini, Robert, *Andrew Jackson and the Bank War* (New York: Norton, 1967).
——, *Daniel Webster* (New York: W. W. Norton, 1997).
Renda, Lex, "Retrospective Voting and the Presidential Election of 1844: The Texas Issue Revisited," *Presidential Studies Quarterly*, 24 (1994), pp. 837–54.
Richardson, Heather Cox, *The Greatest Nation of the Earth: Republican Economic Policies during the Civil War* (Cambridge, Mass.: Harvard University Press, 1997).
Roberts, Richard, *Schröders: Merchants and Bankers* (Basingstoke: Macmillan, 1992).
Roberts, Timothy, and Daniel Walker Howe, "The United States and the Revolutions of 1848," in R. J. W. Evans and Hartmut Pogge Von Strandmann (eds.), *The Revolutions in Europe, 1848–1849* (Oxford: Oxford University Press).
Robson, Maureen, "The *Alabama* Claims and the Anglo-American Reconciliation, 1865–1871," *Canadian Historical Review*, 42 (March 1961), pp. 1–22.
Roeckell, Lelia, "Bonds over Bondage: British Opposition to the Annexation of Texas," *Journal of the Early Republic*, 19 (Summer 1999), pp. 257–78.
Sanders, Neill, "Freeman Harlow Morse and the Forbes-Aspinwall Mission: An Aberration in Union Foreign Policy," *Lincoln Herald*, 80 (Spring 1978), pp. 15–25.
Scherer, Paul. "Partner or Puppet?: Lord John Russell at the Foreign Office, 1859–1862," *Albion*, 19 (Fall 1987), pp. 347–71.
Schmidt, Louis, "The Influence of Wheat and Cotton on Anglo-American Relations during the Civil War," *Iowa Journal of History and Politics*, 16 (July 1918), pp. 400–39.
Schonberger, Howard, *Transportation to the Seaboard: The 'Communication Revolution' and American Foreign Policy, 1860–1900* (Westport, Conn.: Greenwood Press, 1971).
Schoonover, Thomas, *Dollars over Dominion: The Triumph of Liberalism in Mexican–United States Relations, 1861–1867* (Baton Rouge: Louisiana State University Press, 1978).
——, *The United States in Central America, 1860–1911: Episodes of Social Imperialism and Imperial Rivalry in the World System* (Durham, N.C.: Duke University Press, 1991).
Schrader, Frederick, *The Germans in the Making of America* (Boston: Stratford, 1924).
Schroeder, John H., *Shaping a Maritime Empire: The Commercial and Diplomatic Role of the American Navy, 1829–1861* (Westport, Conn.: Greenwood Press, 1985).
Schwab, John C., *The Confederate States of America* (New Haven: Yale University Press, 1901).

Scroggs, William O., *Filibusters and Financiers* (1916; rpt., New York: Russell and Russell, 1969).
Silbey, Joel, *"A Respectable Minority": The Democratic Party in the Civil War Era, 1860–1868* (New York: Norton, 1977).
———, *The American Political Nation, 1838–1893* (Stanford: Stanford University Press, 1991).
Sears, Louis, "August Belmont: Banker in Politics," *Historical Outlook*, 15 (April 1924), pp. 151–4.
Sexton, Jay, "Transatlantic Financiers and the Civil War," *American Nineteenth Century History*, 2 (Autumn 2001), pp. 29–46.
———, "The Funded Loan and the *Alabama* Claims," *Diplomatic History*, 27 (Autumn 2003).
———, "Toward a Synthesis of Foreign Relations in the Civil War Era, 1848–1877," *American Nineteenth Century History*, 5 (Autumn 2004), pp. 50–73.
Sharkey, Robert, *Money, Class, and Party: An Economic Study of Civil War and Reconstruction* (Baltimore: Johns Hopkins Press, 1959).
Shenton, James, *Robert John Walker: A Politician from Jackson to Lincoln* (New York: Columbia University Press, 1961).
Shewmaker, Kenneth, "Daniel Webster and the Politics of Foreign Policy, 1850–1852," *Journal of American History*, 53 (September 1976), pp. 303–15.
——— (ed.), *Daniel Webster: "The Completest Man"* (Hanover, N.H.: University Press of New England, 1990).
Silver, Arthur, *Manchester Men and Indian Cotton, 1847–72* (Manchester: Manchester University Press, 1966).
Smith, Gregor, and R. Todd Smith, "Greenback-Gold Returns and Expectations of Resumption, 1862–1879," *Journal of Economic History*, 57 (September 1997), pp. 697–717.
Sobel, Robert, *Panic on Wall Street* (London: Macmillan, 1968).
Somerville, Col. Duncan S., *The Aspinwall Empire* (Mystic, Conn.: Mystic Seaport Museum, 1983).
Spencer, Donald S., *Louis Kossuth and Young America: A Study of Socialism and Foreign Policy, 1848–1852* (Columbia: University of Missouri Press, 1972).
Spencer, Warren, *The Confederate Navy in Europe* (Tuscaloosa, Ala.: University of Alabama Press, 1983).
Stacey, C. P., "Britain's Withdrawal from North America, 1864–1871," *Canadian Historical Review*, 36 (September 1955), pp. 185–98.
Stephanson, Anders, *Manifest Destiny: American Expansionism and the Empire of Right* (New York: Farrar Straus and Giroux, 1995).
Stevens, Kenneth, *Border Diplomacy: The* Caroline *and McLeod Affairs in Anglo-American-Canadian Relations, 1837–1842* (London: University of Alabama Press, 1989).
Strouse, Jean, *Morgan: American Financier* (New York: Random House, 1999).

Summers, Mark, *Railroads, Reconstruction, and the Gospel of Prosperity: Aid under the Radical Republicans, 1865–1877* (Princeton, N.J.: Princeton University Press, 1984).

Surdam, David, "Cotton's Potential as Economic Weapon: The Antebellum and Wartime Markets for Cotton Textiles," *Agricultural History*, 69 (Spring 1994), pp. 122–45.

Sylla, Richard, "The United States: Financial Innovation and Adaptation," in Michael Bordo and Robert Cortes-Conde, *Transferring Wealth and Power from the Old to the New World* (Cambridge: Cambridge University Press, 2001).

Taylor, Amos, "Walker's Financial Mission to London on Behalf of the North, 1863–1864," *Journal of Economic and Business History*, 3 (February 1931), pp. 296–320.

Taylor, John, *William Henry Seward: Lincoln's Right Hand* (London: Brassey's Press, 1991).

Temin, Peter, *The Jacksonian Economy* (New York: Norton, 1969).

———, "The Panic of 1857," *Intermountain Economic Review*, 6 (Spring 1975), pp. 1–12.

Thistlewaite, Frank, "Atlantic Partnership," *Economic History Review*, 7 (1954), pp. 1–17.

———, *America and the Atlantic Community: Anglo-American Aspects, 1790–1850* (New York: Harper and Row, 1959).

Thompson, Samuel, *Confederate Purchasing Operations Abroad* (Chapel Hill: University of North Carolina Press, 1935).

Todd, Richard, *Confederate Finance* (Athens: University of Georgia Press, 1954).

Trefousse, Hans, *The Radical Republicans* (New York: Alfred A. Knopf, 1969).

Van Deusen, Glydon, *Thurlow Weed: Wizard of the Lobby* (Boston: Little, Brown, 1947).

Van Riper, Robert, *A Life Divided: George Peabody, Pivotal Figure in Anglo-American Finance, Philanthropy and Diplomacy* (London: Lightning Source, 2000).

Van Vleck, George W., *The Panic of 1857* (New York: Columbia University Press, 1943).

Varg, Paul, *United States Foreign Relations, 1820–1860* (Michigan: Michigan State University Press, 1979).

Veenendaal, A. J., *Slow Train to Paradise: How Dutch Investment Helped Build American Railroads* (Stanford: Stanford University Press, 1996).

Vevier, Charles, "American Continentalism: An Idea of Expansion, 1845–1910," *American Historical Review*, 65 (January 1960), pp. 323–35.

Villars, Brougham, and W. H. Chesson, *Anglo-American Relations, 1861–1865* (London, 1919).

Vincent, John, *The Formation of the British Liberal Party, 1857–68* (Harmondsworth: Penguin, 1972).

Warren, Gordon, *Fountain of Discontent: The Trent Affair and Freedom of the Seas* (Boston: Northeastern University Press, 1981).

Weeks, William Earl, *Building the Continental Empire: American Expansion from the Revolution to the Civil War* (Chicago: Ivan R. Dee, 1996).

Weidenmier, Marc, "The Politics of Selective Default: The Foreign Debts of the Confederate States of America," Claremont College Working Papers.

——, "The Market for Confederate Cotton Bonds," *Explorations in Economic History*, 37 (January 2000), pp. 76–97.

Weinberg, Albert Katz, *Manifest Destiny: A Study of Nationalist Expansionism in American History* (Gloucester, Mass.: P. Smith, 1935).

Whitridge, Arnold, "British Liberals and the American Civil War," *History Today*, 12 (October 1962), pp. 688–95.

Wicker, Elmus, *Banking Panics of the Gilded Age* (Cambridge: Cambridge University Press, 2000).

Wienberg, Adelaid, *John Eliot Cairnes and the American Civil War* (London: Kingwood, 1970).

Wilgus, Curtis, "Some London *Times* Comments on Secretary Chase's Financial Administration, 1861–1864," *Mississippi Valley Historical Review*, 26 (December 1939), pp. 395–8.

Wilkins, Mira, *The History of Foreign Investment in the United States to 1914* (Cambridge, Mass.: Harvard University Press, 1989).

Williams, Mary Wilhelmine, *Anglo-American Isthmian Diplomacy, 1815–1915* (Oxford: Oxford University Press, 1916).

Williams, William Appleman, *The Roots of the Modern American Empire: A Study of the Growth and Shaping of Social Consciousness in a Marketplace Society* (New York: Vintage Books, 1970).

——, *The Tragedy of American Diplomacy* (New York: W. W. Norton, 1972).

——, *Empire as a Way of Life* (Oxford: Oxford University Press, 1980).

Wiltse, Charles, "Daniel Webster and the British Experience," *Proceedings of the Massachusetts Historical Society*, 85 (1973), pp. 58–77.

Winkler, Max, *Foreign Bonds: An Autopsy* (Philadelphia: Roland Swain, 1933).

Winks, Robin W., *Canada and the United States: The Civil War Years* (Baltimore: Johns Hopkins Press, 1960).

Wise, Stephen, *Lifeline of the Confederacy* (Columbia, S.C.: University of South Carolina Press, 1988).

Young, Robert, *Senator James Murray Mason: Defender of the Old South* (Knoxville: University of Tennessee Press, 1998).

Zeigler, Philip, *The Sixth Great Power: Barings, 1765–1929* (London: Collins, 1988).

Zorn, Roman. "John Bright and the British Attitude to the American Civil War," *Mid-America*, 38 (July 1956).

Zwerdling, Alex, *Improvised Europeans* (New York: Basic Books, 1998).

UNPUBLISHED THESES

Ashcroft, Neil, "'Uncertain and Unexpected Vicissitudes:' British Maritime Enterprise and the American Civil War, 1856 to 1870," Ph.D. dissertation, University of Hull, 1999.
Fenner, Judith, "Confederate Finances Abroad," Ph.D. dissertation, Rice University, 1969.
Flocks, Sally Ann, "In the Hands of Others: The Development of Dependency by Richmond's Manufacturers on Northern Financiers," Ph.D. dissertation, Yale University, 1983.
Hall, Nigel, "The Cotton Brokers and the Development of the Liverpool Cotton Market c1800 to 1914," D.Phil. dissertation, University of Oxford, 1999.
Hughes, Frank, "Liverpool and the Confederate States," M.Phil. dissertation, Keele University, 1998.
Ley, Douglas, "Expansionists All? Southern Senators and American Foreign Policy, 1841–1860," Ph.D. dissertation, University of Wisconsin, 1990.
Painter, Carvel, "The Recovery of Confederate Property and Other Assets Abroad, 1865–1873," Ph.D. dissertation, American University, 1973.
Roberts, Timothy, "The American Response to the European Revolutions of 1848," D.Phil. dissertation, University of Oxford, 1998.
Roeckell, Lelia, "British Interests in Texas, 1825–1846," D.Phil. dissertation, University of Oxford, 1993.
Woodward, David, "Sectionalism, Politics, and Foreign Policy: Duff Green and Southern Economic and Political Expansion," Ph.D. dissertation, University of Minnesota, 1996.

INDEX

Aberdeen, Lord 40, 50
Adams, Charles Francis 82–3, 102, 126, 131, 140–1
  and *Alabama* claims 202, 204
  and Confederate shipbuilding 105–13
  and Geneva arbitration 226–8
Adams, Charles Francis Jr. 234
Adams, Henry 171
Advance 177
Alabama 177
Alabama 91, 106–8, 143–4, 148, 174
Alabama claims 173, 243
  described and early efforts to resolve 202–5
  Geneva arbitration 226–8
  indirect claims dispute 222–8
  preliminary efforts to resolve 212–16
  relationship to funded loan 206–8, 210–11, 216, 219, 240–1
  significance of resolution 239–41
  Treaty of Washington 215–16
Alexandra 111–12, 174
American Finance and Resources 121
Anglophobia 17–18
Antietam, Battle of 155
Anti-Semitism 249–50
Arman, Lucien 184, 193
arms purchasing, Civil War 104–13, 142
'Aroostook War' 30
Ashburton, Lord (Alexander Baring):
  and Mexican debts 47
  and negotiations with Webster 33–40, 208, 242
  and South 70
Ashley, Evelyn 172

Aspinwall, William 17, 63, 108–12, 114, 131
Atlanta and Chattanooga Railroad 236
Atlantic and Great Western Railroad 93, 234–5

Bagehot, Walter 153–4
Bank Act of 1844 101
Bank of England 24, 77, 206, 223
Bank of the United States (2nd):
  and Andrew Jackson 22, 248
  and the Barings 13
  failure of in 1839 25, 27
Bank of Vienna 237
Bankers' Magazine:
  and Confederate finance 120, 246
  and Union finance 87, 246
  and US during Reconstruction 197, 199, 221, 235, 238
Baring Brothers:
  and *Alabama* claims 206–8
  and coming of Civil War 79–81
  and Confederate shipbuilding 107–12
  and 1842 loan 35–6
  and first funded loan 217–18
  involvement in American politics and diplomacy 12–13, 20–1, 251–2
  and Mexican War loan 56
  and Panic of 1837 25–6
  and post-war loan 195–6, 200, 210
  primacy in American finance 12–13, 20–1, 23
  pro-Northern sympathies and actions 89–91, 141, 159–60, 248–9
  and Northeastern border dispute 30–40

Baring Brothers (*cont.*):
  and restoration campaign 40–5
  and second funded loan 228–9
  and slavery 69–76
  and state debts 28
  and Texas and Oregon, 46–53
  and *Trent* crisis, 98
  and Union loan 114
Baring, Thomas:
  and Civil War 80, 98, 112, 133
  death of 248
  and paper money 197
  and role in American finance and politics 12, 20
  state of US in 1852 60
Bates, Edward 99
Bates, Joshua 75, 77, 81
  and Joint Claims Convention 68–9
  pro-Northern sympathy 89–91
  role in American politics and diplomacy 13–14, 20–1, 250
  and Texas and Oregon 46–53
  and Webster–Ashburton Treaty 31–40
Beecher, Henry Ward 116
Belmont, August 13, 15, 75, 81, 131, 248
  and British intervention in Civil War 152–7
  and Caribbean expansion 73–4
  efforts to smooth over *Alabama* dispute 208
  and indirect claims 226
  and Mexican War loan 56
  mission to Britain in 1861 84–92, 121, 246
  and Mississippi 73, 120
  and Northeastern border dispute 31
  and Pendleton plan 199–200
  and post-war loan 195–7
  and post-war railroad investments 235, 238
  and post-war South 230–1
  and slavery 60, 77
Benjamin, Judah 119, 139, 159, 165, 175, 184–5
Benton, Thomas Hart:
  and foreign creditors 27
  and Oregon 52
Bidlack Treaty 62
Bigelow, John 171, 184
Bills of exchange 127, 144
Bischolffsheim and Goldschmidt 237
Bismarck 125, 237
Bismarck, North Dakota 237
blockade 139, 145, 165–6
blockade running 144, 166, 176, 179–83
Boston Daily Advertizer 42
Bostwick, A. W. 94
Boutwell, George:
  and desire to repay debt in gold 201–2, 210, 249
  and first funded loan 217–21
  and foreign loan 210–11, 217
  and indirect claims 223–8
  and second funded loan 228–9
Brewer, H. O. 172
Bright, John 76, 92, 94, 99, 102, 112, 215
Britain:
  commercial relations with US 3–5
  Confederate shipbuilding 105–13, 174–5
  considers intervention in Civil War 150–6
  in Central America 62–7
  dependence on American cotton 4
  and Kenner mission 185
  Proclamation of Neutrality (1861) 87–8, 141, 143
  revises neutrality laws 209
  seeks to resolve *Alabama* dispute 212–13
  support for Confederacy 146–7

British capitalists:
  interest in American securities 23
  see also under specific banks and
    individuals
Brooks, Preston 78
Brown, John 78
Brown, Shipley and Co. 25, 77
Brown, William 12
Buchanan, James 49, 73
Bull Run, Battle of 91
Bulloch, James 91, 104-5, 174, 180,
    187-9
  activities in France 183-4
  initial operations abroad 142-5,
    147, 181
  needing funds 150, 161, 164, 169
Bulwer, Sir Henry 64-7

Cairnes, John Eliot 121
Calhoun, John C.:
  and Oregon 49, 52
  views on Panic of 1837 24
  as Secretary of State 49
  and state debts 26
Campbell, Lord 146, 148
Canada:
  abandonment of annexation
    plans 210, 215
  commercial relations with US 61
  Northeastern border dispute 29-40
  US desire to annex after Civil
    War 203-4, 206
canals:
  foreign investment in 23
  Isthmian canal 61-7
Carnegie, Andrew 242
Caroline 29-30, 33, 68
Cass, Lewis 18, 66
Chandler, L. 193
Chapters of Erie 234
Chase, Salmon P. 15, 108, 243
  and early war finance 83-5
  and foreign loan in 1863 113-14

  and foreign loan in 1864 128
  Rivalry with Seward 131-2
  and *Trent* crisis 96-100
Chauncey, Elihu 42
Chicora Importing and Exporting
    Co. 180
Civil War:
  and foreign financiers 15-17, 246-8
  see also Union and Confederacy
Clarendon, Lord 204-5
Clay, Henry:
  and annexation of Texas 47
  and Maysville Road 22
Clayton, John:
  as Secretary of State 62-7
Clayton-Bulwer Treaty 61-7, 245
Clews, Henry 218, 251-2
Cobden, Richard 76, 94, 99, 112
Cold Harbor, Battle of 128
Colfax, Schuyler 226
Committee on State Debts 41
Compromise of 1850 60, 62
Confederacy 133-89
  arms purchasing abroad 142
  and cotton loans 157-74
  financial state in 1861 134-9, 144-5
  financial state in 1862 163 157-62
  financial state in 1864-5 175-6
  foundations of diplomatic strategy
    135-50
  international strategy
    evaluated 187-9, 246-7
  Kenner mission 184-6
  merchant marine 180-3
  'New Plan' of finance 174-83
  shipbuilding in Britain 105-13,
    143, 174-5
  shipbuilding in France 183-4
Cooke, Jay:
  and Civil War finance 84, 101, 113,
    128, 130
  and financial failure 238-9
  and first funded loan 217-18, 220-2

Cooke, Jay (*cont.*):
  and post-war finance 194, 196
  and railroads during
    Reconstruction 233–9
  and second funded loan 228–9
copyright agreements 212
Corcoran, William 53–8, 72, 246
Corcoran & Riggs 53
Corn Laws 4, 50–1
Corporation of Foreign
  Bondholders 249
Cotton:
  alternative sources of 137, 149
  alternative strategy 188–9
  British reliance on 4, 135, 138
  during Civil War 89, 137, 145, 151, 156, 159
  Price of and Panic of 1837 24
  see also 'King Cotton'
cotton bonds 159–74, 182–3, 187–9
Credit Mobilier scandal 235
Crenshaw, William 182
Creole 30, 37–8, 69
'Crime of 1873' 249
Crimean War 76, 86, 100, 176
Crossan, Thomas 177
Cuba 73–4
currency contraction 195, 198
Curtis, Benjamin 43
Curtis, J. D. 195
Cushing, Caleb 134, 192–3

Davis, J. C. Bancroft 222, 227
Davis, Jefferson:
  and Confederate diplomacy 139, 144, 182, 184
  and repudiation 117–21
Davis, John 54
Davis, Reuben 117
Dayton, William 184
Debow's Review 135
default, *see* State Debts and
  Repudiation

Delane, John 103, 172
Democratic Review 43
Democratic Party:
  and Civil War 85–6
  and expansion 47, 66, 246
  and foreign investment 18, 195, 246, 249
Denbigh 166
Douglas, Stephen 66
Drew, Daniel 234
'due diligence' clause 215, 240
Dudley, Thomas 106–7, 191
Dutch investors:
  and post-war railroad
    investments 236
  and Union bonds 121–30
  and US bonds after war 197–8

Economist:
  and the *Alabama* claims 190, 223
  and American fidelity 201
  and coming of Civil War 80
  and Confederacy 138, 158, 165, 173
  determinants of bond prices 243
  and intervention in Civil
    War 151–6
  and Jay Gould 234–5
  and Mexican War loan 55
  and Oregon 51
  and post-war loan 211, 219–21
  and post-war South 230
  and repayment of debt in paper
    money 199–200
  and *Trent* 99
  and Union finances 87, 91, 99, 101–2, 114
  and US in Caribbean 73
  and war with the North 89
Eleventh Amendment 26
emancipation 89, 125, 155
  see also slavery
Erie Railroad 234–5

Erlanger Loan:
  in context of Confederate strategy 17, 187-8, 227-8, 247
  floated in 1863 162-74
  holders of the bonds 171-4
  resurgence of in 1864 182-3
  R. J. Walker and 110, 115, 125
Erlanger & Co.:
  and first funded loan 220
  and post-war railroad investments 236
  and Union bonds 164
  see also Erlanger Loan
European Trading Company 166
Evans, William 124
Everett, Alexander 43
Everett, Edward 34
exchange rates 127
expansionism 2-5, 21, 46-58, 73-4, 203-4, 206, 245, 252-3
export expansion 2-5

Fahnestock, Harris 198
Familiar Epistle, A 119
Fenian raids 215, 226, 240
Fessenden, William 128-30, 133
Fillmore, Millard 57
Fingal 181
Fish, Hamilton 18, 240-1, 245-6
  and *Alabama* dispute 209, 212, 214-15
  and Canada 210
  and funded loan 211
  and indirect claims 222-8
  and international gold standard 201
  and recovery of Confederate property 193
  and Sir John Rose 208-9, 214-15
fisheries 212, 215-16, 239-40
Fisk, Jim 234, 239
Florida 106-7, 143-4, 148, 174
Foreign Enlistment Act 106, 147

foreign investment, *see* canals; Confederacy; National debt; state debts; railroads; Treasury Department; Union; *and specific banks, bankers and loans*
Forbes, John Murray 108-12, 115, 131, 197
Forstall, E. J. 159
Forward, Walter 39
Fourteenth Amendment 173-4
Fox, Gustavus 108
France 152, 155, 171, 183-4, 185
Franco-Prussian War 209, 211
Fraser, Trenholm and Co.:
  account overdrafted 175
  and blockade running 180-2
  difficulties after war 191-3
  financial support of Confederacy 143-7, 165, 167, 174, 187
Fremont, John C. 73
funded loans:
  Congressional passage of bill 210-11
  first funded loan 217-21
  rationale behind 194-5
  second funded loan 221, 228-9

Gamble, John 72
Geneva arbitration 216, 226-8, 245
Georgia 174-5
German investors:
  and American securities in 1850s 57
  and post-war railroads 236
  and Union bonds 121-30
  and US bonds after war 197-8
Gettysburg, Battle of 120, 126, 169, 175
Gilliat, J. K. 172, 182
Gilliat, J. S. 172
Gladstone, William 100, 120, 148, 172, 202, 240
  considers intervention in Civil War 150, 154-5

Gladstone, William (*cont.*):
    and indirect claims 222, 225–6
    seeks to resolve *Alabama*
        claims 212–13, 215
Grant, Ulysses S. 183, 214
    and *Alabama* claims 215, 241
    and hard money 200
    and national debt 210
    removes Motley 210
    and second funded loan 228–9
    and success of first funded loan
        220–1
Granville, Lord 209, 213, 215, 222,
    224, 225, 240
Great War 233
Greeley, Horace 128
Greenbacks 101–2, 195
Gregory, William 141
gold premium 128, 197, 207
gold standard 98–102, 127, 195, 199,
    241
Gould, Jay 234–5

Hale, Nathaniel 42
Hamilton, Alexander 32, 245–6
Hammond, James Henry 69, 136
Hartley, Marcellus 105
Hay, John 67
Hise, Elijah 62
Honduras 62
Hope & Co. 28, 41, 123, 163
Hornby, Edward 68
Hottinguer, Henri 123, 127, 163
Hotze, Henry 148–50, 166, 180
Hudson's Bay Co. 50
Hull, F. S. 143
Huse, Caleb 105, 134, 142, 158, 176,
    181

Illinois Central Railroad 60, 76, 116
Importing and Exporting Company of
    South Carolina 180
Index 149–50, 156

indirect claims dispute, 222–8
    see also Alabama claims
'informal imperialism,' British 18–19
Ingersoll, Joseph Reed 67
internal improvements 23, 245–6
    see also canals; railroads; state debts
Irish Potato Famine 51
Isaac, Campbell and Co. 172, 176

Jackson, Andrew:
    aversion to foreign indebtedness 9,
        18, 22–3, 57, 246, 249
    Specie Circular and Panic of 1837
        24–5
Jackson, Stonewall 150
Jackson, William Andrew 116
*Jefferson Davis, Repudiation,
    Recognition and Slavery* 117–21
Jenkins, Roy 240
Johnson, Andrew 198
Johnson, Reverdy 204
Johnson, William Cost 26
Johnson–Clarendon Convention 204–6
Joint Claims Convention (1853–5) 13,
    67–9, 242
Jones, Lloyd & Co. 41

Kansas 77–8, 116
Kenner, Duncan 184–6
Kenyon, Cox and Co. 238
'King Corn' 16, 138
'King Cotton' 16, 135–50, 187–9, 247
    see also Cotton, Cotton bonds and
        Confederacy
Knickerbocker Trust 238
Kuhne, Frederick 127, 130

Laird Rams 111–13, 133, 174–5
Lampson, Curtis 102
Latrobe, John H. B. 42–5
Lawrence, Abbott:
    and isthmian canal 63–7
    and Mexican War loan 55–6

Lee, Robert E. 150
Legal Tender Act 101, 125, 128
letters of marque 109, 111
Lewis, Sir George Cornwall 155–7
Lincoln, Abraham 76, 94, 100, 128
   role in foreign affairs 131–2
Lindsay, William 103, 146, 159, 160, 162, 164, 171, 175
   financial support of Confederacy 159–62, 164, 171
   political support of Confederacy 103, 146, 171, 175
Liverpool 181
London American 93–5, 103, 149
London Armoury 142
Louisiana Purchase 13, 58
Lyons, Lord 95, 111, 139

McClellan, George 248
McCullough, Hugh 173, 192, 194–6, 220, 237–8
McHenry, James 173
Mackenzie, William Lyon 29
McLane, Louis 42–3, 50
McLeod, Alexander 30, 38, 68
McNutt, Alexander 27
McRae, Colin 175–6, 179–80, 182–3, 185, 187, 193
Madawaska 36–7
Maine, *see* Canada
Mallory, Stephen 142–3, 145, 150, 158
Manchester and County Bank 177
Manifest Destiny 18, 21, 46
   see also expansionism
Mann, Dudley 140–1
Martineau, Harriet 75, 92
Maryland:
   State debt of 40–5
Marx, Karl 122
Marx, Ludwig 127
Mason, James:
   and cotton bonds 159–67

   early activities in London 95, 110, 146
   endorses 'New Plan' 180
   and Kenner mission 184–5
   leaves Britain 175
   Predicts success of 'King Cotton' 157
Massachusetts 231
Maury, Matthew 161, 174
Maysville Road 22, 246
Memminger, Christopher 139, 161
Mexican War loan 53–8
Mexico:
   British capitalists and debt 47–8
   French venture in 184
Michigan Central Railroad 109
Mill, John Stuart 199–200
Miskito Indians 62–7
Mississippi Union Bank 118
Monarch 242
Monroe Doctrine 49, 64, 66
Morgan, J. P. 242, 251
Morgan, J. S.:
   and coming of Civil War 75, 77
   and funded loans 217, 228–9
   and loan to France 251
Morrill Tariff 82, 92–3
Morton, Levi 208, 213–14, 217, 220–1, 223–8, 241
Morton, Rose and Co. 208, 252
   and first funded loan 217–18, 220
   and indirect claims 223
   and second funded loan 228–9
Morse, Freeman 106, 108, 192
Mosquito Coast 62–7
Motley, John Lothrop 210
Murphy, William 120, 122–30, 197

Napoleon III 155, 159, 183–4, 185
Nation:
   and costs of aggressive foreign policy 7, 206, 208

National Debt:
  abroad in mid-nineteenth
    century 9–11, 250–1
  abroad in 1853 57–8
  abroad in 1865 130–3
  abroad during
    Reconstruction 197–8, 239
  after Civil War 194
  during Mexican War 57–8
  retirement of under Andrew
    Jackson 22
New York Warehouse and Security
  Co. 238
Nicaragua 61–7
North Carolina 177
North American Review 43
North, James 145, 150, 164, 174
Northern Pacific Railroad 236–9

Ohio Life Insurance and Trust 76
'Open-Door' 61
Oregon dispute 48–53, 215, 243, 245
Ostend Manifesto 73–4
Overend, Gurney & Co. 39, 41, 56,
  196
Overstone, Lord 101

Pakenham, Richard 49
Palmer, Roundell 112
Palmerston, Henry John Temple, third
    Viscount:
  and Bull Run 91
  and defaulted investments 40
  and intervention in Civil
    War 151–6, 185
  and isthmian canal 64
  and Laird Rams 113
  and Northeastern border dispute
    30, 33
  and *Trent* 95
Panic of 1837 21, 24–5, 49
Panic of 1847 53, 55
Panic of 1857 76–8, 135–6, 139

Panic of 1860 79
Panic of 1866 196, 234
Panic of 1873 229, 238–9, 249, 252
Panic of 1907 238
Peabody, George 12, 23, 75, 77, 251
  blackballed from London Reform
    Club 39
  and coming of Civil War 79–81
  death and funeral 242
  and Maryland debt 43
  and Mexican War loan 56
  pro-Union sympathies 102–3, 141,
    247–8
Peabody Trust 103
Pearson, Zachariah 181
Peel, Sir Robert 35, 94
Pendleton, George 199
Pendleton Plan 199–200
Pennsylvania:
  State debt of 28–9, 41–5
Peto, Sir Morton 234–5
Pickens, Francis 81
Pike, James 123–30, 231
Polk, James K.:
  and Oregon 49–53
  views on foreign investment 18, 57,
    246
Pollacky, Ignatius 105
Populist movement 130, 249–50
Porter, Horace 226
Pound, Ezra 248
Pratt, Thomas 43
Prioleau, Charles 144, 164, 169, 182
'Produce loans' 145
Prostrate State 231
Public Credit Act 201, 206

Queen Victoria 103, 226

railroads:
  foreign investment in 1850s 60, 75
  foreign investment in during
    Reconstruction 233–9

Raster, Hermann 122
Rathbone, William 112
Real Estate Bank of Arkansas 118
Reconstruction 14, 196, 229–33
Reed, William 42
Republican Party:
  views on foreign investment 18, 195, 200, 239–40, 245–6
repudiation:
  Jefferson Davis and 117–21
  of Mississippi, Arkansas, and Florida 72–3, 88, 247, 250
  and post-war South 230–3
Restoration Campaign 40–5
Revolutions of 1848 54–6, 245
Rhett, Robert Barnwell 136–7
Ricker, Sam 122
Robinson, William 39–40
Roebuck, John 103, 120, 146, 175
Rose, Sir John:
  and indirect claims 223–8
  negotiations with Fish 214–15
  seeks to broker funded loan 213, 217
  seeks to resolve *Alabama* dispute 208–9, 212–13, 241
  withdraws from first funded loan 220
Rost, Pierre 140–1
Rothschilds 12–13
  and coming of Civil War 79–81
  and Confederate bonds 151, 167, 248
  and first funded loan 217–18
  and indirect claims 224–5
  and intervention in Civil War 151–7
  Investment in Union bonds 123–4, 248
  and Mexican War loan 57
  and post-war investments in railroads 235, 237
  and post-war loan 195–7, 198, 200
  and post-war South 230–1
  and resolution of *Alabama* claims 241
  and second funded loan 221, 228–9
  and state debts 28
  and *Trent* crisis 98
  and Union loan in 1861 86–7
Rothschild, James 39, 152
Rothschild, Lionel 12
  and *Alabama* claims 208, 225, 226, 241
  and Civil War 91, 120, 154
Rothschild, Salomon 81, 87, 152
Ruggles, Samuel 198
Russell, Lord John:
  and *Alabama* claims 202, 225
  and the Confederacy 106–8, 140, 148, 175
  and intervention in Civil War 80, 95, 154–5
  and Joint Claims Convention 67
Russell, William Howard 91

Sanders, George 160
Sanford, Henry 104
San Juan Island 212, 215
Santo Domingo, 210
Schneck, Robert 210
Schröder and Co. 165–7, 236
Schurz, Carl 226
Schuyler, George 90, 104
Scott, Winfield 30
Seligman, J. W. 124
Senior, Nassau 50, 112
Seward, William Henry:
  and *Alabama* claims and Canada 203–4
  and apology for *Trent* 99–100
  and Confederate bondholders 172–3
  and Confederate shipbuilding in Britain 108–13
  and gold standard 198

Seward, William Henry (*cont.*):
  instructions to Adams 82–3
  and *London American* 93–4
  and McLeod 33
  and recovery of Confederate
    property 191–3
  rivalry with Chase 131–2
Seyd, Ernest 249
Sherman, John 248
Sinclair, George 160
slavery:
  influence on foreign investment 60,
    69–76, 121, 125, 141, 167
  and intervention in Civil War 92,
    152, 154, 185
Slidell, John 95
  appointed envoy to France 146
  and cotton bonds and Erlanger
    loan 153, 157, 162–5
  defends Davis 117
  and diplomacy of 1864–5 183–5
Smith, Goldwin 112
Smith, Revd Sydney 28–9
Smithson, James 118
South Carolina 81, 141
Southern Independence Association
  146
Specie Circular 24
Specie payments 98–105, 144, 195,
  252
Spence, James 146, 161–2, 167, 185
Squier, Ephraim 62
Stanley, Lord 203
State debts 9–11
  defaulting of in 1840s 27–9
  during Reconstruction 229–33
  in 1850s 58–9
  foreign indebtedness in 1830s 23, 25
  and restoration campaign 40–5
  southern states during Civil War
    177
Stephens, Alexander 88, 139
Stonewall 184

Sturgis, Russell 81, 89–90, 249
Sumner, Charles 78, 99, 210, 222
  speech on the *Alabama*
    claims 205–8, 243–4
Sumter 110

tariffs 4, 50–1, 61, 82, 92–3, 116
Taylor, Zachary 57, 61, 65
Tenterden, Lord 209, 212, 227
Texas, annexation of 46–8
Thompson, George 117
Thornton, Sir Edward 209, 212
Thouvenel, Edouard 141
Tigre Island 62
The Times (London):
  and Confederate finances 158
  and Mississippi 72–3, 118
  and post-war investments in South
    231
  reporting of Civil War 91, 110, 112,
    123
  and State debts 40
  and Union finances 102, 114, 123
Titus, H. B. 192
Toombs, Robert 140–1
Train, George Francis 93–5, 96
treasurer's checks 219
Treasury Department:
  and *Alabama* claims 240–1
  and 1842 loan 36–40
  first funded loan 217–21
  and Mexican War loan 53–8
  recovery of Confederate property
    191–3
  and refunding loan 190
  relationship between bond prices
    and diplomatic events 243–5
  Report of 1853 58–60
  role in foreign affairs 6
  State of in 1861 83–4
  State of in 1863 113
  State of in 1865 130–3
  State of after Civil War 193–4

and *Trent* crisis 96
Treaty of Guadalupe Hidalgo 54, 57
Treaty of Paris 111
Treaty of Washington (1842), *see*
  Webster–Ashburton Treaty
Treaty of Washington (1871) 13,
  215–16, 239–40, 242, 245
  assists funded loan 215–16
  vague on indirect claims 222–3
Trefouse, Hans 201
Trenholm, George 143, 183, 186
Trent crisis 95–104, 133, 146, 243
Trotter, Alexander 71–2, 118
Tyler, John 28, 33, 40, 48

Uncle Tom's Cabin 116
Union 82–133
  early efforts to acquire foreign
    loan 84–91
  financing of Civil War 82
  foreign indebtedness in 1865 130,
    132–3
  foreign loan in 1863 113–15
  international strategy
    evaluated 130–3, 246–7
Union and Emancipation Society 112,
  117
Union Pacific Railroad 235
United States:
  reliance on foreign
    investment 6–14, 252–3
  toward financial independence 221,
    250–2
  see also Union, Treasury
    Department
US. v Prioleau 191
Upham, Nathaniel 68

Van Buren, Martin 30, 68
Vance, Zebulon 177
Vanderbilt, Cornelius 62–7, 234
Vicksburg, Battle of 120, 126, 169, 175
Virginia 177, 231

Walker, Norman 158
Walker, Robert J.:
  as Secretary of the Treasury 53–8,
    246
  mission to Europe during Civil War
    101, 115–22, 133
Walker Tariff 50, 116
Walker, William 73
Ward, Samuel 107
Ward, Thomas Wren 55, 75
  involvement in American politics
    and diplomacy 13–14, 20–1
  and restoration campaign 40–5
  and state debts 28
  and Texas and Oregon 46–53
Wayland, Francis 42
Webster, Daniel 69, 208
  and Britain 31
  and Oregon 50
  relations with Barings 13, 21,
    32–3
  and state debts 26, 28, 40–5
  Treaty negotiations with Lord
    Ashburton 33–40
  vews on foreign investment 18,
    31–2, 245–6
Webster–Ashburton Treaty 13,
  31–40, 52, 216, 242–5
Weed, Thurlow 90, 98, 102
Welles, Gideon 107, 109
Westminster Review 71
Whig Party:
  and isthmian canal 61–7
  vews on foreign investment 18,
    26–7, 245–6
White, Andrew Dixon 102
White, John 177
Wilkes, Charles 95
Wordsworth, William 29

Yancey, William 140–1
'Young America' 66, 93

www.ingramcontent.com/pod-product-compliance
Ingram Content Group UK Ltd.
Pitfield, Milton Keynes, MK11 3LW, UK
UKHW041951230426
12048UKWH00008B/272